Encounters with Luther

Encounters with Luther

New Directions for Critical Studies

Edited by

Kirsi I. Stjerna
and
Brooks Schramm

WESTMINSTER
JOHN KNOX PRESS
LOUISVILLE · KENTUCKY

Published by Westminster John Knox Press
Louisville, Kentucky

16 17 18 19 20 21 22 23 24 25—10 9 8 7 6 5 4 3 2 1

Scripture quotations from the New Revised Standard Version of the Bible are copyright © 1989 by the Division of Christian Education of the National Council of the Churches of Christ in the U.S.A. and are used by permission.

Scripture quotations marked RSV are from the Revised Standard Version of the Bible, copyright © 1946, 1952, 1971, and 1973 by the Division of Christian Education of the National Council of the Churches of Christ in the U.S.A., and are used by permission.

See acknowledgments, pp. xiii–xiv, for additional permission information.

Book design by Drew Stevens
Cover design by Allison Taylor

Library of Congress Cataloging-in-Publication Data

Names: Stjerna, Kirsi Irmeli, 1963- editor. | Schramm, Brooks, 1957- editor.
Title: Encounters with Luther : new directions for critical studies / edited by Kirsi I. Stjerna and Brooks Schramm.
Description: Louisville, KY : Westminster John Knox Press, 2016. | Includes index.
Identifiers: LCCN 2016006689 (print) | LCCN 2016016929 (ebook) | ISBN 9780664262167 (alk. paper) | ISBN 9781611646900 (e-book)
Subjects: LCSH: Luther, Martin, 1483-1546. | Theology, Doctrinal. | Theology.
Classification: LCC BR333.3 .E53 2016 (print) | LCC BR333.3 (ebook) | DDC 230/.41--dc23
LC record available at https://lccn.loc.gov/2016006689

Contents

Foreword

Stanley Hauerwas

It is, no doubt, odd that I have agreed to write the foreword to this collection of essays exploring the ongoing impact of Luther and Reformation studies. It is odd because I am an outspokenly ambivalent Protestant who identifies with what I have called the "Catholic side of the Reformation." By that description I have tried to indicate that whatever it might have meant to be Protestant since the sixteenth century, today it is no longer self-evident what it means to be Protestant. That it is no longer self-evident what it means to be Protestant is the inevitable result of what became one of the distinguishing characteristics of Protestantism, that is, self-propagation. That is to say, once Protestantism began there was no way to avoid its becoming an end in itself. In 2015 in the American landscape you can drive down any road and see five different Protestant churches, some "mainline" others "non-denominational." What are we to make of this? Is this what Luther had in mind when he hung his theses on the Wittenberg doors? It's hard to imagine Luther would find it any easier to make sense of our current situation than we can.

Yet the above description is all the more reason a collection like this is timely and needed for current theological reflection on Luther and the Reformation legacy. It is fitting that as we approach the anniversary of the Reformation, scholars from around the world continue to reflect on the implications of Luther's theology for us today. In particular, it seems fitting that all Christians reflect on Luther and ecumenism in the twenty-first century. It is not simply ironic that the contributors of this essay, as well as other Luther scholars, have found it worth revisiting Luther's Catholicism. For whatever significance his theology has had for the present divisions that mark the church today, I think it is fair to surmise Luther may be a key figure for helping us better understand what unites us so that the future of the church is marked not by its division but rather by its unity as the body of Christ. The essays in this book are no doubt a wonderful expression of this hope that is shared by all who have been baptized into the life, death, and resurrection of Christ our Lord.

Contributors

B. A. Gerrish is John Nuveen Professor Emeritus and Professor Emeritus of Historical Theology in the Divinity School at the University of Chicago in Chicago, Illinois.

Mary Jane Haemig is Professor of Church History at Luther Seminary in St. Paul, Minnesota.

Douglas John Hall is Professor Emeritus of Christian Theology at McGill University in Montreal, Canada.

Stanley Hauerwas is Gilbert T. Rowe Professor of Theological Ethics in Duke Divinity School at Duke University in Durham, North Carolina.

Kurt K. Hendel is Bernard, Fischer, Westberg Distinguished Ministry Professor of Reformation History at the Lutheran School of Theology in Chicago, Illinois.

Hans J. Hillerbrand is Professor Emeritus of Religion and History and Professor Emeritus of Germanic Languages and Literature at Duke University in Durham, North Carolina.

Eero Huovinen is Bishop Emeritus of Helsinki, Finland, and Docent at the Theological Faculty at Helsinki University.

Denis R. Janz is Provost Distinguished Professor of the History of Christianity at Loyola University in New Orleans, Louisiana.

Peter D. S. Krey is Pastor of Christ Lutheran Church in El Cerrito, California.

Volker Leppin is Chair of Church History at the Eberhard Karls University in Tübingen, Germany.

Carter Lindberg is Professor Emeritus of Church History in the School of Theology at Boston University in Boston, Massachusetts.

Anna Madsen is Director of the OMG Center for Theological Conversation in Sioux Falls, South Dakota.

Mickey L. Mattox is Professor of Historical Theology at Marquette University in Milwaukee, Wisconsin.

Surekha Nelavala is Pastor of Global Peace Lutheran Fellowship and Pastor of Harmony Community Lutheran Church in Frederick, Maryland.

Brooks Schramm is Kraft Professor of Biblical Studies at Lutheran Theological Seminary at Gettysburg in Gettysburg, Pennsylvania.

Kirsi I. Stjerna is First Lutheran, Los Angeles/Southwest California Synod Professor of Lutheran History and Theology at Pacific Lutheran Theological Seminary of California Lutheran University in Berkeley, California.

Deanna A. Thompson is Professor of Religion at Hamline University in Saint Paul, Minnesota.

Vitor Westhelle is Professor of Systematic Theology at the Lutheran School of Theology in Chicago, Illinois, and at the Faculty of Theology of IECLB in São Paulo, Brazil.

John Witte Jr. is Robert W. Woodruff Professor of Law; McDonald Distinguished Professor; and Director, Center for the Study of Law and Religion at Emory University in Atlanta, Georgia.

Acknowledgments

These pages constitute a continuation of the copyright page. Grateful acknowledgment is made to the following for permission to quote from copyrighted material:

- The essays in this book were originally published in the *Seminary Ridge Review* and are used by permission of the publisher.
- Eero Huovinen, "Doctor communis? The ecumenical significance of Martin Luther's Theology," *Lutherjahrbuch* 80 (2013): 13–30. Used with permission.
- Stanley Hauerwas, "Why Is War a Moral Necessity for America," in *War and the American Difference: Theological Reflections on Violence and National Identity* (Grand Rapids, MI: Baker Academic, a division of Baker Publishing Group 2011), 21–34. Used with permission.
- Vitor Westhelle, "The Practice of Resurrection: On Asserting the Openness of Past Victimizations," in *The Scandalous God: The Use and Abuse of the Cross* (Minneapolis: Fortress Press, 2006), 108–124. Used by permission.
- Deanna Thompson, "Becoming a Feminist Theologian of the Cross," in *Cross Examinations: Readings on the Meaning of the Cross Today* (ed. Marit A. Trelstad; Minneapolis: Fortress Press, 2006), 76–90. Used with permission.
- Kirsi I. Stjerna, "Luther on Marriage—Considerations in Light of Contemporary Concerns," in Matthias Heesch, Thomas Kothmann, Craig L. Nessan, eds. *Theologie im Spannungsfeld von Kirche und Politik (Theology in Engagement with Church and Politics), Hans Schwarz zum 75 Geburstag (Hans Schwarz on the Occasion of His 75th Birthday)* (Frankfurt: Peter Lang, 2014), 409–426. Used by permission.
- Kurt Hendel, "Finitum capax infiniti: Luther's radical incarnational perspective," *Currents in Theology and Mission*, 35/6 (December, 2008): 420–433. Used with permission.
- Carter Lindberg, "Luther on the Use of Money," *Christian History* 6, no. 2 (1987) is revised and footnoted and is used by permission.
- Quotations from *Luther's Works*, vols. 1–30, are used with the permission of Concordia Publishing House:

> 250 word quote from Luther's Works, Vol. 1
> Credit: From *Luther's Works* 1 © 1958, 1986 Concordia Publishing House. Used with permission. www.cph.org.

150 word quote from Luther's Works, Vol. 2
  Credit: From *Luther's Works* 2 © 1960, 1988 Concordia Publishing
  House. Used with permission. www.cph.org.
280 word quote from Luther's Works, Vol. 9
  Credit: From *Luther's Works* Vol. 9 © 1960, 1988 Concordia Publishing
  House. Used with permission. www.cph.org.
25 word quote from Luther's Works, Vol. 12
  Credit: From *Luther's Works* Vol. 12 © 1955, 1983 Concordia
  Publishing House. Used with permission. www.cph.org.
180 word quote from Luther's Works, Vol. 16
  Credit: From *Luther's Works* 16 © 1969 Concordia Publishing House.
  Used with permission. www.cph.org.
100 word quote from Luther's Works, Vol. 20
  Credit: From *Luther's Works* 20 © 1973, 2001 Concordia Publishing
  House. Used with permission. www.cph.org.
260 word quote from Luther's Works, Vol. 21
  Credit: From *Luther's Works* 21 © 1956, 1984 Concordia Publishing
  House. Used with permission. www.cph.org.
150 word quote from Luther's Works, Vol. 26
  Credit: From *Luther's Works* 26 © 1963, 1991 Concordia Publishing
  House. Used with permission. www.cph.org.
15 word quote from Luther's Works, Vol. 27
  Credit: From *Luther's Works* 27 © 1964, 1992 Concordia Publishing
  House. Used with permission. www.cph.org.
350 word quote from Luther's Works, Vol. 30
  Credit: From *Luther's Works* 30 © 1967, 2001 Concordia Publishing
  House. Used with permission. www.cph.org.

• Quotations from *Luther's Works*, vols. 31–55, are used with the permission
  of Fortress Press.

Introduction

Kirsi I. Stjerna

Reformation Scholarship Pulsating

Martin Luther continues to excite. The reformer engages scholars from different fields and backgrounds—endlessly, it seems. Ongoing, renewed Reformation research is finding new touchpoints with Luther and his fellow reformers, such as John Calvin—ones that facilitate advantageous conversations between ecumenical partners. Bridges are being built that cross historical divides, not the least thanks to new compassionate and critical scholarship, invoked particularly by the 2017 Reformation Jubilee year.

With new approaches and questions, scholars seek to take a new look at the Reformation's roots and the multifarious heritage that has percolated from the radical developments of the sixteenth century. Study of the Reformation proves time again its relevance not only in enhancing our sense of history and belonging, but also contributing to our theological imaginations and spiritual visions. What was said and done in the sixteenth century mattered greatly, and much of that still matters today in both recognizable and less noticeable ways. The pulsating study of the Reformation provides important ingredients for our continued deliberations on theology, history, and Christian identity today.

In this book, nineteen scholars share their work on Reformation themes. Each scholar writes from his or her expertise and areas of interest and with a passion for the topic. The articles represent natural diversity in terms of methodologies used, the authors' gender, age, language of origin, stages in career, and institutional and ecclesial connections. The result is a delightfully rich chorus of voices that advance Luther and Reformation research individually and collectively.

The Context of the Articles

The articles stand on their own while their birthing context is shared: each contributor has presented from his or her work once upon a time at the Lutheran Theological Seminary at Gettysburg. By invitation to participate in the annual Luther Colloquy, which is offered each October for students, scholars, alumni/alumnae, and "friends," scholars have put aside time and other commitments to drill deeper into a topic about which they have felt passionate and on which they have been currently working. They have delighted in the opportunity both to focus on a topic at stake and to share from the fruits of their labor with a broader audience beyond their customary academic peers. Deep friendships across denominational or institutional divides have been built on these occasions of celebration of scholarship and intellectual discovery regarding the sixteenth-century sources.

The Luther Colloquy has a long history: It was established in 1970 by professors Eric Gritsch and Gerald Christianson. The founding vision stated that "critical reassessment of Luther and his heritage in terms of their significance for modern ecumenical Christianity is enhanced by renewed focus on supportive interdisciplinary scholarship in the field."[1] Since 2000, under the direction of the Institute for Luther Studies, which hosts the Luther Colloquy as part of the seminary's graduate studies program, the original vision has been expanded to embrace ecumenical horizons theologically in a more explicit manner and to initiate partnerships that enhance critical appreciation of the Reformation's traditions around the world, with and beyond Luther.[2] The articles in this book represent this vision in practice.[3] Articles have been previously published in the seminary's faculty journal, *Seminary Ridge Review*, and are here published with the enthusiastic permission of the authors.

The Content of the Book

Encounters with Luther offers in one volume original primary research from an international and ecumenical pool of established scholars in their field. Luther and Lutheran theological tradition, as well as the broader Protestant tradition, are herewith critically re-assessed, with humor and heart. Combined, the articles address both the Reformation's historical foundations and its proper understanding in light of the most recent research, while intentionally moving forward, with an explicit focus on contemporary issues of relevance and ecumenical collegiality, in scholarship and in praxis.

As the table of contents reveals, topics range from sacraments and marriage to violence and the devil, from reassessment of the relations between Calvin and Luther to hopes for ecumenical unity and a reality check on Jewish-Christian relations. The presentations have been offered over the course of the last fifteen years, with an emphasis on the more recent offerings: each author has focused on a specific topic in the field of his/her scholarship, attempting to present a detailed, analytical account. Each author feels passionate about the topics at stake and genuinely seeks for the truth of the matter, striving to articulate findings in convincing and fresh ways.

1. Luther Colloquy and the Institute for Luther Studies has been directed (in this order) by Eric Gritsch, Scott Hendrix, and Kirsi Stjerna. See further: http://www.ltsg.edu/resources-services/resources-for-ministry/institute-of-luther-studies.
2. The planning committee for the Luther Colloquy, in recent years, consisted of Professors B. Bohleke, Brooks Schramm, and Kirsi Stjerna, with input from colleagues and students. Originally a free-standing institution, recently the event was incorporated into the seminary's Graduate Studies program, with the same committee in operation.
3. Only a selection of the presentations are included in this volume. For a complete list and collections, see the *Seminary Ridge Review*: http://www.ltsg.edu/about-us/news/seminary-ridge-review.

One could choose to focus on any of the articles based upon its topic—or its author—and be rewarded with the inquiry. In this regard, the work can serve as a valuable reference tool for a wide-ranging audience. At the same time, the reader could embrace the whole in search for constructive paradigm shifts and programmatic moves toward reforming the Reformation traditions and reclaiming the contemporary relevance of the sixteenth-century reforming visions to be offered in new languages. The reader could begin by reflecting on what are some of the continuing and what are some of the new issues for Reformation scholarship to tackle, and also, in the company of the reformers, name some of the burning issues of our time.

Questions that demand our attention are reflected in the articles: What methods do we use in Reformation scholarship, and what sources do we choose to engage? Are we looking at the ocean of possibilities with broad enough horizons and large enough nets? How do we or should we or could we write about Luther, or Calvin, or any of the personalities involved, in light of our most recent knowledge? What new is there to discover in Luther or his fellow reformers? What are the divides and connectors between different denominational groups? What is the status of our respective practices and theologies with the sacraments and Christian life together? Do the sixteenth-century theological debates still divide or have we moved to a place where altogether different urgencies should grab our attention? E.g., a life-and-death matter for our generation is no longer the agreement on eucharistic theology but rather the rescue of the failing creation we have managed to hurt beyond the imagination of our reforming ancestors. Our urgencies are less in the doctrines and more in the practice, where the reformers' theological vision can be found timelessly empowering.

The reformers' theologies and examples in many ways speak to our conscience and challenge us: In the tradition of the reformation's radical theologies of Christian freedom and equality, how successful or deliberate are we in our efforts to evoke reforms to eradicate relentless poverty and ongoing crimes of violence, and to secure human rights for every child of God? What transformative language can we use to speak to the manifold experiences of the hells of violence and war? Gender and sexuality issues, and relatedly, marriage rights, present an ongoing acute issue: how better to translate into practice the Reformation's radical theologies to secure human rights in this regard and in other matters of human-relations? In addition, in this broken world, what kind of an enduring and life-giving spiritual voice is there to be found in the Reformation theological tradition? How can the spiritual promise of God-based hope for renewal, proclaimed by the reformers with varied dialects, foster true unity and peace and re-adjustment of our priorities today? To paraphrase the words of one of the contributors, have we learned to play with one another, regardless of our differences?

Rather than describing the contents of each article, the articles are offered for the reader to embrace, with the promise of satisfaction and surprise. The following thesis statements suffice to highlight the neuralgic pulse of the research in the weaving together of the threads.

Searching for the Common Ground

[Huovinen:] As *doctor communis*, Luther strives for the unity of the
common faith. Hopes of realizing such unity require digging
deeper into the truth of the matter: what the issues were—
and were not—requires reopening old coffins.

Wrestling with Demons and Violence

[Janz:] As children of faith and doers motivated by God's love,
Christians endure their private hells. Confidence in faith
is the weapon to fight the hopelessness and false security
caused by the devil of despair. Namely, our despair puts us in
very close proximity of grace.

[Leppin:] God does not hate you—that would be the devil talking. We
live with the *Anfechtung* of falling either into despair or false
security. The decisive battle against the devil was precisely
Luther's Reformation discovery.

[Mattox:] If living today, Luther would be against the death penalty per
se. At the same time, he deemed ordered violence a necessary
evil in the fallen world. Luther is best understood in his
pastoral role, in which he interprets the Bible as his mirror of
reality for life before and after the fall.

[Hauerwas:] Attempts to justify wars fought on realist grounds in
the name of just war serve to hide the reality of war.
The American Civil War teaches us what happens when
Christians confuse the sacrifice of war with the sacrifice of
Christ. War is America's altar, but the church is the alternative
to war. When Christians lose the reality of the church as an
alternative to the world's reality, they abandon the world to
the unreality of war.

Reimagining Theologies of the Cross

[Hall:] The compassion and solidarity of God, as the first
principle, is the Christological basis for the theology of the
cross: a theology of faith and not sight, of hope and not
consummation, of love and not power; *theologia crucis* is
viable only when it expresses itself in an *ecclesia crucis*. It is
the theology of faith, which certainly was a positive word for
Luther.

[Westhelle:] Theology of the cross as a dispositional practice stands in
the face of the cross but reacts to it with the confidence that
it is not outside of God's providence, however promising
or terrifying it might be. Theology of the cross is always the
other side of a practice of resurrection, just as the practice
of resurrection is only exercised with the experience of the
cross—sharing the experience of Mary's Magnificat.

[**Thompson:**] Living Christian vocation is about bearing the cross of challenging friendships. The church is a sanctuary for all those friends who are broken and in pain, and an invitation to divinely designed friendships that challenge our identities. This means that suffering is an inevitable by-product of justified existence. Feminist theologians, with Luther, embrace the cross in their and their friends' experience.

Sex and Marriage Matters

[**Witte:**] Lutheran theology has power to transform laws. A brilliant example of that are laws regarding marriage. Even in his late medieval chauvinism, Luther liberated marriage in radical ways, by rejecting laws that forbade clerical and monastic marriage—or other human-made impediments for marriage. And yet, the inequality of the sexes and in human relations still continues, and the impact of the Reformation changes on women's lives is being re-examined.

[**Stjerna:**] If living today, Luther would be pro-gay marriage. He would consider it diabolical to prevent people from God's gift of marriage by any nonsensical human laws that put people in an untenable situation that leads them to sin and hurt. Luther's radical reforms which elevated marital love and union, combined with modern anthropology, give seeds for continuing reforms, in society and in the church.

Sharing the Sacraments

[**Gerrish:**] Let us not keep Luther and Calvin at arm's length, but let them embrace in their mutual appreciation of the mystery of faith and in the celebrating of the sacramental union of sign and thing in the Lord's Supper. Christ is present in faith itself, Luther and Calvin would agree.

[**Hendel:**] The reformers diligent debating on the effect and meaning of the sacrament of the Lord's Supper give us perspective on what is of utmost importance: the mysterious reality of Christ's true presence in the symbol and in the tangible calls Christians to re-focus on the care of creation as the true vehicle of grace.

Spiritual Care

[**Haemig:**] Luther's reformation of prayer is about rediscovering who God is and how God relates to human beings. Using biblical images to put human flesh on his teaching on prayer, Luther urged Christians to pray in all situations, even when knowing that God is angry with us. God hears prayers regardless of our worth or unworth. Short and to the point prayers are the best.

[Krey:] Luther found the value of confident despair and designed theological therapy, pointing to Christ as the internal therapist in our hearts. Truly to appreciate Luther's gift to a humanity struggling with existential issues, we could look at his psychological wisdom and acumen and startlingly relevant instincts.

The Word Transforming the World

[Hillerbrand:] Luther affirmed the relevance of the gospel for social and political order, a relevance that might mean the advocacy of change and reform. Christians who derive from Scripture their legitimation of a just society are called to, in Mary's footsteps, bring the gospel to effect in both individual lives and in the public square, and to do so boldly. In the end, however, they must take their seat with the powerless and the humble.

[Lindberg:] Luther detested the calculating entrepreneur. His doctrine of justification by grace alone apart from works cuts the nerve of the medieval ideology of poverty. With his doctrine of grace and observations on the realities of sin, he names poverty in all its forms as a personal and social evil to be combated. Under the rubrics of justice and equity, Luther and his colleagues promoted new social welfare policies.

[Nelavala:] From a Dalit feminist perspective, Luther advocates liberation and justice with his "Scripture alone" principle: Scripture proclaims Christ and thus necessarily perpetuates liberation and justice. Among other liberationists, Dalit theologians are praxis-oriented and aim for reaching the masses for tangible transformations among the suffering. Otherwise, what would be the point?

Critical Issues to Embrace

[Madsen:] In our life and death experiences, we get our hands dirty with composting matter that once was alive and is now dead; but out of it grows new, different life. To this we can all relate. A feminist theologian of the cross and grace, with Luther, attends to the existential issues of renewed relations and relatedness, and hangs with hope on the promise of new life, even and particularly in encounters with death.

[Schramm:] Luther's thinking on the nature and place of the law of Moses in the lives of Christians demonstrates, in the final analysis, that his thought has no room for the ongoing existence of Judaism in any theologically positive sense.

To paraphrase Luther's words (quoted in Denis Janz's article): We are children of God in faith, in which we receive God's grace, while in God's love we are made doers and actors. The ongoing dilemma and invitation for all Christians is the balance between receiving divine grace and sustenance and renewal of pardoning mercy for our daily faltering, and rejoicing in the gifts already received and boldly moving mountains and changing the world—in faith that believes in the God of the impossible. Reformation traditions underscore this fundamental conviction: God is omnipotent, and in God we stand strong, even in our own fragility.

This volume seeks to invite more traffic in the ocean called reformation studies and traditions. The horizon is endless and there is room for more sailors.

Special thanks are due to our editors at Westminster John Knox Press, Dan Braden and Julie Tonini, without whose professional guidance and expertise this project could not have been completed.

We dedicate this book to the founders of the Luther Colloquy at Gettysburg Seminary: Eric W. Gritsch[†] and Gerald (Jerry) Christianson.

Abbreviations

ARG	*Archiv für Reformationsgeschichte*
BC	*The Book of Concord*
CurTM	*Currents in Theology and Mission*
CWI	Civil War Institute
CWRS	Church of Sweden Research Series
HLQ	*Huntington Library Quarterly*
HTR	*Harvard Theological Review*
JAAR	*Journal of the American Academy of Religion*
JBTh	*Jahrbuch für Biblische Theologie*
JMLB	*Jahrbuch des Martin Luther Bundes*
JSCE	*Journal of the Society of Christian Ethics*
JSNT	*Journal for the Study of the New Testament*
JSOTSup	Journal for the Study of the Old Testament: Supplement Series
KuD	*Kerygma und Dogma*
LCC	Library of Christian Classics
LQ	*Lutheran Quarterly*
LQB	Lutheran Quarterly Books
LS	*Luther's Spirituality*
LuJ	*Lutherjahrbuch*
LW	*Luther's Works*
OTL	Old Testament Library
QFRG	Quellen und Forschungen zur Reformationsgeschichte
SBL	Society of Biblical Literature
SCJ	*Sixteenth Century Journal*
SCSE	Sixteenth Century Studies and Essays
SRR	*Seminary Ridge Review*
STL	Studia Theologica Lundensia
TC	*Concordia triglotta: die symbolischen Bücher der evangèlish-lutherischen Kirche, deutsch-lateinisch-englisch*
TS	*Theological Studies*
USQR	*Union Seminary Quarterly Review*
VIEG	Veröffentlichungen des Instituts für Europäische Geschichte Mainz

WA	Weimarer Ausgabe = *D. Martin Luthers Werke: Kritische Gesamtausgabe*
WA Br	*D. Martin Luthers Werke: Kritische Gesamtausgabe, Briefwechsel*
WA TR	*D. Martin Luthers Werke: Kritische Gesamtausgabe, Tischreden*
WF	Wolfenbütteler Forschungen
WJK	Westminster John Knox Press
WSCF	World Student Christian Federation
WUNT	Wissenschaftliche Untersuchungen zum Neuen Testament
WW	*Word and World*
ZSGRG	*Zeitschrift der Savigny Gesellschaft für Rechtsgeschichte*
ZTK	*Zeitschrift für Theologie und Kirche*

Searching for
the Common Ground

1. A Common Teacher, *Doctor Communis?*
The Ecumenical Significance of Martin Luther

Eero Huovinen

Distinguished participants of the Academy, dear sisters and brothers in Christ. It is a great joy and honor to visit the famous Lutheran Theological Seminary in Gettysburg and especially to be invited by Professor Kirsi Stjerna, with whom I have been able to study theology both in Helsinki and in Rome. Especially I appreciate the honor of offering the George and Janet Harkins lecture. George Harkins graduated from Gettysburg seminary and was the secretary to Franklin Clark Fry, who was elected in Helsinki in 1963 to be the President of the Lutheran World Federation. His wife Janet had a lifelong devotion to the church in a remarkable way, teaching church school for 77 years. Through to their will, much has been donated to Gettysburg Seminary.

Luther's Relation to the Earlier Tradition?

Speaking during this Reformation week, I would like to start by asking together with you, how Martin Luther stands out from his own environment and background, from his contemporaries. What is Luther *specificus?* What relation does he have to the medieval Roman Catholic Church and its theology? This issue can be approached from different angles. For a good while, we looked for the "real" Luther by emphasising the differences and disputes that he had in regard to the mainstream of his time. Many researchers maintained that it was either Luther's fault or to his credit that the western part of Christendom was divided in the sixteenth century.

The viewpoint of this research shifted as late as the middle of last century. While nonetheless admitting the differences, both Catholic and Lutheran scholars now aim to assess how Luther connects with the preceding age and with the classic interpretation of Christianity. This has no doubt happened because of the rise of the Ecumenical Movement since World War II. As the year 2017 draws nearer, we find it appropriate to ask what the ecumenical significance of Martin Luther and his theology is, what they mean a half a millennium after the Reformation.

It was a new spirit of ecumenism when Cardinal Jan Willebrands in 1970 at the Fifth Assembly of the Lutheran World Federation applied the classic Roman Catholic title of *doctor communis* to Martin Luther. Cardinal Willebrands referred to the well-known thought of Luther that justification is the doctrine upon which the church stands or falls. In speaking of this matter, Luther can also be a "common teacher" for the Roman Catholic Church, because Luther desires that "God will remain our Lord and that our most important human response is unconditional trust and respect for God."[1]

This title that the Cardinal used for Luther, *doctor communis*, is one of the honorifics of St. Thomas Aquinas. According to Willebrands, St. Thomas and Luther, the Middle Ages and the Reformation, belong together. Luther represents and continues a common tradition. Nevertheless, *doctor communis* is not simply a historical title, pointing to the past. With this title, the Cardinal wishes to show us that Luther has something to say jointly to the Roman Catholic and Lutheran Churches today.

Cardinal Willebrands' thoughts were continued by Karl Lehmann, then Roman Catholic Bishop of Mainz. Cardinal Lehmann writes of the ecumenical significance of Luther's Small *Catechism*. Lehmann states that the *Small and Large Catechisms*—in contrast to certain other writings of Luther—are an excellent example of the linkage of the Reformer with earlier tradition. Within the history of the church, Luther's *Catechisms* are neither new nor the random contrivance of a single theologian. Rather, they are closely related, both in their structure and their content, to the classical theology of the early church and the medieval church. According to Lehmann, Luther is a "Teacher of the Faith" (*Lehrer des Glaubens*).[2]

Although the churches' evaluations of Luther have differed greatly throughout history in regard to content and estimation, both sides have long held certain features in common. Just as Luther's valuation as *doctor communis* has not been self-apparent to Roman Catholics, it has not been all that clear to Protestants either. Luther has been interpreted as an individual, a person who started something new—whether that was negative or positive. Luther created a new "Protestant" Christian belief—or at least he presented an interpretation of the original belief which differed radically from the faith of earlier centuries.

Roman Catholic Interpretation of Luther: Arch-heretic or Father in Faith?

According to Roman Catholics, Luther departed from the one, catholic tradition—which was his downfall. In the assessment of Protestants, Luther departed from tradition, and that was his accomplishment. Overstating the case only slightly, we can say that Luther was not *doctor communis* for either side.

For Roman Catholics Luther has been one of those deviating from the main tide, in other words, a heretic, while for the Protestants he has been a guiding light whose significance is emphasized against an otherwise dark firmament overshadowing the church. And even when Luther has been studied in relation to his background of ecclesiastical and general history, his qualities, uniqueness, and digression from the norm, that is to say, his significance as an individual, has come to the fore. So it is rather understandable that there has

1. J. Cardinal Willebrands, *Mandatum unitatis: Beiträge zur Ökumene* (Paderborn: Bonifatius, 1989), 124.
2. Karl Lehmann, "Luther als Lehrer des Glaubens? Die ökumenische Bedeutung seiner Katechismen: Lutherische Kirche in der Welt," *JMLB* 45 (1998): 131–146.

not been enough motivation for scrutinizing Luther as *doctor communis*, as a representative of the one, classical Christendom.[3]

During the Reformation, Roman Catholics depicted Luther as an arch-heretic and as a destroyer of the unity of the church. Even at the beginning of the twentieth century, Luther was seen in dark colors, not only to be avoided in doctrine but also to be studied under the typology of a personal pathology. For example, Heinrich Denifle claimed that Luther had created his doctrine of justification simply in order to be able to live a carefree, libertarian life for himself. From these viewpoints, we could say that both Luther the person and Luther the theologian were viewed as the sum of individual flaws and biases.

On the eve of the Second World War, there was a new breakthrough both academically and ecumenically in the publication of Joseph Lortz's book: *Die Reformation in Deutschland.* Lortz critiqued the errors of the medieval church. He strove to understand Luther's own spiritual intentions. He appreciated Luther as a "religious personality." Nonetheless, he concluded that as a theologian Luther was a "subjectivist." In Lortz's view Luther represents a catholicity without being catholic in an authentic sense. In a unique way Luther had stressed the significance of the Apostle Paul. Yet, Luther did not attend fully (*Vollhörer*) to the Holy Bible. The revolutionary Luther was entirely a prisoner of his own deliberations.[4]

The theory of Luther's subjectivism was soon re-evaluated by Roman Catholic scholars. Lortz's own students, in particular Erwin Iserloh and Peter Manns, held that the thesis of subjectivism was overly superficial and denigrating. Manns used the name "Father in Faith" (*Vater im Glauben*) for Luther. Manns examined Luther with special reference to the devotional life of the medieval and early churches. The title "Father in Faith" arises from that spiritual tradition.

In his broad-ranging study of St. Thomas Aquinas and Martin Luther, Otto Hermann Pesch asserted that their understandings of the doctrine of justification were not mutually exclusive. Thus Luther's theology is properly to be situated among the common traditions of Christendom, regardless of the denomination of the person doing the evaluation.[5]

In official Roman Catholic evaluations after Vatican II, the position afforded to Luther is substantially different from those given at the beginning of the twentieth century. In addition to Cardinal Willebrands and other ecumenically minded thinkers, Pope John Paul II on several instances quoted Luther's

3. "Die Bedeutung des überkommenen Dogmas für Luther kann schwerlich überschätzt werden; sie ist in der Forschung weithin zu gering veranschlagt worden." (Bernhard Lohse, *Martin Luther: eine Einführung in sein Leben und sein Werk* [Munich: Beck, 1981] 171; on the history of Luther research, see 207–246).

4. Joseph Lortz, *Die Reformation in Deutschland,* 2 vols (Freiburg: Herder, 1941). See also Eero Huovinen, "Die ökumenische Bedeutung des Luther-Verständnisses von Joseph Lortz für die Lutherforschung in Finnland," in *Zum Gedenken an Joseph Lortz: Beiträge zur Reformationsgeschichte und Ökumene,* ed. Rolf Decot and Rainer Vinke (Stuttgart: Franz Steiner Verlag, 1989), 262–292.

5. Otto Hermann Pesch, "Martin Luther: Reformator und Vater im Glauben," in *Referate aus der Vortragsreihe des Instituts für Europäische Geschichte Mainz,* ed. Peter Manns (Stuttgart: Steiner Verlag, 1985); idem, *Theologie der Rechtfertigung bei Martin Luther und Thomas von Aquin* (Mainz: 1967); idem, *Martin Luther, Thomas von Aquin und die reformatorische Kritik an der Scholastik: zur Geschichte und Wirkungsgeschichte eines Missverständnisses mit weltgeschichtlichen Folgen* (Göttingen: Matthias Grünewald Verlag, 1994); Peter Manns, *Vater im Glauben: Studien zur Theologie Martin Luthers: Festgabe zum 65. Geburtstag am 10. März 1988,* ed. Rolf Decot, VIEG 131 (Stuttgart: Franz Steiner, 1988).

spiritual texts, e.g., the *Commentary on Romans*. Furthermore, he spoke positively of Luther's significance for all of Christendom.

Protestant Interpretation of Luther

Mutatis mutandum, Protestant Luther research has followed the same channels
as Roman Catholic scholarship. Protestant studies either historically or systematically tended to support a view of Luther as "the Reformer". Indirectly, this
research-setting quite possibly led to an emphasis on Luther's distinctiveness
and exceptionality.

In examining the history of Protestant Luther studies,[6] it is rather amazing
how Luther is emphatically viewed as extraordinary and original. During the
period of Lutheran Orthodoxy, Luther was held by many to be unique, even
infallible, as a teacher of correct doctrine. Luther was considered to correspond
to the angel in Revelation, having "an eternal gospel to proclaim to those who
live on the earth—to every nation and tribe and language and people" (Rev
14:6). Pietism regarded Luther's theology as an expression of individual piety,
i.e., from the point of view of regenerated, living faith and sanctification. In
such a view, the significance of the Christian faith lies in the internal and personal experience of belief.

During the Enlightenment, Luther was construed as the precursor of the
freedom of reason and the conscience, the one who freed the Christian faith
from the dark disbelief of the Middle Ages. The general anthropological mode
of thought, characteristic of the era, led to a delineation of Luther as a situation-
bound thinker whose thoughts could not claim normativeness. Luther was
esteemed as a great person and as a fighter, but he too was to be evaluated critically on the basis of reason and the ethical demands of the conscience.

Gotthold Ephraim Lessing boasted of Luther that he had set people free
from the bondage of tradition. The task of the Enlightenment was only to carry
this liberation to its fruition. Frederick the Great was not satisfied even with
this, but rejoiced that Luther, the "poor, damn devil," freed the people from
the yoke of the priests and thus increased the income of the state. Lutheranism
began to change into Protestantism, which then developed into enlightened
subjectivism.

Albert Ritschl strove to place Luther into his own historical framework.
Nevertheless, Ritschl was of the opinion that Luther's value was primarily
in the overturning of old speculative metaphysics and mysticism. Ultimately,
Luther proclaimed freedom and independence of the soul.

More recent Luther research has been deeply influenced by the same Protestant theological models. In popular church discussions Luther is often held to
be a situation-bound dilettante, or an otherwise unrestrained exception in the
history of theology, one to whom Christians following current trends should
not be too committed. Such comments often reflect, in their background, the
same setting of the question: Was Luther a private sage or *doctor communis*?

---

6. See Lohse, *Martin Luther*, 213–240.

Contrary to the previously used paradigm emphasizing the differences between the Catholic Middle Ages and Luther, we find that, for example, in the United States, Robert Jenson and Carl Braaten's theological interpretation of the "Catholicity of the Reformation" has brought up new points of view.[7] In Finland, similar new thoughts were also introduced by Tuomo Mannermaa and his students.[8] Both of these parties delineated the philosophical, theological, and spiritual nature of the Middle Ages, thus attempting to understand the era preceding Luther. Furthermore, they focused their attention on how the modern image of Luther has been influenced by various philosophical preconceptions and trends.

So, back to our fundamental question: Was Luther exceptional, unique, i.e., in some manner a *novum*, or was he rather one link, one witness in the chain of the shared classic Christian faith? Without a doubt, this question is, to the observant academic researcher, quite a generalized one. Nonetheless, answering it may be a justifiable attempt to understand heuristically what is at stake in Luther's theology and, shall we dare to say, the whole of Christian belief. Was Luther simply the father of Lutheranism or was he also, for all of Christendom, *Vater im Glauben? Doctor privatus* or *doctor communis?*

The Ecumenical Significance of Luther's *Catechisms*

In attempting an incipient answer to the question above, I want to adapt the interpretation of Karl Lehmann. According to Lehmann's view, it is particularly the *Catechisms* of Luther that can, for their part, shed light on both Luther's relationship to the tradition preceding him and on his significance for the church today. Lehmann says that he is astonished how little Luther's *Catechisms* have undergone ecumenical evaluation.[9] There appear to be at least six well-founded reasons for giving the *Catechisms* an ecumenical reading.

First, the *Small and Large Catechisms* are examples of Luther's deepest desire to be *doctor communis.* In the *Catechisms,* if anywhere, Luther was *doctor,* a teacher of the ordinary people and a guide of pastors in need of theological knowledge and training. Among Luther's writings, the *Catechisms* emphasize most visibly what is common to the classic Christian faith.

In accord with the basic idea of a catechism, Luther wanted to teach what is necessary in being and living as a Christian. As *doctor,* Luther the catechist was primarily a spiritual teacher. His goals of teaching and learning were not just to increase knowledge for its own sake but to foster faith in God and to strengthen love for one's fellow human being.

---

7. See Carl E. Braaten and Robert W. Jenson, eds., *Catholicity of the Reformation* (Grand Rapids, Mi: Eerdmans, 1996).

8. On Finnish Luther research, see Juhani Forsberg, "Die finnische Lutherforschung seit 1979," *LuJ* 72 (2005): 147–182.

9. Lehmann, "Luther als Lehrer des Glaubens?," 142. In 1999 the Finnish Evangelical Lutheran Church approved a new official *Catechism.* Its base text was written by Eero Huovinen. Due to its historical and ecumenical significance, the *Catechism* included the entire text of Luther's *Small Catechism.* This new *Catechism* has been translated, e.g., into English, Swedish, Latin, Arabic, Russian, Chinese, Hungarian, German, Spanish, Croatian, and French.

Secondly, in his *Catechisms* Luther was *doctor communis* in the sense that he structured his catechetical teaching on the foundation of a long tradition. That is to say, Luther's *Small and Large Catechisms* were firmly and knowingly built on the framework of the tradition of the Jews and of the early church (the Decalogue, the Creed, the Lord's Prayer, and the Sacraments). Even in its own time Luther's catechetical ideas were neither original nor a new plan. The Commandments, Creed, and Lord's Prayer were the didactic heritage of the Middle Ages.

Although catechetical-type books of this form had not been written down, the three primary points mentioned above were the main body of Christian upbringing. Peter Abelard prepared his famous *Commentary on the Apostles' Creed and the Lord's Prayer*, which all Christians were to study together and learn by heart. Erasmus of Rotterdam wrote a catechism soon after 1510. This is the same structure Luther that developed and deepened.

The very framework of the *Catechism* emphasizes continuity with the tradition of the faith. The Ten Commandments are the foundation of the Judeo-Christian way of life. The Apostles' Creed has its roots in the first Christian century. The Lord's Prayer is the model prayer taught by Jesus. The components of Luther's *Catechism* are more those coming from the Jews, the New Testament, and Early Christianity than they are innovations of the Reformation.

Thirdly, Luther's *Catechisms*, especially the explanation of the Third Article of the Creed, are constructed on two classic dogmas of Christianity, i.e., the doctrines of the Trinity and the two natures of Christ. Although justification is not mentioned as a term in the *Catechisms*, it is implicitly a central theme and is firmly based on trinitarian doctrine and christology: Salvation is the work of the triune God, which is grounded in the person and work of Jesus Christ. Currently, the Roman Catholic Church, the World Council of Churches, the Lutheran World Federation, as well as the constitutions of many other ecumenical organizations are built upon these *dogmata*.

Fourthly, Luther's *Catechisms* are also witness to the common faith in the sense that, in them, controversial theology aimed at either Rome or the radical Reformation remains only in a subordinate role. The *Small Catechism* does not include any direct polemic. The *Large Catechism*, intended for pastors, has some critical comments on the "church of the Pope" and on spiritualistic baptismal concepts, but in comparison to Luther's other writings, it does not have anti-ecumenical, controversialist traits.

Fifthly, in line with Karl Lehmann's thoughts, in Luther's *Large Catechism* one can discern a spiritual self-critical ethos, which may also have ecumenical significance. The *Large Catechism* is a good example of what an honest and open-minded analysis of the church and Christendom could be. At the same time the *Catechism* boasts of the breakthrough of the gospel, it appraises not only the problems of its theological opponents but also, in the same measure, the pitiful mediocrity of the Christian life of its own camp.

In the Preface, for example, we read that it is expressly its own "shepherds", that is, the priests who had migrated to the Reformation camp, who were afforded an earful as "lazy bellies" (*faule Wänste, ignavos vetres*) and "presumptuous saints" (*vermessene Heiligen, praesumptuosos sanctos*). They are depicted as being more interested in the perquisites of their office than in the duties of the office, or in such matters as prayer, study, and serving the parishioners: "These shameful gluttons and servants of their bellies are better suited to be swine-herds or keepers of dogs than guardians of souls and pastors." Self-criticism in regard to one's own Church and one's own state of Christianity is a precondition for genuine ecumenical relations.

Sixthly, in the explanations of the Sacraments at the end of the *Large Catechism,* Luther attempts to link up with the teaching of his predecessors. This too has positive ecumenical significance. The sacramental teaching of Martin Luther is characterized by a strong theological realism and an understanding of the effectiveness of the Word of God. Baptism, confession, and Holy Communion do not simply refer to things external to themselves, but they include and give Christ and all his works. They are the efficacious signs (*signa efficacia*) of Christ's presence, God's grace, and the communion of Christians.[10]

The Central Place of the Sacraments

The Holy Sacraments have central standing in the *Catechisms* of Luther as well as in his other texts. Baptism joins one both to Christ and to his church. In accord with the strong words of the *Catechism,* in baptism God donates to the believer "victory over death and the devil, forgiveness of sin, God's grace, the entire Christ and all his Works, and the Holy Spirit with his gifts."[11] Simultaneously, it is made clear that the one who is baptized every single day needs teaching, prayer, exhortation, and the support of other Christians in order to prevail over troubles, to persevere in faith, and to be strengthened in love.

In addition to Baptism, there is a link established to theological realism in the explanation of Holy Communion in the *Catechism*. The Eucharist is the meal of Christ's presence, which joins to other Christians and donates "the forgiveness of sins and everlasting life."

Currently, the doctrine and praxis of Holy Communion remain a central ecumenical issue between Lutherans and Roman Catholics as well as other churches. Holy Communion includes nearly all theological *loci* from creation to redemption and eschatology. The bottleneck that is choking off the visible unity of the Churches is the theology of the ministry, which reaches its culmination in Holy Communion. Thus it is interesting to ask what Martin Luther's concept of Holy Communion could bring to the rapprochement between the churches in our day. Could he also be *doctor communis* for the theology of the Eucharist?[12]

The Sacrament of Christ's Presence

To Martin Luther, the Eucharist was the sacrament of Christ's real presence. Thus it is not only a feast of remembrance where we recall Jesus' teachings

---

10. On the effective character of the sacraments in the theology of Luther, see Eero Huovinen, *Fides infantium: Martin Luthers Lehre vom Kinderglauben,* VIEG 159 (Mainz: Philipp von Zabern, 1997), 45–74.

11. *Large Catechism,* "Baptism," in *The Book of Concord: The Confessions of the Evangelical Lutheran Church,* ed. Robert Kolb and Timothy Wengert (Minneapolis, Mn: Fortress Press, 2000), 41–42.

12. See e.g., *Justification in the Life of the Church: A Report from the Roman Catholic - Lutheran Dialogue Group for Sweden and Finland* (Uppsala, Stockholm and Helsinki, 2010).

and deeds. Neither is it a mere symbolic feast where the bread and the wine might remind us of Christ's body, absent and distant in heaven. Luther frequently repeated the words of institution, that is, "this is my body", *hoc est corpus meum*. These words are to be interpreted simply and realistically. The host does not merely signify the body of the Lord, referring only to a Christ dwelling elsewhere. The words of institution include and effect what they promise.

The concept of the real presence, naturally enough, is not the sole content of Holy Communion in the Bible and tradition. Luther, too, links other motifs to Communion: grace and the forgiveness of sins, the communion of Christians, the remembrance of Christ, the meal of gratitude to and confession of faith in God. It is at one and the same time the representation of the sacrifice given by Christ on Golgatha and the foretaste of the heavenly feast. According to Luther the essence of the Eucharist is, however, the real presence of Christ's body and blood in the bread and the wine. To Luther this faith was no abstract theological theory or philosophical idea. He wanted to rely on the simple Word of God, on the New Testament instituted by Christ himself. Christ gave his own body "for us for the forgiveness of sins" (Matt 26:28).

Faith in the real presence of Christ at the Eucharist has always united Lutherans and Catholics. We have always wanted to have confidence that Christ himself is present at the Holy Eucharist in the bread and the wine "truly and in substance", *vere et substantialiter*, giving the baptized believer the reality of all of salvation. As a community the church lives in the true meaning of the words *de eucharistia*, out of the mystery and gift of the Eucharist. In accordance with the Lutheran theology of the Eucharist, Christ's real presence is based on the doctrine of God, on Christology, and on the doctrine of justification. To Luther God is in his essence the Giver and the Donor.

According to the Creed, the Triune God is not a jealous judge or a merchant demanding compensation, but rather self-sacrificing Love, who loves us and wants good things for us. Luther summed up the message of the Creed by using the metaphor of giving gifts: "We see here in the Creed how God gives himself completely to us, with all his gifts and power.... [T]he Father gives us all creation, Christ all his works and the Holy Spirit all his gifts."[13]

God's love is the reason for Christ's incarnation and the basis for the Sacrament of the Eucharist. Out of love for us God became man in Christ, making peace with us. Out of love for us Christ instituted the Eucharist so that he might continue to be present among us and bring the gifts of reconciliation to our lives.

Christ's real presence at the Eucharist is thus in inseparable union with the gift of the Sacrament, its efficacy. The Eucharist is the feast of Christ's death and resurrection, where we partake of the reconciliation on the cross, the forgiveness

---

13. *Large Catechism* in Kolb-Wengert, *The Book of Concord*, 440. "Here in the Creed you have the entire essence, will, and work of God exquisitely depicted in very brief but rich words.... For in all three articles God himself has revealed and opened to us the most profound depths of his fatherly heart and his pure, unutterable love.... We see here in the Creed how God gives himself completely to us, with all his gifts and power, to help us keep the Ten Commandments: the Father gives us all creation, Christ all his works and the Holy Spirit all his gifts." Ibid., 63–69. On the theology of the Eucharist in Luther, see e.g., Jari Jolkkonen, "Eucharist," in *Engaging Luther: A (New) Theological Assessment*, ed. Olli-Pekka Vainio (Eugene, Or: Cascade, 2010), 108–137.

of sins, life eternal—all in all, we partake of Christ himself. Trust in Christ's real presence in the Sacrament of the Eucharist is such a treasure of faith which could bring Lutherans ever closer to Roman Catholics, the Orthodox, and to other Christians who confess this faith in doctrine and practice.

It is this mystery of faith that Pope John Paul II wrote about in his encyclical *Ecclesia de Eucharistia*. Christ, the true man and the true God is present in the bread and the wine of the Eucharist, really, wholly, and entirely.[14] We Lutherans can also wholeheartedly join in the words of the encyclical concerning Christ's presence and the gift of the Eucharist. Christ's presence is true "in objective reality", *in ipsa rerum natura*, and "independently of our minds", *a nostro scilicet spiritu disiuncta*. The Sacrament of the Eucharist, apart from bringing Christ's person and work into the present, also donates them to us personally. "The Eucharist thus applies (*applicat*) to men and women today the reconciliation won once for all by Christ for mankind in every age."[15]

The Holy Eucharist as a Communal Feast

On the basis of its name (*synaksis, communio*) the Holy Eucharist is a communal feast. St. Paul writes: "Is not the bread which we break a sharing [*koinonia*] in the body of Christ?" (1 Cor 10:16–17). The Holy Eucharist connects Christ and sinner, and a Christian to other Christians. Communion is not only a matter between God and the individual but a communal event with an ecclesiological and ethical dimension. Those who share the consecrated bread and wine also share all joy and sorrow, victory and suffering, concern and comfort. Those who are joined to Christ in the consecrated bread and wine are also joined to one another in faith and love.

The communal nature of this Holy Supper is brought out forcefully in the theology of the Holy Communion of Martin Luther:

> Besides all this, Christ did not institute these two forms solitary and alone, but he gave his true natural flesh in the bread, and his natural true blood in the wine, that he might give a really perfect sacrament or sign. For just as the bread is changed (*vorwandelt*) into his true natural body and the wine into his natural true blood, so truly are we also drawn and changed (*als so warhaftig werden wir vorwandelt*) into the spiritual body, that is, into the fellowship of Christ and all saints and by this sacrament put into possession of all the virtues and mercies of Christ and his saints.[16]

As the Eucharist is a *communio* in Christ, so also the sacrament unites us with other Christians and the whole *Gemeinschaft* of the *communio sanctorum*. Participation in Christ through word and sacrament is, in fact, sharing in the body of Christ, in the community of all saints. The interchange of the love of Christ takes place between all the members of this community.

---

14. *Ecclesia de Eucharistia*, §15.
15. Ibid., §12.
16. *The Blessed Sacrament of the Holy and True Body of Christ and the Brotherhoods* (LW 35:59).

The manner in which Martin Luther here speaks about the communal nature of the Eucharist and faith can open possibilities for new ecumenical convergence in the field of ecclesiology.[17] In the *Large Catechism*, Luther strongly emphasises the role of the Christian church. In creating new spiritual life, the Holy Spirit accomplishes this "through the Christian church." Luther states that: "In the first place he [the Holy Spirit] has a unique community in the world. It is the mother that begets and bears every Christian through the Word of God." When the Holy Spirit sanctifies us, "he first leads us into his holy community, placing us upon the bosom of the church, where he preaches to us and brings us to Christ."[18]

On the above bases where Luther speaks of the presence of Christ, the communal nature of the Holy Eucharist and the role of the church, we Lutherans may join in with the words of Pope John Paul II that the Holy Eucharist has a "unifying power."[19] "Our union with Christ, which is a gift and grace for each of us, makes it possible for us, in him, to share in the unity of his body which is the Church." Communion not only joins Christ and sinner, it also joins together Christians within the same church, young and old, women and men, priests and parishioners. It joins together dioceses and finally also local churches ministering to various parts of the world, churches confessing the same faith.

It is my fervent wish that we Lutherans could come together with our Roman Catholic and other Christian sisters and brothers at the common Communion table. We yearn for a common table because the Holy Eucharist is the feast of Christ's presence and *communio sanctorum*. On the basis of Luther's theology we have no difficulty in joining with those words which Benedict XVI, Bishop of Rome, stated in his inaugural homily: "All of us belong to the communion of Saints, we who have been baptized in the name of the Father, and of the Son and of the Holy Spirit, we who draw life from the gift of Christ's Body and Blood, through which he transforms us and makes us like himself."[20]

There is, however, no shortcut to a joint Holy Eucharist. Unity does not endure without truth; we require "the truth in love", *veritas in caritate*. The goal of visible unity and of a common Communion demand that we dig deeper into the foundation of our common Christian faith. We need patience to delve into revealed truth and we need the courage then to take decisive steps when adequate consensus is achieved.

---

17. Simo Peura, "The Church as a Spiritual Communion in Luther," in *The Church as Communion: Lutheran Contributions to Ecclesiology*, ed. Heinrich Holze, LWF Documentation 42 (Geneva: LWF, 1997), 93–131.

18. Theodore G. Tappert, ed., *The Book of Concord: The Confessions of the Evangelical Lutheran Church* (Philadelphia, Pa: Fortress Press, 1959), 415–416.

19. Stated more fully, "Eucharistic communion also confirms the Church in her unity as the body of Christ. Saint Paul refers to this *unifying power* of participation in the banquet of the Eucharist.... The argument is compelling: our union with Christ, which is a gift and grace for each of us, makes it possible for us, in him, to share in the unity of his body which is the Church. The Eucharist reinforces the incorporation into Christ which took place in Baptism though the gift of the Spirit (cf. 1 Cor 12:13, 27).... The seeds of disunity, which daily experience shows to be so deeply rooted in humanity as a result of sin, are countered by the *unifying power* of the body of Christ. The Eucharist, precisely by building up the Church, creates human community." (*Ecclesia de Eucharistia*, § 23–24).

20. Omelia del Santo Padre per il solenne inizio del Ministero Petrino, Domenica, 24 April 2005.

Conclusion

In summary, may I dare to contend that Martin Luther, in his *Catechisms* and his writings on Holy Communion, speaks as *doctor communis*, not attempting to develop new doctrine but rather striving to express and interpret the common faith of the undivided Christendom. Thus his writings still bear ecumenical fruit.

Wrestling with Demons and Violence

2. To Hell (and Back) with Luther
The Dialectic of Anfechtung *and Faith*

Denis R. Janz

I want to begin this lecture with a short introduction to the way Luther speaks about hell and how he understands it. From there I will turn to the complex theme of *Anfechtung*, in order to show that for Luther, hell at its hottest and *Anfechtung* at its deepest really amount to the same thing. Finally, when all of us are thoroughly depressed, I want to show how Luther speaks of faith as the sole remedy, as the only thing which really has the power to pull us back from the abyss.

Hell

First then, hell. The term "hell" occurs hundreds of times in Luther's writings. Sometimes he uses it vehemently to dismiss people he is unhappy with. Thus he says of "the papists," for instance: "Let them go to hell."[1] What he meant by this is precisely what we mean today when we use the phrase. More often in Luther, "hell" is used in combination with terms like sin and death. Thus the triad "sin, death, and hell" recurs with great frequency: it is Luther's formulaic, short-hand way of referring to all that Christians are "saved" from. "Hell" in this context simply means the negative things about human life.

If we look more closely at other ways in which Luther uses this term, the landscape of his hell acquires sharper features. In his 1535–1545 *Lectures on Genesis*, he makes it clear that the conventional Roman Catholic view is unacceptable. This tradition, he says, posited "five places after death": a hell of the damned, a hell for unbaptized infants, purgatory, a limbo for the "fathers" of ancient Israel, and heaven. This schema he dismisses as "foolishness" and "silly ideas."[2] As for unbaptized infants who die, we do not know what happens to them: we simply commend them "to the goodness of God." And as for any kind of "torment by eternal fire," Luther expresses great hesitation. After pointing out some contradictory biblical passages, he concludes by saying that about this "I am making no positive statement."[3] About the damned mentioned in John 5:29 he adds: "I am unable to say positively in what state those are who are condemned in the New Testament. I leave this undecided."[4]

---

1. Jaroslav Pelikan and Helmut T. Lehmann, eds., *Luther's Works*, American ed., 55 vols. (Philadelphia, Pa: Fortress Press; Saint Louis, Mo: Concordia Publishing House, 1955–86), 34:366 (hereafter, *LW*).
2. *LW* 4:314–315.
3. *LW* 4:315.
4. *LW* 4:316.

Properly speaking, Luther believed, hell is not a place. In his *Lectures on Jonah* from 1524–26 he is explicit on this: "It is not a specific place, but, in Scripture, it is nothingness."[5] For Luther it is an experience, an experience of nothingness. And nothingness, metaphysically speaking, is the opposite of being itself, or God. Thus hell is the experience of the absence of God. Or as Luther puts it, "To be deprived of the vision of God is hell itself."[6]

Essentially, Luther thought, we know nothing about how the absence of God will be experienced after death. But what we do know a great deal about is how the absence of God is experienced in this life, here and now. Thus the only hell we really know about is the one we encounter in our lives. And this is the one Luther speaks about almost exclusively. Thus he describes the experience of *Anfechtung* as hell. Referring to his own "dark night of the soul," he said in 1518, "I myself 'knew a man' [2 Cor 12:2] who claimed that he had often suffered these punishments, in fact over a brief period of time. Yet they were so great and so much like hell that no tongue could adequately express them."[7] Here "hell" is indeed pain—the ultimate, indescribable, emotional pain.

Hell is also for Luther the terror of death which cripples our lives. In his 1519–21 lectures on the Psalms (*Operationes in Psalmos*) he said: "I hold that the sorrow of death and of hell are the same thing. Hell is the terror of death, that is, the sense of death, in which the damned have a horrified dread of death and yet cannot escape."[8] So too, hell can be described as anxiety: "Those who are anxious seem to enter hell, and therefore, when someone finds himself in the most extreme misery of this kind, this experience is also called the most acute hell."[9] And, as a final example, Luther can speak of despair as hell: "The theologian is concerned that man become aware of this nature of his. When this happens, despair follows, casting him into hell."[10] This hell—the experience of *Anfechtung*, or the fear of death, anxiety, despair—this we humans know a great deal about. Ultimately it is the experience of the absence of God, and it is very real.

Here I want to add a brief note on the ancient belief about Christ's "descent into hell." This was a Christian teaching with vague origins in Roman mythology and in certain rather obscure New Testament passages (e.g., 1 Pet 3:19–22; 4:6; Eph 4:8–10). By the mid-fourth century it had found its way into early creedal formulations. In the Middle Ages it provided grist, in a minor way, for the scholastic theological mill. It also furnished a vivid theme for the creative imagination, expressing itself in graphic and dramatic art. Luther accepted the *descensus ad inferos*, as the creeds (Apostles' and Athanasian) called it, as an article of faith. Thus the question of its truth was not at issue. What was open to discussion, of course, was its meaning. Yet, even on this, Luther had surprisingly little to say. Only in a few Easter and Ascension Day sermons, and in a handful of other sources, does Luther express his views.

---

5. *D. Martin Luthers Werke: Kritische Gesamtausgabe*, 69 vols. (Weimar: Hermann Böhlaus Nachfolger, 1883–), 13:232,19–20 (hereafter, WA).
6. *LW* 4:315.
7. *LW* 31:129.
8. WA 5:463,22–25.
9. WA 13:232,17–19.
10. *LW* 12:310–311.

Luther's understanding of this doctrine seems to have been developing throughout the 1520s. In 1523, for instance, we find him expressing considerable puzzlement over what the primary Scriptural source (1 Pet 3:19–22) could possibly mean.[11] He came back to this passage and Eph 4:8–10 in 1527, in a sermon for Ascension Day. What it means, he emphasized, is that Christ went "down" before he went "up." In fact he went as deep as it is possible to go, to "the devil, death, sin, and hell." Thus the triumphant Christ encompasses all things under his rule, from the very lowest to the highest.[12]

By the 1530s Luther's understanding seems to have reached maturity, and he expressed it most fully in his 1532 sermon for Easter Day. The article of faith as he now enunciates it is quite simply that "[Christ] descended into hell that he might redeem us, who should have lay imprisoned there."[13] But the question is: how should this be understood? Luther begins his sermon with a substantial polemic against those who take articles of faith like this literally, and thus make nonsense out of them. "[M]any have wanted to grasp these words with their reason and five senses, but without success. They have only been led further from the faith."[14] Obviously, Luther says, "it did not happen in a physical way, since he indeed remained three days in the grave."[15] Crude literalism, Luther insists, makes nonsense of this.[16] Indeed it is precisely the devil that tries to make us literalists and thus lead us away from the core truth.[17]

How then did it happen? Luther's answer is frankly agnostic: we really don't know. "I would simply leave this subject alone since I cannot even grasp everything that pertains to this life."[18] What it points to, on the other hand, is "that Christ destroyed hell's power and took all the devil's power away from him. When I grasp that, then I have the true core and meaning of it, and I should not ask further nor rack my brain about how it happened or how it was possible."[19] We could learn much from "children and simple people" and artists, when it comes to expressing these things. They are not literalists, but they use their imaginations—create paintings, tell a story, perform in the children's Easter pageant, and so forth.[20] Luther gives an example of such imaginative "explanation": "[H]e went to hell with his banner in hand as a victorious hero, and he tore down its gates and charged into the midst of the devils, throwing one through the window and another out the door."[21] And we shouldn't be afraid (as literalists tend to be) that such imaginative depictions will "harm or mislead us."[22]

Once we have grasped Luther's rejection of the literal, we are in a position to understand his final answer to the question of why Christ descended into hell: to douse the fire! "[N]either all monastic sanctity nor all the world's power

11. WA 12:367,31–32.
12. WA 23:702,12–16.
13. WA 37:62,31–32.
14. WA 37:62,37–63,2.
15. WA 37:62,12–13.
16. WA 37:63,36–41.
17. WA 37:64,16–19.
18. WA 37:63,20–21.
19. WA 37:63,31–34.
20. WA 37:63,5–13; 64,23.
21. WA 37:65,23–25.
22. WA 37:65,38–39.

and might can extinguish one spark of the fire of hell. But it so happened that this man went down with his banner, and then all the devils had to flee as if for their lives. And he extinguished all the fires of hell, so that no Christians need to fear it."[23] Here we have a new soteriological title: Christ as fireman! The threat of hell hovered ominously over the medieval and Reformation periods and it loomed large on Luther's personal horizon. It was in this context that Luther came to understand the descent into hell as a "powerful" and "useful" article of faith.[24]

Anfechtung

With this in mind, I return now to the theme of *Anfechtung* for a closer look. This term, which Luther used throughout his career, has no exact equivalent in English. It refers not to an idea or a belief but to an experience. Literally, it means a kind of assault or attack. The Latin term Luther most often used to refer to the same thing is *tentatio*. But to translate this simply as "temptation," as many have done, is seriously to distort what he meant. In short, the term is problematic.

At the same time, it is of major importance. This is because Luther's theology has experience, more precisely religious experience, as its starting point. The subject matter of theology is the human person—his/her guilt and redemption. Theologians try to understand this with the help of revelation. But they are driven to this task in the first place by religious experience—their own and that of others. This is what Luther meant when he said that "experience alone makes the theologian."[25] Of course, human religious experience comes in multiple, almost infinite, varieties. But Luther's analysis categorized all of it into two basic types: the negative and the positive, the experience of our sinfulness and separation from God, on the one hand, and the experience of faith, on the other. *Anfechtung* is Luther's term for the first type of experience, especially in its more intense forms. This primal religious experience "taught" Luther theology: "I didn't learn my theology all at once. I had to ponder over it ever more deeply, and my *Anfechtungen* [*tentationes*] were of help to me in this, for one does not learn anything without experience [*sine usu*]."[26]

This provisional definition can give us an initial orientation to the subject, but it must be tested against the many other things Luther said about *Anfechtung*. He was not reluctant to speak and write about this aspect of his personal inner life. It was a recurring experience for him: he felt it in varying degrees of intensity at every stage of his life—as a young monk, as a beginning professor at Wittenberg, at the Wartburg, in the late 1520s, and so on, into old age. Obviously this was not the kind of experience which is finally and decisively overcome once and for all in a dramatic conversion event. Moreover, his many descriptions and definitions vary widely. They leave the distinct impression

---

23. WA 37:66,29–34.
24. WA 37:63,30.
25. *LW* 54:7, #46.
26. *D. Martin Luthers Werke: Kritische Gesamtausgabe, Tischreden*, 6 vols. (Weimar: Hermann Böhlaus Nachfolger, 1912–1921), 1:146,12–14, #352 (hereafter, WA TR).

that mere words are inadequate to define it. We should not be surprised: often people's most deeply felt experiences elude precise delineation in ordinary language.

Luther realized that some of his bouts of *Anfechtung* were related to physical illnesses. They can be, he says, the cause of headaches and stomach problems.[27] They can also result from physical ailments which force us to face our mortality.[28] But the "spiritual anguish exceeds bodily suffering by far."[29] And *Anfechtung* can strike when we are in perfect health. So too, Luther understood that *Anfechtung* is related to depression.[30] Severe depression can be a kind of *Anfechtung*.[31] But on the other hand, *Anfechtung* is by no means reducible to depression, from his point of view.

Sometimes Luther describes *Anfechtung* as an experience of God's anger—a horrifying anger because it is eternal: "[I]n this present agony, a person sees nothing but hell, and there seems to be no way out. He feels that what is happening to him/her is endless, for it is not the wrath of a human person but of the eternal God."[32] Elsewhere Luther describes this fear that God's anger is unending in other terms: "My *Anfechtung* [*tentatio*] is this, that I think I don't have a gracious God…. It is the greatest grief, and, as Paul says, it produces death [2 Cor 7:10]."[33] Even worse, perhaps, is when one senses that he/she faces it alone. "When persons are tormented by *Anfechtungen*, it seems to them that they are alone. God is irreconcilably angry only with them."[34]

Sometimes the theme of *human* anger rises to the fore in Luther's discussion. His own early experience of *Anfechtung* in the monastery made him "angry with God."[35] The experience can lead to hatred of God, the "wish that there were no God at all!"[36] and ultimately, blasphemously, to the desire to kill God.[37]

The person who experiences *Anfechtung*, Luther thought, approaches the gates of hell. "[T]he entrance of hell … is near despair."[38] Already in his *Ninety-five Theses* of 1517, Luther had mentioned the "horror of despair."[39] In the following year, in his *Explanations of the Ninety-five Theses*, he elaborated on this despair in a passage that was to become his most famous description of *Anfechtung*. Here is the full text of the passage I began to quote earlier:

> I myself "knew a man" [Luther is referring to himself] who claimed that he had often suffered these punishments, in fact over a very brief period of time. Yet they were so great and so much like hell that no tongue could adequately express them, no pen could describe them, and one who had not himself experienced them could not believe them. And so great were they that, if they had

27. *LW* 54:74, #461.
28. *LW* 14:141.
29. *LW* 54:276, #3799.
30. *LW* 54:17, #122; 54:275, #3798.
31. *D. Martin Luthers Werke: Kritische Gesamtausgabe, Briefwechsel*, 18 vols. (Weimar: Hermann Böhlaus Nachfolger, 1930–1985), WA Br 11:112,7–10, #4120 (hereafter, WA Br).
32. WA 5:210,13–16.
33. WA TR 1:200,6–8, #461.
34. WA 5:79,14–15.
35. *LW* 34:337.
36. *LW* 22:142.
37. WA 5:210,1–2.
38. *LW* 31:130.
39. *LW* 31:27.

been sustained or had lasted for half an hour, even for one tenth of an hour, he would have perished completely and all of his bones would have been reduced to ashes. At such a time God seems terribly angry, and with him the whole creation. At such a time there is no flight, no comfort, within or without, but all things accuse. At such a time, as the Psalmist mourns, "I am cut off from thy sight" [cf. Ps 31:22].... All that remains is the stark naked desire for help and a terrible groaning, but it does not know where to turn for help. In this instance the person is stretched out with Christ so that all his bones may be counted, and every corner of the soul is filled with the greatest bitterness, dread, trembling, and sorrow in such a manner that all these last forever.[40]

This "abyss of despair" remained for Luther one of the standard ways of describing what he meant by *Anfechtung*.[41]

If despair brings us near to the gates of hell, there is another form of *Anfechtung* that takes us into hell itself. And that is the experience of the silence of God. Sometimes God "withdraws his anger" and disappears.[42] He abandons us: "To be abandoned by God—this is far worse than death."[43] Here is the ultimate anguish, what Luther calls the "most perfect *Anfechtung*,"[44] the very worst human experience imaginable—hell itself.

Luther did not think that the experience of *Anfechtung* was universal. Some, such as Staupitz, Luther's early spiritual mentor, did not seem to understand.[45] Sebastian Münster, a Hebraist on whom Luther relied for help in translating the Old Testament, had no such experience, in Luther's opinion.[46] Erasmus and Luther's "sacramentarian" opponents would change their minds if they ever experienced this.[47] The indulgence preachers could never so crassly trivialize the gospel if they felt this.[48] The "reprobate," Luther says, feel no such thing.[49] Then too, "self-assured, coarse, untested, inexperienced people know and understand nothing about this."[50]

At the same time Luther took comfort in the fact that he wasn't alone: many people *do* in fact experience something similar. And some of these have left us with their attempts to describe it. The book of Job is one example of this.[51] Even more poignant, from Luther's perspective, is the story of Jonah. What greater abandonment could there be than to be "cast into the deep" (Jonah 2:3)?[52] What greater silence than to be in "the belly of the fish" (Jonah 2:1)? And Jonah's story was Luther's: "I sat with Jonah in the whale where everything seemed to be despair."[53] Most eloquent of all in expressing the experience of *Anfechtung*, Luther thought, were the Psalms. In fact this is what the whole book is about.[54]

40. *LW* 31:129.
41. *LW* 33:190; 54:16–17.
42. WA TR 1:585,3–10, #1179.
43. WA 45:237,23.
44. WA 5:204,26.
45. *LW* 54:133, #1288.
46. WA TR 3:363,4–6, #3505.
47. *LW* 49:173.
48. *LW* 31:130.
49. *LW* 25:378.
50. WA 45:237,23–26.
51. WA 5:78,36–37; 45:239,18–19.
52. *LW* 19:18–19.
53. WA TR 3:363,4–6, #3503.
54. WA TR 5:592,26–27, #6305.

From the divine wrath of Psalm 6,[55] to the "despairing spirit" of Psalm 51,[56] to the "faint spirit" of Psalm 142,[57] to "the depths" of Psalm 130—"where," Luther asks, "do you find deeper, more sorrowful, more pitiful words of sadness? There again you look into the hearts of all the saints, as into death, yes, as into hell itself."[58] Above all, the theme of abandonment is powerfully expressed in Psalm 22: "My God, my God, why have you forsaken me?"

With this we come to the supreme sufferer of *Anfechtung*, Jesus himself. Luther often alludes to this, but he addresses it most directly in sermons on the passion.[59] Following Matthew's narrative (Matt 26:36–46), Luther recounts how Jesus entered the Garden of Gethsemane with his disciples. There Jesus experienced an anguish (*Angst*) so great he felt he could die from it.[60] Faced with this *Anfechtung*, he prayed "Let this cup pass from me" three times according to Matthew. And the Father's answer? Silence! (In Luke's version, Luther notes, God sends an angel to "strengthen" Jesus.[61] But still, God's silence is not broken (Luke 22:41–44). No wonder then that shortly thereafter, from the cross, we hear his cry of dereliction, "My God, my God, why have you forsaken me?" (Matt 27:46). Silence and abandonment—Jesus experienced "the most perfect *Anfechtung*,"[62] or what Luther elsewhere calls "the high *Anfechtung*, which is called being forsaken by God,"[63] a "high, spiritual suffering" which is unimaginable.[64]

Horrifying as the experience of *Anfechtung* can be, it can also be salutary. Without this, for instance, one cannot really understand the Scriptures[65]—not David, or Jonah, or Job, or Christ. Luther wonders whether "smug people, who have never struggled with any temptation [*tentatio/Anfechtung*] or true terrors of sin and death" can really know what faith is.[66] Moreover, Luther thought, this experience is essential for theologians. In his 1539 prescription for "a correct way of studying theology," *Anfechtung* plays a major role: "[It] is the touchstone which teaches you not only to know and understand, but also to experience how right, how true, how sweet, how lovely, how mighty, how comforting God's word is, wisdom beyond all wisdom."[67] Without experiencing the depths, in other words, the immensity of the heights can scarcely be grasped.

There is also a deeper sense in which the experience of *Anfechtung* is beneficial for us. The "broken spirit" which the Psalmist calls "the sacrifice acceptable to God" (Ps 51:17), Luther thinks, is the *Anfechtung* of despair.[68] In fact, our despair puts us in very close proximity to grace.[69] God's kindness and love

55. *LW* 54:275, #3798.
56. *LW* 25:377.
57. *LW* 42:184–185.
58. *LW* 35:256.
59. E.g., *WA* 52:734–742.
60. *WA* 52:734,26–28.
61. *WA* 52:742,8–9.
62. *WA* 5:204,26.
63. *WA* 45:240,26–27.
64. *WA* 45:239,23.
65. *WA TR* 1:472,22–24, #941.
66. *LW* 26:127.
67. *LW* 34:286.
68. *LW* 25:377.
69. *LW* 33:190.

lie hidden beneath his anger, as Jonah discovered.[70] When we experience the silence and the absence of God, Christ is "with" us: "If … you have been three days in hell, this is a sign that Christ is with you and you are with Christ."[71] Resurrection is at hand.

Is there anything that can be done to alleviate or mitigate this experience for oneself and for others? Luther offers a very substantial repertoire of advice in this regard. Some of it is found in short treatises such as his 1521 work, *Comfort for a Person Facing High Anfechtung.*[72] Even more is found in personal letters to friends and acquaintances. For instance, in 1530 Luther wrote a series of rather substantial letters to one Jerome Weller, who was going through a prolonged period of *Anfechtung.*[73] Likewise in 1531 he sent a letter of advice on this theme to Barbara Lisskirchen.[74] And in 1545 he circulated a letter to pastors, detailing a kind of semi-liturgical procedure for dealing with this very common problem.[75] References to his own personal bouts of *Anfechtung* and how he dealt with them are found in various writings, but above all throughout his *Table Talk.* What is notable in all this is the enormous variety. No single piece of advice is appropriate in every case. People differ, and *Anfechtung* manifests itself in a whole range of forms and levels of intensity.

One can easily compile a list of techniques he suggested to one or another sufferer and ones he himself used: 1. private confession to a pastor or friend;[76] 2. pray, using Psalm 142;[77] 3. tell the devil, "Kiss my ass";[78] 4. flee solitude;[79] 5. drink heartily (though for some, abstinence is better);[80] 6. eat sumptuously; 7. think of sex;[81] 8. tell jokes and laugh; 9. commit a sin to spite the devil;[82] 10. yield to God's will: focus not on "Let this cup pass from me," but rather on "Not my will, but yours."[83] And so on. This list could easily be extended. All of these things, Luther thought, work in certain circumstances.

Yet he also knew that in another sense, none of them work. We can begin to understand this if we focus for the moment solely on the "most perfect" or "high" *Anfechtung.* Lesser *Anfechtungen* are really only weaker versions of the same thing. And this high *Anfechtung* is, as we have seen, the experience of God's silence, his abandonment of us, our God-forsakeness, hell. Luther can also speak of it as our sense that God is not really "for us" but "against us": "My *Anfechtung* [*tentatio*] is this, that I think I don't have a gracious God…. It is the greatest grief, and, as Paul says, it produces death (2 Cor 7:10). God hates it, and he comforts us by saying, 'I am your God.' I know his promise, and yet should some thought that isn't worth a fart nevertheless overwhelm me, I have the

70. *LW* 19:73; WA TR 1:585,3–10, #1179.
71. *LW* 10:373.
72. WA 7:784–791 = *LW* 42:183–186.
73. WA Br 5:373–375, #1593; 518–520, #1670; 546–547, #1684.
74. WA Br 12:134–136, #4244a.
75. WA Br 11:111–112, #4120.
76. *LW* 51:98.
77. *LW* 42:184–185.
78. WA TR 1:64,16–17, #144.
79. *LW* 54:277, #3799.
80. *LW* 54:18, #122; WA 40/2:115,14–116,2; *LW* 50:48.
81. *LW* 54:18, #122.
82. WA Br 5:519,42–46, #1670.
83. *LW* 42:183.

advantage ... of taking hold of his word once again. God be praised, I grasp the first commandment which declares, 'I am your God (Exod 20:2). I am not going to devour you. I am not going to be poison for you.'"[84] Here we see what is, to Luther's way of thinking, the only real remedy. It is the confidence that God is "for us." This confidence or trust is what Luther called "faith."

Faith

There is nothing more fundamental for an understanding of Luther than his concept of faith. For him it was at the same time the profoundest and the most important mystery of human life. In a real sense his theological career was a lifelong struggle to grasp and explain it. At the mid-point of that career, in 1531, he confessed, he had barely made a start: "For in my heart there resides this one doctrine, namely, faith in Christ. From it, through it, and to it all my theological thought flows and returns day and night; yet I am aware that all I have grasped of this wisdom in its height, width, and depth are a few poor and insignificant firstfruits and fragments."[85] By the end of his career he had approached the subject from every conceivable angle, seeing ever new dimensions and implications, explaining it hundreds of times in scores of different ways, searching always for a more adequate language, and finally acknowledging the poverty of the human intellect in the face of this, one of life's ultimate mysteries.

To begin to understand what Luther meant by faith, we must have a firm grasp of definitions he rejected. Trained in scholasticism, he had inherited the dominant medieval understanding of faith as an infused intellectual virtue or habit from which the "act of faith" proceeds. Such an act of faith, then, is essentially the assent of the intellect to propositional truths. Luther's early marginal notes on Augustine and Peter Lombard of 1509/10 indicate his agreement with this traditional view.[86] But already by 1515 he regarded this understanding of "faith as belief" as an impoverished, superficial distortion of what it really means.

Of course, he did not simply make up a new definition. Rather his new understanding emerged from a deeply personal engagement with the text of Scripture, and especially the writings of St. Paul. Here he found a language of faith which, in his view, overturned the traditional one. Simply acknowledging certain events to be true, for instance, falls far short of what St. Paul meant by "faith" in his letter to the Romans: "Faith is not the human notion and dream that some people call faith.... [W]hen they hear the gospel, they get busy and by their own power create an idea in their heart which says, 'I believe'; they take this then to be a true faith. But it is a human figment."[87] In an academic disputation of 1535, Luther used the example of beliefs about Jesus to illustrate the point. "[T]he infused faith of the sophists [scholastics], says of Christ: 'I believe that the Son of God suffered and rose again,' and here it stops. But true faith says: 'I certainly believe that the Son of God suffered and rose, but he did

84. *LW* 54:75, #461.
85. *LW* 27:145.
86. E.g., WA 9:92,38–93,7.
87. *LW* 35:370.

this all for me, for my sins, of that I am certain'.... Accordingly, that 'for me' or 'for us', if it is believed, creates that true faith and distinguishes it from all other faith which merely hears the things done. This is the faith that alone justifies us."[88] Or, as the *Augsburg Confession* had put it in 1530, faith does indeed acknowledge these events, but then so does the devil. True faith goes beyond this by believing the effect of this history.[89] Simple belief that these things happened (*fides historica*) certainly does not justify: Luther's slogan "justification by faith alone" makes no sense if this is what faith means.

Luther's understanding of faith has rightly been called "existential": knowledge of God or Christ is not real knowledge but rather it remains useless information until we see its implications for us. This is what Luther had in mind when he said in his 1535 *Lectures on Galatians* that "[f]aith is the creator of the Deity, not in the substance of God, but in us."[90] It is in faith that God becomes real for us. In those same lectures, Luther explained that for Christians this happens through Christ. The "doctrine [or content] of faith," he says, "proclaims that Christ alone is the victor over sin, death, and the devil."[91] Faith itself then "is a sure confidence that takes hold of Christ."[92] In other words, faith is the confidence that "sin, death, and the devil" have been overcome for me. It is the subjective appropriation of what has objectively happened; and until there is such a subjective appropriation, what has happened objectively (Christ's victory) does me no good.

This appropriating, or apprehending, or grasping, or accepting is what Luther means by "faith." "Faith apprehends Christ," Luther says,[93] and he means that in faith the entire being of the person recognizes, grasps, and accepts the ultimate import of Christ for him or her. And who is Christ? Most fundamentally for Luther, Christ is "a mirror of the Father's heart."[94] To "apprehend Christ" means therefore to grasp that I am the object of the divine love. As the *Augsburg Confession* put it, faith is the belief that we "are received into grace [i.e., into divine favor];" it is by faith that "forgiveness of sins and justification are taken hold of."[95] Or as Luther says in his 1522 Preface to St. Paul's letter to the Romans, "Faith is a living daring confidence in God's grace, so sure and certain that the believer would stake his life on it a thousand times. This knowledge of and confidence in God's grace makes men glad and bold and happy in dealing with God and with all creatures. And this is the work which the Holy Spirit performs in faith."[96] In the final analysis, faith is for Luther the confidence that, because we are objects of an infinite and unconditional love, the negativities of human existence can have no finality or ultimacy for us: fear, despair, death, and all troubles have been conquered. They are stripped of their power by the conviction that the very deepest of all human longings has been

---

88. *LW* 34:110.
89. Robert Kolb and Timothy J. Wengert, eds., *The Book of Concord* (Minneapolis, Mn: Fortress Press, 2000), 57 (hereafter *BC*).
90. *LW* 26:227.
91. *LW* 26:224.
92. *LW* 26:348.
93. *LW* 34:153.
94. *BC*, 440.
95. *BC*, 41.
96. *LW* 35:371.

fulfilled. For if we really are loved infinitely and unconditionally by an omnipotent being, nothing can hurt us.

To live one's life with such a trust, according to Luther, makes all the difference in the world. But before describing Luther's view of this "new creature," we must emphasize that for him, faith exists very often in tension with experience. There are "mountaintop" moments in life when humans have a profound sense that all is right with the world. But there are other moments, Luther knew all too well, when bitter experience suggests that "sin, death, and the devil" (i.e., all the evils that oppress humans) will have the last word. At such times, Luther said, "faith slinks away and hides."[97] This was the experience of Christ on the cross, and so too is it our experience. Reason, at such moments, interprets experience so as to contradict faith, and only faith can overcome it: "It [reason] can be killed by nothing else but faith, which believes God…. It [faith] does this in spite of the fact that he speaks what seems foolish, absurd, and impossible to reason [namely, that he loves us]."[98] The miracle is that faith, weak as it now may be, persists. Only in the life of the world to come will our experience cease to contradict faith: then what we believe now, that all evil has been overcome, will be apparent.

Faith, this trust that death and all troubles have been conquered, can sometimes seem as self-evident to us as "three plus two equals five."[99] But more often in real life it coexists, in a complex relationship, with doubt. In his Preface to his 1535 *Lectures on Galatians*, Luther warns that we have little hope of understanding St. Paul here unless we too are "miserable Galatians in faith," that is, "troubled, afflicted, vexed, and tempted."[100] The presence of doubt does not imply the absence of faith. Faith is a mysterious reality which hides itself beneath doubt and even beneath its absolute opposite, despair. So it is difficult to tell where faith is. "For it happens, indeed it is typical of faith, that often he who claims to believe does not believe at all; and on the other hand, he who doesn't think he believes, but is in despair, has the greatest faith."[101] Faith sometimes "crawls away and hides" beneath doubt and despair, and then it reemerges. And ultimately, Luther thinks, humans do not control this. If they did, faith would be little more than "the power of positive thinking."

It is, Luther insists, a gift. Having true faith is really a divine work[102] which comes to us through the proclamation of the gospel—the good news that God loves us though we are unworthy of that love.[103] Some—not all—who hear it accept it, and that acceptance is what Christians call the work of the Holy Spirit in us.[104] In other words, when humans receive and accept God's grace, that itself is the result of grace. "For here we work nothing, render nothing to God; we only receive and permit someone else to work in us, namely God."[105] Faith thus comes to us, Luther says, as the dry earth receives the rain, in utter passivity.[106]

97. WA 17/1:72,17.
98. *LW* 26:231.
99. WA 10/3:260, 23–261,1.
100. *LW* 27:148.
101. *LW* 40:241.
102. WA 12:442,4–9.
103. *LW* 35:368.
104. *LW* 21:299.
105. *LW* 26:4–5.
106. *LW* 26:6.

Human striving cannot induce it to fall, but when it does, new life erupts. And whenever we see signs of this new life, we can be sure that it has fallen: "True faith is not idle. We can, therefore, ascertain and recognize those who have true faith from the effect or from what follows."[107]

Luther was explicit in spelling out the consequences of faith for human emotional life, and in this he very directly brought his own experience into play. As I have shown, throughout his life and fairly frequently he was vigorously assaulted by *Anfechtungen*. Luther vividly described his *Anfechtungen* as the experience of hell itself. And ultimately the only answer, he thought, was faith: "[T]he afflicted conscience has no remedy against despair and eternal death except to take hold of the promise of grace offered in Christ, that is, this righteousness of faith."[108] Losing faith means losing Christ as savior, and from this "sure despair and eternal death follow."[109] Losing faith, in other words, means losing confidence that the source and heart of all reality is an infinite love, and losing trust that we are unconditionally objects of that love. Hence, Luther says, when assaulted by fear and death, "we must look at no other God than this incarnate and human God.... When you do this, you will see the love, the goodness, and the sweetness of God."[110] Faith alone is what enables us to experience life as sweet, in the deepest sense. It brings peace and happiness—in short, salvation.[111]

This topic of faith has brought us to the very heart of Luther's understanding of Christianity. Its meaning, according to him, cannot be exhausted. "[The one] who has had even a faint taste of it can never write, speak, meditate, or hear enough concerning it."[112] If one were forced to choose a summary statement from Luther, the following one from 1522 may well be the best. And it is noteworthy that it comes not from a theological lecture or academic disputation but from a sermon.

> All Christian teaching, works and life can be summed up briefly, clearly, and fully under the two categories of faith and love: humans are placed midway between God and their neighbor, receiving from above [faith] and dispensing below [love], and becoming as it were a vessel or a tube through which the stream of divine benefits flows unceasingly into other people. How clearly those are conformed to God who receive from God everything he has to give, in Christ, and in their turn, as though they were gods to others, give them benefits.... We are children of God through faith, which makes us heirs to all the divine goodness. But we are gods through love, which makes us active in doing good to our neighbor; for the divine nature is nothing other than pure goodness ... and friendliness and kindness, pouring out its good things every day in profusion upon every creature, as we can see.[113]

---

107. *LW* 34:182.
108. *LW* 26:5–6.
109. *LW* 26:11.
110. *LW* 26:29–30.
111. *LW* 26:11.
112. *LW* 31:343.
113. *WA* 10/1/1:100,8–101,2.

Faith, ultimately, is the ability to understand and accept ourselves as the objects of God's love. This, Luther thought, is the key to finding happiness in life.

If this is what faith really is, then it is also what rescues us from hell. As we have seen, hell at its very hottest is nothing but the ultimate extremity of human dread and despair, the terror of feeling abandoned by God, the horror we feel when *our* cry of dereliction is answered by silence. This is the abyss, and only faith, Luther believed, has the power to drag us back from its edge.

3. Luther on the Devil

Volker Leppin

Luther's memory in Germany is a difficult and somehow strange phenomenon.[1] There are so many places that are supposed to be genuine witnesses to the reformer's life and actions. A number of these will be the destinations of large numbers of tourists and pilgrims leading up to 2017, and perhaps after, but there are significant questions regarding their authenticity. We can start with the house in Eisleben, which has for a long time been regarded as Luther's birth house. Recent research, however, has shown that this house is far too young to have been the actual house, and as result the house is now referred to as the *Geburtshausmuseum*[2] (the birth house museum)—a linguistic invention that might be possible in no other language except German. Even worse is another case in the very same town of Eisleben. The house that claims to be the place where Luther died is actually the wrong building. The real one lies one or two blocks away, and it is used as a restaurant and hotel rather than as a Luther memorial. And let me be quite frank about the famous *Thesenanschlagstür* (the Theses door) in Wittenberg. The legend has it that it was here that Luther nailed his 95 Theses against indulgences in 1517, but apparently this never happened.[3]

One of the most famous legends, albeit detected long ago, is one that deals with the devil. I am thinking here about the story of the ink stain at the Wartburg Castle. Generations of visitors were able to see it and hear the story of Luther mocking the devil by throwing his inkwell against the wall.[4] Currently, the stain is dulled and no efforts are being made to renew it for the sake of curious tourists. Many Protestants may actually feel good about this fading of memory, happy with the knowledge that Luther's struggle with a real devil was only a matter of legend.

The devil is not so popular nowadays in Protestant theology. One of the most decisive theological disputes during the Enlightenment, however, was concerned precisely with the devil. Many theologians were distressed about Luther's *Taufbüchlein* (baptism booklet), because the reformer had not

---

1. With this paper, I am following the lines of my study, Volker Leppin, "'Der alt böse Feind': Der Teufel in Martin Luthers Leben und Denken," *JBTh* 26 (2011): 291–321. I am deeply grateful to Brooks Schramm for correcting my English text. Translations from WA are my own.

2. See Annemarie Neser, "Luthers Geburtshaus in Eisleben: Ursprünge, Wandlungen, Resultate," in *Martin Luther und Eisleben*, ed. Roesemarie Knape, Schriften der Stiftung Luthergedenkstätten in Sachsen-Anhalt 8 (Leipzig: Evangelische Verlagsanstalt, 2007), 87–119.

3. For recent discussion see Joachim Ott and Martin Treu, eds, *Faszination Thesenanschlag: Faktum oder Fiktion* (Leipzig: Evangelische Verlagsanstalt, 2008).

4. For this, see Johannes Luther, *Legenden um Luther* (Berlin: Walter de Gruyter, 1933).

abolished the practicise of exorcism. For enlightened Protestants, it was simply an act of superstition to presuppose the reality of the devil in this way, and to regard a newborn child as a part of the realm or reign of the great enemy. As a result, they attacked the liturgical text of the reformer himself so as to create an up-to-date version of Protestant belief. At a remove of some centuries, however, I would like to suggest that it may now be possible to speak of Luther's more realistic, concrete conception of the devil, without simultaneously being accused of trying to rehabilitate a mere superstitious belief. Let me begin with the reality of the devil in Luther's life.

Luther was convinced of the devil's reality from a very young age. We do not know much about his father's piety, but one peculiar aspect seems to be quite clear. Hans Luder believed in the devil's willingness and ability to interfere into human life. When Luther argued with his father about his decision to enter the monastery in Erfurt, Hans at least pondered the possibility that it might have been the devil who had drawn his son in this direction.[5] This sheds some light on the atmosphere in which the young Luther was raised. In large part, it was one of severe and anxious belief, as can be seen in the few remarks that Luther made about his parents.[6]

As critical as he was, Luther never lost his parental heritage totally. The devil remained a companion in his life, and he could describe with precision those moments when he encountered him. Those brief phases between sleeping and being awake were the time when the devil would come. When Luther was dozing off to sleep, or when he was in the process of waking up, the devil would come to him: "For, it is like this with me. When I am awaking, the devil quickly comes and disputes against me, until I admonish him: Lick my ass!"[7]

Obviously, Luther was not overly shy about using uncouth words and phrases. Even more, as Heiko Oberman has shown, there is a strong connection between vulgar speech and the devil.[8] Actually, far more important for the struggle against the devil was the word of God, and so Luther gave the following advice: "When the devil comes by night to bother me, my answer is: Devil, now I have to sleep, for this is God's command: working by day and sleeping by night."[9] As situations like these show, the Stotternheim event[10] that was argued about between Luther and his father was an exceptional example of the way that the devil enters human lives. But in reality it is at every second that we have to be aware of the devil's attacks. The entire life of the human being is, as Oberman has pointed out, a life between God and the devil.[11]

---

5. See Volker Leppin, *Martin Luther*, 2nd ed. (Darmstadt: Wissenschaftliche Buchgesellschaft, 2010), 34.
6. For this see Leppin, *Martin Luther*, 16–21.
7. "Leck mich in dem a." D. *Martin Luthers Werke: Kritische Gesamtausgabe, Tischreden*, 6 vols. (Weimar: Hermann Böhlaus Nachfolger, 1912–1921), WA TR 2:15,35–37, #1263 (hereafter, WA TR).
8. Heiko A. Oberman, *Luther: Man between God and the Devil*, trans. Eileen Walliser-Schwarzbart (New Haven, Ct and London: Yale University Press, 1989), 154–156.
9. WA TR 2:132,4–7, # 1557); cf. 1:204,30f, #469); 4:409,20f, # 4630); 6:215,39–216,2, #6827. On the role of God's word in the struggle against the devil, see Hans-Martin Barth, *Der Teufel und Jesus Christus in der Theologie Martin Luthers* (Göttingen: Vandenhoeck & Ruprecht, 1967), 113–121.
10. Slightly north of Erfurt, Stotternheim was where Luther had been caught in the terrible thunderstorm.
11. Oberman, *Luther: Man between God and the Devil*.

Thus it is not only sadness and melancholy that derive from the devil's offences but also war,[12] disease,[13] and even the great plague as well.[14] This is not merely a metaphorical way of speaking. Luther himself was convinced that the theologian, by recourse to the devil, can explain diseases better than a physician: With respect to diseases, physicians only observe natural causes. They try to help with their own facilities, and they do quite well with this. But they do not think about Satan, the founder of the material causes in the illness itself. He can immediately change causes and diseases, warm to cold, and vice versa. So, one needs a higher medicine, meaning faith and prayer.[15]

Even for himself, Luther stressed that his own diseases could never be cured by medicine alone, because their cause was not natural.[16] His view of life took into account the possibility of God's directly curing a disease, as well as the devil's potency to interfere in any part of our life whenever he wanted to do so. He was convinced that the Bible forced him to see the world in this way. It was not only the book of Job that showed this, but also Jesus Christ himself: "And if Christ himself may say, this woman is possessed by Satan, or Peter is bound by Satan (Acts 10:38), why should the devil not be able to harm our eyes or anything else?"[17]

For the reformer, it is not only disease that is caused by the devil, but also bad weather.[18] This is the point where witchcraft comes in. The devil uses sorceresses for causing tempests.[19] His whole life long, Luther envisaged the existence of witches, even if his thoughts were somewhat transformed by Reformation ideas. In his early expositions of the Decalogue, he wrote much about witchcraft and sorcery as acts against God himself. Later on, it was mainly the wrong use of the name of God that he attacked in this. Even if he did not pick up the image of a *Teufelsbuhlschaft*, the marriage and intimate relationship of a woman with the devil himself, he was convinced: "They [i.e., the witches] do much harm, so they should be put to death, not only because they harm, but also because they are in contact with the devil."[20] Still during Luther's lifetime, in 1540, there was a process against a witch in Wittenberg. Luther himself was not involved in this particular process, but he also was not opposed it. Without being one of the worst haters and persecutors, Luther shared the common belief in witches and their contact with the devil in his times. In this complex, he also shared the animosities against the medical or philosophical explanations that we saw earlier in his attitude toward diseases and their causes. Regarding severe weather he said: "Philosophers and physicians ascribe it to nature, but I don't know by what reason."[21] By this he meant that he himself knew the real reason for tempests and storms, namely, the devil. In this aspect of his thinking, Luther's

---

12. WA TR 2:79,3, #1379 [*LW* 54:145–146]; 6:208,5, #6813.
13. WA TR 1:150,31, #360 [*LW* 54:53–54]; 1:347,14f, #722; 5:443,38f, #6023; 6:207,39–208,2, #6813; 6:212,8–10, #6819.
14. WA TR 1:347,30f, #722; cf 2:70,3, #1379 [*LW* 54:145–146].
15. WA TR 4:501,20–24, #4784.
16. WA TR 6:212,8–10, #6819.
17. WA TR 1:274,15–17, #588.
18. WA TR 4:620,17–24, #5027.
19. WA TR 2:504,22–23, #2529b; 4:31,26, #3953 [*LW* 54:298].
20. *D. Martin Luthers Werke: Kritische Gesamtausgabe*, 69 vols. (Weimar: Hermann Böhlaus Nachfolger, 1883–), 16:552,22–23 (hereafter, WA).
21. WA TR 23:10,9–10, #2829 [*LW* 54:172].

thoughts were obviousy different from our contemporary conceptions. It is science and modernity that he sees as going wrong by removing human beings from insights into the real world, which is not the world of natural causes and effects but of the struggle between God and the devil. Max Weber's description of modernity as somehow a disenchanting of the world (*Entzauberung der Welt*) does not link up easily with Luther. His world might not be enchanted in a strict sense, but it is full of powers that transcend it and that move it in this or that direction. Mainly, it is a world in the hands of God—but at all times it is in danger of falling into the devil's reign or power.

This becomes even more obvious if we examine those situations where Luther speaks not only about the devil's effects but about encounters with Satan himself as a real, visible, and tangible person. It makes no difference if we think of Luther in his medieval youth or of the older one, the great reformer. In the summer of 1540, a table talk took place in Wittenberg.[22] Andreas Osiander, the Nuremberg reformer, denied the existence of poltergeists, but Luther then began a long report of encounters with them, stressing his own experience in this. Both during his monastic period and later on, he had heard the devil clattering with something, he had seen him coming as a black sow, and in his time on the Wartburg as a black dog. This dog was bold enough to creep into Luther's bed, but he took him and threw him out of the window, happy to get rid of him.[23] This seems not to be the Luther of our confirmation classes or our seminary lessons—but it is a real Luther, one who sees the devil as more than an enlightened idea of evil. And it was not only his own experience that underlined this perception; he also could set forward easily the medieval tradition of the *Physiologus*, from which he learned that the devil could become incarnate in a monkey—possibly being happy that in middle Europe monkeys were not all that widespread. To be sure, the devil did not use foreign masks at all times. He could also appear in the classical image with his threating stick in his hands, exactly as people had depicted him.[24] There are some tender modern souls who want Luther to be one of those who never used classical images like this for the devil[25]—but actually he did. He was not a modern rationalist, rather he shared numerous medieval perspectives on the world.

The devil's deeds could even become worse. He could come into our world in human form. Thus Luther knew and reported the story of a child who in reality was the devil himself and who tortured his parents all the time by his disobedience.[26] This may not be the best pedagogical counsel for our days, but it does show Luther's participation in the common convictions of his time. In another table talk, he referred to a story that the duke himself had reported in order to show the nastiness of the devil, how he uses human countenance and even seemingly good advice to play his game with people. The story goes as follows: A buried woman came back alive to her widower, a nobleman. She

22. Actually, the historical background of the Table Talks is not as certain as we normally assume. See now Katharina Bärenfänger et al. eds. *Martin Luthers Tischreden: Neuansätze der Forschung* (Tübingen: Mohr Siebeck, 2013).

23. WA TR 5:87–88, #5358b.

24. WA TR 6:217,37–38, #6830.

25. See Gerhard Ebeling, *Lutherstudien*, vol 2: *Disputatio de homine, Part 3: Die theologische Definition des Menschen: Kommentar zu These 20–40* (Tübingen: Mohr Siebeck, 1989), 267, n. 182.

26. WA TR 2:503–505, #'s 2528b, 2529a–b.

promised to stay longer with him, if he would abandon his curses—a hint that did not make her seem to be the devil's pawn. So, they were married anew and even produced three children—until the nobleman pronounced a curse again. At once his wife disappeared, and the man, now a widower for the second time, remained with his children who had been born by a ghost.[27] In conclusion, Luther sighed, saying: "What a shocking example of Satan deceiving human beings, such that he even procreates children. The sons are nothing else than devils, because they had the same body as their mother had had."[28] We might shake our heads about this superstitious story, but it is far more than superstitious, for the image sketched here shows the devil as the direct counterpart of the creating God, himself bringing human beings to life and making real what actually is not more than a mere semblance. A ghost in our understanding should not be able to bring forth real human beings with flesh and bones, but the devil's creature was able to do it. For pious believers this also means: Whatever you think to be real could in fact be the devil's mocking.

The threefold devil in the sons also reminds of the fact that the devil is not just one and unique. There are—as there were in the Middle Ages—numerous representations of the devil. Listen to Luther from a table talk:

> But the devil goes with me to bed, and I myself do have one or two devils. They run to me and are quite pretty little devils. And when they cannot win in my heart, they grab my head and torture it. And if my head no longer suffices, I will show them my ass. That's where he [the devil] belongs.[29]

Luther did not think of the devil(s) as being confined to his personal life; he also thought of them as present in the forests, in the waters, and in the marshes.[30] The whole of nature is the devil's playground in a way that strongly reminds of magical conceptions. Luther can even explain why there are so many devils. If a devil is defeated, he himself will not come back, but in his place many poltergeists will appear, about which we heard before.[31]

Why do I relate all of these disconcerting stories? It is not merely to present the strange and far away Luther. Rather, within them, one can perhaps see how important it was for Luther that in this world God's reign was always questioned by another destructive power, the devil's attacks. However strange he was, the devil was a danger for all piety. In his concrete manifestations Luther saw the realization of the eternal struggle between God and the devil.

This is why the devil had one special victim in this world: Luther himself. Insofar as Luther could see his own life as a way to reveal God's ultimate will for this world, he also could speak about the devil disturbing him, whenever he could. The stories mentioned before were only the outer side of this impatient fighting against the living prophet of God, Martin Luther. This provides the background for less anecdotal, more spiritual accounts of the devil in Luther's remembrances. This special prophetic role as the devil's target is what is meant when Luther reports that the devil visited him from his early youth on, and that

27. WA TR 3:516,3–9, #3676.
28. WA TR 3:516,10–12, #3676.
29. WA TR 1:216,7–11, #491 [*LW* 54:82–83].
30. WA TR 1:608,21–22, #1222; 3:10,7–8, #2829 [*LW* 54:172]; cf 5:105,1–2, #5375e.
31. WA TR 6:208,17–20, #6814.

he only interrupted these visits during the first year after his entrance into the order as well as in the first year after his ordination,[32] which as we know took place within the medieval church. When Luther reports this he does not mean black sows or dogs visiting him, rather he means the one great tempter, whose aim is to destroy all faith and all hope, especially in the shape that Reformation theology gave to it.

> What I say, I experienced myself at least partly. Since I know the devil's deceit and quick and malicious stratagem quite well. He does not only whisper to us the Law. With this, he wants to terrify us, making large beams out of little slivers, which means, out of things which are no, or only little, sins, he makes a real hell; since he is a real miraculous master who is able to make the sin large and heavy, even making sin where no sin is, just to frighten our conscience.[33]

Remembrances like this were not only reports; Luther also used them to comfort others.[34] With them he spoke about the spiritually destructive power of the devil, which was far more important than the material manifestations. With this the devil obstructs Jesus Christ in a twofold, somehow contradictory manner. First, he brings human beings into security, moving them away from the right and good fear of God. Second, he brings human beings into temptation or *Anfechtung*.[35] The second is the decisive one for Luther's own experience. The distressing thing is that temptation itself can be good and important for the spiritual path of a Christian, so as to protect him/her from false security. But if it is not Christ but the devil who brings the temptation, it is distorted. Thus it does not prepare one to listen to the saving gospel, but the devil instead leads from temptation to desperation, which means into absolute remoteness from the saving God. This ambivalence of temptation makes it possible for Luther to say that God himself allows the devil to attack human beings.[36] This shows in a very intricate way the limits of the devil. Precisely in his most mighty action, when he is bringing human beings into temptation, he is not a full-value counterpart of God himself. The power of the devil does not go further than God allows it.

Thus the nature of spiritual temptation leads to central questions of theology, and this brings us to the heart of Luther's own convictions. The temptation, the devil's pronouncing of the law instead of the gospel, is strongly connected to Luther's teaching on justification. The devil questions nothing less than exactly this delightful preaching of God, which endows us with salvation by grace alone, through faith alone. In the devil's temptations, the savior Christ is made into a judge,[37] and human beings, saved believers, are made into hated persons and objects of accusation. "This is the worst temptation of Satan, when he says: God hates the sinners. But you are a sinner. Ergo

32. WA 8:660,31–32.
33. WA TR 6:88,36–41, #6629.
34. WA TR 2:27,11–30, #1288 [LW 54:132–133]; cf WA TR 2:29,11–14, #1289.
35. WA TR 3:174,11, #3108. On the devil and "Anfechtung," see Barth, *Der Teufel und Jesus Christus in der Theologie Martin Luthers*, 124–153.
36. WA TR 2:172,23–25, #1671; cf 2:430,4–6, #2353; 2:536,3–5, #2597; and Barth, *Der Teufel und Jesus Christus in der Theologie Martin Luthers*, 153–183.
37. WA TR 1:5, #9; cf WA TR 6:88, #6629.

God hates you."[38] Perhaps you can see the devil arguing here like a scholastic theologian in syllogistic manner, starting with a general sentence, then subsuming a special sentence, and then drawing a conclusion. This conclusion obviously contradicts the central Reformation conviction of *simul peccator et iustus*, which means that the Christian is at the same time a real sinner and nevertheless righteous in the eyes of the saving God. God's actions overwhelm the boundaries of logic that the scholastics place upon him. Behind this background, Luther can use the famous word he used in 1545 to report on his Reformation breakthrough also to describe the devil's activities. "The devil does not want anything else in us than active justice. But we have the passive one and shall not have the active one."[39] Actually, the devil is the author of a false doctrine of justification, stressing the human being's own works instead of the mere passivity to receive God's grace.

Stated the other way around, this means that the decisive battle against the devil was precisely Luther's Reformation discovery. In the moment when he learned that God does not want any human deeds but rather endows us with his grace without any presuppositions, there was no more place for the devil's insinuations.

Since the new theology does not found a new world all at once, the devil remains active. But there is a weapon in our hands, or our hearts, against him: the true and pure doctrine of justification. Whenever the devil claims human beings such that they follow the law as if they could gain salvation in this way, human beings are in danger of losing their trust in God's grace.[40] Thus Luther held against the devil that Christians are without the law and above it.[41] To make his position clear, in his *Table Talks* Luther distinguishes two so-called chanceries: God's and the devil's. In God's chancery, human beings are terrified first, only to be raised afterwards. But the devil makes the human being enjoy his/her sins so as then to bring him/her into desperation.[42] Theologically, God's chancery and the devil's have different uses of the law. While God uses it in the theologically correct way, the convicting use that shows us that we are sinners, the devil's use is the deadly one that brings us to the end of all our means and makes us remote from God. The devil uses the law to bring us into the "nowhere," while Christ leads us to the real Christian liberty.[43] Thus in the opposition of the devil it is Jesus Christ who gives us the possibility of withstanding the devil's persecutions and attacks:

> But we do have Christ who came not to destroy us, but to save us. If one watches him, there is no other God in heaven or on earth than the God who is justifying and saving us; the other way around, if one loses sight of him, there is no help, comfort or peace. But when you come to the teaching: 'God sent his son to us,' our heart receives peace.[44]

---

38. WA TR 1:61,19–21, #141; cf WA TR 2:13,11–12, #1263.
39. WA TR 1:63,29–30, #141; 2:15,18–20, #1263.
40. WA TR 2:429,26, #2353.
41. WA TR 1:204,32–205,1 #470.
42. WA TR 1:602–603, #1210.
43. WA TR 2:11–13, #1353 [*LW* 54:143].
44. WA TR 1:63,10–14, #141.

In this text one can immediately see the consequences of Luther's early conversations with his confessor, John of Staupitz. It was he who had said to the
young Luther despairing over the question of predestination: "One has to look
at the one who is called Christ."[45] With this advice, Staupitz made Luther, as the
reformer later said, "newborn in Christ."[46] This can remind us that Luther not
only derived his concrete imagination of a material devil from the Middle Ages,
but also his hope in Jesus Christ.

Following this Christological centering, Jesus Christ is not only content but
also example of the struggle against the devil.[47] This spiritual battle does not
happen once but again and again in the life of a Christian. The starting point,
however, is baptism. Into a line from the medieval liturgy, Luther integrated
exorcism into the baptismal ritual:

> I conjure you, impure ghost, by the name of the father † and of the son † and
> of the Holy Spirit: Get out of this minister of God N., since he is your Lord,
> you awful one, who walked over the sea on foot and who reached out his
> hand to Peter when he was sinking down.[48]

After baptism the entire life of Christians should be devoted to dispelling the
devil.[49] Nevertheless, Luther still knew the rite of exorcism in Christian life.[50]
This can be seen in the fate of Valerius Glockner from Nuremberg.[51] He admitted to Luther that he had dedicated himself to the devil five years prior. But
now, he confessed and renounced Satan:

> I myself, Valerius, confess before God and all his holy angels and before the
> assembly of the church, that I had renounced my belief in God and devoted
> myself to the devil. This I regret from my heart. From now on, I will be the
> devil's enemy and follow God my Lord voluntarily and amend myself.
> Amen.[52]

As stated before, this example was exceptional. Luther's primary aim was to
renounce the devil with one's whole life, in all thoughts, words, and deeds. The
only help here was to look at Christ himself and to hold oneself by the word
of God.[53]

From Christ himself the believer receives the power to resist the devil and
even to mock him, just as the devil does with the Christians: "I said," Luther
reports, "Devil, I also took a shit in my pants. Have you recorded that alongside
my other sinful deeds?"[54] As Heiko Oberman pointed out, it is not by chance
that Luther uses vulgarisms in this context. And it is not only defecation but

45. WA TR 1:245,11–12, #526 [*LW* 54:97].
46. *D. Martin Luthers Werke: Kritische Gesamtausgabe, Briefwechsel*, 18 vols. (Weimar: Hermann Böhlaus Nachfolger, 1930–1985), 11:67,7–8, #4088 (hereafter, WA Br).
47. WA TR 1:63,15–19, #141; 2:15,5–7, #1263.
48. WA 12:44,25–28.
49. WA TR 1:401,21–25, #830.
50. Cf. WA Br 11:111–112, #4120.
51. WA TR 3:581–582, #3739.
52. WA TR 3:582,5–10, #3739.
53. WA TR 1:64,4, #141; cf WA TR 1:458,4–5, #907; and Barth, *Der Teufel und Jesus Christus in der Theologie Martin Luthers*, 82–123.
54. WA TR 1:392,3–4, #812.

also farting that can help against the devil,[55] or one can shout at him: "Lick my ass, or: shit in your britches and hang them around your neck."[56]

However the struggle with the devil appears, human beings do not fight for themselves but are rather soldiers of God. The real struggle happens between God himself and the devil.[57]

> Here follows: Where God's finger does not expel the devil, there is the devil's reign; and where the devil's reign is, is not the reign of God. So, it concludes strongly: As long as the Holy Spirit does not come into us, we are inept for good and are inevitably in the devil's reign; but whenever we are in his reign, we cannot do any other than what he wants us to do."[58]

This also provides the background for what is perhaps Luther's most famous dictum about the devil's impact on us. In his debate with Erasmus of Rotterdam over free will, which was denied by Luther while Erasmus upheld it, Luther writes:

> Thus the human will is placed between the two like a beast of burden. If God rides it, it wills and goes where God wills, as the psalm says: "I am become as a beast [before thee] and I am always with thee" [Ps. 73:22–23]. If Satan rides it, it wills and goes where Satan wills; nor can it choose to run to either of the two riders or to seek him out, but the riders themselves contend for the possession and control of it.[59]

Even if this passage sounds like it, Luther never thought in terms of a strict dualism,[60] as if God and the devil were fighters on the same level. Luther does not speak about cosmic alternatives but only about the salvation or misery of human beings. Here, human beings are not able to decide on their own. Human beings on their pilgrimage do not see or feel the limits that God has set for the devil; they only feel the harsh and seemingly inevitable offence of the devil. Being under the devil means to be on the way to misery, and human beings themselves cannot find a way out. The situation becomes even worse, because in human afflictions the devil uses nothing less than the word of God, mainly the word of God as the ultimate judge. Thus as in the story of the nobleman and his wife, the devil takes on godly appearance to bring human beings to perdition—and since human will is not free, he or she can do no other than follow the devil willingly.

But the point is this. The individual experience described here makes human beings part of a universal scenario, beginning with the creation of the world and then onward to its end. Actually, Luther is not heavily invested in the beginnings of this battle. He does not deny the traditional myth of the devil as a fallen angel,[61] but this is not overly important for him. Rather, he stresses the

---

55. WA TR 1:205,1, #469 [*LW* 54:78].
56. WA TR 2:306,13–14, #2059.
57. Cf. Uwe Rieske-Braun, *Duellum mirabile: Studien zum Kampfmotiv in Martin Luthers Theologie* (Göttingen: Vandenhoeck & Ruprecht, 1999).
58. WA TR 6:120,24–29, #6685).
59. *LW* 33:65–66 [WA 18:635,17–22].
60. Cf. Barth, *Der Teufel und Jesus Christus in der Theologie Martin Luthers*, 196–201.
61. WA TR 2:429,12–13, #2353; cf 2:28,10, #1289.

devil's efforts to rule human beings from the beginning onward. The serpent in paradise, for Luther as for his forerunners, was no one else than the devil himself. "Satan ... seduced Eve from the word that God had spoken"[62]—actually, from here we also find an explanation of why the devil, as said before, could be seen as the author of diseases. The consequence of his seduction, as is well known, was that death came to humankind, and all diseases are an aftermath of exactly this moral situation.[63] Thus from the beginning of the world, the devil is present and effects his own deeds, combining himself with sin and death.[64] This is "Luther's unholy triumvirate," as Scott Hendrix points out.[65]

Moving from prehistory to history, in Luther's view, the devil is always at the side of those who are intent on the law. It is from here that Luther's aggressive view of the Jews derives—insofar as it belongs to theological argumentation. Luther's central biblical authority for this was John 8:44: "You are from your father the devil, and you choose to do your father's desires. He was a murderer from the beginning and does not stand in the truth, because there is no truth in him. When he lies, he speaks according to his own nature, for he is a liar and the father of lies."[66] On the basis of this text, Luther regarded the Jews as worshippers of the devil:[67] "The devil with all his angels has obsessed this people. So they do nothing else than boast of outer things, their own gifts, deeds and works before God."[68] Statements like this show that Luther's late anti-Jewish polemic is not merely generated by a peculiar situation or by the frustrations of an old man, but rather it has its theological foundations, as abtruse as they are. To be honest, it is the Reformation discovery itself that frames his anti-Judaism. Thus, for Luther, the parallel between Jews and Catholics—as he saw them—is evident, and he can use inner-Christian terms to describe what he wanted to criticize in Jewish devotion: "The same [as with the Catholics] happened with the people of Israel. They always highlighted circumcision as an *opus operatum*, their own work, against the word of God, and they persecuted the prophets, through whom God wanted to speak to them."[69] In this horizon, for Luther, the Jews were the representatives of the devil's power in history, perverted by trusting in their own deeds and the law.

This leads to a deeper understanding of the cross, which constitutes the final victory of Christ over the devil and death. With this, it also opened a way for human beings to develop faith in a manner that feels God's grace as being the center of all devotion. Luther knew how difficult it was to understand the cross—if not on his own, he could learn it from his dear wife, as can be seen in a table talk:

> "The devil slays us all, for the Scripture states that he causes death and is the author of death [John 8:44]. Satan put God's Son to death." The doctor's wife

---

62. WA 42:111,18–19 [*LW* 1:147–148]; cf. WA TR 1:24–25, #991; 6:104,31–34, #6662.
63. WA TR 6:104,34–37, #6662.
64. See Barth, *Der Teufel und Jesus Christus in der Theologie Martin Luthers*, 68–69.
65. Scott H. Hendrix, *Martin Luther: A Very Short Introduction* (Oxford: Oxford University Press, 2010), 83.
66. WA 53:420,26–31 [*LW* 47:141].
67. WA 53:605,4–8.
68. WA 53:447,20–21 [*LW* 47:174]; 580,1–2; 587,10–15.
69. WA 53:437,5–8 [*LW* 47:161].

said, "Oh, no, my dear Doctor! I don't believe it!" Then the doctor said, "Who would love our Lord God if he himself had a mind to kill us?"[70]

The short dialogue gives a feeling for the deeper truth: Jesus' death, at least in the way in which it happened, cannot follow God's will—and nevertheless it is the foundation for the salvation of all human beings and the core of the gospel.

Besides these somehow skeptical reflections, Luther wants us to know one thing: that the cross brings victory over death and the devil, while it cannot stop the devil's advances all at once. As a result, the devil changes his medium. After having fought against Christ from creation onward, he now gives birth to the Antichrist. Again we see how deeply rooted Luther's polemics are in his theology. This is the reason why he could denounce the papacy as the Antichrist, while he never referred to the Jews in this manner. Their place in history was before the birth of Christ; the Antichrist could only occur after this event.

Properly speaking, after Jesus' death there was a brief time when the Antichrist was not yet on Earth. Luther was not exactly sure when the Antichrist began to reign over the Church. For the most part, he regarded Gregory the Great as the last bishop of Rome, while his successors became Popes and, with this, the Antichrist.[71] How perfidious the devil is, we can see from 2 Thessalonians 2 that the Antichrist rose precisely in the temple of God, which for Luther referred allegorically to the Church.[72]

Astonishing as it may sound, the devil plays a similar game as in his individual encounters. In the same way in which he could adopt the deceased wife's figure, he (meaning his creature, the Antichrist) can appear as the head of the terrestrial church, thus making the pope "the devil's mask."[73] Not surprisingly, and even as predicted in Matt 24:24, the Antichrist can even perform miracles and similar signs,[74] as one can see in the stories of the saints and others.

Thus there is no clear shelter against the devil in history. Satan can cheat and betray, not only by means of the Pope, but also by means of the so-called "fanatics," the "Schwärmer."[75] This again gives Luther himself an exceptional role in the story of salvation. Mocked from his youth onward by the devil, he was able to detect his malice. What he experienced individually was something like a mirror of the larger history: "If Satan had not agitated me, I would not have become his enemy and would not have been able to harm him in this way."[76] As a result, therefore, the new reformed church becomes a medium against the devil. The church and the ministry of preaching are determined by God as aides against the devil.[77] After what we have heard before, this is not surprising in

70. *LW* 54:145 [*WA TR* 2:78,24–26, #1379].

71. See Ernst Schäfer, *Luther als Kirchenhistoriker: Ein Beitrag zur Geschichte der Wissenschaft* (Gütersloh: C. Bertelsmann, 1897), 327–329.

72. *WA* 38:220,28–31; 251,27–36; 40/1:619,18–31.

73. *WA* 54:229,31 [*LW* 41:291].

74. *WA TR* 5:279, #5622. See Hans Preuß, *Die Vorstellungen vom Antichrist im späteren Mittelalter, bei Luther und in der konfessionellen Polemik: Ein Beitrag zur Theologie Luthers und zur Geschichte der christlichen Frömmigkeit* (Leipzig: J.C. Hinrichs, 1906); William R. Russell, "Martin Luther's Understanding of the Pope as Antichrist," *ARG* 85 (1994): 32–44; Volker Leppin, "Luthers Antichristverständnis vor dem Hintergrund der mittelalterlichen Konzeptionen," *KuD* 45 (1999): 48–63.

75. *WA TR* 2:385,27–28, #2267a; cf 1:246,1–7, #528 [*LW* 54:97].

76. *WA TR* 1:62,5–6, #141.

77. *WA TR* 1:205,3–5, #469 [*LW* 54:78].

any way. If the devil is the representative of the belief in the law, it must be the proclamation of the gospel—in the manner characteristic of the Reformation churches—that stands over against him.

Thus, and following the line of his battle with the devil, we come to the principal background of Luther's late polemics. It is not merely an expression of bitterness when Luther, in parallel to his anti-Jewish treatises, also writes against the papacy as a "donation of the devil."[78] It also shows that Luther found himself in an eschatological situation. The detection of the Antichrist by means of the Reformation message had brought the last raging of the devil.[79] In Reformation times, therefore, he becomes even worse than under the papacy,[80] notwithstanding that for Luther the papacy itself was "the last adversary on earth, and the most obvious thing that all devils with all their power could do."[81]

Luther saw himself, his personal existence and his message, as standing in the middle of God's last battle with the devil. "The old wicked enemy means it now in earnest"[82]—this famous song lyric expresses both Luther's activity as well as his motivation. It was he, the reformer in Wittenberg, where all threads—individual, theological, historical—came together. It was in Luther himself where the devil found his target. Not surprisingly, when Luther ended the famous report of his life, which he wrote for the preface to his Latin works, he stated: "Vale, lector, in Domino et ora pro incremento verbi adversus satanam" ("Farewell in the Lord, reader, and pray for the growth of the Word against Satan").[83]

78. WA 54:206–299 [*LW* 41:263–376].

79. *D. Martin Luthers Werke: Kritische Gesamtausgabe, Deutsche Bibel*, 18 vols. (Weimar: Hermann Böhlaus Nachfolger, 1906–1961), 11/2:113,11–12.

80. WA TR 1:404,9–11, #831.

81. WA 54:299,6–8 [*LW* 41:376].

82. From the hymn, "A Mighty Fortress Is Our God." *Archiv zur Weimarer Ausgabe der Werke Martin Luthers: Texte und Untersuchungen*, 10 vols. (Cologne, Germany: Böhlau Verlag, 1985–2011), 4:247.

83. WA 54:187,3–4 [*LW* 34:338].

4. Warrior Saints

Warfare and Violence in Martin Luther's Readings of Some Old Testament Texts

Mickey L. Mattox

It is a story Lutherans love to tell. In early 1535, answering a request from his barber Peter Beskendorf, a man he had known since 1517 and considered a close friend, Martin Luther brought forth a sweet and practical booklet touchingly entitled *A Simple Way to Pray, Written for a Good Friend*. Today this work is justly celebrated as a minor classic that both epitomizes Luther's spirituality and powerfully suggests what a deep and lasting impact he would make on the lives of his many followers. The after story, however, is less well known. In late summer that same year a letter from Luther made its way to Prince-Elector John Frederick's vice chancellor, the honorable Franz Burkhard, who was handling a criminal matter. In the letter Luther asked Burkhard to show clemency toward a convicted murderer: exile rather than execution. Ironically, this work too was written on behalf of Peter Beskendorf, who in late March, only weeks after the publication of *A Simple Way to Pray*, had stabbed to death his son-in-law, Dietrich von Freyenhagen. Luther's appeal had the desired effect: Beskendorf—whose crime had apparently been committed while inebriated—was exiled. As Luther had recommended, the man kept his life and suffered no violent punishment, but lost his home and possessions.[1]

The after story of Luther's *Simple Way to Pray* reminds us first of his conviction that the application of the law should always be tempered by the jurist's sensitivity to the particulars of the case. He never tired of repeating the old adage that "the strictest law is the highest injustice" (*summum ius summa iniuriae*). The law should serve both the individual and the common good, and equity (*epieikeia*) demands that justice be ever tempered to fit the facts. Dr. Luther clearly brought these convictions to the aid of Mr. Beskendorf.[2] More importantly for present purposes, this story also reminds us that violence was not for Martin Luther merely a theoretical question. Indeed, Luther lived in an age characterized by a good deal of institutionalized violence, violence, that is, that was being carried out by civil and ecclesiastical rulers for a variety

---

1. The best English-language biographies of Martin Luther include: H. G. Haile, *Luther: An Experiment in Biography* (New York, Ny: Doubleday, 1978); Heiko A. Oberman, *Luther: Man between God and the Devil*, trans. Eileen Walliser-Schwarzbart (New Haven, Ct & London: Yale University Press, 1989). The authoritative biography is Martin Brecht, *Martin Luther*, 3 vols., trans. James L. Schaff (Minneapolis, Mn: Fortress Press, 1985, 1990, 1993). For two more recent studies that challenge aspects of the long-settled conventional narrative of the young Luther's development, see Volker Leppin, *Martin Luther*, 2nd ed (Darmstadt: Wissenschaftliche Buchgesellschaft, 2010); Franz Posset, *The Real Luther: A Friar at Erfurt and Wittenberg* (Saint Louis, Mo: Concordia Publishing House, 2011).

2. For Luther and *epieikeia*, see Haile, *Luther: An Experiment in Biography*, 345–50. I am also indebted to the work of my graduate student, Jason Gehrke, "The Virtue of *Epieikeia*: A Study in Luther and his Sources," *SRR* 17/1 (2014): 68–101.

of purposes, including, e.g., the extension of kingdoms, the establishment of dynasties, the settling of border disputes, and, at least some of the time, the maintenance of social order. Indeed, wars of one kind or another proliferated in this period until they led at last to the Thirty Years War and related conflicts in the seventeenth century.[3] For groups that rose up to challenge the existing social order the emerging early modern states of Luther's day were already beginning to amass standing armies, which could be used to put down rebellions of one kind or another.[4]

Against lawbreakers such as Beskendorf, moreover, the early modern civil authorities had ready to hand the tool of capital punishment, which could be administered in a number of horrific ways, and this tool was also used to punish religious dissenters. In Reformation times, for example, one might be burned as a Lutheran heretic in Belgium, as happened to two Augustinian friars who had become followers of Luther in 1522; for that matter, one could suffer the same fate as a Jewish *converso* (crypto-Jew) in an *auto-da-fé*, as were hundreds of Spanish Jews between 1481 and 1530. Or one could be drowned as an Anabaptist in Switzerland, as happened to Felix Manz in Zurich in 1527, or drawn and quartered as a Catholic priest in England, as happened to St. John Houghton in 1535, when he refused to recognize King Henry VIII as supreme head of the church. One of the most ironic markers of Christian Europe in the early modern period is the witness of martyrdom, which these religiously divided Christian peoples both gave and imposed, to and on one another.[5]

This is not to say that violent events such as the occasional war or the imposition of the death penalty were everyday occurrences in Luther's world. To the contrary, then as now, most men and women who were motivated to action by Christian faith and piety gave themselves over to quite different kinds of work, spending their lives teaching others about God's love, devoting themselves to daily prayer (as among the religious), feeding and housing the poor, or attempting to relieve the suffering of the sick or dying. Then as now, faith in the Good News of Jesus the Christ motivated many to lives of heroic service that left only faint traces in the historical records. These undeniable fruits of Christian faith typically receive much less attention today than do the acts of violence that marred early modern Christendom, for violence, after all, is much on *our* minds. Indeed, for increasing numbers of us today the fact of religiously motivated violence, the apparent capacity of religion to make some people feel very good about behaving very badly, calls the entire enterprise of religion into question. What good is religion, some ask, if it produces the sorts of people who do such things?[6]

---

3. For a withering attack on the secularist narrative that labels these the "wars of religion," see William T. Cavanaugh's provocative work, *The Myth of Religious Violence: Secular Ideology and the Roots of Modern Conflict* (New York, Ny: Oxford University Press, 2009). Cavanaugh methodically deconstructs the notion that the Thirty Years War and related conflicts had primarily to do with religion, pointing instead to the rise of the modern nation state as the source of the violence.

4. For warfare and the development of arms in this period, see Michael E. Mallett, "The Art of War," in *Handbook of European History 1400–1600: Late Middle Ages, Renaissance, and Reformation*, Vol. 1: *Structures and Assertions*, ed. Thomas A. Brady et al. (Leiden: Brill, 1994), 535–62.

5. On this topic, see Brad S. Gregory, *Salvation at Stake: Christian Martyrdom in Early Modern Europe* (Cambridge, Ma: Harvard University Press, 1999).

6. This criticism is frequently voiced by representatives of the "new atheism." For a learned and insistent rejoinder, see David Bentley Hart, *Atheist Delusions: The Christian Revolution and Its Fashionable Enemies* (New Haven, Ct: Yale University Press, 2009).

Today's worries about religion and violence, an unmistakable marker of post-9/11 existence, will surely not leave Martin Luther and his Reformation unexamined, even if his response to violence has been criticized many times before. In his own day, for example, many quite understandably found his reactions to the Peasants' uprising excessively harsh, legitimating the princes' excessively violent response.[7] Going all the way back to Friedrich Engels this criticism was magnified in the Marxist literature on Luther and the Reformation, which somewhat implausibly made Thomas Müntzer the true hero of the age.[8] More recently, all of us have fretted about the extent of Luther's responsibility for the sad fate of the Jews at the hands of the National Socialists.[9] Did Luther's "Two Kingdoms" doctrine so compartmentalize Christian righteousness within the spiritual and hidden kingdom of God's right hand as to leave it no earthly good in the physical and tangible kingdom of the left hand?[10] Did Luther's political theology leave a legacy of ethical complacency? Thankfully, some of the shadows cast over Lutheran ethics by the last Great War have finally begun to fade. The urgency with which the latter question was once posed has been defused somewhat by a steadily developing recognition of Luther's joy, as one scholar recently put it, in the Law of God.[11] However fallibly he may have lived and acted in the events of his own time, Luther readily sang with the Psalmist, "Oh, how I love thy Law," and he did his best to hold Christian people accountable to it, as anyone familiar with his two great Catechisms, particularly their treatment of the Ten Commandments, can readily affirm. As a theorist, so to speak, of the Christian life, Luther seems to have left little room for ethical complacency.

The former question, however, abides. The status of Jews and Judaism in Luther's thought remains neuralgic, as a spate of recent works can well attest.[12]

---

7. For a selection of Luther's writings on some of these problems, see the new *Martin Luther on the Freedom of a Christian, with Related Texts*, trans. Tryntje Helfferich (Indianapolis, In: Hackett, 2013), which offers, inter alia, a translation of Thomas Müntzer's *Highly Provoked Defense* alongside Luther's *Against the Robbing, Murdering Hordes of Peasants*.

8. For an interesting study of the place of Luther in the thought of Karl Marx and Friedrich Engels, see Roland Boer, "Reformation and Revolution: Concerning the Interpretation of Luther in Marx and Engels," *Sino-Christian Studies* 11 (2011): 45–72. The classic study of the problem is Abraham Friesen, *Reformation and Utopia: The Marxist Interpretation of the Reformation and its Antecedents* (Wiesbaden: Steiner, 1974). A perceptive analysis of Luther's theology in relation to Marxist thought may be found in Paul R. Hinlicky, "Passion and Action in Christ: Political Theology between the Times," in *Luther and the Beloved Community: A Path for Christian Theology after Christendom* (Grand Rapids, Mi: Eerdmans, 2010), 301–57.

9. Assessments of Luther's thought in this difficult area abound, but the considered judgment of Heiko A. Oberman, included in a last collection of his essays and published posthumously, stands out. "From Luther to Hitler," in *The Two Reformations: The Journey from the Last Days to the New World*, ed. Donald Weinstein (New Haven, Ct: Yale University Press, 2003), 81–85, 212.

10. On Luther's "two kingdoms doctrine" and its long and problematic reception in Lutheran theology, see William J. Wright, *Martin Luther's Understanding of God's Two Kingdoms: A Response to the Challenge of Skepticism* (Grand Rapids, Mi: Baker Academic, 2010), esp. ch. 1.

11. See Andreas Wöhle, *Luthers Freude an Gottes Gesetz: eine historische Quellenstudie zur Oszillation des Gesetzesbegriffes Martin Luthers im Licht seiner alttestamentlichen Predigten* (Frankfurt: Haag & Herchen, 1998).

12. See, e.g., Thomas Kaufmann, "Luther and the Jews," in *Jews, Judaism, and the Reformation in Sixteenth-Century Germany*, ed. Dean Philip Bell and Stephen G. Burnett (Leiden: Brill, 2006) 69–104; Eric W. Gritsch, *Martin Luther's Anti-Semitism: Against His Better Judgment* (Grand Rapids, Mi: Eerdmans, 2012). For a selection of original texts in translation, with helpful introductions, see Brooks Schramm and Kirsi I. Stjerna, eds., *Martin Luther, the Bible, and the Jewish People: A Reader* (Minneapolis, Mn: Fortress Press, 2012).

We could add to it the difficulty of Luther's ill treatment of the "false brethren," so effectively showcased by Mark Edwards.[13] Indeed, with abiding problems like this one in mind, Paul Hinlicky has urged that theological appropriation of Luther today must become a self-consciously *critical* enterprise, one that repeatedly endeavors to become aware of and excise the strategy of demonization he so often employed in controversy with his opponents, including not just the Jews, but Catholics, Protestants, and Muslims as well.[14] Luther's rhetoric and invective were not infrequently violent and abusive, and for that reason must be handled today with great care.

Many of us remain convinced, nevertheless, that Luther is still a vital conversation partner, a man whose thought and history remain in many ways yet to be discovered[15] and whose potential contribution to theology and exegesis today therefore also remains at least somewhat unexplored. He was after all one of the greatest biblical expositors in the long Catholic tradition, and applied himself with energy and singular insight not only to the Scripture itself, but also to the events and controversies of his day. Scripture and life—no, Scripture and Luther's life—informed and interpreted one another, and that dynamism made him a wondrously imaginative and exciting reader of the stories of the biblical saints, as we shall see below. Luther was contextual both as a theologian and as an exegete, which makes his exegetical writings, as Julius Köstlin observed long ago, an especially rich source of both Luther's theology as well as his "practical wisdom of life."[16]

Of course, we could bypass Luther's exegesis and examine his theological evaluation of war and violence as found in occasional treatises that addressed the problem directly.[17] For example, his important writing of 1523, *Temporal Authority: To What Extent It Should Be Obeyed*, lays out what has traditionally been understood as a "two kingdoms" approach to balancing the authority of the state with that of the church so that they mutually support one another. The treatise provides state authority over against that of the church with compelling biblical grounding, notably Romans 13.[18] The fallen world, Luther concluded, cannot be ruled by the gospel, so the civil authorities must rule through pre/proscription and as well as through violent coercion, through the law, that is, and the sword.[19] Far from offering rulers carte blanche, however, Luther moved

13. See Mark U. Edwards, Jr., *Luther and the False Brethren* (Stanford, Ca: Stanford University Press, 1975).
14. See Paul Hinlicky, "The Problem of Demonization in Luther's Apocalyptic Theology," in *Luther and the Beloved Community*, 379–85. For Luther's approach to Islam, see Adam S. Francisco, *Martin Luther and Islam: A Study in Sixteenth-Century Polemics and Apologetics* (Leiden: Brill, 2007); Gregory J. Miller, "Luther on the Turks and Islam," *Lutheran Quarterly* 14 (2000): 79–97.
15. For support of my claim for a Luther yet to be discovered, a good starting point is Risto Saarinen, "Luther the Urban Legend," in *The Global Luther: A Theologian for Modern Times*, ed. Christine Helmer (Minneapolis, Mn: Fortress Press, 2009), 13–31. For a more programmatic attempt to destabilize the traditional Luther narrative, see Christine Helmer and Bo Kristian Holm, eds., *Transformations in Luther's Theology: Historical and Contemporary Reflections* (Leipzig: Evangelische Verlagsanstalt, 2011).
16. See Julius Köstlin and Gustav Kawerau, *Martin Luther: sein Leben und seine Schriften*, vol. 2 (Berlin: A. Duncker, 1903), 425.
17. For a collection of Luther's political writings, see J. M. Porter, ed., *Luther: Selected Political Writings* (Lanham, Md: University Press of America, 1974).
18. Interestingly, Luther advised Christians to be obedient citizens, even in the event of a Muslim conquest, which seemed a distinct possibility in his day. See Francisco, *Martin Luther and Islam*.
19. Note well, however, Svend Anderson's argument that while Luther would not allow that the state could be ruled by the gospel, he nevertheless recognized it as an arena for the concrete application of

to moderate official acts of violence, arguing, for example, against the execution of heretics (although he hedged on that one later), and admonishing Christian princes to preserve the peace and avoid war. In this advice, perhaps he had in mind the example of his own Christian prince, Frederick the Wise, whose reputation as a peacemaker had earned him, from the German *Friedrich*, the nickname *Friedensreiche*: "peace lover."

Instead of limiting myself to important texts like this one, however, I want to turn now instead to some of Luther's exegetical writings, where he did the biblical spadework out of which occasional treatises like *Temporal Authority* grew. As will be shown below, when we examine Luther's understanding of warfare and violence in the Christian life from the vantage point of biblical interpretation, where his pastoral instincts are on high alert for biblical support for the Christian struggling for faith and holiness, we find him at his best, also regarding the question of war and violence. Here he attempts a balancing act, in which he recognizes first of all that violence itself is necessary only because the assertion of evil has rendered the creation itself a site of conflict. Importantly, this reminds us that violence does not belong to the original condition of humankind in Luther's thought. Indeed, in an unfallen world—which Luther often imaginatively sketches out, particularly in his work on Genesis—war and violence would have had no place.[20]

Peaceable Origins

The backdrop, then, to Luther's conflicted view of life in this fallen world is an irenic vision of the original creation, where an unfallen Adam and Eve once feasted their eyes on the "garden of delights" and found their hearts and minds elevated by every created thing to the love and contemplation of their Creator. Adam's imposition of names upon the animals, and perhaps later upon his wife as well, was therefore in no way arbitrary, as if what he called each of them lacked any connection to their being, their purpose, their inherent beauty or goodness. Instead, Adam called things what they really were, for he, and later Eve as well, was so utterly suffused with the knowledge of God as to see through created things to their created end, their *telos*, and to their uncreated Source as well, as their final cause.[21] Eden, as the elder Martin Luther imagined it, was unambiguously good in every way, and this inherent goodness left no room for violence of any kind. No force, no coercion, no dominance or submission could obtain within the human family, especially not between our "first

---

the law of Christian love, in which the Christian acts in service to the neighbor in need, extending the "happy exchange" given in justification so as to make Christ present in self-giving love in this world. See Svend Anderson, "Lutheran Political Theology in the Twenty-First Century," in *Transformations in Luther's Theology*, 245–63.

20. Recent works on Luther's Genesis lectures include: Juhani Forsberg, *Das Abrahambild in der Theologie Luthers: Pater Fidei Sanctissimus* (Stuttgart: Franz Steiner Verlag, 1984); John A. Maxfield, *Luther's Lectures on Genesis and the Formation of Evangelical Identity*, SCSE 80 (Kirksville, Mo: Truman State University Press, 2008); Mickey Leland Mattox, *"Defender of the Most Holy Matriarchs:" Martin Luther's Interpretation of the Women of Genesis in the* Enarrationes in Genesin, *1535–1545* (Leiden: Brill, 2003).

21. For some further detail on this point, see Mickey L. Mattox, "Hearer of the Triune God: Martin Luther's Reading of Noah," in *Luther Digest: Volume 20 Supplement* (Saint Louis, Mo: Luther Academy, 2012), 49–70, esp 52–56.

parents."[22] Eve, he averred, was her husband's equal, a conviction he expressed in predictably patriarchal terms when he described her as a woman "who does things like a man."[23] These two, moreover, were created for a life, and a spiritual body, that lay beyond what was given in the garden. Indeed, death was somehow natural to them, but only as the last step before their "translation" into the "spiritual body."[24] This eschatological vision of the original and definitively peaceable kingdom of Eden must be kept ever in view, because it renders violence and coercion—about which Luther can be sometimes almost shockingly blunt—alien to the realities and purposes of the original creation, and just to that extent entirely unnatural.

In this fallen world, however, Luther unhesitatingly affirms that if violence must be done—and again he has no doubt that it must—then it is best done by people of faith. There can be no avoidance of this sad necessity. Here as in so many other areas of his thought Luther leaves the Christian no pious option to check out and leave the difficult responsibilities incumbent on life in the world to the "seculars." To the contrary, the world is God's own creation, and the struggle for faith and faithfulness as Luther describes it takes place in the concrete spheres of Christian existence that God has established, including not only the church with its pastors and preachers, the Christian home with its mothers and fathers and children, but also the state, where God grants to Christian rulers distinctive gifts for keeping the peace, including the application of violence through war and capital punishment.[25] One can find therefore an authentic Christian faithfulness not only in the preacher or the parent, but also in the Christian ruler, the Christian soldier, or even the Christian executioner.[26]

To be sure, on Luther's account, the civil rule, including the maintenance of order by coercive means, is less glorious than that offered in either the domestic or the ecclesial spheres, but it is not for that reason un-Christian. Good work in the kingdom of the left hand can therefore be truly good, including the good work of upholding the social order and effecting a measure of social justice by means of violence, even if such acts are not proper, so to speak, in terms of God's original intentions for an unfallen humanity.[27] As with the preacher

22. See Mattox, *Defender*, chs. 1–2.

23. "Heuam autem dicit vocandam *Ischa*, perinde ac si dicas a Vir Vira, quod sit uxor, *heroica Mulier, quae virilia gerit.*" D. *Martin Luthers Werke: Kritische Gesamtausgabe*, 69 vols. (Weimar: Hermann Böhlaus Nachfolger, 1883–), 42:103,12–13 [italics added] (hereafter, WA).

24. "Cessassent autem ista corporalia praefinito tempore post impletum numerum Sanctorum, et Adam cum posteritate sua esset translatus ad aeternam et spiritualem vitam." ["At a predetermined time, after the number of saints had been filled up, these bodily matters would have come to an end, and Adam with his posterity would have been carried up to an eternal and spiritual life."] (WA 42:42,26–8).

25. For Luther's "three estates doctrine," see Wilhelm Maurer, *Luthers Lehre von den drei Hierarchien und ihre mittelalterliche Hintergrund* (Munich: Verlag der Bayerische Akademie der Wissensschaften, 1970). Some ethical implications are examined in Risto Saarinen, "Ethics in Luther's Theology," in *Moral Philosophy on the Threshold of Modernity*, ed. Jill Kraye and Risto Saarinen, The New Synthese Historical Library 57 (Dordrecht: Springer, 2005), 195–215.

26. See, e.g., Luther's 1526 writing *Whether Soldiers Too Can Be Saved* (LW 46:87–137; WA 19:623–62).

27. See, e.g., Luther's remarks in the confession of faith appended at the end of his *Confession concerning Christ's Supper*, 1528 (LW 37:364):
But the holy orders and true religious institutions established by God are these three: the office of priest, the estate of marriage, the civil government.... Moreover, princes and lords, judges, civil officers, state officials, notaries, male and female servants and all who serve such persons, and further, all their obedient subjects—all are engaged in pure holiness and leading a holy

or the parent so too the ruler or soldier should turn to the Scripture itself for instruction and inspiration for faithfulness within his calling. When we recall that in his *Address to the Christian Nobility of the German Nation* of 1520 Luther had appealed to the civil rulers by virtue of their status as their society's first Christians (i.e., as both secular rulers and Christians baptized into the common priesthood) to take responsibility for the reform of the church, then it is perhaps somewhat less surprising to find him looking to the Scriptures for instruction for the good Christian prince or magistrate. In this way, the Bible is an eminently practical book, one that answers just the questions a good Christian prince or magistrate should ask: for what reasons should I wage war, and how should I do it? On whom, and for what crimes, must I impose the death penalty?[28]

War and the Biblical Saints

To shed further light on the problem of war and violence in Luther's thought I turn now to a few of his readings of the Old Testament. It is true, as readers have often noted, that Luther took comfort in the failings of the biblical saints. God's gracious dealing with the fallible figures portrayed in the biblical narratives suggests hope for every struggling Christian. At the same time, however, it is equally true that his portrayal of the biblical saints was often saintly in a much more conventional way, which means that one regularly finds in his readings of the lives of the patriarchs and matriarchs of the Old Testament paradigmatic examples of men and women who epitomized the struggle for faith and faithfulness, including—mostly for the men—the Christian exercise of worldly authority, also by means of violence and coercion. Viewed through Luther's interpretive lens the heroes and heroines of the Old Testament became, in effect, like Luther's own namesake, St. Martin of Tours, warrior saints, in both a literal and a figurative sense.

In the four brief exegetical vignettes set forth below, I examine some important aspects of Luther's approach to the question of war and violence. The first two are early exegeses of texts from the Pentateuch, which Luther had translated for the *Wittenberger Sonderausgabe des Pentateuchs*, published in August 1523, less than a year after the better known edition of the New Testament, the so-called "September Testament."[29] Turning first to his 1523–24 sermons on Genesis, we look in on his reading of the story of murderous Cain's exile, and the city he built. Next I examine the broad advice about war he offers in an interpretation of Deuteronomy 20 found in lectures from 1525. Afterwards we

---

life before God. For these three religious institutions or orders are found in God's Word and commandment; and whatever is contained in God's Word must be holy, for God's Word is holy and sanctifies everything connected with it and involved in it.

28. Here we discover the rationale behind Luther's peculiar commentary on the Song of Songs, which he interpreted neither as a tribute to marital love, nor as an allegory of the relationship between Christ and the soul or the church, but as a manual for the Christian prince. Luther seems to have thought that the reading of the Song of Songs as an allegory of the soul supported the dominance of the church over the state, and the superiority of monastic life to life in the world. On this topic, see Jarrett A. Carty, "Martin Luther's Political Interpretation of the Song of Songs," *The Review of Politics* 73/3 (2011): 449–67, with further bibliography.

29. See vol. 8 of *D. Martin Luthers Werke: Kritische Gesamtausgabe, Deutsche Bibel*, 18 vols. (Weimar: Hermann Böhlaus Nachfolger, 1906–1961).

zoom out for a wider perspective offered in some of his lectures on Zechariah of 1527, which enable us to sketch out Luther's vision of violent conflict in the cosmos as a whole. Finally we leap ahead a decade or so to eavesdrop on the lectures on Genesis for a moment to see what Luther thought could be learned from one biblical example of a warrior saint, father Abraham.

Luther on Cain: The Origins of Arms and Defenses

In the sermons on Genesis of 1523–24 (published in Latin and German editions in 1527),[30] Luther asks and answers the question of the origins of war. Examining the story of Cain's expulsion from Adam's household following his murder of Abel, Luther notes that Cain afterwards "built a city." Why, he wonders, does the Scripture first mention a city in association with this man? Why build a city? Luther's answer: fear.[31] Cain had been expelled from the peaceable household of Adam (*die versamlung der gleubigen*),[32] an assembly of love and friendship that in Luther's understanding was *ecclesia* and *oeconomia* at the same time. Departing this community, the exiled Cain became a "citizen of the earth." Unlike the non-violent people he left behind, the murderous Cain figured he needed "arms and defenses"—that is, weapons and city walls—to protect his people. Arguing, as he is wont at times to do, from silence, Luther magnifies Cain's need by contrast to the situation in Adam's household, which he figures built neither weapons nor walls. Entering imaginatively into saintly Adam's psyche he explains that these good Christians [sic] did not even think about that, and their confident faith looked ahead to the promised Messiah, whom they expected to arrive soon.[33] They trusted in God and therefore had no need of arms or defenses.[34] Cain, on the other hand, had been exiled into a sad and alien land, driven out from the "countenance of God" (*Gottes angesicht*), i.e., away from the household of faith in which, through the Word, God was present (*da ist Gott gegenwertig*).[35]

---

30. *Reihenpredigten über das erste Buch Mose // In Genesin Mosi librum sanctissimum D. Martini Lutheri Declamationes* (WA 24:1–710).

31. WA 24:143a,1–3, where the Latin version makes the division between the two households clear: "Hic sunt duo populi, facti separati a se: qui cum Adam sunt, non aedificant civitatem, sed qui cum Cain, qui timent: timuit Cain, ne ob homicidium occideretur, ideo constituit Rempublicam aedificata urbe."

32. WA 24:143b,11–12.

33. Maxfield argues persuasively that one of Luther's achievements in the later *Enarrationes in Genesin* was to recover a biblical and apostolic sense of the imminent *parousia*. See his *Luther's Lectures on Genesis*, chap. 5.

34. Luther states:
Da beschreibt Moses Kains geschlecht bis ynns siebend gelied, Sonderlich sagt er, das Kain eine stad gebawet habe, Die stad hat er gebawet als ein buerger auff erden, Denn wenn es also stuende, das wir alle Christen weren, doerfft man nicht des weltlichen schwerds und schutzs. Die bey Adam blieben sind, haben keine stad gebawet noch sich gedacht zu schuetzen und weren. Dieser aber hat freylich daruemb gebawet, das er etwas sicher moechte sein, weil er sich furchtet und zaget. (WA 24:143b,28–34).

35. Luther states:
Wie ist Kain von Gottes angesicht gangen, so yhm doch niemand entlauffen kan? Antwort: Es ist soviel gesagt: Er ist geflohen vom vater yns elende und ynn ein frembde land komen, da niemand gewonet hat, Das heist von Gottes angesicht geflohen, Denn wo Christen sind, die Gottes wort haben und predigen, da ist Gott gegenwertig, da sihet er hin, wie die schrifft viel mal sagt. (WA 24:143b,6–11).

So it is that the younger Luther locates the origins of the coercive rule of one human being over another, as well as the fear that motivates the building of a fortified city and the forging of swords, outside the first household of faith, in what immediately becomes the false church of the apostate Cain. Here the story of Cain's exile functions, so to speak, as a second fall after the Fall. In this way, Luther rhetorically maximizes the distance between the fearful citizens of Cain's city with the true Christians who remained in Adam's fearless and therefore unfortified household, a sort of town versus country tension, if you will.[36] This early interpretation of Cain's story suggests that in the young Luther's understanding a properly Christian society would be, not to put too fine a point on it, *pacifistic*, that is, lacking arms or defenses. If the civil estate is understood as by its very nature as concerned with the coercive power that protects a people and punishes the wicked among them, then in the long ago history of the most ancient fallen human societies Luther positions *politia* on Cain's side, in agonistic relationship to the original peaceable order, which remained intact despite the fall in the faith-filled household of Adam and Eve.

This retelling of the story contrasts markedly with what is found in Luther's better known lectures on Genesis delivered about 10 years later, where he shifted the origins of coercive state power back a generation into fallen Adam's rule over his wife,[37] a movement that seems to reflect his growing concern more effectively to validate sixteenth-century political authority, or at the very least not to make it seem as if true Christians should be without arms or defenses. In 1525, after all, the peasants had revolted against the established authorities in the name of "godly law," and Luther in response had urged their violent suppression.[38] Ten years after the earlier Genesis sermons had been preached, moreover, Luther's reform movement had come increasingly to rely not only on the political cover provided by his stalwart prince elector, John Frederick (1503–54; ruled, 1532–47), but also on the League of Smalcald, a defensive alliance of the Protestant princes formed in response to the Imperial Congress held at Speyer in 1529, which had called not only for a cessation of church reform but for the enforcement of the Edict of Worms as well. The fate of Luther's movement rested, in short, upon the military might and political savvy of the princes who protested this edict of Speyer. This is not the place to explore these questions further, but the difference between the younger and the older Luther on the emergence of coercive civil government as a means of preserving godly order—whether later with Cain's exile, or earlier with Eve's subjection to her husband—seems to reflect both the unsettling experience of the violent disorder occasioned by the Peasants' uprising of 1525,[39] and the pressing need to validate duly established Protestant political authority after 1529.

---

36. Further to Cain's relationship to the *ecclesia/oeconomia* of Adam, one may consult Mickey L. Mattox, "*Fortuita Misericordia*: Martin Luther on the Salvation of Biblical Outsiders," *Pro Ecclesia* 17/4 (2006): 423–41.

37. See Mattox, *Defender*, 92–98.

38. For the treatise *Against the Robbing and Murdering Hordes of Peasants*, see Porter, *Selected Political Writings*, 85–88.

39. Maurer sees a connection, too: "Der Bauernkrieg brachte eine revolutionäre Erschütterung dieses Ordnungsgefüges. Bald nach seiner Beendigung—um den 1. November 1525 herum—hat Luther in zwei Predigten die regierende Gewalt am Elternamt illustriert." (*Luthers Lehre von den drei Hierarchien*, 21).

Luther on Deuteronomy 20: Making War the Right Way

In May of 1526 Luther's treatise *How Christians Should Regard Moses* was published by Hans Weisz in Wittenberg. There he argued that the Ten Commandments should be understood as the expression of a universally recognizable natural law, the Jewish version, as he put it, of what one could also find in ancient Roman law, as well as the German *Sachsenspiegel* (code of law).[40] His commentary on Deuteronomy, published in 1525, evidences a similar spirit, where Luther attempts to identify which elements of the law belong solely to Israel's history and which embody enduring principles. Among the latter, he includes the Mosaic prescriptions for the application of the death penalty and the proper conduct of war.

Luther's task was not easy. Deuteronomy 20 presents the reader with difficult questions about God's election of Israel and violence. The Lord God is giving Israel a promised land, but their taking possession of it depends on first violently dispossessing it from its current inhabitants, including in some cases killing all the males among them, and in other cases destroying those peoples entirely. Deuteronomy 19 introduces the topic of killing, where the law parses the differences between intentional and unintentional homicidal acts. Luther reads chapter 20 as a continuation of that topic. At this point, he surmises, Deuteronomy has completed its treatment of duties related to the First Table of the law, the duty to worship and obey God, and moves on to those related to the Second Table, the duties one owes to other people in one's community. The overarching rule of the latter, he claims, is *the law of love*, which functions to bind people together in community with all the benefits appertaining thereunto, especially peace and security, because all the members of the community cast their lot together for mutual support and defense.

This communal law of love seems a curious contrast to the fear that Luther had found just a year earlier at the root of the community gathered in the city of the exiled Cain. In this case, the city and its defenses are an expression of the law of love, and of one's service of the community's common good. The historical situation dictates this change, it seems, for the community of Israel finds itself threatened from within and without. The love that preserves the bond of community must be "severe and merciless," he insists, because it recognizes the necessity of strict law for the maintenance of order and the preservation of life. Though the principle of equity may at times call for moderation, in other cases the good of the community requires that the law should be applied severely and without mercy. For that reason, Luther here unequivocally endorses the death penalty for intentional murder—"because he who kills intentionally has sinned out of malice and has disturbed the public peace"—arguing that murderers cannot take sanctuary even in a holy place but ought rather to be "seized from the altar of the Lord and killed."[41] Clearly Luther is reading this text not just as a story about the particular laws and practices of the people of ancient

---

40. *LW* 35:161–174. This "treatise" was originally a sermon that Luther preached as an introduction to Exodus 19–20 during his 1524–1525 sermon series on Exodus. The sermon was delivered on Aug. 27, 1525.
41. *LW* 9:195.

Israel, but as a reflection as well of the general principles by which societies of all times should be ordered and ruled.

This early reading of Deuteronomy is also punctuated by occasional excurses on the text's allegorical meaning. In later times, Luther would insist that the spiritual meaning of the text was to be sought in the letter,[42] but in this case he moves more conventionally from a literal exegesis to a figural one. Literally, so Luther, this text relates Israel's "law of war." This law is special and peculiar in so far as it depends first and foremost on Israel's abiding recognition that victory depends not upon strength of arms but upon faith in the Word of God. Armor and weapons are only the outer masks (*larvae dei*) under which the Lord, who fights for them, hides himself. Armor and weapons, therefore, were only necessary for Israel insofar as they prevented the people from tempting God by, for example, attempting to fight without any weapons at all. History, then, including all the vicissitudes of war, is a mask beneath which God works in a hidden way to achieve God's own purposes.

Luther is also deeply impressed in this text by what we might call Moses' preferential option for peace. Even when foreign nations do not accept Israel's proffer of peace, moreover, the law demands moderation: a "civil and fine moderation should be observed in war," Luther writes. "He wants this people to be civil and not barbarous, and to wage war, not to devastate a land which has not sinned but to sweep away the godless."[43] Israel should wage war, moreover, with self-control so that their soldiers will not "rage against women and girls in debauchery, lust, and other violence after conquering the enemy, as happens nowadays in our barbarity."[44] This line suggests that Luther recognizes a certain distance between the world of ancient Israel and his own. He does not, however, draw from that fact the implication that these rules of war were time bound, laid down only with Israel's invasion of the Promised Land in view. To the contrary, for Luther they express general principles applicable to war and the maintenance of the public peace. Deuteronomy 20 as Luther reads it prescribes the faith, humility, and moderation proper to the waging of war.

Luther then turns to allegory, where his reading of this text spiritualizes the honorable warfare described above so that it morphs into a vision of the militant Christian, who, like Luther himself, is engaged in the struggle for faith against the church's enemies. This reading ratchets down some of the tension inherent in any Christian reading of the text, insofar as it explains away some of the blood and gore. The wars in which Luther is interested here are not the ones fought between nations, but those that pit the true faith against heresy. The text provides him with a typology. Israel, he notes, had faced three kinds of enemies: first, the foreign nations that accepted Israel's offer of peace, then those that rejected it, and, finally, the enemies within, whom Luther likens to the Canaanites and Amorites, i.e., those who lived within the boundaries of

42. For the Reformation insistence on the spirituality of the letter as an extension of developments that marked later medieval exegesis, see Christopher Ocker, *Biblical Poetics before Humanism and Reformation* (New York, Ny: Cambridge, 2002). For Luther's explicit rejection of allegory and his insistence that the spiritual meaning is to be found in the story level of the text, see, e.g., "Luther's Preface to Justus Menius, *Commentary on the First Book of Samuel*" (LW 60:7–10).
43. LW 9:204.
44. LW 9:204.

Israel's own Promised Land. The first type symbolizes heretics or outsiders to the faith who hear the Word of God and right away give up their belief in works righteousness and make peace with the Gospel; their reception of the offer of peace epitomizes the surrender with which every Christian life begins. The second type represents those who employ the weapons of Scripture to oppose the Gospel. Of these only "the males are to be killed," which according to Luther means only that the leaders among them must be defeated and slain, that is, condemned and cast out of the church. Finally, there are those who are hardened and obstinate enough in their heresy that they must be anathematized and excluded from the community, cursed, in other words, and exiled.

The violent history of Israel's occupation of the Promised Land is thus made a figure of the violence which theologians must do as their contribution to the Christianization of their own lands and societies. Again, this is not physical violence. Indeed, Luther insists here that the church conquers through the Word that smites consciences, not through the physical sword that ruins bodies. He rejects, in other words, the violent coercion of those who will not convert to the evangelical cause, or at least capital punishment for heresy, a fearsome prospect to which he himself was no stranger, and which he had argued against in his *Appeal to the Christian Nobility* in 1520.[45] The Christian, then, is a warrior in so far as he fights with the weapons of the Word of God to see the Gospel rightly preached and widely accepted. Thus Luther's allegorical reading of this "hard text" from the Old Testament supports a significant curb on the state's use of violent coercion in the case of religious conflict when he prescribes exile for heresy rather than the death penalty. Although Luther was not a forerunner of the early modern states' religious toleration, then at least in this case he does argue for a lesser penalty for religious non-conformity. In later years Luther would endorse the death penalty against the Anabaptists on grounds that they were guilty of both blasphemy and sedition.[46] Once again, the trajectory of his development is toward identification and support for the secular authorities in their vocation of keeping order, especially in seeing to it that the Word of God is rightly taught and practiced.

Cosmic Conflict: The Lectures on Zechariah

In Luther's understanding, as Heiko Oberman reminded us not so long ago, conflict is much more than a this-worldly matter.[47] Indeed, in a series of lectures on Zechariah published in 1527, we discover that this conflict extends,

---

45. Writing in 1520, Luther rejected capital punishment for heretics. Considering the burning of John Hus in the *Address to the Christian Nobility of the German Nation*, he said:

> The devil made the Romanists mad and foolish so that they did not know what they had said and done. God has commanded that a promise of safe-conduct shall he kept. We should keep such a commandment though the whole world collapses. How much more, then, when it is only a question of freeing a heretic! We should overcome heretics with books, not with fire, as the ancient fathers did. If it were wisdom to vanquish heretics with fire, then the public hangmen would be the most learned scholars on earth. We would no longer need to study books, for he who overcomes another by force would have the right to burn him at the stake. (*LW* 44:196; cf WA 6:455,19–25).

46. Luther associated the Anabaptists with both Müntzer and the Sacramentarians. For an analysis, see John S. Oyer, *Lutheran Reformers against Anabaptists: Luther, Melanchthon, and Menius, and the Anabaptists of Central Germany* (The Hague: M. Nihjoff, 1964), 126ff.

47. Oberman, *Luther: Man between God and the Devil.*

so to speak, from the top all the way down. Zech1:7ff. recounts the prophet's vision of angels riding horses.[48] Luther interprets the angelic discussion related there as an example of "how God rules the world through the angels."[49] God has instituted, he claims, a four-fold government (*vierley regiment*)—which is actually, as we shall see, five-fold—at the highest level of which is the *regiment* of God, who works all in all without anyone's help, as, for example, when he makes or multiplies his creatures "durch seine macht alleine."[50]

Beneath the level of God's own immediate government, however, he also rules over humankind through a series of four further governments (*Regimenten*). The first of these is the angelic government, in which the holy angels "do their part" (*das yhr dazu*) and watch over humankind "from the outside" (*von aussen*).[51] They do so through "understanding and reason" (*verstand und vernunfft*), by which Luther means that the angels' knowledge of God, unlike that of fallen human beings, is unobscured by the fall.[52] The unfallen angels, who already perceive God face to face, are established as external caregivers for fallen humankind, mediators of his grace and providential care. Most fundamentally, they preserve people from the consequences of the fall, not only by preventing physical harm but also by inspiring "useful and helpful thoughts" and in that way preserving them spiritually.[53]

The angels' ministry also includes a mediating role in the present administration of human affairs.[54] Zechariah mentions the prophet's encounter with a rider on a red horse, apparently an angel, who speaks of those who have been sent to "patrol the earth." Riders on other horses—red, sorrel, and white—report to the first angel that "the earth remains at peace." In an earlier version of this commentary Luther explains that the riders are the angels, "through whom God manages this visible world,"[55] while the horses are the nations over whom the angels rule. The peace the riders report, then, pertains to the very horses they sit astride.

Beneath the angelic rule Luther positions a third kind of government (*das dritte regiment*), namely, God's rule over human beings through apostles and preachers, who exercise their divinely appointed office through the external (*eusserlich*) proclamation of the Word of God. Here God makes human beings his co-workers. Alongside their work of preaching and teaching the external Word, God once again does his own work, unseen and interior (*ynnwendig*),[56] instructing both the preachers and their hearers through the Holy Spirit. By God's ordination, however, saving faith in the gospel depends on the external human proclamation of the Word carried out by this "third government."

The home and secular authority (*weltliche regiment*) constitute the fourth and fifth governments, with the secular authority ranked as the lowest (*das unterste*,

---

48. *Der Prophet Sacharja ausgelegt* (WA 23:485–664; LW 20:153–347).
49. WA 23:511,34; LW 20:169. On Zech 1:7.
50. Ibid.
51. WA 23:512,5.
52. WA 23:513,39.
53. WA 23:512,6–7.
54. The earlier Latin version of the Zechariah lectures that derives from the original lectures of 1525–26 confirms as much. *In Zachariam Prophetam* (WA 13:546–669; LW 20:1–152).
55. WA 13:558,3–4: "Equites haud dubie sunt angeli, per quos administrat deus hunc mundum visibilem." (LW 20:15). On Zech 1:8.
56. WA 23:512,8–9.

which seems to support my surmise that Luther's support for secular government grows as does the dependence of the Reformation upon it).[57] Parents,
he notes, imitate God, for God also plays the role of parent, as in the case of
Adam and Eve or even with orphan children. In this world God, however, has
assigned his own parental role to human parents, who nurture and care for
their young, and also exercise authority over them. Alongside this "home government" (*haus regiment*) one also finds the worldly government, which, Luther
says, rules by "the sword and the fist," violence and coercion.

He then makes clear the mutual interdependence of the orders. With the
exception of the direct rule of God, each of these governments serves to rein-
force all the others: "the sword serves the Gospel," for example, because it
demands respect and obedience, which creates a peaceful public space within
which the Word of God can be preached and believed. The angelic regiment, in
turn, is ordered to the working of both the Word and the sword, for the angels
move people toward obedience to both. Likewise, as Luther puts it, "the Word
and the sword are ordered to the angelic rule, for they make room and prepare
people through peace, so that the angels may all the better approach them and
promote their rule [*regiment*]."[58] The four governments thus lead believers into
proper conformity with divine order and reason; in this way God's appointed
ends are achieved not just in the midst of conflict, but through and by means
of it.

It is crucial to note that with the exception of God's own immediate rule
over all things, conflict characterizes Luther's orders of government at every
level. Against the four governments of angels, preachers, parents, and magistrates the devil ever rages, doing everything possible to destroy all God's
good creation.[59] The fourfold government thus constitutes a rule in the midst
of opposition: the fallen angels oppose the good, heretics and false teachers
oppose the apostles and prophets, disobedient children oppose their parents,
and rebellious or lawless people oppose the worldly regiment. When such evils
seem to gain the upper hand, the failure of divinely instituted government
reflects nothing so much as a temporary but providential withdrawal of God's
own rule as a means of punishment. As God effects the good through external
means, so the withdrawal of God's internal power and effect allows evil to
advance, through both the fallen angels and sinful human beings. In short, the
divine order and rule are contested. Not this earth only, but the cosmos itself is
an arena of conflict, of battle, of violence and war.

The Genesis Lectures: Abraham's Just and Moderate War

We turn now to Abraham as an example of one who embodies much of what
has been sketched out above. As Juhani Forsberg has observed, Luther praised
Abraham highly, as a *pater fidei sanctissimus*, and made him a great hero and
example of the Christian faith. More than that, Abraham was simultaneously
paterfamilias, priest, and prince over his extended family. To that extent, he

---

57. WA 23:514,19.
58. WA 23:514,27–31; translation from *LW* 20:172, slightly amended.
59. WA 23:514,32–4: "Widder solche Gotts regimente tobet nu der Satan, des ampt nichts anders ist
denn alles zubrechen und zurstoeren, was Gott durch diese regimente schafft und thut."

exercised a position of authority in all three spheres of this-worldly rule identified in the Zechariah lectures: church, home, and state. As if those three offices were not enough, in both his *Supputatio annorum mundi* (computation of the years of the world) and in the *Enarrationes* on Genesis Luther also identified Abraham as an eschatological figure, the *"gubernator"* who introduced the world's third age (*tertii millennarii gubernator*) following the destruction of the old world in the flood.

The *gubernatores* of the changing ages of world history were in Luther's understanding heroes, that is, saints. Before Abraham they included Adam, who lived by faith in the promise of God after his tragic fall into sin, and was the *gubernator* of the first millennium,[60] as well as holy Noah, a prophet of God through whose eyes the righteous God saw and judged the wickedness of the world.[61] As *gubernator* of the world's third age, holy Abraham symbolized the announcement of a new promise and with it the arrival of a new day in which it became clear that the Messiah would come from Abraham's own flesh. He signals the Christian hope for a new and better world, and the fulfillment of that hope, Luther surmised, is coming very soon. Abraham, then, is not only for Luther a paradigm of the call to faith through the Word of God, but also a reminder that things do not always stay the way they have been. This point also has a particular poignancy for Luther, because he saw himself, too, as an eschatological figure, or at least as caught up in a great eschatological struggle. Biography and autobiography are ever a jumble in Luther's exegesis.

Genesis 14 recounts the story of St. Abraham's victory over Chedorlaomer, when he restored Lot and his household from captivity. Luther finds much to praise in Abraham's conduct of this war. It was only some 30 years or so after the great flood, he calculates, and already men were rushing headlong into sin, with a group of some nine tyrannous kings gathered here to wage war against one another for domination in the land. God "wants there to be government [*imperia*]," Luther assures us, for both the defense of the godly and the damnation of the wicked, "but Satan corrupts their hearts, and the magistrates degenerate into tyrants."[62] Following the great battle between these tyrants, Lot and his clan were carried off into captivity, at which point they become for Luther a type of the Christian who faces adversity: life, that is, under the cross. It seems to Lot and his family that all is surely lost, but God has in mind a miraculous rescue, one that will confirm their trust in God. "This game, with its perpetual reversals, he [God] ever plays with his saints."[63] Attending to the wondrous reversal about to come, Luther notes that Abraham is called here for the first time a "Hebrew," which he thinks identifies Abraham as one who had kept to the pure religion and the true church of the patriarchs. This great man had no concern for the fate of the five wicked kings and their peoples, but he determined to rescue his kinsman Lot and his family on account of their shared faith in the true God.

---

60. WA 53:38.
61. WA 53:39. To this topic one may consult my "Hearer of the Triune God," cited above.
62. WA 42:526,19–21.
63. WA 42:527,4. For these "reversals," in which God sometimes appears as the devil and the devil as God, see Mattox, *Defender*, 227–31.

The military attack led by holy Abraham, Luther figures, was both brave and cunning, and this from a man who not long before had identified his wife as his sister out of fear of Egypt's Pharaoh. The inspiration of the Holy Spirit in this case gave Abraham a courage and confidence greater than that of any Hannibal or Scipio. Adopting a brilliant strategy, he fell upon his enemy by night, and from many different directions, routing them from the field. He drew the sword, Luther notes, to protect his kinsman, that is, as a textbook example of the proper application of the coercive power of government to protect its citizens. The angel of the Lord, too, fought on Abraham's side in this battle, joining forces, so to speak, with the civil government embodied in Abraham, in order to strike fear into the hearts of his enemies.[64] Afterwards, moreover, Abraham was magnanimous in victory, refusing to make it a pretext to claim the whole of the land of Canaan as his own. Inwardly, Luther surmises, Abraham interpreted the promise of that land as a blessing to be fulfilled in Christ, for as the Savior says in John 8:56, "Abraham rejoiced that he would see my day; he saw it and was glad." Still, Luther wonders, how did Abraham know that God would be with him and give him the victory? His answer? Abraham acted at the command of the Holy Spirit. His action provides no example, Luther hastens to add, to be imitated in the present, as those like Thomas Müntzer and other "seditious rubes" would like to think.[65]

From this remark we can better appreciate the fine line Luther is attempting to walk here. On the one hand, he wants to praise Abraham for the military action he took in defense of his kinsman, and to give God credit for the victory, just as he had insisted in his interpretation of Deuteronomy 20. Abraham used arms and violence, but he did not trust in them for the victory. On the other hand, however, Luther is well aware that conceding even to such a great man as Abraham the inspiration of the Holy Spirit to justify an obviously violent episode is a theological hot potato, for claims to the inspiration of the Spirit could be used to justify a wide variety of rash or rebellious deeds, like those he associates with Müntzer. The deeds of an Abraham should therefore be wondered at, Luther insists, but not imitated.[66] In the end, then, Abraham is established in Luther's reading of this text as a man of "distinguished faith and a truly heroic spirit."[67] He was both a saint and, at just the right time and to just the right degree, a warrior. Moreover, the violent acts that were required in order to free his captive kinsman did not separate him from the Spirit of God. Indeed, the Spirit led him, and the angel of the Lord fought on his side.

Conclusions

We began with a series of questions regarding violence in Luther's theology, perhaps most importantly whether Luther somehow promoted religious

64. WA 42:531,28–30.
65. WA 42:531,7–10.
66. On this "narrative barrier" between the acts of the biblical saints and the lives of contemporary Christians, which Luther admits becomes permeable in the challenges to faith the believer faces in this life, see Mattox, *Defender*, 250–251.
67. WA 42:532,3–4.

violence. As has been shown, his vision for the original creation leaves no room for violence and coercion, which become realities in this life only after the fall. Thereafter, however, violence is unmasked as a cosmic reality, one that antedates the peaceable kingdom of Eden, with the sounds of conflict echoing up and down the great chain of being so to speak, as reflected in his lectures on Zechariah. For this reason, violence is unavoidable. Though his early reading of the story of Cain seems to suggest a peaceable and even pacifistic Christian kingdom in this world after the fall, his later exegesis steps back from that conclusion and he more consistently grants the secular powers their place as good gifts from God. Still, Luther typically works very hard to restrain the application of violence even in this fallen world, developing a model of princely rule that is at once firm and threatening toward lawbreakers but gentle and even magnanimous toward those who accept correction, as seen in his lectures on Deuteronomy, and as witnessed to in his plea for clemency for Peter Beskendorf. Though he would later change his mind, in these early exegetical vignettes he also opposes the application of the death penalty, even for persistent theological error.

Though the reading of Abraham examined above was given many years later, still we find in it a textbook case of the application of Luther's principles regarding war and violence. As a warrior saint, Abraham epitomizes simultaneously the faithfulness of the pastor, the practical wisdom of the *Hausvater*, and the steadfastness of the prince. When Abraham fought, God fought on his side. This image of the militant saint comports quite well with Luther's broader conception of the Christian life, which is marked indelibly by a certain kind of spiritual violence. On Luther's account it is the task of every Christian so to let Christ be born in her as to rise anew each day and begin the battle all over again. The terrible malady of sin, however—the conflict and disorder that characterize human life this side of Eden—requires a severe mercy. The agent of grace must be merciless to sin in order to effect the mercy of renovation in the believer. The converse of the Christian's daily rising in Christ, then, is the daily putting to death of the old Adam, living a life, in other words, in which sin is ruled over and conquered, through faith and the Holy Spirit. For this metaphorical battle Scripture and especially the stories of the biblical saints provide, on Luther's account, a sure and certain guide.

5. Why War Is a Moral Necessity for America, Or, How Realistic Is Realism?

Stanley Hauerwas

The Idealism of Realism

Pacifists always bear the burden of proof for their ideology, because as attractive as nonviolence may be, most people assume pacifism just will not work. You may want to keep a few pacifists around for reminding those burdened with running the world that what they sometimes have to do is a lesser evil, but pacifism simply cannot and should not be, even for Christians, a normative stance. To call for the abolition of war, as Enda McDonagh and I have, is then viewed as an unrealistic proposal made possible by our isolation as academics from the real world. Nonviolence is unworkable, or to the extent it works, it does so only because it is parasitic on more determinative forms of order secured by violence. Those committed to nonviolence, in short, are not realistic.

In the first part of this chapter I will explore the evidence for "just war" theory. In contrast to pacifism it is often assumed that just war reflection is "realistic." It is by no means clear, however, whether advocates of just war have provided an adequate account of what kind of conditions would be necessary for just war to be a realistic alternative for the military policy of a nation. In the second part, in order to raise questions about how realistic it is to think war can be limited, I will explore the American understanding of war as sacrifice. The understanding of war as sacrifice, I believe, was forged in the American Civil War and continues to shape how Americans morally comprehend war. War is necessary for America's moral well-being, which means it is by no means clear what it would mean for Americans to have a realistic understanding of war.[1]

---

1. WWI is equally important for the American sacralization of war as sacrifice. Jonathan Ebel has recovered how the American soldiers understood their participation in the war as redemptive in his *Faith in the Fight: Religion and the American Soldier in the Great War* (Princeton, Nj: Princeton University Press, 2010). Drawing on letters and poetry written by those who fought in the war, he documents that participants "believed that by involving themselves in the war, assenting to its demands, and achieving victory, they would attain at least this more general redemption of the world and of America. By exposing themselves to the mysterious and powerful forces of combat, many believed they would achieve a personal redemption of great metaphysical consequence" (27). The significance of WWI for underwriting the sacrificial character of war cannot be overestimated. See, for example, Richard Koenigsberg's *Nations Have the Right to Kill: Hitler, the Holocaust, and War* (New York, Ny: Library of Social Science, 2009) for the effect WWI had on Hitler's understanding of the sacrificial character of war. Koenigsberg argues that Hitler understood war as a sacrifice necessary for the renewal of the German people. "The Aryan" was therefore understood as someone willing to sacrifice himself or herself for the nation. The Jew, in contrast, was individualistic and selfish. Accordingly, the Jew could be sacrificed for the good of the nation (7). The destructive character of war is crucial for the moral purpose war should serve, from Hitler's perspective. For war is form of sacrifice "whereby human beings give over their bodies and possessions to the objects of worship with names like France, Germany, Japan,

In Christian tradition, realism is often thought to have begun with Augustine's account of the two cities, hardened into doctrine with Luther's two kingdoms, and given its most distinctive formulation in the thought of Reinhold Niebuhr. Thus Augustine is often identified as the Christian theologian who set the stage for the development of just war reflection, which enables Christians to use violence in a limited way in order to secure tolerable order.[2] It is assumed, therefore, that just war is set within the larger framework of a realist view of the world.

With his customary rhetorical brilliance Luther gave expression to the realist perspective, asking:

> If anyone attempted to rule the world by the gospel and to abolish all temporal law and sword on the plea that all are baptized and Christian, and that, according to the gospel, there shall be among them no law or sword—or the need for either—pray tell me friend, what would he be doing? He would be loosing the ropes and chains of the savage wild beasts and letting them bite and mangle everyone, meanwhile insisting that they were harmless, tame, and gentle creatures; but I would have the proof in my wounds. Just so would the wicked under the name of Christian abuse evangelical freedom, carry on their rascality, and insist that they were Christians subject neither to law nor sword as some are already raving and ranting.[3]

Luther is under no illusions. War is a plague, but it prevents a greater one. Of course slaying and robbing do not seem the work of love, but "in truth even this is the work of love."[4] Christians do not fight for themselves, but for their neighbor. So if they see that there is a lack of hangmen, constables, judges, lords, or princes, and find they are qualified, they should offer their services and assume these positions.[5] That "small lack of peace called war," according to Luther, "must set a limit to this universal, worldwide lack of peace which would destroy everyone."[6]

Reinhold Niebuhr understood himself to stand in this "realist" tradition. In 1940 in his "Open Letter (to Richard Roberts)," Niebuhr explains why he left the Fellowship of Reconciliation: he did not believe that "war is merely an 'incident' in history" but rather that it "is a final revelation of the very character of human history."[7] According to Niebuhr the incarnation is not "redemption"

America, etc." (xv). War, in short, is the human activity in which "human bodies are sacrificed in the name of perpetuating a magical entity, the body politic" (42).

2. Needless to say, I think the Niebuhr's use of Augustine to justify war in the name of "realism" to be a simplification of Augustine. Robert Dodaro provides a much more complex understanding of the two cities in his *Christ and the Just Society in the Thought of Augustine* (Cambridge, UK: Cambridge University Press, 2004).

3. Martin Luther, *On Temporal Authority: To What Extent It Should Be Obeyed*, in *Luther: Selected Political Writings*, ed. J.M. Porter (Philadelphia, Pa: Fortress Press, 1974), 56.

4. Luther, *Whether Soldiers, Too, Can Be Saved*, in Porter, *Luther*, 103.

5. Luther, *Temporal Authority*, 58.

6. Luther, *Whether Soldiers*, 103. For a fuller account of Luther on the ethics of war, see Joel Lehenbauer, "The Christological and Ecclesial Pacifism of Stanley Hauerwas: A Lutheran Analysis and Appraisal" (PhD diss., Saint Louis, Mo: Concordia Seminary, 2004). Lehenbauer's dissertation is an extremely fair account of my (and Yoder's) work in comparison to Luther's thought on war.

7. Reinhold Niebuhr, "An Open Letter (to Richard Roberts)," in *Love and Justice: Selections from the Shorter Writings of Reinhold Niebuhr*, ed. D.B. Robertson (Louisville, Ky: Westminster/John Knox, 1957), 268.

from history as conflict because sinful egoism continues to express itself at every level of human life, making it impossible to overcome the contradictions of human history. Niebuhr, therefore, accuses pacifists of failing to understand the Reformation doctrine of "justification by faith." From Niebuhr's perspective, pacifists are captured by a perfectionism that is more "deeply engulfed in illusion about human nature than the Catholic pretensions, against which the Reformation was a protest."[8]

"Just war" proponents argue that war is justified because our task as Christians and as citizens is first and foremost to seek justice. Paul Ramsey understood his attempt to recover just war as a theory of statecraft to be "an extension within the Christian realism of Reinhold Niebuhr."[9] Ramsey saw, however, that there was more to be said about "justice in war than was articulated in Niebuhr's sense of the ambiguities of politics and his greater/lesser evil doctrine of the use of force."[10] That "something more," Ramsey asserted, is the principle of discrimination, which requires that war be subject to political purpose through which war might be limited and conducted justly, that is, that noncombatants be protected.

Yet it is by no means clear if just war reflection can be yoked consistently to a Niebuhrian realism. Augustine's and Luther's "realism" presupposed there was another city that at least could call into question state powers. For Niebuhr, realism names the development of states and an international nation-state system that cannot be challenged. Niebuhrian realism assumes that war is a permanent reality for the relation between states because no overriding authority exists that might make war analogous to the police function of the state.[11] Therefore each political society has the right to wage war because it is assumed that to do so is part of its divinely ordained work of preservation. "Realism," therefore, names the reality that at the end of the day in the world of international relations, the nations with the largest army get to determine what counts for "justice." To use Augustine or Luther to justify this understanding of "realism" is in effect to turn a description into a recommendation.

In an article entitled, "Just War Theory and the Problem of International Politics," David Baer and Joseph Capizzi admirably try to show how just war requirements, as developed by Ramsey, can be reconciled with a realistic understanding of international relations. They argue that even though a certain pessimism surrounds a realistic account of international politics, that does not mean such a view of the world is necessarily amoral. To be sure, governments

---

8. Ibid., 269.

9. Paul Ramsey, *The Just War: Force and Political Responsibility* (New York, Ny: Rowman & Littlefield, 2002), 260.

10. Ibid.

11. For the best defense of this view, see Philip Bobbitt's *The Shield of Achilles: War, Peace, and the Course of History* (New York, Ny: Anchor, 2003). Bobbitt puts it starkly by observing: "War is not a pathology that with proper hygiene and treatment can be wholly prevented. War is a natural condition of the State, which was organized in order to be an effective instrument of violence on behalf of society. Wars are like death, which, while they can be postponed, will come when they will come and cannot finally be avoided" (819). I admire Bobbitt's analysis of the development of constitutional orders that war makes possible, as well as his account of the transition from nation-states to market states. I do not think, however, that he shows how the latter can sustain the ethos necessary to produce people capable of sustaining the kind of military he admires. Why should consumers care about honor?

have the right to wage war because of their responsibility to a particular group of neighbors, but that does not mean that governments have carte blanche to pursue every kind of interest. "The same conception that permits government to wage war also restricts the conditions of legitimate war making. . . . Because each government is responsible for only a limited set of political goods, it must respect the legitimate jurisdiction of other governments."[12]

Yet who is going to enforce the presumption that a government "must respect the legitimate jurisdiction of other governments"? Baer and Capizzi argue that Ramsey's understanding of just war as the expression of Christian love by a third party in defense of the innocent requires that advocates of just war favor the establishment of international law and institutions to better regulate the conduct of states in pursuit of their self-interest.[13] Yet Baer and Capizzi recognize that international agencies cannot be relied on because there is no way that such an agency can judge an individual government's understanding of just cause. As they put it, "absent effective international institutions, warring governments are like Augustine's individual pondering self-defense, moved by the temptation of inordinate self-love."[14]

Baer and Capizzi argue that a more adequate understanding of just war will combine a realist understanding of international politics with a commitment to international order by emphasizing the importance of just intention.[15] Which means a war can be undertaken only if peace, which is understood as a concept for a more "embracing and stable order," be the reason a state gives for going to war. The requirement that the intention for going to war be so understood is an expression of love for the enemy just to the extent that a lasting order be one that encompasses the interests of the enemy.[16]

---

12. Helmut David Baer and Joseph E. Capizzi, "Just War Theory and the Problem of International Politics: On the Central Role of Just Intention," *JSCE* 26/1 (2006):167–168. George Weigel argues in a similar fashion in his article, "World Order: What Catholics Forgot," *First Things* 143 (May 2004): 31–38. Weigel argues the Catholic tradition insists that "politics is an arena of rationality and moral responsibility. Unlike those theories of international relations which insisted that world politics is amoral or immoral, classic Catholic thinking about international relations taught that every human activity, including politics, takes place within the horizon of moral judgment, precisely because politics is a human activity and moral judgment is a defining characteristic of the human person. That is true of politics among nations, the Catholic tradition insisted, even if there are distinctive aspects to the moral dimension of world politics" (31). I could not agree more, but it is one thing to make such a claim and quite another to suggest that is the way the world works.

13. Baer and Capizzi, "Just War Theory," 164–166.

14. Ibid., 168.

15. Baer and Capizzi argue that this means that going to war requires increasing reliance on international agencies. Weigel, in the article mentioned above, argues exactly the opposite. Indeed, Weigel wrote his article in response to the Vatican's deferral to the United Nations concerning the legitimacy of the war against Iraq. Weigel defends the preemptive war strategy of the Bush administration in the name of preserving a more nearly just world order.

Martha Nussbaum argues that the very idea of a world state is not desirable because it is very unlikely that such a state could be held accountable. Moreover, such a state would be dangerous. "If a nation becomes unjust, pressure from other nations may prevent it from committing heinous crimes (whether against its citizens or against other nations). If the world state should become unjust, there would be no corresponding recourse; the only hope would be for rebellion from within" (Martha Nussbaum, *Frontiers of Justice: Disability, Nationality, Species Membership* [Cambridge: Belknap Press, 2006], 313).

16. Baer and Capizzi, "Just War Theory," 170–171. One wonders what empirical tests might exist to test this requirement of enemy love. Would the "enemy" need to say after being defeated that they were glad to lose the war?

And pacifists are said to be unrealistic? The idealism of such realist justifications of just war is nowhere better seen than in these attempts to fit just war considerations into the realist presuppositions that shape the behavior of state actors.[17] Ramsey, Baer and Capizzi, and Oliver O'Donovan are to be commended for trying to recover just war as a theory of statecraft rather than as a checklist to judge whether a particular war satisfies enough of the criteria to be judged just.[18] Yet by doing so they have made apparent the tensions between the institutions necessary for just war to be a reality and the presumptions that shape international affairs.

For example, what would an American foreign policy determined by just war principles look like? What would a just war Pentagon look like? What kind of virtues would the people of America have to have to sustain a just war foreign policy and Pentagon? What kind of training do those in the military have to undergo in order to be willing to take casualties rather than conduct the war unjustly?[19] How would those with the patience necessary to ensure that a war be a last resort be elected to office? Those are the kinds of questions that advocates of just war must address before they accuse pacifists of being "unrealistic."

To put the challenge more concretely, we could ask, why was it possible for the United States to conduct the second war against Iraq? The answer is very simple. America had a military left over from the cold war, a war that was fought according to an amoral realism, and therefore America could go to war in Iraq because nothing prevented America from going to war in Iraq—a war that is, moreover, justified as part of a "war against terrorism." Yet, in spite of the title of Jean Bethke Elshtain's book, *Just War against Terror*, it is by no means clear that you can fight a just war against terrorism.[20] If one of the crucial conditions of a just war is for the war to have an end, then the war against terrorism clearly cannot be just because it is a war without end.

---

17. It would be quite interesting, for example, for Baer and Capizzi to address Bobbitt's claim that the deepest immorality is to be found in those who attempt to avoid war. To make going to war "a last resort" would only make the world more dangerous. Bobbitt argues the issue is never whether we ought to avoid war, but rather "we must choose what sort of war we will fight, regardless of what are its causes, to set the terms of the peace we want." The avoidance of war, therefore, cannot and should not be an objective because such a policy "counsels against the preparations for war that might avert massive, carefully planned, large-scale attacks by one state on another." Such a view rightly rejects those who assume war is a pathology of the state.

18. O'Donovan's account of just war can be found in his *The Just War Revisited* (Cambridge, UK: Cambridge University Press, 2003).

19. There is a complex relation between the public reasons given for war and the reasons that actually shape those who fight the war. This is explored in fine detail by Nancy Sherman in her book *The Untold War: Inside the Hearts, Minds, and Souls of Our Soldiers* (New York, Ny: W.W. Norton, 2010). She begins the book with an observation from Anthony Miller, who warned, as he was preparing to write a Hollywood movie in 1940 about G.I. Joe, that soldiers abhor an ideological vacuum. Miller accordingly argued that "unless the American people can explain and justify this war, they are going to injure and sometimes destroy the minds of a host of their returning veterans" (39). There are no doubt many reasons for post-traumatic stress disorder (PTSD), but one cannot help but think part of the problem for many who return from combat so affected is due to the failure of American soldiers' ability to match the reality of war with the reasons for which the war is being fought. One cannot help but wonder, moreover, if the tension is not endemic to a just war position.

20. Jean Bethke Elshtain, *Just War against Terror: The Burden of American Power in a Violent World* (New York, Ny: Basic Books, 2003). The subtitle of Elshtain's book is revealing just to the extent the subtitle suggests that America's role in the world, a role shaped by a realistic foreign policy shaped by American self-interest, is the necessary condition for fighting a just war.

I think the lack of realism about realism by American just war advocates has everything to do with their being American. In particular, American advocates of just war seem to presume that democratic societies place an inherent limit on war that more authoritarian societies are unable to do. While such a view is quite understandable, I want to suggest that democratic societies, or at least the American version of democracy, are unable to set limits on war because they are democratic.[21] Put even more strongly, for Americans, war is a necessity to sustain our belief that we are worthy to be recipients of the sacrifices made on our behalf in past wars. Americans are a people born of and in war, particularly the Civil War, and only war can sustain our belief that we are a people set apart.

Upon the Altar of the Nation[22]

In his extraordinary book, *Upon the Altar of the Nation: A Moral History of the Civil War*, Harry Stout tells the story of how the Civil War began as a limited war but ended as total war. He is well aware that the language of total war did not exist at the time of the Civil War, but he argues that by 1864 the *spirit* of total war emerged and "prepared Americans for the even more devastating total wars they would pursue in the twentieth century" (xv). Stout's story of the transformation of the Civil War from limited to total war is also the story of how America became the nation we call America. According to Stout,

> Neither Puritans' talk of a "city upon a hill" or Thomas Jefferson's invoca-
> tion of "inalienable rights" is adequate to create a religious loyalty sufficiently
> powerful to claim the lives of its adherents. In 1860 no coherent nation com-
> manded the sacred allegiance of all Americans over and against their states
> and regions. For the citizenry to embrace the idea of a nation-state that *must*
> have a messianic destiny and command one's highest loyalty would require
> a massive sacrifice—a blood sacrifice. . . . As the war descended into a kill-
> ing horror, the grounds of justification underwent a transformation from a
> just defensive war fought out of sheer necessity to preserve home and nation

21. In his article, "Authority, Lies, and War: Democracy and the Development of Just War Theory," *TS* 67 (2006) 378–394, David DeCosse argues that Catholic deference to political authority has inadequately integrated democratic ideas into just war theory as is evident by the lying that justified the Iraq war. Though I am sympathetic with DeCosse's claim that lying is analogous to the use of physical force, I am not at all convinced that by paying more attention "to the rights, responsibilities, and virtues of democratic citizens in time of war" (393) means we will ensure more truthful speech about war.

22. The following account is dependent on Harry S. Stout's, *Upon the Altar of the Nation: A Moral History of the Civil War* (New York, Ny: Viking, 2006). (Page references will appear in the text.) Stout is to be commended for his courage as a historian to make candid that he is writing a "moral history" of the Civil War. He does not elaborate in this book what it means methodologically for him to assume a moral stance other than to accept just war as normative for the story he tells. One can only hope in the future he might tell us more about what it means for a historian to acknowledge that history is a moral endeavor. Though he ends his book by making clear that he does not use the Civil War to justify pacifism, he nonetheless remains deeply ambiguous about the reality of war. It remains true for him that "at its most elemental, war is evil. War is killing. War is destroying. War may be a necessary evil, and in that sense 'right,' but it is nevertheless lethally destructive" (xii). Stout dedicates his book to his father, who he says fought in a "just war," but if that was WWII, there are very real questions if in fact WWII was fought justly. Of course it does not mean that those that fought in that war were unjust. I am hesitant to call attention to Stout's regard for his father's military service, but I think his ambiguity about war reflects the tendency we all have to justify war because of our love of those who fought in past wars.

to a moral crusade for "freedom" that would involve nothing less than a national "rebirth," a spiritual "revival." And in that blood and transformation a national religion was born. Only as casualties rose to unimaginable levels did it dawn on some people that something mystically religious was taking place, a sort of massive sacrifice on the national altar. The Civil War taught Americans that they were a Union, and it absolutely required a baptism of blood to unveil transcendent dimensions of that union (xxi).[23]

The generals on both sides of the Civil War had not only been trained at West Point to embody American might and power; they were also taught to be gentlemen. The title of "gentlemen" not only carried with it expectations that the bearers of the title would be honorable, but that they would also pursue their profession justly. They "imbibed" the code of limited war, which demanded that they protect innocent lives and minimize destructive aspects of war. According to Stout they were even taught by Dennis Mahan, a professor of civil engineering, to use position and maneuver of interior lines of operations against armies rather than engaging in crushing overland campaigns that would involve civilian populations (21).

Stout argues that Lincoln, as early as 1862, and prior to his generals, realized that the West Point Code of War would have to be abandoned. After Bull Run, and frustrated by McClellan's timidity, Lincoln understood that if the Union was to be preserved, the war would need to escalate into a war against both citizens and soldiers. In response to Unionists in New Orleans who protested his war policy, Lincoln replied,

What would you do in my position? Would you drop the war where it is? Or would you prosecute it in future with elder-stalk squirts charged with rose water? Would you deal lighter blows than heavier ones? I am in no boastful mood. I shall not do more than I can, and I shall do all I can, to save the government, which is my sworn duty as well as my personal inclination. I shall do nothing in malice (139).[24]

23. Stout documents how during the Civil War the flag became the central symbol of American patriotism. Prior to 1860 the flag was barely visible, flying primarily on ships, but after 1861 the flag was flown on churches, storefronts, homes, and government buildings to signify loyalty and support (28). The title of Stout's book, as well as his understanding of the flag as a totem, is supported by Carolyn Marvin and David Ingle in their book *Blood Sacrifice and the Nation: Totem Rituals and the American Flag* [Cambridge, UK: Cambridge University Press, 1999). They argue "that violent blood sacrifice makes enduring groups cohere, even though such a claim challenges our most deeply held notions of civilized behavior. The sacrificial system that binds American citizens has a sacred flag at its center. Patriotic rituals revere it as the embodiment of a bloodthirsty totem god who organizes killing energy" (1).

In *Redeemer Nation: The Idea of America's Millennial Role* (Chicago, Il: University of Chicago Press, 1968), Ernest Tuveson traces the background of millennial theological categories for shaping American national identity. Accordingly he observes "that the apocalyptic vision of the Civil War was far more than a spontaneous response to a great crisis by a nation of Bible-readers, who naturally saw it as a moral conflict. It seemed to fit exactly into a pattern long established, and seemed to confirm the validity of that pattern. Thus it was more than just another war about a moral issue, even if a great one, it was *the* crisis of mankind, even if only one nation was involved" (196). Tuveson's book is essential reading if we are to understand the rhetoric that shapes American foreign policy after September 11, 2001. For an astute and informative analysis of that rhetoric, see Michael Northcott, *An Angel Directs the Storm: Apocalyptic Religion and American Empire* (New York, Ny: I.B. Tauris, 2004).

24. Grant and Sherman are, of course, those who are most associated with pursuing a brutal strategy in the war, but Stout makes clear that each was in quite different ways doing Lincoln's bidding. In a letter to General Halleck about his destruction of Atlanta, Sherman concluded, "If the people raise a howl against my barbarity and cruelty, I will answer that war is war, and not popularity-seeking. If

Crucial to Lincoln's strategy for the prosecution of the war against the population of the South was the Emancipation Proclamation, which Lincoln signed on September 22, 1862. Lincoln's primary concern was always the preservation of the Union, but the Emancipation Proclamation made clear to both sides that a very way of life was at issue, requiring a total war on all fronts.[25] Emancipation blocked any attempt to reconcile the North and South, because now the war by necessity stood for moral aims which could not be compromised. Stout quotes Massachusetts's abolitionist senator Charles Sumner, who supported the Emancipation Proclamation as a "war measure" in these terms:

> But, fellow-citizens, the war which we wage is not merely for ourselves; it is for all mankind. . . . In ending slavery here we open its gates all over the world, and let the oppressed go free. Nor is this all. In saving the republic we shall save civilization. . . . In such a cause no effort can be too great, no faith can be too determined. To die for country is pleasant and honorable. But all who die for country now die also for humanity. Wherever they lie, in bloody fields, they will be remembered as the heroes through whom the republic was saved and civilization established forever (174–175).[26]

Stout's book is distinguished from other books on the Civil War by his close attention to what religious figures on both sides were saying about the war. It was ministers of the gospel who supplied the rhetoric necessary for the war to achieve its mythic status. To be sure, the South represented a more conservative form of Christianity than the North, as Christianity was recognized as the established religion in the Confederacy's Constitution, but for both sides "Christianity offered the only terms out of which national identity could be constructed and a violent war pursued" (43).

Stout provides plenty of examples of how Christians narrated the bloody sacrifice of the war, but Horace Bushnell's contribution is particularly noteworthy

---

they want peace, they and their relatives must stop the war" (369). Stout provides a very illuminating account of how the generals, and in particular Stonewall Jackson, in the Civil War were seen as "saviors." Indeed he notes that Jackson became a "messianic figure" who could "never die" because he incarnated the Confederate civil religion through a violent atonement (229). For a depiction of the complex character of Sherman, see E.L. Doctorow's, *The March* (New York, Ny: Random House, 2006). *The March* is a novel, but it may give us a better sense of the anarchy of Sherman's march across the South than many of the histories on the same subject.

25. On August 22, 1862, Lincoln sent a letter to Horace Greely that was printed in the *New York Tribune* in which he made clear his primary purpose in pursuing the war:

> My paramount object in this struggle is to save the Union, and is *not* either to save or to destroy slavery. If I could save the Union without freeing *any* slave I would do it, and if I could save it by freeing *all* slaves I would do it, and if I could save it by freeing some and leaving others alone I would also do that. What I do about slavery, and the colored race, I do because I believe it helps to save the Union; and what I forbear, I forbear because I do *not* believe it would help to save the Union. . . . I have here stated my purpose according to my view of *official* duty; and I intend no modification of my oft-expressed *personal* wish that all men everywhere could be free (184).

26. Tuveson calls attention to the significance of Julia Ward Howe's "Battle Hymn of the Republic" for giving the war its apocalyptic cast. What makes Howe's hymn so significant is her identification with such liberal thinkers as Theodore Parker, Ralph Waldo Emerson, and Oliver Wendell Holmes. Tuveson observes that though Howe had no use for faith in a special revelation, she could still write lines like

> I have seen Him in the watch-fires of a hundred circling camps;
> The have builded Him an altar in the evening dews and damps;
> I can read His righteous sentence by the dim and flaring lamps:
> His day is marching on (Tuveson, *Redeemer Nation*, 197–198).

for no other reason than that his Christianity was liberal. Early in the war Bushnell suggested that morally and religiously a nation was being created by the bloodshed required by the war. According to Bushnell, through the shed blood of soldiers, soldiers of both sides, a vicarious atonement was being made for the developing Christian nation.[27] Such an atonement was not simply a metaphor, "but quite literally a blood sacrifice required by God for sinners North and South if they were to inherit their providential destiny" (249).[28] Shortly after Gettysburg, Bushnell identified those who gave their lives in the war with the martyrs, writing:

> How far the loyal sentiment reaches and how much it carries with it, or after it, must also be noted. It yields up willingly husbands, fathers, brothers, and sons, consenting to the fearful chance of a home always desolate. It offers body and blood, and life on the altar of devotion. It is a fact, a political worship, offering to seal itself by martyrdom in the field (251).[29]

As the toll of the war mounted, the most strident voices calling for blood revenge came from the clergy. Thus Robert Dabney, at the funeral of his friend, Lieutenant Carrington, CSA, told his listeners that Carrington's blood "seals upon you the obligation to fill their places in your country's host, and 'play the men for your people and the cities of your God,' to complete vindication of their rights" (201). One Confederate chaplain even prayed, "We should add to the prayer for peace, let this war continue, if we are not yet so humbled and disciplined by its trials, as to be prepared for those glorious moral and spiritual gifts, which Thou designest it should confer upon us as a people" (197). Such a prayer makes clear that the war had become for both sides a ritual they had come to need to make sense of their lives.

27. Lincoln shared Bushnell-like sentiments most clearly articulated in the Second Inaugural. Yet as early as 1862 Lincoln is reflecting on the imponderable purpose of God in relation to the war. Lincoln says, "In the present civil war it is quite possible that God's purpose is something different from the purpose of either party—and yet the human instrumentalities, working just as they do, are of the best adaptation to effect this purpose. I am almost ready to say this is probably true—that God wills this contest, and wills that it shall not end yet" (146). Stout observes that Lincoln's sense of destiny "provided for Lincoln a Christlike compassion for his foes; in death, it would render him a Christlike messiah for the reconstituted American nation" (146).

28. Stout quotes from a sermon by N. H. Chamberlain concerning the flag, preached after Lincoln's assassination. Chamberlain said:

> Henceforth that flag is the legend which we bequeath to future generations, of the severe and solemn struggle for the nation's life. . . . Henceforth the red on it is deeper, for the crimson with which the blood of countless martyrs has colored it; the white on it is purer, for the pure sacrifice and self-surrender of those who went to their graves up bearing it; the blue on it is heavenlier, for the great constancy of those dead heroes, whose memory becomes henceforth as the immutable upper skies that canopy our land, gleaming with stars wherein we read their glory and our duty (454–455).

29. The language of laying lives on the altar is repeated often in sentiments expressed by wives on hearing of their husbands' deaths (200) as well as soldiers reflecting on the deaths of their friends (340). Stout quotes a pastor at a funeral for two soldiers crying out: "We must be ready to give up our sons, brothers, friends—if we cannot go ourselves—to hardships, sufferings, dangers and death if need be, for the preservation of our government and the freedom of the nation. We should lay them, willing sacrifices, upon the altar" (341). Drew Gilpin Faust observes that the way of death in the Civil War transformed not only the individuals directly affected by the loss, but the entire American nation. The was created, in the words of Frederick Law Olmstead, a veritable "republic of suffering." As a result, "sacrifice and the state became inextricably intertwined. . . . Death created the modern American union—not just by ensuring national survival, but by shaping enduring national structures and commitments" (*The Republic of Suffering: Death and the American Civil War* [New York, Ny, Alfred A. Knopf, 2008], xiii–xiv).

Stout's account of the religious character of the Civil War, perhaps, is best illustrated by the most celebrated speech ever given by an American: the Gettysburg Address. Stout observes that something "emerged from Gettysburg that would become forever etched in the American imagination. A sacralization of this particular battlefield would mark it forever after as the preeminent sacred ground of the Civil War—and American wars thereafter" (269). Stout is surely right, making these words all the more chilling:

> It is for us the living, rather, to be dedicated here to the unfinished work which they who fought here have thus far so nobly advanced. It is rather for us to be here dedicated to the great task remaining before us—that from these honored dead we take increased devotion to that cause for which they gave the last full measure of devotion—that we here highly resolve that these dead shall not have died in vain—that this nation, under God, shall have a new birth of freedom—and that government of the people, by the people, for the people, shall not perish from the earth.

A nation determined by such words, such elegant and powerful words, simply does not have the capacity to keep war limited.[30] A just war that can only be fought for limited political purposes cannot and should not be understood in terms shaped by the Gettysburg Address.[31] Yet after the Civil War, Americans think they must go to war to ensure that those who died in our past wars did not die in vain.[32] Thus American wars are justified as a "war to end all wars" or "to make the world safe for democracy" or for "unconditional surrender" or "freedom." Whatever may be the realist presuppositions of those who lead America to war, those presuppositions cannot be used as the reasons given to justify the war. To do so would betray the tradition of war established in the

---

30. Charlie Pinches rightly argues that the Lincoln Memorial is the proper place for the Gettysburg Address to be read, because there it is complemented and qualified by Lincoln's Second Inaugural Address. The rousing end of Gettysburg, according to Pinches, is enabled by the appeal that we "cherish a just, and a lasting peace, among ourselves, and with all nations" (*A Gathering of Memories: Family, Nation, and America in a Forgetful World* [Grand Rapids, Mi: Brazos, 2006], 103–104).

31. In essay after essay Paul Ramsey insisted that at the heart of the just war was the requirement that a war have a recognizable political purpose. Indeed from Ramsey's perspective a failed nation is one unable to fight a "good war," that is, "a war in which force begins and ends in subordination to national purpose and policy, even the purpose of the arbitrament of a civil war waged to determine what a national purpose shall be" (*Just War*, 15). Accordingly, Ramsey thought a nation's "self-interest" should be constitutive of any reason given for going to war, and therefore he argued that the goal of American foreign policy should be the creation of a system of free and independent nations (8). Yet in a "democracy" it proves quite difficult to convince civilians that they should go to war to maintain what a national purpose shall be" in Asia.

32. Ramsey recognizes that war has a sacral quality. On the same page he argues that war can only be fought by nations capable of disciplining war to a national purpose; "but who can deny that there is a strong feeling for the sacred in the temporal person at work delaying and weakening political resolve until a more inclusive entity is vitally challenged—the nation which is felt to be immortal and transcendent over the individual in value and in the perdurance of its life? Thus the nation affords a provisional solution of the ambiguity of finite sacrifice, and only if this is the case does the nation or any other political entity become the 'subject' of political agency capable of legitimating finite sacrifice" (*Just War*, 15). But Ramsey does not tell us what keeps finite sacrifice finite. Interestingly enough I suspect you can only keep the sacrifice of war finite if you have a church strong enough to discipline a nation's ambition, which presents an interesting challenge to just war thinkers; that is, do they think the church in America has the strength to keep the finite finite? Critical though I may be of Constantinianism, at least the Constantinian churches at one time had the power to keep the finite finite by reminding those who ruled that they were destined to die. Once "the people" are said to rule themselves, the church, at least the church in America, seems to have lost that ability.

Civil War. Wars, American wars, must be wars in which the sacrifices of those doing the dying and the killing have redemptive purpose and justification. War is America's altar. Confronted by such a tradition of war, the attempts to justify war using just war considerations, no matter how sincerely done, cannot help but be ideological mystifications.[33]

In his book, *The Civil War as a Theological Crisis*, Mark Noll asks why the Civil War, in contrast to past wars, produced no "deep theological insights from either elites or the masses."[34] At least one of the reasons may be, as Noll amply documents, that religious thinkers in America assumed that the people of America had a covenantal relationship with God.[35] America was identified with the tribes of Israel in which it was assumed that the federal union "created a higher bond than the bond constituted by the unity of all Christian believers in the church."[36] This was combined with the confidence of the Enlightenment that the common man was capable of reading Scripture without guidance from any other authority, which meant that it was a simple matter to read God's providential will for political events.[37] The war did not force American Christians to deeper theological insights because the war was, for America, our church.[38]

Pacifism as Realism

Where has all this gotten us? I think it helps us recognize that we live in the worst of all worlds. Realism is used to dismiss pacifism and to underwrite some version of just war. But it is not at all clear that the conditions for the

33. In an essay on Martin Luther King, Timothy Jackson distances himself from King's pacifism, observing that "in a fallen world, at any rate, I believe that protecting the innocent may move some Christians, properly, to take up the sword against evil, as in the American Civil War." ("Martin Luther King," in *The Teaching of Modern Christianity on Law, Politics, and Human Nature: Volume 1*, ed. John Witte and Frank Alexander [New York, Ny: Columbia University Press, 2006], 456). One would like to know what "evil" Jackson assumes the sword was taken up against in the Civil War. Was it the "evil" of secession? Was it the "evil" of slavery? Does the reality of the "cause" of the war matter for Jackson-like appeals to the Civil War to justify the use of the sword? I think Jackson's appeal to the Civil War to justify Christian participation in war exemplifies the presumption that finally "pacifism" just will not do. Yet show me how, in the light of Stout's history of the Civil War, the Civil War can be used as a justification for just war reasoning. Of course I think slavery should have been brought to an end. I think, moreover, pacifists should have been more prominent in that struggle. We can point to the example of John Wolmann and other Friends who tirelessly worked to convince slave holders of the evil of slavery, but obviously slavery was and is a judgment on Christians. But to say war is the alternative form of faithfulness is surely a mistake.

34. Mark Noll, *The Civil War as a Theological Crisis* (Chapel Hill, Nc: University of North Carolina Press, 2006), 15.

35. Ibid., 18.

36. Ibid., 61.

37. Ibid., 19. I argued a similar case in *Unleashing the Scripture: Freeing the Bible from Captivity to America* (Nashville, Tn: Abingdon, 1993).

38. One of the great virtues of Noll's study is his chapter on Catholic viewpoints on the Civil War and, in particular, French and Italian Catholic responses to the war. Noll thinks conservative Catholics rightly assessed American inability to disentangle race from slavery or to free the Bible from the certainties of "common sense" because they saw that American culture was characterized by a set of elective affinities: "fundamental principles of the Protestant Reformation linked to a liberal economic order linked to unfettered access to the Bible linked to liberal democracy linked to practical material- ism linked to a bloated and dangerous republican government linked to theological confusion" (Noll, *Civil War*, 157).

possibility of just war are compatible with realism. At least it is not clear that just war considerations can be constitutive of the decision-making processes of governments that must assume that might makes right. Attempts to justify wars begun and fought on realist grounds in the name of just war only serve to hide the reality of war.

Yet war remains a reality. War not only remains a reality, but if Stout's account of the ongoing significance of the Civil War is even close to being right, war remains for Americans our most determinative moral reality. How do you get people who are taught that they are free to follow their own interest to sacrifice themselves and their children in war? Democracies by their very nature seem to require that wars be fought in the name of ideals, which makes war self-justifying. Realists in the State Department and Pentagon may have no illusions about why American self-interest requires that a war be fought, but Americans cannot fight a war as cynics. It may be that those who actually have to fight a war will have no illusions about the reality of war, but the rest of the nation justifies war, using categories that require there be a "next war."

Pacifists are realists. Indeed we have no reason to deny that the "realism" associated with Augustine, Luther, and Niebuhr has much to teach us about how the world works, but that is why we do not trust those who would have us make sacrifices in the name of preserving a world at war. We believe a sacrifice has been made that has brought an end to the sacrifice of war. Augustine and Luther thought Christians might go to war because they assumed a church existed that provided an alternative to the sacrificial system war always threatens to become. If the Civil War teaches us anything, it is that when Christians no longer believe that Christ's sacrifice is sufficient for the salvation of the world, we will find other forms of sacrificial behaviors that are as compelling as they are idolatrous. In the process, Christians confuse the sacrifice of war with the sacrifice of Christ.

If a people does not exist that continually makes Christ present in the world, war will always threaten to become a sacrificial system. War is a counter-church. It is the most determinative moral experience many people have. That is why Christian realism requires the disavowal of war. Christians do not disavow war because it is often so horrible, but because war, in spite of its horror, or perhaps because it is so horrible, can be so morally compelling. That is why the church does not have an alternative to war. The church *is* the alternative to war. When Christians no longer see the reality of the church as an alternative to the world's reality, we abandon the world to war.

Reimaging Theologies
of the Cross

6. The Theology of the Cross
A Usable Past

Douglas John Hall

Among those who have read some of my work it is fairly well known, I think, that I am an admirer of Martin Luther. I have even been introduced—in print—as "a Lutheran theologian." Alas, I am not a Lutheran. Insofar as these distinctions are still relevant and meaningful, I am a member, minister, and theologian of the United Church of Canada—which, historically, ought to bring me closer to the Reformed than to the Lutheran side of the Reformation, since the union of churches that brought my denomination into being in 1925 included both Presbyterian and Congregational components. But somehow these distinctions, while not meaningless, are far less meaningful than they were even two or three decades ago. The question today is not what confessional tradition we adhere to but whether we are able—in the face of the many problems that confront our species—really to *confess* the faith at all: not merely to profess it, but to confess it, that is, to engage the world at the level of its real crises and to confer upon it the blessings of both truth and hope.

Two Preliminary Observations

My topic is "The Theology of the Cross: A Usable Past," and before I turn to the primary substance of my presentation I would like to make two preliminary observations. First, a brief comment on the term *theology of the cross*. It was part of the genius of Martin Luther that he detected, quite brilliantly, the difference between this biblically-based conception of the theology appropriate to our faith, and the culturally and philosophically-based *theology of glory* that has colored most of the history of Christendom. Luther named this distinction, and the naming of things is of vital importance for the corporate thinking of the church. But, of course, he did not invent the theology of the cross. Luther himself depended, as we must, upon a tradition: the tradition particularly of Paul, but behind that the tradition of the Hebraic prophets and poets who understood the highest consciousness of Hebrew faith to consist in the awareness of the "pathos of God"—as Abraham Joshua Heschel insisted.

But when we ourselves want to draw upon the tradition named *theology of the cross*, we—if we go deeply enough—will find ourselves drawing not only on this biblical and classical past but, in addition to Luther himself, on a modern host of exemplars of this tradition that is both numerous and impressive. It includes, certainly, Kierkegaard, the early Karl Barth, Paul Tillich, Reinhold

Niebuhr, Dietrich Bonhoeffer, Kazuo Kitamori, Kornelis Miskotte, Hans-Joachim Iwand, Jürgen Moltmann, Kosuke Koyama, Dorothee Soelle, Elisabeth Moltmann-Wendel, and many others—persons who, in their particular times and places, have grasped essential aspects of this theological tradition and applied them to their analyses of and messages to their social and ecclesiastical contexts. Luther in many ways stood alone when he first introduced this term and this distinction, though the German mystics Tauler and Nicholas of Cusa and others were certainly there in the background, along with Augustine of Hippo. But Luther has not been alone in the exemplification of this tradition in subsequent centuries, and I will draw upon some of these in what follows.

The second preliminary observation concerns Luther himself, or rather our appropriation of his thought—though it could be applied to any great thinker of the past (for instance, Karl Rahner applies something like this same observation to St. Thomas Aquinas[1]). When as Christians in the here and now we turn to the great figures of our faith's past, there are two attitudes that can be taken: one is a strictly historical attitude which asks, "What did this thinker actually say and do?" The other is an attitude which, while wishing to take history seriously, is asking for something more than history alone can give. Standing in the present and wanting to be a faithful witness in that present, this second attitude asks, "What would this thinker say and do if he or she were here with us"—here, therefore, as one conscious not only of the problems and possibilities of the past to which he or she belonged, but conscious also of our present-day context in all its specificity.

My interest in Luther is chiefly of this second type. In fact, I have found Luther as interesting as I have (for decades now) because from the first I sensed, in what I learned of him, that this was indeed a figure from our common Christian heritage who could understand something of our present situation, and who could be shown to have some very important things to say to us. In short, his life and work was such that it could constitute for us "a usable past." Not all that makes up the past of the Christian sojourn through history is usable today. In fact a great deal of it, when not simply useless, is positively misleading for us, and a hindrance. For instance (to consider a recent period) nineteenth-century utopian liberalism is at least misleading today, and the nineteenth-century Fundamentalist reaction to that liberalism and modernism is more than misleading, it is dangerous—a fact that is illustrated for us on this continent daily, in spades. The need for a past, which is an *essential* need for Christians (for we do not invent our message arbitrarily as we go along!), cannot be satisfied with any and every testimony from the past. Theological judiciousness is nowhere more vital than in our choice of pasts on which to meditate in our search for foundations. I have found Luther a trustworthy guide in most things, but my interest in him is not that of a historian, who only wants to know what Luther did and said then; I want him to help me know what to do and say now. I hope to have grasped his own person and thought with something like a reasonable intuition, but my purpose is quite clearly not that of the historian or Luther scholar, but that of the theologian; and (linking this with the first

---

1. See Karl Rahner, *Spirit in the World*, trans. William Dych, S.J. (Montreal: Palm Publishers, 1968), especially the author's introduction, xlix–l.

observation), as a theologian I am bound to hear his "theology of the cross" (which is a term I would apply to his theology as a whole) in tandem with those later and earlier witnesses to this tradition who tried in their own times and places to comprehend and apply this tradition.

A Spirit and Method

This being said by way of presupposition, I turn now to the main part of this address. If our purpose is to find in the theology of the cross such a "usable past," it is essential that we attempt to achieve some grasp of this theology that can be shared by as wide a spectrum of Christians as possible. It is certainly not a theology that lends itself to popularity—as Jürgen Moltmann said of it, "There is a good deal of support in the tradition for the theology of the cross, but it was never much loved."[2] But while it will likely never be a theology with wide popular appeal, neither ought we who feel its power and relevance imagine, in our pride of ownership, that it is so far above the ordinary grasp of church folk that it is unprofitable to make the attempt. The truth, as I have experienced it, is that minorities within all the once-mainline churches of this continent, disillusioned with the pompous Christian triumphalism of popular religion and sickened by the religious and cultural imperialism that that triumphalism inevitably begets, are extraordinarily open to the alternative that this submerged theological strain represents. But of course it needs to be cast in language that can be grasped by persons without a great deal of theological and historical background, and above all it needs really to engage the real problems and possibilities of the present.

What *is* the theology of the cross? I have tried on many occasions, in both sustained argument and more metaphoric ways to describe this "thin tradition"—as I called it in my first book on the subject, *Lighten Our Darkness*. I know that I will never do justice to it because, to begin with, the theology of the cross is not an "it"—not a specific and objectifiable set of teachings or dogmas; not "a theology"—it is, rather, a spirit and a method that one brings to all one's reflections on all the various areas and facets of Christian faith and life. I have never been able to improve on Moltmann's metaphor when he says that the theology of the cross is "not a single chapter in theology, but the key signature for all Christian theology."[3] This is a theological approach that is not easy to pin down, as one can (with care) pin down terms like "orthodoxy," or "neo-orthodoxy," or "liberalism," or "fundamentalism." But *theologia crucis* as a spirit and method of theological thought cannot be stated in a formula. It may, however, be recognized when it is heard or experienced, whether in sermon, serious theological writing, or artistic expression. With regard to the latter, I have found it interesting that some of the best expressions of this very classical Protestant approach to the Christian message are found in plays and novels by Roman Catholics—like Shusaku Endo's *Silence*, Graeme Green's *The Power and*

2. Jürgen Moltmann, *The Crucified God*, trans. R.A. Wilson and John Bowden (London: S.C.M. Press Ltd., 1973), 3.
3. Ibid., 72.

the Glory, or George Bernanos' *Diary of a Country Priest.* It is also representable in art. The great figure of modern ecumenism, W.A. Visser t'Hooft, wrote a beautiful book about his countryman, Rembrandt, in which he presents Rembrandt as an "artist *of the cross,*" and in letters to me he reinforced this connection between Rembrandt's painting and sketches and the theology of the cross. I think one could make a similar observation about Georges Rouault, Kaethe Kollwitz, Ernst Barlach, and many other artists.

If one cannot exactly codify the theology of the cross, what one can perhaps do is to identify certain informing or overarching principles that inform this thin tradition. And in what remains of my presentation I should like to attempt just that.

Informing Principles of This Theology

The Compassion and Solidarity of God

This must be thought the "first principle" of this theology. The *christological* basis of the theology of the cross is at the same time its *theological* basis (and I am using theology here in the more restrictive sense, meaning our understanding of the nature of the deity). For this theological approach, the cross of the Christ is not only Jesus' cross, it is also and simultaneously God's cross. As Jon Sobrino writes:

> Our theology of the cross becomes radical only when we consider the presence (or absence) of God on the cross of Jesus. It is at this point that we face the alternative posed by Moltmann: Either the cross of Jesus is the end of all Christian theo-logy [by which he means the end of speculation concerning the being and acting of God] or else it is the beginning of a truly Christian theology.[4]

This is indeed a radical affirmation in the light of the entire theological background of the church triumphant, especially from the time of its establishment in the fourth century. The need of all self-declared high religion, particularly when it is politically and culturally established, to keep God absolute in power and transcendence, and therefore free of contamination by earthly involvements and passions, is so strong in the whole history of Christian theology—also today!—that it is astonishing and unacceptable to many Christians whenever God is too closely associated with the crucified son. Curiously, especially in the Christian West, we characteristically accentuate the second person of the Trinity—to the point, as H. Richard Niebuhr complained, of ending with a "unitarianism of the second person of the trinity"; and yet when it comes to assumptions about God "the Father," we fail to apply this same christomonistic tendency and accentuate attributes of magnificence, especially of power, that scarcely reflect either the God of Israel, who is so deeply involved with his people, or the God and Father of Jesus, the Christ.

Luther (and in this I think he has been followed by all who took up the theology of the cross subsequently) dared to break with this hold of classical

---

4. Jon Sobrino, *Christology at the Crossroads,* trans. John Drury (Maryknoll, Ny: Orbis Books, 1978), 182.

philosophic-theology, as it was held especially by the school of Alexandria, and in the spirit of the school of Antioch accentuated the themes of compassion and solidarity. One could say, using other terms, that he christologized the Deity, even going so far as to speak of "the crucified God." As Moltmann characterizes this: "Christian faith stands and falls with the knowledge of the crucified Christ, that is, with the knowledge of God in the crucified Christ, or, to use Luther's even bolder phrase, with the knowledge of the 'crucified God.'"[5]

The implications of this radical identification of God with the crucified Christ are manifold, for it means not only that the famous "distinctions" between the persons of the Trinity are radically qualified and their tendency to devolve into tritheism checked, it means also that theories of the *work* of Christ (soteriology) that depend upon these distinctions, as does that of Anselm of Canterbury, are implicitly called in question. And in that connection I think that Gustaf Aulén was entirely justified when—in his famous little study, *Christus Victor*, he affirmed that Luther did not follow the general tendency of the Christian West in picturing Christ's work as satisfaction offered to a holy, remote, and implacably righteous God for the sins of the many. Such a conception of the atonement depends upon keeping God strictly differentiated from the substitutionary victim, Jesus; and it is one of the anomalies of Western Protestantism that most of it has nevertheless clung to an Anselmian soteriology indistinguishable in essentials from the very Catholic theology (doctrine of God) that Luther questioned. Calvin, of course, did not help very much in this process!

The Cross as World-Commitment

If the cross of Jesus is first of all a statement about the nature of the Deity, it is in the second place—but not even as a second step, but implicitly and necessarily—a statement about the world and God's abiding love for the world and all its creatures. It is not strange to faith, however astonishing or incredible it may seem to unbelief (which is always at base cynicism about the worthwhileness of the world), that when the author of the fourth Gospel, allegedly the most hellenistic of the four Gospels, wished to state in a sentence the whole intention of God in the Christ, he wrote, "For God so loved the world that he gave his only Son, so that everyone who believes in him may not perish but may have eternal life" (John 3:16). Nor is it surprising that this same verse of scripture is the best-remembered New Testament sentence of them all; for despite the rhetoric and the activity of Christians and churches, which often betray precisely such a sentiment, that which is best in all of us remembers that at the centre of this faith there is an extraordinary affirmation of creation. Doctrine must never become so drunk on redemption, or rather on its own superlatives and exaggerations of the redeemed estate, that it ends by denigrating the creation that God "so loved" and loves.

The cross is at once, for Christians, the ultimate statement of humankind's movement away from God and of God's gracious movement towards fallen humankind. I think of the cross of Golgotha as the divine determination to *claim* this world, however wretched its history and however costly its redemption. I

---

5. Moltmann, *The Crucified God*, 65.

will be *your* God and you will be *my* people! Against the clear tendency of the creature to degrade itself and abuse its environs, God in Christ reinstates the divine ownership of creation and commits Godself to creation's fulfilment, its flourishing.

It was this sense of the divine commitment to the world that made the young prisoner, Dietrich Bonhoeffer, perhaps the best advocate of the theology of the cross in our epoch, call in question the interpretation of Christianity as a religion of "redemption." He writes:

> The redemption myths try unhistorically to find an eternity after death. . . . [For them] redemption . . . means redemption from cares, distress, fears, and longings, from sin and death, in a better world beyond the grave. But is this really the essential character of the proclamation of Christ in the gospels and by Paul? I should say it is not. The difference between the Christian hope of resurrection and the mythological hope is that the former sends [a person] back into . . . life on earth in a wholly new way. . . . The Christian, unlike the devotees of the redemption myths, has no last line of escape available from earthly tasks and difficulties into the eternal, but, like Christ himself . . . he must drink the earthly cup to the dregs, and only in his doing so is the crucified and risen Lord with him, and he crucified and risen with Christ. This world must not be prematurely written off; in this the Old and New Testaments are at one.[6]

Honesty about Experience (Christian Realism)

As a third principle at work in the theology of the cross I would name an extraordinary commitment to truth-telling, a rare determination to be honest in one's faith-claims—rare, I mean, in the whole realm of "religion." For me at least, the twenty-first thesis of the *Heidelberg Disputation* has been vital: "A theologian of glory calls evil good and good evil. A theologian of the cross calls the thing what it actually is."[7] This is in some ways an enigmatic statement, but only if we fail to grasp the critique of religious triumphalism that is being contrasted with the theology whose character Luther is attempting to depict. A theology that seeks to show the obviousness of the divine power and glory has to end in exaggeration and untruth. Why? Because in order to uphold its exaggerated positive it must downplay or neglect everything by which that positive is negated or called in question—which is to say, the "evil" that manifests itself in everyday life. By contrast, he says, the *theologia crucis* names the negating realities openly, beginning with the cross of Christ itself: the cross and all that it stands for by way of human degradation and suffering is not good, not *in se*—in itself! We are not called to laud and embrace this symbol of violence and torture and death as though it were something splendid. What is good lies hidden underneath or behind this dreadful reality, namely, God's concealed presence and determination to mend the creation from within. The theology of the cross is thus not only allowed but commanded to draw the attention of church and world to that, in both, which contradicts and demeans the glory of

---

6. Dietrich Bonhoeffer, *Letters and Papers from Prison*, ed. Eberhard Bethge, trans. Reginald Fuller, 3rd ed. (New York, Ny: The Macmillan Company, 1967), 185–186.
7. LW 31:53.

God. The theologian of the cross is not (as is childishly alleged) a pessimist, but he or she is also not the congenital optimist who must repress every thought of doubt, despair, the demonic and death. The theology of the cross therefore leads to a prophetic stance on the part of the church, a boldness which "calls a spade a spade." It is here that Reinhold Niebuhr's "Christian realism" has its foundations.

But thesis 21 has another connotation that is easily overlooked. It means not only that faith is called upon to be honest about the reality of historical experience but that it must be modest about its own claims. For if God's triumph is indeed "hidden beneath its apparent opposite," we dare not imagine that we have captured the truth of God in our theology! That is precisely the error of the theology of glory! We, rather, who live "under the cross," are able only to point to the mystery of the divine *agape* that is manifested in this strange, paradoxical manner. As von Loewenich writes in his biography of Luther: "Luther's view appears to be complex, but basically it is quite simple. The apparent paradoxes prove to be true in experience. It is a question of honesty whether we acknowledge the reality of this experience or whether we reject it. Luther calls this honesty *humility*."[8]

This humility has always been mandatory for those who have grasped the fact that God is *Person*, "Thou" (in Buber's terms), and who have contemplated in all seriousness the mystery of God's compassion and solidarity with us *in Christo*. But today it is of the very essence of Christianity, for like all religion our religion too, as religion, is sorely tempted to make grandiose claims for itself, and in that direction—in our pluralistic world—lies violence and death. Whatever else may be said of the monumental theology of Karl Barth, his ties with Luther's *theologia crucis* are no more clearly in evidence than when, in his *Evangelical Theology*, his Chicago lectures, he insists: "Evangelical theology is *modest* theology, because it is determined to be so by its object, that is, by him who is its subject."[9]

The Contextual Character of This Theology

In my book, *The Cross in Our Context*,[10] I argued that the theology of the cross is inherently and fundamentally a contextual theology. I suppose such a claim could be interpreted as an attempt, on my part, to justify by reference to an authority-figure whom I respect, a predilection of my own for contextuality in theology. I am a sinner, also intellectually, and therefore I shall not seek to argue for the purity of my motives. Yet I do not see how one can immerse oneself in this theological tradition, not only Luther but the whole tradition, without coming to that kind of conclusion. As for Luther himself, it is of course perfectly obvious that he did not think of his work in modern contextual terms. Contextuality in theology is a by-product—rather late in time, actually!—of historical

---

8. Walter von Loewenich, *Martin Luther: The Man and His Work*, trans. Lawrence W. Denef (Minneapolis, Mn: Augsburg, 1982), 123.

9. Karl Barth, *Evangelical Theology: An Introduction*, trans. Grover Foley (New York, Ny: Holt, Rinehart and Winston, 1963), 7.

10. Douglas John Hall, *The Cross in Our Context: Jesus and the Suffering World* (Minneapolis, Mn: Fortress Press, 2003), 35ff.

consciousness, which is a Modern mindset. Nevertheless Luther acted in a contextual manner, as one intensely aware of the fact that he was—for instance,
a German; an Augustinian; and a critic of Aristotelianism and its ascendency
in the official theology; and so on. That Aristotelianism, as James M. Kittelson
notes in his biography of Luther, assumed as its primary methodological presupposition that "all important truths ... were universal. Circumstances of time
and place made no difference to the truth of propositions that could be developed by the exercise of right reason."[11] Precisely that assumption, which in the
hands of religious authority was no innocent teaching but a potent tool for the
suppression of difference, was what Luther had to challenge—and not only
because he had been influenced by the so-called *Via Moderna*, but because as
a German conscious of his own and his people's particularity he simply could
not accept as binding truths that were "made in Rome," a quite different context from his own. One could argue, surely, that the whole Reformation was
steeped in a place-consciousness that could not be fitted easily into the religious
ideology of external authority.

But in addition to such historical reasons for concluding that this theological approach is inevitably contextual, there are (in my estimation at least) solid
theological grounds for such a conclusion. It follows irrevocably from all three
of these principles: (1) A conception of God as one having compassion for and
desiring solidarity with the creature would be an empty sentiment unless "the
creatures" for whom such love is intended were seen in all their particularity—which only represents, in fact, a return to the tradition of Jerusalem, with
its historical consciousness, and away from the kind of abstractionism belonging to that side of the tradition of Athens that loves universals at the expense
of particulars. (2) To speak of the cross of Christ in terms of God's world-
orientation and commitment could only be an empty claim if "the world"
remains at the level of an intellectual construct and does not become explicit.
"The world" that God loves is not a construct but a reality, constantly in flux, rich
in variety, old in sin but redolent of potentiality. Love itself, whether divine or
human, is never love for generalities but for specifics; and it becomes an absur-
dity and a pretense if it indulges in generalities that defy specificity—which
unfortunately happens all too often in religion ("I love the world, it's only these
wretched people I can't stand"). (3) A theology that is committed to truth-telling,
realism about evil, modesty about itself, can only be a contextual theology. Its
honesty (*Wahrheitsorientierung*—its orientation towards truth) is nothing but a
determination to pay attention (in Simone Weil's sense) to what is actually there
in front of it. It is not permitted to contemplate an ideal that is wholly unrelated
to the here and now. It entertains change, certainly, and even strives for change
with every fiber of its being, but it wishes to change what actually is, and (as in
the famous serenity prayer of Reinhold Niebuhr) "can be changed."

To translate all of this into other terms, the theology of the cross is at base a
practical theology. It is not interested in pure theory. It is inherently critical of
ideology. It drives always towards incarnation, towards enactment. This at least
it has in common with liberation theology, that it is never satisfied with being

---

11. James M. Kittelson, *Luther the Reformer: The Story of the Man and His Career* (Minneapolis, Mn:
Augsburg, 1986), 47.

theology but must become an ethic. Yet never an ethic separable from its own theological base and point of departure. Bonhoeffer, the Lutheran, complained about the Lutheranism that nurtured the theology of justification because it did not find its inherent goal in just action but rested in the security of a doctrinalized grace. One could complain just as appropriately of the Christian activism that never ponders the why of the act and, therefore, perennially complicates the very problems it would address.

The Refusal of Finality

It would be difficult to grasp the character of this theological tradition without paying a good deal of attention to the eschatological dimension that runs through its length and breadth. One could even say that the chief difference between the theology of the cross and the antithesis that Luther uses as his contrast, the *theologia gloriae*, is their eschatology. The theology of glory depends on an eschatology that is fully realized, namely, realized in the church, realized in theology as true and irrefutable doctrine. There is a realized dimension in the theology of the cross, too; but it is not a realization to which the church and its theology can lay claim. The purposes of God are realized *in Christ*, and faith looks to God in trust and hope. But the faithful live without finality, without closure, without certitude. All our ancestors were "under the cloud," says Paul. "Nevertheless, God was not pleased with most of them, and they were struck down in the wilderness.... So if you think you are standing, watch out that you do not fall" (1 Cor 10:1, 5, 12). In confidence (*con-fide*) we may feel that we are on the right road, but woe to any who imagine they have arrived. The following statement seems to me typical of Luther: "Christian living does not mean to *be* good but to *become* good; not to *be* well, but to get well; not *being* but *becoming*; not rest but training. We are *not yet*, but we shall be. It has *not yet* happened, but it is the way. Not everything shines and sparkles as yet, but everything is getting better."[12] This kind of statement does not deny progress or betterment, but neither does it affirm the kind of perfectionism that John Wesley courted. We are living, it is true, after the victory of God in the risen Christ; but while the Christ is risen we ourselves live in hope and not fulfilment—we live, as the late Alan Lewis put it, on holy Saturday, between cross and resurrection.

And this is perhaps the best place to address the question: What is the relationship of the resurrection to the theology of the cross? Contrary to many critics of the theology of the cross, this theology does not overlook or downplay the victory of the third day; what it critiques is the use, or rather the misuse, of the resurrection to render the cross null and void. And that misuse is by no means a minor thing. Especially in North American popular Christianity the resurrection—or what I call resurrection-ism—functions to turn the religious away from the cross as a thing well and truly overcome. And that means not only the cross of Jesus, but the cross of reality; so that the religion thus mythically bolstered becomes a primary factor in the deadening of otherwise sensitive people to the pain of God in the world. I suspect there is no greater theological task

---

12. *D. Martin Luthers Werke: Kritische Gesamtausgabe*, 69 vols. (Weimar: Hermann Böhlaus Nachfolger, 1883–), 7:336; trans. by Edward Furcha; emphasis added.

in North America today than to refuse and redirect this false and dangerous functioning of Easter in this society. Rightly to grasp the meaning of Christ's resurrection is to be turned towards the cross, with understanding, not away from it. Moltmann puts it this way:

> [Easter] does not overcome the story of Christ's passion so that we no longer remember it. Rather, it establishes Christ's cross as a saving event. The one who goes before us into the glorious and liberated future of God's resurrected is also the one who died for us on the cross. We come face to face with the glory of the coming God beholding the features of the crucified and not through infinite demands or flights of fancy.[13]

Being turned by resurrection faith and hope towards the cross of Jesus is not merely an act of piety; it is also an act of human and ethical solidarity with all who suffer. For Jesus is never alone, never just Jesus. He is this representative of the suffering God and of suffering creation and creatures. A religion that in the name of faithfulness to Jesus turns away from, or becomes smug and indifferent in relation to the world, is a blasphemy in the service of false religion, the religion of glory without the cross. We are living in a society that walks very close to this blasphemy.

Conclusion

I must bring this to an end, and I can only do so reluctantly, for I could have wished to cover all the aspects and facets of this theological tradition in a persuasive and final way. But that too indicates the temptation of theology always to covet glory for itself. If it is the theology of the cross that we are treating, there can be no final statement. Final statements in Christian theology are invariably to be mistrusted. That is the frustration of this discipline whenever it wishes to be a theology of the cross.

In concluding, I will leave you once again—as I did in *The Cross in our Context*—with a kind of meditation on the three Pauline virtues, faith, hope, and love. The best way that I have found of conveying what I think this theological method and spirit is all about is by considering these so-called virtues in the light of what they are each negating. Unless the negation of each is understood, the positive statement (the virtue) of each is cheapened and made into a cliché. We do not have to speculate about what these virtues negate, for in each case the negation is clearly present in the collected works of Paul; and as the New Testament's chief exemplar of this "thin tradition" Paul speaks, I believe, not only for Luther but for all who have been grasped by the principles of this tradition.

Faith. What does this term negate? The metaphor that crops up time and again in Paul's writings is "sight." Faith, which "comes by hearing" and is precisely a not-seeing. "Now faith is the assurance of things hoped for, the conviction of things not seen," (Hebr 11:1)—one of Luther's favorite texts. The

---

13. Jürgen Moltmann, *Theology of Play*, trans. Reinhard Ulrich (New York, Ny: Harper and Row, 1972), 30.

eschatological element—especially the "not yet" side of Christian eschatology—is here strongly present. The theology of the cross is a theology of *faith*, and while faith is certainly a positive term for Luther it must not be elevated beyond its proper limit. In the act of trusting, the One trusted is glimpsed—as through a glass darkly; but not seen. Faith that is not sight is thus a faith warned against presumption. It is also a faith that is able to live with its antithesis, doubt, and that is in fact dead faith (as Unamuno said) when doubt is no longer allowed a hearing.

Hope. Hope is at once an orientation to the future and a recognition that the present is still lacking its promised fulfilment. Hope realized is no longer hope. The stance that we call hope is one constantly made conscious of the fact that the present, the *hic et nunc*, is a falling-short of what is most to be desired. So the hope that is faith's future dimension is always "hoping against hope" (Rom 4:18). As faith must live with doubt, so hope must live with its antithesis, hopelessness, despair. What is hoped for must not be taken for granted, as though it were already experienced reality, already seen—for here too Paul resorts to the metaphor of sight: "For in hope we were saved. Now hope that is seen is not hope. For who hopes for what is seen? But if we hope for what we do not see, we wait for it with patience" (Rom 8:24–25).

Love. Love negates many things, as Paul makes plain in the famous hymn to love in 1 Corinthians 13. But I think that what must receive priority where this discussion is concerned is power. "[Love] does not insist on its own way (1 Cor 13:5). "The crux of the cross," wrote Reinhold Niebuhr, "is its revelation of the fact that the final power of God over man is derived from the self-imposed weakness of his love."[14] This, I think, is of the essence of this theology, and it is hard for all to accept who think of deity chiefly in terms of power—omnipotence, almighty-ness. But if God is love, then the divine power must accommodate itself to divine love, and not vice versa. And that, for the theology of the cross, is basic. Paul Tillich writes (and I will quote the entire thought because I think it is wonderfully illuminating):

> One of Luther's most profound insights was that God made himself small for us in Christ. In doing so, He left us our freedom and our humanity. He showed us His heart, so that our hearts could be won. When we look at the misery of our world, its evil and its sin, especially in these days which seem to mark the end of a world period, we long for divine interference, so that the world and its daemonic rulers might be overcome. We long for a king of peace within history, or for a king of glory above history. We long for a Christ of power. Yet if *He* were to come and transform us and our world, we should have to pay the one price we could not pay: we would have to lose our freedom, our humanity, and our spiritual dignity. Perhaps we would be happier; but we should also be lower beings, our present misery, struggle and despair notwithstanding. We should be more like blessed animals than men made in the image of God. Those who dream of a better life and try to avoid the Cross

---

14. Robert McAfee Brown, *The Essential Reinhold Niebuhr: Selected Essays and Addresses* (New Haven, Ct: Yale University Press, 1986), 22.

as a way, and those who hope for a Christ and attempt to exclude the Crucified, have no knowledge of the mystery of God and of man.[15]

To summarize: the theology of the cross is a theology of faith (not sight);
a theology of hope (not consummation); and a theology of love (not power).
And if you want to understand what the theology of glory is, you just have to
turn this ordering of the virtues around: it is a theology of sight (not faith), of
consummation (not hope), and of power (not love).

The one aspect of the theology of the cross that I have omitted from this
characterization concerns its consequence as an ecclesiology. This is a serious
omission, because the *theologia crucis* is only a viable theology as and when it
expresses itself in an *ecclesia crucis*. To make up for this omission, besides referring you to Part 3 of my book, *The Cross in Our Context*, I want to quote the final
paragraph of Paul Tillich's best-read book, *The Courage to Be:*

> [A] church which raises itself in its message and its devotion to the God above
> the God of theism without sacrificing its concrete symbols can mediate a cour-
> age which takes doubt and meaninglessness into itself. It is the Church under
> the Cross which alone can do this, the Church which preaches the Crucified
> who cried to God who remained after the God of confidence had led him in
> the darkness of doubt and meaninglessness. To be as a part in such a church
> is to receive the courage to be in which one cannot lose one's self and in which
> one receives one's world.[16]

---

15. Paul Tillich, *The Shaking of the Foundations* (New York, Ny: Charles Scribner's Sons, 1953), 148
(from the sermon entitled, "He Who Is the Christ").
16. Paul Tillich, *The Courage to Be* (London: Nisbet and Co. Ltd., 1952), 178.

7. Usus Crucis

The Use and Abuse of the Cross and the Practice of Resurrection

Vitor Westhelle

Es ist eyn unterscheyd praedicare passionem Christi et usus passionis. Diabolus primium eciam praedicat, secundum vero spiritussanctus tantum.

—Martin Luther

Luther in a sermon in 1525 wrote: "There is a difference between the discourse, or preaching, about the passion of Christ and the practice of passion. The devil foremost preaches [passion], but the [practice] is the true work of the Holy Spirit."[1] This difference is what is being examined here. What is constitutive of a practice as opposed to a discourse? And what is being proposed here is that this *difference* is precisely something that interrupts the discourse, even the discourse about the cross itself. In other words, it is the incision of an ironic gesture that suspends and severs the smoothness of analogical reasoning that rules the discourse and seeks to know the unknown by the akin. The ironic gesture is the moment of pondering that disturbs the unequivocal attempt of closing meaning and settling the issues in a manageable orderly manner.

Luther is now known for his theology of the cross. But what he said *about* it is in fact less significant than the way he practiced it in his theological struggles (*Anfechtungen*) and endeavors. For example, consider this text, unlikely to appear in any treatment of Luther's "theology of the cross":

> Suppose a group of earnest Christian laymen were taken prisoner and set down in a desert without an episcopally ordained priest among them. And suppose that they were to come to a common mind there and then in the desert and elect one of their number, whether he were married or not, and charge him to baptize, say mass, pronounce absolution, and preach the gospel. Such a man would be as truly a priest as though he had been ordained by all the bishops and popes in the world.[2]

This passage in Luther's *To the Christian Nobility of the German Nation* suggests some interesting observations. First, Luther invites a comparison between the context in which the Reformation came about and that wilderness where stranded people had to find a way of carving out their own freedom, of charting a space of possibilities; the Reformation was an uncharted "territory."

---

1. *D. Martin Luthers Werke: Kritische Gesamtausgabe*, 69 vols. (Weimar: Hermann Böhlaus Nachfolger, 1883–), 17/1:71,25–28 (hereafter, WA).

2. Jaroslav Pelikan and Helmut T. Lehmann, eds., *Luther's Works*, American ed., 55 vols. (Philadelphia, Pa: Fortress Press; Saint Louis, Mo: Concordia Publishing House, 1955–86), 44:128 (hereafter, *LW*).

Second, he claims the right of people under those conditions to find their own legitimate way of organizing themselves, without the necessary sanction of the ecclesial and political establishment. But on what grounds does he make this claim? Would he be advancing a defense of human autonomy as it would be put forward during the Enlightenment? This is not the case. We might notice that his example appeals not for a right to anarchy, but rather to an insurgent right and legitimacy of claiming the very powers that the hierarchical ecclesial system of his day had organized within orders of privilege. Those in the hierarchy self-entrusted themselves with the deposit of the revelation, which supposedly contained the available and inerrant knowledge of the divine.

In speaking of this hypothetical group Luther does not appeal for an exception to the rule, as if he would be saying: "In spite of the irregular conditions we should make an exception and recognize them as having established a legitimate office." Instead, he vindicates a radical catholicity that exceeds the catholicity of those who claimed to administer it. The man chosen to be a priest in the imaginary example he offers is not merely an acceptable exception to the rule, he is "truly a priest as though he has been ordained by *all the bishops* and *popes*." Such is the ethos that characterizes the ironic gestures of the Reformer: that which is an exception, a group set apart and thus defined as heretical (for this is what heresy primarily means: to be set apart), has more legitimacy than that which is considered to be the rule and the norm; values are subverted. Finally, the very image of a displacement as an opening for the *new*-formation to come about, suggests that this new, the *novum* that the West has so often projected into the future,[3] might indeed be somewhere else. Western utopian thinking, which translates the no-place (*u-topos*) into a future to come, is in Luther's spatial imagery moved to another-place (*hetero-topia*). If we speak of the eschatological vision as another world that comes about, this other world might be the very world of the other, the one who is different and is excluded from our world.

What frames such a vision is the eschatological ethos, an understanding of revelation, indeed an apocalyptic one, that knows the end, and owns it, which then also becomes a place for a beginning. This eschatology, what Walter Benjamin called "Messianic gate,"[4] which for the powers represents only the unthinkable limit, are for those who inhabit it, those who are at the limit, the medium in which condemnation is experienced and yet only there is liberation a possibility. Condemnation and liberation meet each other at that liminal moment that is at the same time a "limit-to" (to the edges of our world) and also a "limit-of" (of a world to come).[5] As the poet Hölderlin expressed it: "Near is God, but where danger lies, grows also that which saves."[6] United by the experience of liminality, both the Reformation and the movements inspired by liberation theologies are committed to a reorientation of the whole theological endeavor. This can be expressed in the famous definition of Luther: *crux sola est nostra theologia*, the cross alone is our theology, or rephrased: "our theology lies

---

3. Robert Nisbet, *History of the Idea of Progress* (New York, Ny: Basic Books, 1979).
4. Walter Benjamin, *Illuminations*, ed. Hannah Arendt (New York, Ny: Schocken, 1969), 264.
5. For the theological definition and usage of these categories, see David Tracy, *Blessed Rage for Order: The New Pluralism in Theology* (New York, Ny: Seabury, 1975), 92–94.
6. Friedrich Hölderlin, *Gedichte-Hyperion* (Augsburg: Wilhelm Goldmann, 1978), 138.

in the crossing."[7] The radical importance of such a theology is to make plain once more that it is neither a theology among others, nor a doctrine, but a way of doing theology, which does not cancel any other theology but comes to it with a provoking ironic gesture that disturbs discursive continuities; it is an allergy within the order of discourse.[8] It is a way of recognizing the other and hidden side of history, the margins, the excluded, the stranded ones, the "crucified people" (I. Ellacuría), the "nonpersons" (G. Gutiérrez), as the privileged space of God's self-revelation.

In the *Heidelberg Disputation*, in which we find the most used and abused utterances that Luther made about the theology of the cross, we read:

> 19. That person does not deserve to be called a theologian who looks upon the invisible things of God as though they were clearly perceptible in those things which have actually happened.
> 20. He deserves to be called a theologian, however, who comprehends the visible and manifest things [*posteriora*] of God seen through suffering and the cross.
> 21. A theologian of glory calls evil good and good evil. The theologian of the cross calls the thing what it actually is. This is clear: He who does not know Christ does not know God hidden in suffering.[9]

Luther's indictment of the theology of his day was also a critique of the theories of the cross (atonement theories), either ontological or moral, in the plea for a theology done as a practice of passion (*in usus passionis*), an engaging experience, and an intentional disposition, as he described it in a sermon on Matt 27:47ff. in 1525.[10] As such, more than a past event in which atonement was accomplished, and also more than a moral example for a virtuous life, the cross becomes an epistemological locus, the privileged place of God's own self-revelation. But this dispositional practice was not an invention of Luther. Before he named it as a theology of the cross, *theologia crucis*, this motif was clearly presented by Paul in 1 Corinthians 1, where he speaks about the message of the cross as scandal (*skandalon*), foolishness (*moria*), and weakness (*asthenes*), a message about life that is found in death, a message about liberation that can only be seen and found through the lenses of oppression, a message about God hidden in the mask of a devil, a message about goodness that can only shine when evil is named for what it is. Maximus the Confessor (seventh century), a forerunner of the later named "theology of the cross," phrased it like this:

> The more [God] becomes comprehensible through [Incarnation], so much more through it is he known to be incomprehensible. For he is hidden ... in his revelation. And this mystery of Jesus in itself remains hidden, and can be

---

7. WA 5:176,32–33.
8. Luther preferred to use the expression "theologian of the cross" instead of "theology of the cross" in order to lift up the fact that such a theology is a praxis and not a doctrinal locus. One could also say that for Luther "theology of the cross," *theologia crucis*, is to be read primarily as a subjective genitive, as a theology done from the perspective of the cross, and not a theology about the cross, which would be the objective sense of the genitive. See Gerhard Forde, *On Being a Theologian of the Cross: Reflections on Luther's Heidelberg Disputation, 1518* (Grand Rapids, Mi: Eerdmans, 1997), 70–71.
9. LW 31:40.
10. *Es ist eyn unterscheyd praedicare passionem Christi et usus passionis. Diabolus primium eciam praedicat, secundum vero spiritussanctus tantum.* (WA 17/1:71,26–28).

drawn out by no reason, by no intellect, but when spoken of it remains ineffable, and when understood unknown. What could do more to demonstrate the proof of the divine transcendence of being than this: revelation shows that it is hidden, reason that it is unspeakable, and intellect that it is transcendentally unknowable, and further, its assumption of being that it is beyond being.[11]

And even more sharply: "The Lord, who wanted us to understand that we should not look for natural necessity in what is above nature, wanted to bring about his work by means of opposites. He therefore fulfilled his life by death and accomplished his glory by means of dishonour."[12]

Such a perspective recognizes what Latin American theologians have called the "battle of gods,"[13] which suggests that in such experiences no discernment can be made at the theoretical level, at the level of orthodoxy, about who the real God is. It is in this sense that we can read Luther's statement that "God cannot be God unless He becomes a devil; and the devil will not be the devil before being God."[14] "Orthopraxis" is the word used to describe this methodological approach that for Luther was the way of the theologian of the cross, but we might better call it a practice of solidarity with the pain of the world, which follows the encounter with Christ crucified. This means that one is unable to decide whether it is God or the devil one is serving unless one's position and disposition or perspective, one's location, is that of cross and suffering. Hence the revelation of God—that which God allows us to see—is not only indirect in the sense that God's self-revelation is not only given by means other than the divine itself (it is not an epiphany) but it is also doubly elusive insofar as it even appears contrary to what is divine. The ironic gesture keeps coming back. There is a double indirectness as Karl Barth called it in his reading of Luther's notion of "revelation hidden under its opposite" (*revelatio sub contraria specie*). According to Barth, "the nerve of Luther's thought is that the *larva Dei* [mask of God], the indirectness of his self-communication, is a double one issued not only through its created character, but also through the sinfulness of the creature."[15]

"Were you there when they crucified my Lord?"

The distinction earlier elaborated between the theology of the cross as a theory or discourse (in either the moral sense of an example to be followed or the ontological sense in which it describes an event between God and sinful humanity) and the theology of the cross as a practice can now be elucidated. This practice (*usus*), in the search for a better word, is really not to be understood only as an action or an operation, but also a disposition or a *habitus* in the sense that it entails, more than action, also an involvement in the midst of the circumstances in which the practice takes place. It is a dispositional practice. This can

---

11. "Difficulty 5," in Andrew Louth, ed., *Maximus the Confessor* (London: Routledge, 1996), 173.

12. Cited by Yves Congar, *I Believe in the Holy Spirit*, 3 vols. (New York, Ny: Crossroad, 1983), 3:15.

13. Pablo Richard et al., *La lucha de los dioses: los ídolos de la opresión y la búsqueda del Dios liberador* (San José/Managua: DEI/CAV, 1980).

14. *LW* 14:31.

15. Karl Barth, *Die kirchliche Dogmatik* I/1 (Zürich: Evangelischer Verlag Zollikon, 1952), 173–174.

be further exemplified by the expression *theologia crucis*. There is a difference between the subjective and the objective sense of the genitive in the expression. Luther's preference for using the expression "theologian of the cross" instead of "theology of the cross" is indicative of his predilection for the subjective sense of the genitive. In this sense theology is done from the point of view or perspective of the cross, as a disposition, instead of being *about* the cross, which would be the objective sense of the genitive.

What allows us to establish this distinction is our *position*, our location vis-à-vis the cross out of which we *dis-pose*. "Were you there when they crucified my Lord?" The question of the old spiritual implies, as in Kierkegaard, a sense of contemporaneousness with Jesus, that one can be there where God is being crucified, even today. But the question can be taken even further to ask what our location or placement is in relationship to the cross. This location establishes whether we are theologians of the cross or theologians of glory. Different circumstances and contexts establish different narratives, different possibilities to theologize. Luther's use of the distinction between the theologian of the cross and the theologian of glory seems and has become "jargonish" and too narrow a typology to account for more subtle ways in which we might relate to the cross. Four different possibilities, producing four different theological voices, will serve to illustrate this point. Obviously, typologies, even expanded ones, are still simplifications, indeed, oversimplifications. They do not account for the complexities of real life situations, but they can help to discern distinct courses of action, to signal possibilities, to detect realities, and to situate different voices coming from different epistemic locations.

(a) *The Theology of the Crucified*. Mary, as Luther sees her in his *Commentary on the Magnificat*, is a good example of the first circumstance. She is the one who "looks not to the result of humility but with simple heart regards things of low degree, and gladly associates with them."[16] Or, then, in Luther's words:

> You must feel the pinch of poverty in the midst of your hunger and learn by experience what hunger and poverty are, with no provision on hand and no help in yourself or any other man, but in God only; so that the work may be God's alone and impossible to be done by any other. You must not only think and speak of a low estate but actually come to be in a low state and caught in it, without any human aid, so that God alone may do the work. Or if it should not go to pass, you must at least desire it and not shrink from it.[17]

In the cross, in suffering and humiliation, we can only utter the story of this suffering that God will deliver us from, while with the same confidence cry out the lament of forsakenness. The theologian of the cross, from the standpoint of the cross itself cannot speak *about* the cross; she can only speak from the cross in sheer faith without evidence, in complete trust amidst abandonment, in her radical refusal to say that evil is good. This location calls us to "simply be honest about the world"[18] and not buffer the cries that come from the crosses even today, not to stifle the "deafening cry" of the oppressed, as Medellín, the

---

16. *LW* 21:315
17. *LW* 21:347–48
18. Jon Sobrino, *Jesus the Liberator* (Maryknoll, Ny: Orbis, 1993), 234.

1968 Latin American Episcopal Conference, called it, when we hear them echoing still as it did then in Calvary: "My God, my God, why have you forsaken
me." Faith and the "deafening cry" do not cancel each other. Or else, consider
the short dialogue between Jesus and the criminal being executed by his side
(Luke 23:39–43). The scene itself, as it is narrated by the evangelist, produces
the mixture of styles typical of biblical literature, the extreme "pendulation"
between *sublimitas* and *humilitas*, as Auerbach has argued, is original to biblical narration in all of Western literature.[19] There is such simplicity in the scene
that surprises us in turning the worst fate into unimaginable lustrous promise
of glory. Jorge Luis Borges' poem, "Luke XXIII", serves as a commentary on a
"theology of the crucified" which is as pertinent as any ever produced.[20] In the
poem, cross and paradise, shame and glory meet each other. The same blunt-
ness that led the robber time and again into sin and crime was that which made
him ask and be granted paradise, nothing else was required from him that he
did not have before, even if it had been employed for sinful ends. As it reads
so well in the original "*...ese candor que hizo que pediera y ganara el Paraíso ... era
el que tantas vezes al pecado lo arrojó y al azar ensangrentado.*"[21] The theologian of
the cross, as the one being on the cross, does not pronounce a theology of the
cross, in the objective sense of the genitive. From the cross comes only a plea:
"remember me."

   (b) *Theology at the Cross Deriding.* The second form of location in relationship to the cross is most exemplified by the other robber who challenges Jesus'
credentials as well as by those at the foot of the cross who were mockingly
telling the physician to heal himself. Be it sarcasm, as in the gospel narratives,
or a pious practice from medieval Christendom to modern-day spiritual techniques that promise prosperity, the basic attitude seems to be the same. It is
tempting God in Christ, or placing Christ on trial. This is the *angefochtene Christus*, the tempted Christ, who is asked to deliver the signs of power and glory
at his moment of trial. He already knew from his desert experience who the
tempter was and also that "It is said, 'Do not put the Lord your God to the test'"
(Luke 4:12). Here one of the basic characteristics of the theologian of glory is
manifested in the precise reversal of the relationship between what God does
and who God is. The *angefochtene Christus* is the tempted God in the sense that
the theologian of glory not only speculates behind the visible in search for the
invisible, but, in doing so, looks for something visible that would serve as an
indication of the invisible. Such theology prioritizes the work produced, both
human and divine, above the knowledge of God. The theologian of glory is
the one who says: "show me what you do and I will believe who you are." The
theologian of the cross says: "I know who you are for I have seen you there in
the midst of brokenness."

   The parable of the great judgment of Matthew 25 is a shocking narrative for
those who pretend to know who Christ is (Christians!) by what Christ does and
reveals in his glory. The parable is not a moral instruction to feed the poor, cloth
the naked, visit the sick and so forth. It is rather about a cognitively dissonant

---

19. Erich Auerbach, *Mimesis: The Representation of Reality in Western Literature*, trans. Willard R. Trasu
(Princeton, Nj: Princeton University Press, 1953), 72, 151.
   20. Jorge Luis Borges, *Selected Poems* (New York, Ny: Viking, 1999), 131.
   21. Ibid., 130.

surprise. Those who attended the needs of the little ones did it without knowing that they were doing it to Christ himself. They did not recognize Christ
in the faces of those they helped. Those who were condemned plead their
case saying that also they did not recognize Christ in the faces of those little
ones, implying, obviously, that they supposedly knew who Jesus was. In their
"knowledge" of Christ, they missed Jesus, for they could see in that cross only a
criminal who boasted to be a king being executed. If only, instead of being poor,
sick, jailed, hungry, Christ had shown some of his glory, they would then, only
then, see him. As Barth remarked, Christ is not only God in the flesh, but under
the condition of utter sinfulness.

(c) *Theology Away from the Cross.* The third location in relation to the cross
is the one taken by most of the disciples according to the Gospel narratives.
Here there is no theology of the cross. Those who ran from the cross saw it
as a tragic event, a death that no longer belonged to the world, a tragic end
with no intrinsic meaning except the one of pointing back to the life of Jesus.
Their explanation and interpretation is that the true prophet dies, as we can
find in the dominant motif accounting for Jesus' death in the speech of Stephen
in Acts 7:52: "Which of the prophets did your ancestors not persecute? They
killed those who foretold the coming of the Righteous One, and now you have
become his betrayers and murderers." Most of the disciples stayed away from
the cross, carrying with them the memories of the life of Jesus; the rest was left
behind in a tomb.

Exemplary is the story of the two disciples who took off to go to Emmaus
as recounted in Luke 24. On their way Jesus was certainly remembered as the
one who walked over water; a Jesus who was alive in the stories about him
before or even apart from having gone through death. He resurrects, so to say,
in the tales told about him. In this case the cross does represent the closing of
the meaning of one's life, but lies outside of it, and is, most importantly, not its
fulfillment, only its consummation.

They are going away from the cross as if saying that this is the way things
are and it is over. They are joined by a fellow traveler who tells them the story
that leads to the cross as the prophets foretold it. They are given a frame within
which the meaning could be attained. They need the story to be brought back
to the cross. But the story itself does not do it, because the point was not its
immanent meaning, the "ah-ha-experience" of saying, "Oh, now I see." The
cross does not end or does not even start at its portrayed meaning, whatever
it might be. The point is to encounter the living God concealed in its opposite,
as Luther, working with his apocalyptic reversals, would say. And this they
will understand only after the story is over and the body is once more, albeit
symbolically, broken.

This lifts another important implication of the theology of the cross. The
theology of the cross is not an intra-textual event. It is not the discourse, the
explanation, or the interpretation that brings about the revelation of meaning,
even if the hermeneutist is Jesus himself. It is an event that does not embed
itself within the frame of meaning of the narrative. Though their hearts were
"burning within" them while they were being instructed about the Scriptures,
it was only after the hermeneutics ended that the revelation happened in the
breaking of the bread. As the nineteenth century Cuban writer and nationalist

hero, José Martí, used to say, "sometimes the best way to say something is to do it." The story is a propaedeutic, but its meaning lies beyond its own confines; or better said, what it reveals happens at the exact moment after the discourse is interrupted, happens outside the text, or in its ironic interstices. Not even in the story of the cross is there a theology of the cross. It becomes a theology of the cross when the story ends, and the present broken body is presented and beheld. The theologian that runs from the cross has the story of Jesus but is unable to read it in the light and darkness of the cross itself. It is only the darkness of the approaching night (v. 29) that reveals the "light" with the breaking of the bread. Then the disciples return immediately to Jerusalem, to the place they left behind, the place of the crucifixion, even as they had retired for the night to rest. The story is about a conversion, a turning around and engaging a new dispositional practice.

(d) *Theology of the Cross as a Practice of Resurrection.* Theology of the cross as a dispositional practice (*usus*) is a theology that stands in the face of the cross but reacts to it with the confidence that it is not outside of God's providence, promising or terrible as it might be. An example is again found in Luther's *Magnificat* of 1521: the description of the lowly maid who recognizes, without yet having the evidence that God raises her and all those of low degree because she saw her own self as meriting nothing but God's own infinite empowerment and grace while still under disgrace. But more importantly, she was the one who with other women is reported to have been there at the foot of the cross. Even if no *Magnificat* was sung there, her actions were a testimony to what could be called a practice of resurrection, for that cross for them was not yet the end of it all, there was still a labor to be done. As that lowly womb of that poor peasant girl from an insignificant Galilean village could bear God (*theotokos*), so also the tomb in which the body of Jesus was laid should be praised with the best that they could offer. The one who had died that shameful death was not yet done for them. Luke tells us that the women, who were at the foot of the cross, went to see where his body was laid. After the dead body of Jesus had been laid in the tomb, they went home in order to prepare ointment and spices for the broken body. And after preparing spices and oils at home and observing the Shabbat, they go to anoint a putrescent dead body, only to be themselves surprised and terrified to find the tomb empty and that very body alive. (Needless to say, we also are often scared of novelty, as were those women, in face of experiences of redemption and resurrection; it is always easier to administer grief than the unexpected, for it lies outside of our control.) The surprise is there when a labor of love and mourning is carried through. In the midst of the pain, in the face of the slain body of the beloved one, those women practiced the unlikely act of love not expected to be ever returned. A theology of the cross is always the other side of a practice of resurrection, and the other way around.

This practice of resurrection has been put remarkably well by Wendell Berry in his poem entitled "The Way of Pain."[22] This practice is what connects the resurrection to the cross, which prefigures the community of those who in proclamation and communion hope against all hope. This is the practice that keeps history open, open to revisit even its past of victimization and suffering. This is

---

22. Wendell Berry, *Collected Poems* (San Francisco, Ca: North Point, 1985), 210.

the task of the followers of Christ: not to allow history to end in calamity, and not to allow the past to be closed, but keep it open, against all evidence, against all hope.

In 1937 the Jewish German philosopher Walter Benjamin wrote the following in an article published in a journal edited by his friend and colleague Max Horkheimer: "The work of the past is not closed for the historical materialist. He cannot see the work of an epoch, or any part of it, as reified, as literally placed on one's lap."[23] A sharp criticism ensues from Horkheimer in which he writes to Benjamin: "The supposition of the unclosed past is idealistic.... Past injustice has occurred and [history] is closed. Those who were slain in it were truly slain.... In the end, your statements are theological."[24] Benjamin retorts establishing a discussion that is one of the most significant theological debates of the twentieth century even as—and perhaps because—it took place outside the faculties of theology:

> The corrective for this sort of thinking lies in the reflection that history is not simply a science but a form of empathetic memory [Eingedenken]. What science has "settled," empathetic memory can modify. It can transform the unclosed (happiness) into something closed and the closed (suffering) into something unclosed. That is theology, certainly, but in empathetic memory we have an experience that prohibits us from conceiving history completely non-theologically.[25]

This empathetic memory is capable of opening the closed past. Horkheimer played the role of the disciples on the way to Emmaus. He left the tragedy closed and behind; Calvary was no longer redeemable. Benjamin, like the women in the Gospels, kept the empathetic memory, against all evidences, against all science, in a practice of resurrection that carried those women to the Easter Sunday.

The connection of the resurrection to the cross is a pilgrimage to the tomb. The surprise comes when a labor of love and mourning is carried through. Only after one prepares the spices for a body that will not be able to even utter a word of thanks, only then might a surprise come about. But there is no guarantee issued in advance. As Wendell Berry said: "Unless we grieve like Mary at His grave, giving Him up as lost, no Easter morning comes." Such a grief, such a labor of love and mourning grows out of the faith and hope that no gesture of love will ever be lost even if nothing can be changed, even if the wrong must be accepted for the sake of love. Danish theologian Anna Marie Aagaard speaks, in this regard, of a theology of tears in a lecture entitled "Cry of Agony and Bread of Tears," and she states:

> The moaning over the wrong that is accepted is visible in the faces of human beings, even when the tears have gone. It leaves its traces. It is holy; it belongs to God, for no human being can share it. No-one but I can, by myself, decide to preserve the love to the one or those who trample on my life so that I for

23. Walter Benjamin, *Ausgewählte Schriften II* (Frankfurt am: Suhrkamp, 1955), 311.
24. Cited by Helmut Peukert, *Science, Action, and Fundamental Theology: Toward a Theology of Communicative Action* (Cambridge, Ma: MIT Press, 1984), 206–207.
25. Ibid., 207.

the sake of love accept to be wretched—and that without hope of change in
the state of things. For, should they be changed, I would have to betray love,
and that is the sin that cannot be forgiven. There is nothing else to do but to
love—and to weep! This is to save the world for the sake of love. It happens
around us—with immense costs. Theologically, we call this "to save," and
faith senses God's presence therein.[26]

A short story by García Márquez conveys well this idea of a labor of mourning and love that is expressed here. The story, published in 1968, is called "The
Handsomest Drowned Man in the World." The author wrote this only some
years after the first of the military coups took place that would spread all over
Latin America (Brazil: 1964, Argentina: 1965, and Chile: 1971) with their practice of dumping enemies of the régime on the high sea. Many would eventually be washed ashore (before Chile improved the "technology" by placing a
large piece of metal in the bowels of the victims before throwing them into the
ocean). García Márquez might have had this in mind when he wrote the story,
which makes it really a story about reclaiming a past, of unclosing it by an
empathetic memory. So goes the story:

In a small village of fishermen off the Colombian coast of the Caribbean Sea
a drowned man is washed to shore. He is found by the villagers and brought
into town. While the women start preparing his body for a proper funeral the
men go around nearby villages to see if someone is missing. They come back
with the news that he was not a habitant of the region. The women were already
imagining places and experiences he had been through, filling that corpse with
a fantastic life, giving him a name, Esteban, and assigning him parents and relatives so that the whole village was, through him, related to each other. When
the news came that he did not belong to any of the villages nearby, there was
jubilation in the midst of tears: "'Praise God,' they sighed, 'he's ours!'" After
preparing the body of the drowned man who "was the tallest, strongest, most
virile, and best built man they have ever seen," they return him to the ocean
dressed in new clothes they had to tailor, for his size was larger than any one
they knew. Fully adorned with flowers, the body is carried in procession to
the cleft on the rocks by the ocean where their dead ones where released to the
waters. And so the story ends:

> While they fought for the privilege of carrying him on their shoulders . . . men
> and women became aware for the first time of the desolation of their streets.
> . . . They let him go without anchor so that he could come back if he wished
> and whenever he wished, and they all held their breath for the fraction of
> centuries the body took to fall into the abyss. They did not need to look at one
> another to realize that they were not whole, and they would never be. But
> they also knew that everything would be different from then on, . . .[27]

Returning to the Gospel narrative, one sees that in the midst of pain and des-
olation, in the face of the slain body of the beloved one, those women practiced

26. Else Marie Wiberg Petersen, "'The Holy Spirit shall come upon you': Mary—the Human 'Locus'
for the Holy Spirit," in *Cracks in the Walls: Essays on Spirituality, Ecumenicity and Ethics*, ed. Else Marie
Wiberg Pedersen and Johannes Nissen (Frankfurt *am*: Peter Lang, 2005), 24.
27. Gabriel García Márquez, "The Handsomest Drowned Man in the World," in *Collected Stories*
(New York, Ny: Harper Collins, 1984), 253–254.

the unlikely act of love not expecting any return. This is a labor of love and mourning. In the words of Kirkegaard,

> If one wants to make sure that love is completely unselfish, he eliminates every possibility of repayment. But precisely this is eliminated in the relationship to one who is dead. If love nevertheless remains, it is in truth unselfish.... *The work of love in remembering one who is dead is a work of the* MOST UNSELFISH *love.*[28]

But most important: it is only such love that can open the history of past victimization, as Benjamin insisted. A theology of the cross (*in usus passionis*) is always the other side of a practice of resurrection, and the other way around: a practice of resurrection can only be exercised in the face of the dismal experience of the cross that in the Shabbat of prayer and weeping is remembered and thus brought back.

---

28. Søren Kirkegaard, *Works of Love*, trans. Howard and Edna Hong (New York, Ny: Harper & Row, 1962), 320; my emphases.

8. Becoming a Feminist Theologian of the Cross

Deanna A. Thompson

"The cross alone is our theology."
—Martin Luther

"No one was saved by the execution of Jesus."
—Rebecca Parker

Contemporary theology plays host to a chorus of voices calling theology to account for its long and thriving history of using the cross of Christ to inflict suffering upon the innocent. Among the alleged perpetrators littering the historical Christian landscape, few loom as large as the Reformers of sixteenth-century Europe, those fathers of Protestantism obsessed with God's wrath toward deservedly damned human beings. Indeed, we need not wade far into the writings of reformer Martin Luther before becoming submerged in what author Kathleen Norris calls the "scary vocabulary" of Christian speech.[1] Does speaking rightly about God today demand that we abandon the theologizing of by-gone thinkers like Martin Luther?

Feminist and other contemporary theologians proclaim that speaking rightly of God requires radical reform of traditional theologies like Luther's. We are often reminded today that all theology is contextual, and that Luther's own contextual preoccupation with wrath, sin, and guilt, many argue, adds real insult to real injury when spoken to those whose lives bear marks of real crucifixions. Even more pointedly, traditional theories of atonement and theologies of the cross are under attack by feminists and others who work to unmask the damage of these theologies to the wounded, the vulnerable, and the oppressed. Where is the good news preached to the victimized? The responsibility for such oppression and suffering is being laid at the feet of the patriarchal Christian tradition, of which Luther is a card-carrying member. Cries for reform rise up, and they deserve a hearing.

But cries of reform also rose up over five hundred years ago from the mouth and pen of Martin Luther over the oppressive theology and church practices of his own day. Theologians of his day, Luther proclaimed, had bypassed the cross of Christ and were following instead glory theologies which pursued disingenuous paths to God, paths controlled by religious decrees of the seemingly all-powerful medieval church. Diametrically opposed to any theology of glory that

---

1. See Kathleen Norris, *Amazing Grace: A Vocabulary of Faith* (New York: Riverhead Books, 1998).

called good evil and evil good, Luther glimpsed an alternate reality through the cross of Christ, an alternative vision of what counted as authority, wisdom, and salvation. What Luther accomplished in his Reformation was nothing less than a new way of imaging church, theology, and the Christian's role in society.

The divide between contemporary feminist theologians and Martin Luther is wide. Is it possible to claim both feminism and Luther? Is the divide that separates them crossable? On good days, I believe that both Luther's vision for life with the cross at the center, and feminist visions for Christian repentance and healing, can be brought together in ways that preserve the integrity of both sides. If Luther's theology of the cross is revisited, feminists will be surprised to meet in Luther an ally for thinking through *how* theologians re-imagine and reform dominant, abusive forms of Christianity, and move toward a more faithful, liberating portrait of life lived in response to the gospel message. Those who reside firmly on the side of Luther can learn more from feminists about the nightmarish realities of human suffering and about theology's complicity in the persistence of unnecessary suffering. The divide can be crossed, and this paper is an exercise in crossing and bridge building.

My understanding of Luther's theology of the cross is indebted to several formative influences. Early in graduate school, I was introduced to Douglas John Hall's work on an indigenous theology of the cross.[2] Hall held up this "not much loved" theological tradition and wagered that it could ignite reform within North American Christianity. His insightful application of Luther's theology to our context is what planted the seed for this project. Second, I build upon Walther von Loewenich's argument that Luther's cross-centered approach was integral to his life-long career as a reformer, rather than a passing preoccupation of his monastic days.[3] Third, I am persuaded by Gerhard Forde's recent rereading of Luther's *Heidelberg Disputation*, the foundational text for Luther's theology of the cross, and his claim that taken in its totality the treatise tells the cross-to-resurrection story of the sinner brought low, justified, and saved through the cross and resurrection of Christ.[4] If I had more time, I would lay out my understanding of Luther as a contextual theologian of the cross whose amazing life reflects both faithful and not-so-faithful lived applications of this subversive theological approach. Since our time is short, however, I will move right into the conversation between feminists and Luther and propose how one becomes a feminist theologian of the cross.

The Conversation Begins

A growing number of scholars are claiming dialectical allegiance to both feminism and Luther's theological vision.[5] This scholarship is part of a larger trend

2. See Douglas John Hall, *Hope Against Hope: Toward an Indigenous Theology of the Cross*, WSCF 1/3 (Geneva, Switzerland: World Student Christian Federation, 1971).

3. See Walther von Loewenich's groundbreaking study, *Luther's Theology of the Cross* (Minneapolis, Mn: Augsburg Publishing, 1976).

4. Gerhard Forde, *On Being a Theologian of the Cross: Reflections on Luther's Heidelberg Disputation, 1518* (Grand Rapids, Mi: Eerdman's, 1997).

5. The 1996 gathering of "Lutheran Women in Theological Education" at the annual meeting of the American Academy of Religion was devoted to "Luther and Feminist Theology," resulting in a

in feminist theology, the subject of a recent *Christian Century* cover story by Emory Professor Joy McDougall.[6] McDougall suggests that this new wave of feminist theologies—and happily she includes my work in this new wave—is about feminists "taking back" their confessional traditions. "Like Jacob wrestling with the angel," McDougall observes, feminists refuse to let these traditions go "until they wrestle a feminist blessing from them."[7] Applying that principle to this project, this feminist theologian of the cross remains within the Lutheran confessional tradition and aims to combine the best of both Lutheran and feminist theological visions. I see this new wave of feminist theologians as standing in the strong and defiant tradition of Luther and other sixteenth-century reformers in their laying claim to Luther's vision of *ecclesia semper reformanda*, the church as always reforming itself.

Unlikely Allies

As more scholars engage in mutually enhancing conversations between Luther and feminist theological visions, method becomes an obvious point of connection. It can be argued that Luther shares with feminists a three-fold methodological approach: critique, retrieval, and re-imaging. I offer here some shared sensibilities that suggest the possibility of a feminist theology of the cross. More suggestive than exhaustive, they begin to reveal points at which both sides converge, and set the stage for deeper, more substantive interaction.

To begin, both Luther and feminists utilize what feminists commonly call a hermeneutics of suspicion, a process of interpretation that recognizes the provisional nature of interpretation and the way in which interpreters presuppose and enforce cultural norms and ideologies. According to feminists, Christian thought and practice overflow with particular theologies of glory—patriarchy, demonarchy,[8] kyriarchy[9]—that employ matrixes of domination in which women live, move, and struggle to be. Feminist theology, in line with Luther's persistence in calling a thing what it is, calls the patriarchal assumptions underlying Christian claims by their real names. Just as Luther's theology of the cross puts everything to the test, including the dominant theological tradition he inherited, so feminists mirror this testing of tradition, scrutinizing its faithfulness to and respect for women.

---

subsequent issue of the Lutheran journal, *CurTM* 24/1 (February 1997), devoted entirely to the same topic. One of the contributors to that issue now has a book devoted to the creative, mutually enhancing pairing of Luther and feminist philosophy. See Mary M. Solberg, *Compelling Knowledge: A Feminist Proposal for an Epistemology of the Cross* (Albany, Ny: State University of New York Press, 1997).

6. Joy Ann McDougall, "Women's Work: Feminist Theology for a New Generation," *The Christian Century* (July 26, 2005), 20–25.

7. Ibid., 20.

8. Delores Williams prefers "demonarchy" to "patriarchy" because it highlights the structures that benefit white women and men while simultaneously harming women and men of color. See her illuminating article, "The Color of Feminism: Or Speaking the Black Woman's Tongue," *Feminist Theological Ethics: A Reader*, ed. Lois K. Daly (Louisville, Ky: WJK, 1994), 42–58.

9. Elisabeth Schüssler Fiorenza also dislikes the limitations of the term patriarchy and instead introduced the neologism "kyriarchy" into feminist theological conversation, to underscore the pyramidal shape of oppression, and to focus on those women at the bottom of a multi-dimensional structure of oppression. See her description in *Jesus: Miriam's Child, Sophia's Prophet* (New York, Ny: Continuum, 1995), 14.

Second, feminist theologians employ a critique similar to Luther's constant warning of the seductive power of any and all versions of theologies of glory. That which attracts and seduces in a patriarchal milieu is often the same as that which oppresses and suppresses those on the margins. In response, feminist theologians set forth a theological vision from the underside of society, of history, an approach not unlike Luther's destabilizing move to the cross of Christ. Luther returns to scripture, to Paul's cross-centered vision, retrieving this critical, subversive approach to counter scholasticism's seductively misleading claims. The God Christians come to know through the cross of Christ is the antithesis of the majestic God of the scholastics, who lives and reigns in power and glory. For Luther, God is met in the basest of places, hidden within suffering, pain, and death. In a similar vein, feminist theologians call attention to the forgotten and ignored elements of Christian tradition that highlight the power of women as agents and recipients of God's love. In a tradition guilty of repeatedly denigrating women, feminists uncover and expose God's hidden presence in the most unpredictable of places: in the lives and experiences of women.

Third, Luther and feminist theologians both witness to theology's experiential dimensions. Both understand that theological reflection must be done in constant conversation with the contexts in which they live, responding to the challenges and struggles confronting them. For Luther, theology always stretched beyond mere intellectual exercise to faithful existence under the cross, and this required him to address the unsentimental realities of suffering and death. Similarly, feminists rely on the contextual category of experience to analyze and assess practical implications of normative claims. Just as Luther determined that attention to the existential dimension of faith was missing from the prevailing theological imagination of his day, so feminists regard concrete experiences of women as missing from dominant theological discourse.

Where Luther and feminist theologians stand most closely together is in their reforming sensibility that gets worked out through shared methodological commitments. Both Luther and feminists are allied in their stinging critiques of dominant traditions. Both are well practiced in leveling a "No!" against the theologies of glory running rampant in their contexts.

When we allow the conversation between Luther and feminist theologians to move beyond shared methodological commitments, however, points of difference quickly emerge. What follows here is an imaginative engagement between Luther and feminists that should help move us forward toward a feminist theology of the cross.

Deepening the Discussion: Sin, Suffering, and the Cross

Several feminist theologians have argued against Luther's and other traditional readings of sin, insisting that they represent decidedly masculine patterns of sinfulness. Stated briefly, if the diagnosis misses the mark for women, feminists insist, then Luther's call to break the self's curvature in upon itself is not only off the mark but potentially harmful for women. As one convinced by Luther's view of human beings as chronically disposed to sin, I am wary of embracing this feminist critique too quickly, for it often leads, as in the work of Daphne Hampson, to an exaltation of feminist empowerment. While such empowerment certainly has its place, feminist ethicist Sally Purvis casts doubt on such optimistic feminist soteriologies, stating that in many of our feminist groups, "commitments to cooperate degenerate into attempts to dominate, the common good is lost in cliques, horizontal violence abounds as the powerless attack one another, and the most commonly shared experience can be a sense of betrayal."[10] Purvis' point is by no means anti-feminist. In fact, this intra-feminist critique has been deepened by black feminist bell hooks who makes visible the way in which privileged white women fail to attend to the vertical violence that persists among women in their complex identities of race, class, and sexuality. Purvis and hooks lend credence to the cross-centered affirmation that all human beings are ensnared in a complex web of sin and are continuously subjected to the temptation to replicate patterns of domination. Women, like men, experience temptation to sin through the abuse of power, as well as through the trials of broken, wounded relationships. Writer Kathleen Norris suggests we need to communicate these abuses through our language. Norris—in decidedly Lutheran fashion—worries that omitting words like "wretch" from contemporary theological discourse means we encourage neglect of a basic human reality. She asks, "Who never lies awake regretting the selfish, nigh-unforgivable things that he or she has done?... It seems to me that if you can't ever admit to being a wretch, you haven't been paying attention."[11] A feminist theologian of the cross must pay attention to women's experiences of personal sin, as well as for collusion with sinful structures external to the self.

But a deeper issue still lurks within this discussion of sin. Many feminist theologians root their understanding of sin not in some generic notion of "woman" but specifically in women whose lives have been shattered by experiences of abuse and oppression. Rebecca Parker, in her book with Rita Brock entitled *Proverbs of Ashes*, recounts in horrifying detail the experiences of being raped as a preschooler by her neighbor. Just as horrifying is her Christian family's—and her Christian community's—inability to help her deal with this violence committed against her. Parker's indictment against her church and her theology is this: "What my community could not name it could not see. And what the community could not see, I could not integrate. My religious community, most of all, could not see [this violence] because it could not name clearly the violence that happened to Jesus."[12] Parker and others demand that theology respond not just to the "sinner," but to the lived reality of those who are gravely sinned against.

From the vantage point of women like Parker, Serene Jones evaluates Luther's story of justification, noting that the first scene in the drama—and indeed in Luther's theology of the cross—depicts God's wrath fully undoing (crucifying) the subject. This drama begins with a harsh movement against "the pretensions of self-definition and pride," which results in "fragmentation" of

---

10. Sally B. Purvis, *The Power of the Cross: Foundations for a Feminist Ethic of Community* (Nashville, Tn: Abingdon, 1993), 16.

11. Norris, *Amazing Grace*, 167.

12. Rebecca Parker, "The Unblessed Child: Rebecca's Story," in *Proverbs of Ashes: Violence, Redemptive Suffering, and the Search for What Saves Us*, ed. Rita Nakashima Brock and Rebecca Ann Parker (Boston, Ma: Beacon Press, 2001), 199.

the arrogant self. In assessing this drama through a feminist lens, Jones asks, "What happens to the woman who enters this tale having spent her life not in the space of narcissistic self-definition but in the space of fragmentation and dissolution?"[13] She suggests one of two possibilities: in the first scenario, Luther's narrative falls on deaf ears; the story is so foreign that the woman is incapable of seeing herself present in it (i.e., unable to identify with its masculine patterns). In the second, more pernicious option, this woman adopts the narrative as her own story, taking upon herself "a script designed for the prideful sinner." She likely will "recapitulate the dynamics of her oppression and self-loss."[14] Again if she adopts the mis-diagnosis of her condition, she will mis-appropriate the cure.

In response to these problematic and potentially destructive scenarios, it is crucial that a feminist theologian of the cross make distinctions among different kinds of suffering. Luther's concern was primarily with description rather than prescription of the situation in which humans find themselves. At the heart of Luther's cross-centered vision was the rejection of the way in which "bearing the cross," as prescribed by medieval Christendom, had lost its rootedness in biblical narrative. Suffering under one's own cross should never become a technique or a "work." Christians are not called to sacrifice and suffer in order to be made worthy before God. This is the religious vision Luther experienced and denounced as virtually unbearable; it is precisely the vision he came to reject through his theology of the cross.

The type of suffering of which Luther primarily speaks is the spiritual suffering we experience in light of God's work "against the presumption of our work." We want to heal ourselves, work out our own salvation, and Luther's talk of suffering mirrors quite vividly the Psalmist's lament of bottoming out, of acknowledging our utter dependence upon God. Further, Luther's dialectical approach to human existence and God's alien and proper work allows the possibility to take a deeper accounting of sin as harm done to others. We look to Luther's dialectical approach to scripture as law and gospel, which he first articulated as letter and spirit. Gerhard Ebeling suggests that Luther realized early on that

> understanding scripture is not something that can be preserved and passed on. As existential life continues, so the understanding of scripture is a continuous task which can never be brought to a conclusion. For there is constant threat that an understanding once achieved will cease to be spirit, and return to being the mere letter, unless it is constantly attained anew and made one's own.[15]

Faced with a woman whose life has been shattered by violence, then, it is conceivable that instead of commending her to be crucified by the law, a theologian of the cross could instead preach a word of comfort regarding God's presence: in Luther's biblical exegesis, for example, he expresses deep concern

---

13. Serene Jones, *Feminist Theory and Christian Theology: Cartographies of Grace* (Minneapolis, Mn: Fortress Press, 2000), 62.
14. Ibid., 63.
15. Gerhard Ebeling, *Luther: An Introduction to His Thought,* trans. R.A. Wilson (Philadelphia, Pa: Fortress Press, 1970), 99.

for the healing of the sinned against. Much in his Genesis lectures affirms that God knows the victims, rages with anger over injustices committed against the innocent, and that God is the One who comforts the wounded, the shattered, as a mother comforts her child.[16]

These aspects of Luther's thought coincide with Jones' vision of retaining Luther's justification drama without having it further damn the crucified woman. Jones suggests that for someone reeling from the effects of sin done against her, she enter the drama in a different scene, namely in the one where she becomes a new creation. Jones argues that "this inversion does not replace or destroy the logic of justification; narrating the story of a sturdy and resilient new creation before turning to the moment of dismantling and forgiveness simply allows the most problematic aspects of justification (its first decentering moment) to be tempered."[17]

This inversion helps preserve what I find at the heart of Luther's theology of the cross: a clarity and conviction that can only be spoken from the resurrection side of the cross. This cross-centered vision for Luther emerges alongside his intensely personal experience of being saved by the Word of God spoken through the cross of Christ. And we cannot forget Luther's dialectical approach to scripture as law and gospel. In light of this dialectic, I propose that the first word a feminist theology of the cross will speak to the wounded, the vulnerable, the oppressed, is the gospel, the word of hope, without losing sight that each life must also inevitably undergo the undoing by the letter, the law, of any and all attempts at self-sufficiency before God.

But we still have yet to cross the most difficult divide—the view of atonement. In the face of forceful and varied critiques leveled against traditional atonement theories, contemporary Lutheran theologians attempt to demonstrate that Luther's understanding of atonement differs from traditional satisfaction, *Christus Victor*, or moral influence theories.[18] What is radical about Luther's understanding of the gospel, it is argued, is that Luther reverses the direction of atonement. The message of Christ on the cross is that God comes to us. If a theology of the cross is going to hold to some version of Luther's understanding of the depth of human sinfulness, then humanity must be viewed as incapable of voluntarily moving toward God, unable to overcome its own limitations and secure its own salvation. The message of the cross for Luther is what God does for us.

For Luther, understanding the meaning of the cross is more like looking in a mirror than it is an intellectual assent to this or that theory. Luther claimed that "Christ mirrors our sin, demonstrating what should have happened to us." Because Christ actually became sin for us, Luther asserts, we are freed from having to do the same. In his stressing the uniqueness of Christ's suffering, Luther was delivering the death knell to medieval religious proscriptions

---

16. Jaroslav Pelikan and Helmut T. Lehmann, eds., *Luther's Works*, American ed., 55 vols. (Philadelphia, Pa: Fortress Press; Saint Louis, Mo: Concordia Publishing House, 1955–86), 2:145 (hereafter, *LW*).

17. Jones, *Feminist Theory*, 63.

18. See Gerhard O. Forde, "The Work of Christ," in *Christian Dogmatics*, ed. Carl E. Braaten and Robert W. Jensen, vol. 2 (Philadelphia, Pa: Fortress Press, 1984), 5–99; Mary Knutson, "Toward a Contemporary Theology of the Cross," Convocation Address (October 5, 1995), Luther Seminary, St. Paul, Minnesota.

that suffering is necessary to become worthy in God's sight. I am drawn here to Luther's invocation of the biblical story of the woman caught in adultery. Luther focused on Jesus' reaction, noting that he did not demand suffering, payment, or sacrifice. Rather Jesus tells her, "Go and sin no more." Luther then described this pronouncement of Jesus as "laying on her the cross." To live faithfully under the reality of the cross is to live as one who has been justified by God and opened to the brokenness and needs of the world in which one lives.

Feminist theologians are concerned not just with theological language itself, but also with the "effective history" of the images and symbols contained in the discourse. Feminists test Luther not only on his theological claims, but also on how his theology functioned in concrete situations. While Luther's pastoral, devotional orientation succeeded in offering words of comfort to those whose existence was marked by unjust sufferings, we cannot overlook his brutish approaches to the Peasants and—later in life—the Jews, often taken in the name of Christ. The feminist theological sensibility of keeping those suffering ones at the forefront of this vision will help mitigate the possibility of following Luther down those destructive paths.

For a feminist theologian of the cross committed to naming the violence specifically toward women that has been justified through appeal to traditional atonement images, a shift in describing the atoning work of Christ becomes necessary. Specifically, I suggest a revisioning of Luther's use of the metaphor of a *fröhlicher Wechsel*, or "happy exchange" between the bridegroom and bride, to understand atonement. Luther lifts up the image of Christ the bridegroom marrying the "poor wicked harlot," thus taking on all her grievous sins and saving her from rightful damnation. Arguably the power of this biblical image comes from Luther's articulation of the gift character of the husband freely taking on all sins of his wife, thereby endowing her with eternal righteousness. In our contemporary setting, however, much of the power of this metaphor is muted or lost for women and men who cannot move past its sexism. The model of Christ rescuing humanity in the form of a deviant woman needs to be replaced in a cross-centered theology with a feminist sensibility.

Rather than a happy exchange between Christ and the wicked harlot bride, I suggest a metaphor that communicates several key aspects of a feminist theologian of the cross' understanding of atonement. It is the model of friendship; that God's atoning work for us on the cross is done through Jesus' befriending humanity. Drawing on Luther's most beloved Gospel of John, we hear Jesus telling his disciples that "no one has greater love than this, than to lay down one's life for one's friends" (John 15:13). This model is suggested in the spirit of Luther's use of various images—from the devil capturing the bait to the bridegroom taking on the sins of his bride—to convey the meaning of the cross. Luther's theology of the cross was constantly applied and adapted to various occasions, and this occasion for a feminist theology of the cross calls out for another image that communicates the message more effectively to contemporary women and men. In John, the image of friendship is privileged to explain the meaning of Jesus' life and specifically, his death on the cross. The image of Jesus laying down his life for his friends highlights the gift character that is crucial to Luther's understanding of what God did on the cross. Sallie McFague emphasizes the freely chosen nature of friendship that has not always been a part of the understanding of marriage.[19] Friends freely choose to be in relation to one another. Is that not an appropriate image of Jesus' willingness to give of himself? Jesus was not paying a debt to God. Jesus the Friend acted freely, giving his very life on behalf of his friends. In a related vein, Gerhard Forde argues that the "for us" notion that was so important to Luther

> should be interpreted more on a sense of "on our behalf," "for our own good," or "for our benefit," rather than "instead of us" . . . [which is] oriented solely toward the past. But Jesus' work "for us" in the New Testament is oriented also toward the future. He died not only to repair past damage but to open a new future "for us."[20]

This image of Jesus as intimate friend of his disciples opens up avenues for talking about Jesus' suffering and atonement in ways tightly connected to the biblical story of Jesus' life and actions. The Matthean narrative reports that Jesus' friends included tax collectors and sinners (Matt 11:19), suggesting that when Jesus lays down his life on behalf of his friends, he bears their sins as well. The image of friendship also points to the role that sin played in placing Jesus on the cross. Jesus' words to Judas in the Garden of Gethsemane are, "Friend, do what you are here to do" (Matt 26:50). Jesus' friend betrays him with a kiss. Jesus lays down his life for the friends who betray as well as those who remain faithful to him.

Returning briefly to Luther's understanding of the joyous exchange between Christ and his bride, we see that because of Christ's exchange of righteousness, "[the bride's] sin cannot now destroy her." Luther explained that the bride is now "free from all sins ... secure against death and hell," but there is little guidance for her or for us about how we are to live in the world in response to what God has done for us.[21] In his *Treatise on Good Works*, Luther insists that the faith in the marriage relationship is a wonderful illustration of how guide books are not needed in order to live faithfully. Yet Luther's critics fault him for saying too little about just what faithful living in the temporal world looks like. The story of Jesus the Friend laying down his life does not provide a guidebook, but it includes some powerful images for how we should live in light of God's work on the cross. In John's Gospel, we hear from Jesus that his friends are to remain in the love of Christ, which means loving as Christ has loved us (cf. John 15:11–17). Here is a way of seeing God's atoning work on the cross as undeniably "future oriented." Remaining in the love of Christ suggests the possibility of a healing vision for those whose present reality is dominated by suffering, negation, and hate, while loving as Christ has loved us beckons all Christians to open ourselves up to the devouring needs of others[22] and even to participate in the process of healing. For in the end, Jesus the friend is not forsaken by God, and therefore, we as friends of Jesus witness to the empowering reality

---

19. Sallie McFague, *Metaphorical Theology: Models of God in Religious Language* (Philadelphia, Pa: Fortress Press, 1982), 159.
20. Forde, "The Work of Christ," 16.
21. *LW* 31:352.
22. Rowan Williams, *Resurrection: Interpreting the Easter Gospel* (London: Darton, Longman and Todd, 2002), 154.

of hope given us by the resurrection, a hope beyond all pain and suffering that surround and sometimes swallow us whole.

In the concluding theses of the *Heidelberg Disputation*, Luther speaks of how, after dying and being raised with Christ, we are freed to look to Jesus' life as a "stimulant" for loving action in the world. Turning to John's Gospel, where we hear of Jesus laying down his life for his friends, we see that the narrative lingers with the image of friendship, and contains the commands given by Jesus to his friends to "love one another as I have loved you" (John 15:12). That Jesus gives this command to the gathering of friends suggests that vocational identity is not just personal in character, but corporate as well. Remaining in the love of Christ entails doing so with others. In fact, one can argue that these words become the identifying marks of the Christian community.[23] Let us turn to the role and responsibility of the followers of Christ both corporately and individually in our vocation under this mark of loving as Christ first loved his friends.

The Vocation of Friendship

Living in the space opened up by justification given through Christ's death and resurrection means living in freedom, called to a vocation of relationship with others in the world. "Faith finds expression in works of freest service, cheerfully and lovingly done ... without hope of reward," Luther wrote.[24] Remaining in Christ's love, Luther believed, meant freedom for the Christian, freedom from bondage to authority as well as freedom to serve all without regard for merit. In assessing Luther's limitations with respect to social reform, critics often point to both his reliance on the language of service, as well as his vision of existence as lived out in two kingdoms, where the importance of the temporal realm fades behind the prominence of the realm of God. A feminist theologian of the cross highlights the whole person as wholly present in both realms, and to avoid slippage into dualisms, advocates for reform in the language of vocation. While a reformation of language does not guarantee reform in action, a feminist theologian of the cross follows the Johannine shift from "servant" to "friend" language. This linguistic shift in turn affects the understanding of vocation within a cross-centered vision.

A feminist theologian of the cross appreciates the subversive character of friendship as an operative image for vocation in our contemporary context. As Mary Hunt suggests, "Everyone has friends, but by reading contemporary theology one would never know it."[25] Why has the image of friendship been so neglected in theological reflection, especially when it figures prominently in the Gospel of John? One possibility is that friendship is often viewed as too ordinary a relationship to image or bear the divine. If one wants to downplay the seriousness of a relationship, one reports "they're just friends."[26] Despite this

---

23. Gail R. O'Day, "Commentary on John," in *The Women's Bible Commentary*, ed. Carol A. Newsom and Sharon H. Ringe (Louisville, Ky: WJK, 1992), 302.

24. *LW* 31:365.

25. Mary Hunt, *Fierce Tenderness: A Feminist Theology of Friendship* (New York, Ny: Crossroad, 1991), 1.

26. This point is made by Hunt, *Fierce Tenderness*, 2; and McFague, *Metaphorical Theology*, 156.

neglect, a feminist theology of the cross views friendship as an unexpectedly insightful image for Christian vocation. This image can express God's hidden presence in a backside manner, through mundane and ordinary relationships.

To understand the ramifications of this shift for an understanding of Christian vocation, we must examine what John's Gospel means by friendship as embodied by Jesus. If we look to Jesus as our friend and understand him as having died for his friends—indeed, for the world—we are confronted with a necessarily harrowing image of friendship. If we are called to love as he first loved us, then our free choice of friendship cannot, must not, be limited to like-minded folk; it must stretch to embrace those toward whom we harbor profound resentment, even contempt. To embrace the reciprocal character of friendship with someone very unlike ourselves might, in the end, bring us closer to Luther's radical insistence that service to the neighbor means service to the most lowly among us, regardless of personal comfort with neighbors we might want to pretend we do not have. Christians are called to be with others in the body of Christ; more explicitly, Christians are called to be nothing other than the church.

Church as a Community of Friends

Interestingly, feminist theologians have recently called for the church to understand itself as a community of friends, a vision that builds on the Johannine passages informing a feminist theology of the cross. A feminist cross-centered vision of church builds on Luther's understanding of church as radically other than the hierarchical institution of his day. To call the church a priesthood of all believers gives church a communitarian shape. In the Johannine claim that Jesus laid down his life *for his friends,* we are confronted with a view of friendship that challenges conventional understanding. Remaining in Christ's love means not only living in fellowship with all of Christ's friends, but it also means Christ's friends can never distance themselves from the cruciform reality of Christ's risen existence.

Within the church community, our vocation is first given to us through baptism. We are baptized into Christ's death, baptized into the story of the cross and resurrection that promises death to the power of sin in our lives. The sacrament of the Lord's Supper also binds the church to the crucified and risen Christ. A tight connection exists between the sacrament and Jesus' relationship to his friends, for sharing a meal "is the oldest ritual of friendship, [and] it is also a ritual so basic to Christianity that a case could be made that it is a if not *the*, central motif in Jesus' ministry and in the early church."[27] Jesus' friendships often included a shared meal, culminating in the last meal shared with his closest friends. The last supper before his crucifixion, however, is marked not only by friendship, but also by betrayal. The sacrament of communion recapitulates that meal, including the betrayal and the cross, but, as Rowan Williams asserts,

---

27. Sallie McFague, *Models of God: Theology for an Ecological, Nuclear Age* (Philadelphia, Pa: Fortress Press, 1987), 172.

"it does so as the Easter feast."[28] To claim Christ's real presence in the Lord's Supper points to the objective status of Christ's presence as the risen crucified victim, the one in whom hope is also embodied. The Christ encountered in the meal is the one we encounter as a stranger, as our victim, to whom we confess our sins, admit our brokenness. The hope experienced in the Last Supper comes from standing before the risen Christ as a restored betrayer, a beloved friend.[29] We are opened to a vocation that calls us into friendship with any and all friends of Christ.

The church as a community of friends gathers to die to old patterns of existence and rise with Christ to new life, a life organized around the forgiveness of sins.[30] This new organization of life around forgiven existence involves being called to a vocation of friendship, not only for us as individuals but also for the church as community. God's Word, met in the risen Christ, judges the church's predisposition to deny its own vocation as the body of Christ, as community of friends. For the church to accept its vocation of friendship demands repentance and openness to transformed existence.

This cross-centered vision of vocation as friendship gives us a sense of what it means to live as a follower of the crucified and risen Christ in the world today. It also helps us understand how a theologian of the cross cannot help but be involved in the temporal affairs. By destabilizing the medieval imagination over what spirituality and Christian vocation are and where they reside, Luther rendered Christ necessary not only for justification before God but also—and just as significantly—for works of love in the realm governed by law.[31] To understand vocation today in terms of friendship, then, takes us into the depths of the left hand of the kingdom, into the depths of our world.

Living Christian vocation, both individually and corporately, is about bearing our own crosses. This is not an appeal to imitate Christ's suffering or death. Rather, to be the church and to remain in Christ's love for his friends is to be with those who suffer, those who are broken, those who are in pain. At its best, the church is a sanctuary for all such persons. At the same time, Christian vocation calls us into friendships that challenge our identities, both within and outside church walls. Laboring to make ordination more just for our friends who are currently excluded, working for affordable housing with our friends in the community who lack an adequate place to live, lobbying for systemic change in laws for medication distribution for our HIV-positive friends abroad and at home, we are called to embody the friendship of Christ. Living out our vocation of harrowing friendships leads us not into reigning with Christ but rather to conformity to his compassionate, healing humanity as he lived on earth. Bearing the cross of friendship in this world means that suffering comes as an inevitable by-product of justified existence.

This feminist theology of the cross represents one attempt at crossing the divide that exists between reformers in the tradition like Martin Luther and contemporary feminist reformers. Potential exists for new forms of theological, ecclesial, and social reform when contemporary theological

---

28. Williams, *Resurrection*, 40.
29. Ibid., 68.
30. See James Wood, "Two Kingdoms—in America?" *CurTM* 14 (1989): 176.
31. Ibid., 162.

thought—particularly in feminist form—rediscovers Luther's turn away from theologies of glory beholden to gods of our own construction toward a theology of the cross and the God hidden in the crucified and risen Christ. This project is just one piece within a much larger conversation between the rich resources of the Christian tradition and the challenging, prophetic forces of feminist theological thought. Let us not pass by this occasion for reform.

Sex and Marriage Matters

9. "The Mother of All Earthly Laws"

The Lutheran Reformation of Marriage

John Witte Jr.

Questions of sex, marriage, and family life occupied Lutheran theologians and jurists from the very beginning of the Reformation.[1] The leading theological lights in Germany—Martin Luther, Philip Melanchthon, Martin Bucer, Johannes Bugenhagen, and Johannes Brenz—all prepared lengthy tracts on the subject in the 1520s. A score of leading jurists took up legal questions of marriage in their legal opinions and commentaries, often working under the direct inspiration of Lutheran theology and theologians. Virtually every German and Scandinavian polity that converted to the Lutheran cause in the sixteenth century had new marriage laws on the books within a decade of its acceptance of the Reformation, which they then heavily revised in subsequent generations.

The reformers' early preoccupation with marriage reform was driven in part by their theology. Many of the core theological issues of the Reformation were implicated by the prevailing Catholic theology and canon law of marriage. The church's jurisdiction over marriage was, for the reformers, a particularly flagrant example of the church's usurpation of the magistrate's authority. The Catholic sacramental concept of marriage, on which the church predicated its jurisdiction, raised deep questions of sacramental theology and biblical interpretation. The canonical prohibition on marriage of clergy and monastics stood sharply juxtaposed to Lutheran doctrines of the priesthood and of the Christian vocation. The canon law impediments to marriage, its prohibitions against complete divorce and remarriage, and its close regulations of sexuality, parenting, and education all stood in considerable tension with the reformers' interpretation of biblical teaching. That a child could enter marriage without parental permission or church consecration betrayed, in the reformers' views, basic responsibilities of family, church, and state to children. Issues of marriage doctrine and law thus implicated and epitomized many of the cardinal theological issues of the Lutheran Reformation.

The reformers' early preoccupation with marriage was also driven, in part, by their jurisprudence. The starting assumption of the budding Lutheran theories of law, society, and politics was that the earthly kingdom was governed by the three natural estates of household, church, and state. *Hausvater,*

---

1. This article is drawn, in part, from my *Law and Protestantism: The Legal Teachings of the Lutheran Reformation* (Cambridge, UK: Cambridge University Press, 2002), ch. 6 and *From Sacrament to Contract: Marriage, Religion, and Law in the Western Tradition,* 2d ed. (Louisville, Ky: WJK, 2011), ch. 7, and is used with permission of the publishers.

Gottesvater, and *Landesvater*; *paterfamilias*, *patertheologicus*, and *paterpoliticus*: these were the three natural offices through which God revealed himself and reflected his authority in the world. These three offices and orders stood equal before God and before each other. Each was called to discharge essential tasks in the earthly kingdom without impediment or interference from the other. The reform of marriage, therefore, was as important as the reform of the church and the state. Indeed, marital reform was even more urgent, for the marital household was, in the reformers' view, the "oldest," "most primal," and "most essential" of the three estates, yet the most deprecated and subordinated of the three. Marriage is the "mother of all earthly laws," Luther wrote, and the source from which the church, the state, and other earthly institutions flowed. "God has most richly blessed this estate above all others, and in addition, has bestowed on it and wrapped up in it everything in the world, to the end that this estate might be well and richly provided for. Married life therefore is no jest or presumption; it is an excellent thing and a matter of divine seriousness."[2]

The reformers' early preoccupation with marriage reform was also driven, in part, by their politics. A number of early leaders of the Reformation faced aggressive prosecution by the Catholic Church and its political allies for violation of the canon law of marriage and celibacy.[3] Among the earliest Protestant leaders were ex-priests and ex-monastics who had forsaken their orders and vows, and often married shortly thereafter.[4] Indeed, one of the acts of solidarity with the new Protestant cause was to marry or divorce in open violation of the canon law and in defiance of a bishop's instructions. This was not just an instance of crime and disobedience. It was an outright scandal, particularly when an ex-monk such as Brother Martin Luther married an ex-nun such as Sister Katharina von Bora—a *prima facie* case of double spiritual incest.[5] As Catholic Church courts began to prosecute these canon law offenses, Protestant theologians and jurists rose to the defense of their co-religionists—producing a welter of briefs, letters, sermons, and pamphlets that denounced traditional norms and pronounced a new theology and law of marriage.

---

2. *Concordia triglotta: die symbolischen Bücher der evangelish-lutherischen Kirche, deutsch-lateinisch-englisch* (Saint Louis, Mo: Concordia Publishing House, 1921), 639–641 [hereafter, TC]; *D. Martin Luthers Werke: Kritische Gesamtausgabe*, 69 vols. (Weimar: Hermann Böhlaus Nachfolger, 1883–), WA 30/1:152 (hereafter, WA); *D. Martin Luthers Werke: Kritische Gesamtausgabe, Tischreden*, 6 vols. (Weimar: Hermann Böhlaus Nachfolger, 1912–1921), 3:378, #3528, (hereafter, WA TR); Jaroslav Pelikan and Helmut T. Lehmann, eds., *Luther's Works*, American ed., 55 vols. (Philadelphia, Pa: Fortress Press; Saint Louis, Mo: Concordia Publishing House, 1955–86), 54:222–223 (hereafter, LW). See similar views in TC 611ff; WA 49:297ff; WA 2:734; LW 44:81ff; TC 363–383.

3. See several examples in Martin Brecht, *Martin Luther*, trans. James L. Schaaf, 3 vols (Minneapolis, Mn: Fortress Press, 1985–1993), 2:91–92.

4. One of the earliest examples was the Wittenberg wedding of ex-monk Wenzeslaus Linck in April, 1523, a lavish ceremony which Luther and several other early reformers attended and celebrated. See Bernd Moeller, "Wenzel Lincks Hochzeit: Über Sexualität, Keuscheit und Ehe in der frühen Reformation," *ZTK* 97 (2000): 317. The wedding two years later of ex-monk Luther to ex-nun Katharina von Bora was considerably more modest. See Brecht, *Martin Luther*, 2:195ff.

5. See Carter Lindberg, "The Future of a Tradition: Luther and the Family," in *All Theology Is Christology: Essays in Honor of David P. Scaer*, ed. Dean O. Wenthe et al. (Fort Wayne, In: Concordia Theological Seminary Press, 2000), 133–151, at 134.

The Case of Johann Apel

Let's begin with a concrete case. Our case comes from 1523. This is six years after Luther posted his 95 Theses, three years after his excommunication, two years after the Diet of Worms. Luther is back in Wittenberg from the Wartburg Castle. The Lutheran Reformation is gaining real revolutionary momentum in Germany and beyond.

Our case involves a priest and lawyer named Johann Apel.[6] Apel was born and raised in Nürnberg, an important German city, still faithful to Rome at the time of the case. In 1514, Apel enrolled for theological study at the brand new University of Wittenberg, where he had some acquaintance with Luther. In 1516, Apel went to the University of Leipzig for legal studies. Like many law students in his day, he studied for a joint degree in canon law and civil law. He was awarded the doctor of both laws in 1519. After a brief apprenticeship, Apel took holy orders and swore the requisite oath of clerical celibacy. One of the strong prince-bishops of the day, Conrad, the Bishop of Würzburg and Duke of Franken, appointed Apel as a cathedral canon in 1523. Conrad also licensed Apel as an advocate in all church courts. Apel settled into his home in Würzburg and began his pastoral and legal duties.

Shortly after his appointment, Apel began romancing a nun at the nearby St. Marr cloister. (Her name is not revealed in the records.) The couple saw each other secretly for several weeks. They carried on a brisk correspondence. They began a torrid romance. She evidently became pregnant. Ultimately, the nun forsook the cloister and her vows and secretly moved in with Apel. A few weeks later, the couple were secretly married and cohabited openly as a married couple.

This was an outrage. Clerical concubinage was one thing. The surviving records show that at least three other priests in Conrad's diocese kept concubines and paid Conrad the standard concubinage tax for that privilege. Earlier that very same year of 1523, another priest had fathered a child and paid the bishop the standard cradle tax. Clerical concubinage, even fatherhood, was known and was tolerated by some obliging Catholic bishops of the day. But clerical marriage: that was an outrage, particularly when it involved both a priest and a nun.

Thus upon hearing of Apel's marriage, Bishop Conrad privately annulled the marriage and admonished Apel to confess his sin, to return his putative wife to her cloister, and to resume his clerical duties. Apel refused, insisting that his marriage, though secretly contracted, was valid. Unconvinced, the bishop privately indicted Apel for a canon law crime and temporarily suspended him from office. Apel offered a spirited defense of his conduct in a frank letter to the bishop.

Bishop Conrad, in response, had Apel publicly indicted in his own bishop's court, for breach of holy orders and the oath of celibacy, and for defiance of his episcopal dispensation and injunction. In a written response, Apel adduced

---

6. The case is recounted in Theodor Muther, *Doctor Johann Apell: Ein Beitrag zur Geschichte der deutschen Jurisprudenz* (Königsberg: Universitäts- Buch- und Steindruckerei, 1861), 14ff., 72ff. Excerpts from the pleadings and court records are included in *Politische Reichshandel: Das ist allerhand gemeine Acten Regimentssachen und weltlichen Discursen* (Frankfurt am Main: Johan Bringern, 1614), 785–795, and in Johann Apel, *Defensio Johannis Apelli ad Episcopum Herbipolensem pro svo conivgio* (Wittenberg 1523). The quotes that follow in this section are from these two sources. See also Martin Luther's correspondence about the case in *D. Martin Luthers Werke: Kritische Gesamtausgabe, Briefwechsel*, 18 vols. (Weimar: Hermann Böhlaus Nachfolger, 1930–1985), 2:353; 354; 357 (hereafter, WA Br).

conscience and Scripture in his defense, much like Luther had done two years before at the Diet of Worms. "I have sought only to follow the dictates of conscience and the Gospel," Apel insisted, not to defy episcopal authority and canon law. Scripture and conscience condone marriage for fit adults as "a dispensation and remedy against lust and fornication. My wife and I have availed ourselves of these godly gifts and entered and consummated our marriage in chasteness and love."

Contrary to Scripture, Apel continued, the church's canon law commands celibacy for clerics and monastics. This introduces all manner of impurity among them. "Don't you see the fornication and the concubinage?" Apel implored Conrad. "Don't you see the defilement and the adultery in your bishopric—with brothers spilling their seed upon the ground, upon each other, and upon many a maiden whether single or married." My alleged sin and crime of breaking "this little man-made rule of celibacy," Apel insisted, "is very slight when compared to these sins of fornication against the law of the Lord, which you, excellent father, will cover and condone if the payment is high enough." "The Word of the Lord is what will judge between you and me," Apel declared to the Bishop, "and such Word commands my acquittal."

Bishop Conrad took the case under advisement. Apel took his cause to the budding Lutheran community. He sought support for his claims from Luther, Melanchthon, and other Protestant leaders who had already spoken against celibacy and monasticism. He published his remarks at trial adorned with a robust preface by Martin Luther. This became an instant hot seller.

Shortly after publication of the tract, Bishop Conrad had Apel arrested and put in prison, pending further proceedings. Apel's family pleaded in vain with the bishop to release him. The local civil magistrate twice mandated that Apel be released, again to no avail. Jurists and councilmen wrote letters of support. Even Emperor Charles V sent a brief letter urging the bishop not to protract Apel's harsh imprisonment in violation of imperial law, but to try him and release him if found innocent.

Apel was tried three months later and was found guilty of several violations of the canon law and of heretically participating in "Luther's damned teachings." He was defrocked—literally his clerical robes were torn from him in open court—and he was excommunicated and evicted from the community. Thereafter Apel made his way to Wittenberg where, at the urging of Luther and others, he was appointed to the law faculty at the University. Two years later, Apel served as one of the four witnesses to the marriage of ex-monk Martin Luther to ex-nun Katharina von Bora.

Catholic vs. Protestant Views of Celibacy and Marriage

Bishop Conrad's position in the Apel case was in full compliance with the prevailing Catholic theology and canon law of marriage and celibacy, in place since the twelfth century.[7] The medieval church regarded marriage as "a duty

---

7. See a detailed account of medieval marriage theology and law, with detailed citations to the literature, in Witte, *From Sacrament to Contract*, chap. 4.

for the sound and a remedy for the sick," in St. Augustine's famous phrase. Marriage was a creation of God allowing man and woman to become "two in one flesh" in order to "be fruitful and multiply" (Gen 1:28; 2:24). Since the fall into sin, marriage had also become a remedy for lust, a channel to direct one's natural passion to the service of the community and the church. When contracted between Christians, marriage was also a sacrament, a symbol of the indissoluble union between Christ and the church. As a sacrament, marriage fell within the social hierarchy of the church and was subject to its jurisdiction, its law-making power. The church developed a comprehensive canon law of marriage after the twelfth century, administered by a vast hierarchy of church courts and officials throughout Western Christendom, stretching from Italy to Ireland, Portugal to Poland.

The church did not regard marriage as its most exalted estate, however. Though a sacrament and a sound way of Christian living, marriage was not considered to be so spiritually edifying. Marriage was a remedy for sin, not a recipe for righteousness. Marriage was considered subordinate to celibacy, propagation less virtuous than contemplation, marital love less wholesome than spiritual love. Clerics, monastics, and other servants of the church were to forgo marriage as a condition for ecclesiastical service. Those who could not were not worthy of the church's holy orders and offices.

This prohibition on marriage, first universally imposed on clerics and monastics by the First Lateran Council of 1123, was defended with a whole arsenal of complex arguments. The most common arguments were based on St. Paul's statements in 1 Corinthians 7. In this famous passage, Paul did allow that it was "better to marry than to burn" with lust. But Paul also said that it was better to remain single than to marry or remarry. "It is well for a man not to touch a woman," he wrote. For those who are married "will experience distress in this life." It is best for you to remain without marriage "to promote good order and unhindered devotion to the Lord." (1 Cor 7:1, 28, 35). These biblical passages, heavily glossed by the early Church Fathers, provided endless medieval commentaries on and commendations of celibacy. They were buttressed by newly discovered classical Greek and Roman writings extolling celibacy for the contemplative as well as by the growing medieval celebration of the virginity of Mary as a model for pious Christian living.

Various philosophical arguments underscored the superiority of the celibate clergy to the married laity. It was a commonplace of medieval philosophy to describe God's creation as hierarchical in structure—a vast chain of being emanating from God and descending through various levels and layers of reality down to the smallest particulars. In this great chain of being, each creature found its place and its purpose. Each institution found its natural order and hierarchy. It was thus simply the nature of things that some persons and institutions were higher on this chain of being, some lower. It was the nature of things that some were closer and had more ready access to God, and some were further away and in need of mediation in their relationship with God. Readers of Dante's *Divine Comedy* will recognize this chain of being theory at work in Dante's vast hierarchies of hell, purgatory, and paradise.

This chain of being theory was one basis for medieval arguments for the superiority of the clergy to the laity. Clergy were simply higher on this chain of being, laity lower. The clergy were called to higher spiritual activities in the realm of grace, the laity to lower temporal activities in the realm of nature. The clergy were thus distinct from the laity in their dress, in their language, and in their livings. They were exempt from earthly obligations, such as paying civil taxes or serving in the military. They were immune from the jurisdiction of civil courts. And they were foreclosed from the natural activities of the laity, such as those of sex, marriage, and family life. These natural, corporal activities were literally beneath the clergy in ontological status and thus formally foreclosed. For a cleric or monastic to marry or to have sex was thus in a real sense to act against nature (*contra naturam*).

By contrast, Johann Apel's arguments with Bishop Conrad anticipated a good deal of the Lutheran critique of this traditional teaching of marriage and celibacy. Like their Catholic brethren, the sixteenth-century Lutheran reformers taught that marriage was created by God for the procreation of children and for the protection of couples from sexual sin. But, unlike their Catholic brethren, the reformers rejected the subordination of marriage to celibacy. We are all sinful creatures, Luther and his followers argued. Lust has pervaded the conscience of everyone. Marriage is not just an option, it is a necessity for sinful humanity. For without it, a person's distorted sexuality becomes a force capable of overthrowing the most devout conscience. A person is enticed by nature to concubinage, prostitution, masturbation, voyeurism, and sundry other sinful acts. "You cannot be without a [spouse] and remain without sin," Luther thundered from his Wittenberg pulpit. You will test your neighbor's bed unless your own marital bed is happily occupied and well used.[8]

"To spurn marriage is to act against God's calling . . . and against nature's urging," Luther continued. The calling of marriage should be declined only by those who have received God's special gift of continence. "Such persons are rare, not one in a thousand [later he said one hundred thousand] for they are a special miracle of God."[9] The Apostle Paul has identified this group as the permanently impotent and the eunuchs; very few others can claim such a unique gift.

This understanding of marriage as a protection against sin undergirded the Lutheran reformers' bitter attack on traditional rules of mandatory celibacy. To require celibacy of clerics, monks, and nuns, the reformers believed, was beyond the authority of the church and ultimately a source of great sin. Celibacy was a gift for God to give, not a duty for the church to impose. It was for each individual, not for the church, to decide whether he or she had received this gift. By demanding monastic vows of chastity and clerical vows of celibacy, the church was seen to be intruding on Christian freedom and contradicting Scripture, nature, and common sense. By institutionalizing and encouraging celibacy the church was seen to prey on the immature and the uncertain. By holding out food, shelter, security, and economic opportunity, the monasteries enticed poor and needy parents to oblate their minor children to a life of celibacy, regardless of whether it suited their natures. Mandatory celibacy, Luther taught, was hardly a prerequisite to true clerical service of God. Instead it led to

8. *LW* 54:31.
9. *LW* 28:27–31; *LW* 45:18–22.

"great whoredom and all manner of fleshly impurity and . . . hearts filled with thoughts of women day and night."[10]

Furthermore, to impute higher spirituality and holier virtue to the celibate contemplative life was, for the reformers, contradicted by the Bible. The Bible teaches that each person must perform his or her calling with the gifts that God provides. The gifts of continence and contemplation are but two among many, and are by no means superior to the gifts of marriage and child-rearing. Each calling plays an equally important, holy, and virtuous role in the drama of redemption, and its fulfillment is a service to God. Luther concurred with the Apostle Paul that the celibate person "may better be able to preach and care for God's word." But, he immediately added: "It is God's word and the preaching which makes celibacy—such as that of Christ and of Paul—better than the estate of marriage. In itself, however, the celibate life is far inferior."[11]

Not only is celibacy no better than marriage, Luther insisted; clergy are no better than laity. To make this argument cogent, Luther had to counter the medieval chain of being theory that placed celibate clergy naturally above married laity. Luther's answer lay in his complex theory of the separation of the earthly kingdom and the heavenly kingdom.[12] God has ordained two kingdoms or realms in which humanity is destined to live, the earthly kingdom and the heavenly kingdom. The earthly kingdom is the realm of creation, of natural and civic life, where a person operates primarily by reason and law. The heavenly kingdom is the realm of redemption, of spiritual and eternal life, where a person operates primarily by faith and love. These two kingdoms embrace parallel forms of righteousness and justice, government and order, truth and knowledge. They interact and depend upon each other in a variety of ways. But these two kingdoms ultimately remain distinct. The earthly kingdom is distorted by sin, and governed by the Law. The heavenly kingdom is renewed by grace and guided by the Gospel. A Christian is a citizen of both kingdoms at once and invariably comes under the distinctive government of each. As a heavenly citizen, the Christian remains free in his or her conscience, called to live fully by the light of the Word of God. But as an earthly citizen, the Christian is bound by law, and called to obey the natural orders and offices of household, state, and church that God has ordained and maintained for the governance of this earthly kingdom.

For Luther, the fall into sin destroyed the original continuity and communion between the Creator and the creation, the natural tie between the heavenly kingdom and the earthly kingdom. There was no series of emanations of being from God to humanity. There was no stairway of merit from humanity to God. There was no purgatory. There was no heavenly hierarchy. God is present in the heavenly kingdom, and is revealed in the earthly kingdom primarily through "masks." Persons are born into the earthly kingdom, and have access to the heavenly kingdom only through faith.

Luther did not deny the traditional view that the earthly kingdom retains its natural order, despite the fall into sin. There remained, in effect, a chain

10. LW 12:98.
11. LW 45:47.
12. See Witte, *Law and Protestantism*, chap. 3.

of being, an order in creation that gave each creature, especially each human creature and each social institution, its proper place and purpose in this life. But, for Luther, this chain of being was horizontal, not hierarchical. Before God, all persons and all institutions in the earthly kingdom were by nature equal. Luther's earthly kingdom was a flat regime, a horizontal realm of being, with no person and no institution obstructed or mediated by any other in access to and accountability before God.

Luther thus rejected traditional teachings that the clergy were higher beings with readier access to God and God's mysteries. He rejected the notion that clergy mediated the channel of grace between the laity and God—dispensing God's grace through the sacraments and preaching, and interceding for God's grace by hearing confessions, receiving charity, and offering prayers on behalf of the laity.

Clergy and laity were fundamentally equal before God and before all others, Luther argued, sounding his famous doctrine of the priesthood of all believers. All persons were called to be priests to their peers. Luther at once "laicized" the clergy and "clericized" the laity. He treated the traditional "clerical" office of preaching and teaching as just one other vocation alongside many others that a conscientious Christian could properly and freely pursue. He treated all traditional "lay" offices as forms of divine calling and priestly vocation, each providing unique opportunities for service to one's peers. Preachers and teachers in the church must carry their share of civic duties and pay their share of civil taxes just like everyone else. And they should participate in earthly activities such as marriage and family life just like everyone else.

The Goods and Gifts of Marriage in Lutheran Thought

Virtually all adults, clerical and lay alike, are called to marriage, Luther argued, because this institution offers two of the most sublime gifts that God has accorded to humanity—the gift of marital love, and the gift of children.

Luther wrote exuberantly about this first gift. "Over and above all [other loves] is marital love," he wrote. "Marital love drives husband and wife to say to each other, 'It is you whom I want, not what is yours. I want neither your silver nor your gold. I want neither. I want only you. I want you in your entirety, or nor at all.' All other kinds of love seek something other than the loved one: this kind wants only to have the beloved's own self completely. If Adam had not fallen, the love of bride and groom would have been the loveliest thing."[13] "There's more to [marriage] than a union of the flesh," Luther wrote, although he considered sexual intimacy and warmth to be essential to the flourishing of marriage. "There must [also] be harmony with respect to patterns of life and ways of thinking."[14]

> The chief virtue of marriage [is] that spouses can rely upon each other and with confidence entrust everything they have on earth to each other, so that it is as safe with one's spouse as with oneself. . . . God's Word is actually

13. WA 2:167; see also WA 13:11; WA 17/2:350ff.
14. WA TR 5, #5524; LW 54:444.

inscribed on one's spouse. When a man looks at his wife as if she were the only woman on earth, and when a woman looks at her husband as if he were the only man on earth; yes, if no king or queen, not even the sun itself sparkles any more brightly and lights up your eyes more than your own husband or wife, then right there you are face to face with God speaking. God promises to you your wife or husband, actually gives your spouse to you, saying: "The man shall be yours; the woman shall be yours. I am pleased beyond measure! Creatures earthly and heavenly are jumping for joy." For there is no jewellery more precious than God's Word; through it you come to regard your spouse as a gift of God and, as long as you do that, you will have no regrets.[15]

Luther did not press these warm sentiments to the point of denying the traditional leadership of the *paterfamilias* within the marital household. Luther had no modern egalitarian theory of marriage. But Luther also did not betray these warm sentiments to the point of becoming the grim prophet of patriarchy, paternalism, and procreation *über alles* that some modern critics make him out to be. For Luther, love was a necessary and sufficient good of marriage. He supported marriages between loving couples, even those between young men and older women beyond child-bearing years or between couples who knew full well that they could have no children.[16] He stressed repeatedly that husband and wife were spiritual, intellectual, and emotional "partners," each to have regard and respect for the strengths of the other. He called his own wife Katharina respectfully "Mr. Katy" and said more than once of her: "I am an inferior lord, she the superior; I am Aaron, she is my Moses."[17] He repeatedly told husbands and wives alike to tend to each other's spiritual, emotional, and sexual needs and to share in all aspects of child-rearing and household maintenance—from changing their children's diapers to helping their children establish their own new homes when they had grown up.[18]

In addition to the divine gift of love, marriage also sometimes bestowed on the couple the divine gift of children. Luther treated procreation as an act of co-creation and co-redemption with God. He wished for all marital couples the joy of having children, not only for their own sakes but for the sake of God as well. Childrearing, he wrote,

is the noblest and most precious work, because to God there can be nothing dearer than the salvation of souls. . . . [Y]ou can see how rich the estate of marriage is in good works. God has entrusted to its bosom souls begotten of its own body on whom it can lavish all manner of Christian works. Most certainly, father and mother are apostles, bishops, [and] priests to their children, for it is they who make them acquainted with the Gospel. See therefore how good and great is God's work and ordinance.[19]

15. WA 34:52,5–9; 12–21 using the translation of Scott Hendrix, "Luther on Marriage," *LQ* 14/3 (2000): 335–350. See also *LW* 31:351ff.

16. See, e.g., WA TR 4, #5212; *LW* 2:301ff.

17. Quoted by Steven E. Ozment, *Ancestors: The Loving Family in Old Europe* (Cambridge, Ma: Harvard University Press, 2001), 36–37. See the interesting portrait of Katharina and other Reformation women in Kirsi Stjerna, *Women and the Reformation* (Malden, Ma: Blackwell, 2009).

18. *LW* 45:39ff.

19. *LW* 45:46.

This last image—of parents serving as priests to their children—was a new and further application of the familiar Protestant doctrine of the priesthood of all believers. It added further concreteness to the Protestant effort to soften the hard medieval distinction between a superior clergy and a lower laity: all persons are priests to their peers, and all parents are priests to their children, called to care for them in body, mind, and soul alike.

The education of children fell not only to parents. The Lutheran reformers were pioneers in creating public schools for the religious and civic education of all children, and producing a welter of catechisms, textbooks, and household manuals to assist in the same. For the reformers, each child was called to a unique Christian vocation, and it was the responsibility of the parent, priest, and prince alike to ensure that each child was given the chance to discern his or her special gifts and prepare for the particular vocation that best suited those gifts. This teaching drove the creation of public schools in early modern Protestant lands—Lutheran, Calvinist, and Anglican alike. It added a crucial public dimension to the parents' private procreation and nurture of their children. Philip Melanchthon, the so-called "teacher of Germany," called the public school a "civic seminary" designed to allow families, churches, and states alike to cooperate in imbuing both civic learning and spiritual piety in children.[20]

Marriage Is Not a Sacrament but a Social Estate

While marriage was a gift of God for the couple and their children, for the Lutheran reformers marriage was a social institution of the earthly kingdom, not a sacrament of the heavenly kingdom. Marriage was, in Luther's words, "a natural order," "an earthly institution," "a secular and outward thing."[21] "No one can deny that marriage is an external, worldly matter, like clothing and food, house and property, subject to temporal authority, as the many imperial laws enacted on the subject prove."[22]

To be sure, Luther agreed, marriage can symbolize the union of Christ with his church, as St. Paul wrote in Eph 5:32. The sacrifices that husband and wife make for each other and for their children can express the sacrificial love of Christ on the cross. A "blessed marriage and home" can be "a true church, a chosen cloister, yes, a paradise" on earth.[23] But these analogies and metaphors do not make marriage a sacrament on the order of Baptism and the Eucharist. Sacraments are God's gifts and signs of grace ensuring Christians of the promise of redemption which is available only to those who have faith.[24] Marriage carries no such promise and demands no such faith. "[N]owhere in Scripture," writes Luther, "do we read that anyone would receive the grace of God by getting married; nor does the rite of matrimony contain any hint that the ceremony is of divine institution."[25] Scripture teaches that only Baptism and the Eucharist

20. See Witte, *Law and Protestantism*, chap. 7.
21. *LW* 21:93.
22. *LW* 46:265.
23. *LW* 44:85.
24. See *LW* 36:11; *TC* 310ff.
25. *LW* 36:92–93.

(and perhaps penance, the early Luther allowed) confer this promise of grace. All other so-called sacraments are "mere human artifices" that the Church has created to augment its legal powers and to fill its coffers with court fees and fines.[26]

The Catholic Church, Luther continued, has based its entire sacramental theology and canon law of marriage on a misunderstanding of Eph 5:32: "This is a great mystery (*mysterion*), and I am applying it to Christ and the church." The Greek term *mysterion* in this passage means "mystery," not "sacrament." St. Jerome had just gotten it wrong a millennium before when he translated the Greek word *mysterion* as the Latin word *sacramentum* and included that in his Latin translation of the Bible, the Vulgate. The Catholic Church has gotten it wrong ever since. In this famous Ephesians passage, Luther argued, St. Paul is simply describing the loving and sacrificial union of a Christian husband and wife as a reflection, an echo, a foretaste of the perfect mysterious union of Christ and his church. But that analogy does not make marriage a sacrament that confers sanctifying grace. The Bible is filled with analogies and parables that are designed to provide striking images to drive home lessons: "Faith is like a mustard seed": it grows even if tiny. "The kingdom of heaven is like yeast": it leavens even if you can't see it. Or "the Son of Man will come like a thief in the night." So be ready at all times for his return. And the examples go on. The marriage analogy is similar: "Marital love is like the union of Christ and the church." So be faithful and sacrificial to your spouse. Ephesians 5 is not divining a new sacrament here, Luther insisted, but driving home a lesson about marital love that much of the chapter has just explicated.[27]

Moreover, Luther argued, it made no sense for the Catholic Church to call marriage a sacrament without giving the clergy a role in this sacrament or providing a mandatory liturgy of preparation and celebration.[28] Neither the husband nor the wife are clerics—nor can they be if they seek marriage in the Catholic Church. Yet, regardless of what they know or intend, both perform a sacrament just by making a present promise to marry, or making a future promise to marry and then having sex. And that purported sacramental act binds them for life. This just piles fiction upon self-serving fiction, Luther concluded. The Catholic Church forbids its clergy to marry because it is a natural association beneath them in dignity. Yet it pretends that marriage is a sacrament even if the clergy do not participate in its formation or if the marriage does not take place in the church. "This is an insult to the sacraments," Luther charged. The church's "real goal is jurisdictional not theological" in declaring marriage to be a canonical sacrament. There is no valid biblical or theological basis for this claim.[29]

Denying the sacramental quality of marriage, had dramatic implications for how a marriage should be formed, maintained, and dissolved. First, the Lutheran reformers argued, there should no formal religious or baptismal tests for marriage. Parties would certainly do well to marry within the faith for the

26. LW 36:97ff.
27. LW 36:97ff.
28. The Catholic Council of Trent added these clerical and liturgical requirements for Christian marriage only in 1563, well after Luther's passing.
29. LW 36:97.

sake of themselves and their children. But this is not an absolute condition. Religious differences should not be viewed as an impediment to a valid marriage that can lead to annulment, but a challenge to be more faithful within marriage and to induce proper faith in each other.

> [M]arriage is an outward, bodily thing, like any other worldly undertaking. Just as I may eat, drink, sleep, walk, ride with, buy from, speak to, and deal with a heathen, Jew, Turk, or heretic, so I may also marry and continue in wedlock with him. Pay no attention to the precepts of those fools who forbid it. You will find plenty of Christians—and indeed the greater part of them— who are worse in their secret unbelief than any Jew, heathen, Turk, or heretic. A heathen is just as much a person—God's good creation—as St. Peter, St. Paul, and St. Lucy, not to speak of slack or spurious Christians.[30]

Second, because marriage was not a sacrament, divorce and remarriage were licit, and sometimes even necessary. To be sure, the reformers, like their Catholic brethren, insisted that marriages should be stable and presumptively indissoluble. But this presumption could be overcome if one of the essential marital goods were chronically betrayed or frustrated. If there were a breach of marital love by one of the parties—by reason of adultery, desertion, or cruelty—the marriage was broken. The innocent spouse who could not forgive this breach could sue for divorce and remarry. If there were a failure of procreation—by reason of sterility, incapacity, or disease discovered shortly after the wedding—the marriage was also broken. Those spouses who could not reconcile themselves to this condition could end the marriage and at least the healthy spouse could marry another. And if there were a failure of protection from sin—by reason of frigidity, separation, desertion, cruelty, or crime—the marriage was again broken. If the parties could not be reconciled to regular cohabitation and consortium, they could divorce and seek another marriage.[31] In each instance, divorce was painful, sinful, and sad, and it was a step to be taken only after ample forethought and counsel. But it was a licit, and sometimes an essential, step to take.

Third, because marriage was not a sacrament, it also did not belong primarily within the jurisdiction of the church, that is, within the law-making authority of the clergy, consistory, and congregation. Luther underscored this several times in his sermons and instructions to fellow pastors:

> First, we [pastors] have enough work to do in our proper office. Second, marriage is outside the church, is a civil matter, and therefore should belong to the government. Third, these cases [of marital dispute] have no limits, extend to the height, the breadth, and the depth, and produce many offences that bring disgrace to the gospel. . . . [W]e prefer to leave this business to civil officials. The responsibility rests on them. Only in cases of conscience should pastors give counsel to godly people. Controversies and court cases [respecting marriage] we leave to the lawyers.[32]

---

30. *LW* 45:25.
31. WA Br 3:288–290; WA 15:558ff; Brecht, *Martin Luther*, 2:93–94.
32. WA TR 3, #4716; *LW* 54:363–364. See also WA TR 2, #3267; *LW* 54:194.

This did not mean that marriage was beyond the pale of God's authority and law, or that it should be beyond the influence and concern of the church. "It is sheer folly," Luther opined, to treat marriage as "nothing more than a purely human and secular state, with which God has nothing to do."[33] Questions of the formation, maintenance, and dissolution of marriage remain important public concerns, in which church officials and members must still play a key role.

First, Luther and other reformers took seriously the duty of pastoral counseling in marriage disputes that raised matters of conscience. As pastors themselves, many of the reformers issued scores of private letters to parishioners who came to them for counsel. Second, theologians and preachers were to communicate to magistrates and their subjects God's law and will for marriage and the family, and press for reforms when prevailing marital laws violated God's law. As a theologian, Luther published an ample series of pamphlets and sermons on questions of marriage and marriage law, sometimes wincing about how often his interventions were still needed. Third, to aid church members in their instruction and care, and to give notice to all members of society of a couple's marriage, the local parish church clerk was to develop a publicly-available marriage registry which all married couples would be required to sign. Fourth, the pastors and teachers of the local church were to instruct and discipline the marriages of its church members by pronouncing the public banns of betrothal, by blessing and instructing the couple at their public church wedding ceremony, and by punishing sexual turpitude or egregious violations of marriage law with public reprimands, bans, or, in serious cases, excommunication. Fifth, it was incumbent upon all members of the church to participate in the spiritual upbringing and counsel of all new children, as their collective baptismal vows required.

The Legal Reformation of Marriage and Family Life

While the church still had a role to play in the guidance and governance of marriage and family life, chief legal authority, the Lutheran reformers insisted, now lay with the Christian magistrate. The civil magistrate holds his authority from God. His will is to reflect God's will. His law is to reflect God's law. His rule is to respect God's creation ordinances and institutions. His civil calling is no less spiritual than that of the church. Marriage is thus still completely subject to godly law, but this law is now to be administered by the state, not the church.

This new Lutheran marital theology was something of a self-executing program of action for the creation of a new state law of the family in Lutheran lands. Just as the act of marriage came to signal a person's conversion to Protestantism, so the Marriage Act came to symbolize a political community's acceptance of Protestantism. Hundreds of new state marriage acts or ordinances emerged in Lutheran Germany and Scandinavia in the first decades of the Reformation.[34]

---

33. *LW* 21:95.
34. Most of these laws are collected in Amelius L. Richter, ed., *Die evangelischen Kirchenordnungen des sechszehnten Jahrhunderts*, repr. ed., 2 vols (Nieuwkoop: B. de Graaf, 1967); Emil Sehling, ed., *Die evangelischen Kirchenordnungen des 16. Jahrhunderts* (Leipzig: O.R. Reisland, 1902–1913), vols. 1–5, continued under the same title (Tübingen, 1955–), vols. 6–16. For overviews, see Hartwig Dieterich, *Das*

These new Protestant state laws took over a number of basic principles and rules of marriage inherited from medieval canon law, classical Roman law, and ancient Mosaic law. These laws assumed: that marriage was formed by a two-step process, first of engagement then of marriage; that a valid engagement and marriage contract required the mutual consent of a man and a woman who had the age, fitness, and capacity to marry each other; that marriage was a presumptively permanent union that triggered mutual obligations of care and support for the other spouse, their children, and their dependents; that marriage often involved complex exchanges of betrothal gifts and dowry and triggered presumptive rights of dower and inheritance for widow(er)s and legitimate children; that marriages could be annulled on the discovery of various impediments and upon litigation before a proper tribunal; and that in the event of dissolution, both parents remained responsible for the maintenance and welfare of their children, and the guilty party bore heavy financial obligations to the innocent spouse and children alike. All these assumptions remained common both to the new Protestant civil laws and to the traditional Catholic canon laws of marriage.

But the Lutheran Reformation also made crucial legal changes—beyond the critical shift of marital jurisdiction from the church to the state. Because the reformers rejected the subordination of marriage to celibacy, they rejected laws that forbade clerical and monastic marriage, that denied remarriage to those who had married a cleric or monastic, and that permitted vows of chastity to annul vows of marriage. Because they rejected the sacramental nature of marriage, the reformers rejected impediments of crime and heresy and prohibitions against divorce in the modern sense. Marriage was for them the community of the couple in the present, not their sacramental union in the life to come. Where that community was broken, for one of a number of specific reasons (such as adultery or desertion), the couple could sue for divorce. Because persons by their lustful natures were in need of God's remedy of marriage, the reformers removed numerous legal, spiritual, and consanguineous impediments to marriage not countenanced by scripture. Because of their emphasis on the godly responsibility of the prince, the pedagogical role of the church and the family, and the priestly calling of all believers, the reformers insisted that both marriage and divorce be public. The validity of marriage promises depended upon parental consent, witnesses, church consecration and registration, and priestly instruction. Couples who wanted to divorce had to announce their intentions in the church and community and petition a civil judge to dissolve the bond. In the process of marriage formation and dissolution, therefore, the couple was subject to God's law, as appropriated in the civil law, and to God's will, as revealed in the admonitions of parents, peers, and pastors.

On account of all these changes, marriages in Lutheran lands were easier to enter and exit. Family life was more public and participatory. Children were afforded greater rights and protections. Abused spouses were given a way out

---

protestantische Eherecht in Deutschland bis zur Mitte des 17. Jahrhunderts (Munich: Claudius Verlag, 1970); Roland Kirstein, *Die Entwicklung der Sponsalienlehre und der Lehre vom Eheschluss in der deutschen protestantischen Eherechtslehre bis zu J.H. Böhmer* (Bonn: H. Bouvier, 1966), 39ff; Walter Köhler, „Die Anfänge des protestantischen Eherechtes," *Zeitschrift der Savigny-Stiftung für Rechtsgeschichte: Kanonistische Abteilung* 74 (1941): 271.

of miserable homes. Divorcees and widow(er)s were given a second chance to start life anew. Ministers were married, rather than single, and better able to exemplify and implement the ideals of Christian marriage and sexual morality.

Many of the legal reforms of marriage introduced by the Lutheran reformers would remain at the heart of the Western legal tradition until the later twentieth century. But not all was sweetness and light in the Lutheran Reformation of domestic life. Yes, the Protestant reformers did outlaw monasteries and cloisters. But these reforms also ended the vocations of many single women and men, placing a new premium on the vocation of marriage. Ever since, adult Protestant singles have chafed in a sort of pastoral and theological limbo, objects of curiosity and pity, even suspicion and contempt. These are stigmata which adult singles still feel today in more conservative Protestant churches, despite the avalanche of new singles ministries to help them.

Yes, the Protestant reformers did remove clerics as mediators between God and the laity, in expression of St. Peter's teaching of the priesthood of all believers. But they ultimately interposed husbands between God and their wives, in expression of St. Paul's teaching of male headship within the home. Ever since, Protestant married women have been locked in a bitter struggle to gain fundamental equality both within the marital household and without—a struggle that has still not ended in more conservative Protestant communities today.

Luther's legal legacy therefore should be neither unduly romanticized nor unduly condemned. Those who champion Luther as the father of liberty, equality, and fraternity might do well to remember his ample penchant for elitism, statism, and chauvinism. Those who see the reformers only as belligerent allies of repression should recognize that they were also benevolent agents of welfare. Prone as he was to dialectic reasoning, and aware as he was of the inherent virtues and vices of human achievements, Luther would likely have reached a comparable assessment.

10. Luther on Marriage, for Gay and Straight

Kirsi I. Stjerna

Introduction

Martin Luther knew all about marriage.[1] He wrote, "The estate of marriage and everything that goes with it in the way of conduct, works, and suffering is pleasing to God."[2] Luther was also fully aware of how complicated marriage could be on the human front; he even used the word "bitterness" to discuss different marriage-related issues.[3] Regardless of the Hollywood stories of happily-ever-after, and (thankfully) regardless of the reality shows exposing outrageously dysfunctional family systems, people continue to get married, our societies still respect marriage as a worthy institution and see it important to legalize and control it; the churches continue to be invested in the ceremonies celebrating marital unions, and in shaping people's thinking about marriage.

In this article, (1) I will first reflect on the urgency of the Lutheran church to move theologically to a place where our church affirms the marriage of gay and lesbian persons on par with the marriage of heterosexual persons. (2) I propose that the issue of gay and lesbian persons' "right to marry" and the church's joyful blessing of such unions are a "priority reformation concern" today, similar to the sixteenth-century Reformations' promotion of clergy marriage over the church's celibacy rules. (3) I will engage Luther's argumentation on marriage and sexuality and the nature of his reforms in order to build a foundation for continued constructive reforms regarding marriage matters today.

---

1. An earlier form of this article appeared as "Luther on Marriage—Considerations in Light of Contemporary Concerns," in *Theologie im Spannungsfeld von Kirche und Politik / Theology in Engagement with Church and Politics: Hans Schwarz zum 75. Geburtstag / Hans Schwarz on the Occasion of His 75th Birthday*, ed. Matthias Heesch et al. (Frankfurt *am*, Bern, Bruxelles, New York, Oxford, Warszawa, Wien: Peter Lang, 2014), 409–426. It it used here with permission of the publisher.

2. *Vom Ehelichen Leben* // *The Estate of Marriage* [1522] in *D. Martin Luthers Werke: Kritische Gesamtausgabe*, 69 vols. (Weimar: Hermann Böhlaus Nachfolger, 1883–), 10/2:294,30 (hereafter, WA); Jaroslav Pelikan and Helmut T. Lehmann, eds., *Luther's Works*, American ed., 55 vols. (Philadelphia, Pa: Fortress Press; Saint Louis, Mo: Concordia Publishing House, 1955–86), 45:38 (hereafter, *LW*).

3. *LW* 45:39, 42; WA 10/2:295,7–298,9.

Human Sexuality and the Right to Marry—a Reformation Concern[4]

Today the Lutheran church has an important responsibility to take an active role in the conversations on marriage and human sexuality.[5] These questions have wide-ranging ramifications in the life of the church, in Lutheran ethics, and in the quality of life for people in all walks of life. These questions have a theological background and a contemporary impact. How we deal theologically with the issue of human relations, sexuality, and human rights, in implicit and explicit ways, "translates" or communicates to the world the church's doctrine of God and grace. How we deal with these human issues is revealing and exposes the foundations of our faith and how we interpret the gospel of Jesus—and also how we chronically fail in this task.

The church and its theologians have important opportunities and challenges here with the current debates about marriage and sexuality. To name just a few: Informed by new theological hermeneutics as well as scientific advances, theologians can work towards a healthy and theologically sound contemporary Lutheran understanding of marriage and sexuality. The church and its theologians cannot stay apart from the conversations on what is considered "normal" and what is "biblical"; it is a tender, vital task to address the problems between the two considerations. The church has a stake in the hotly debated question of who has the right to marry. Theologians are called to task to reassess what exactly is the church's role in marriage matters today and properly advise the church to do its "job," with the support of theological and anthropological perspectives that employ both the Scriptures and the scientific wisdom of the day, and to do so with compassion for the people whose lives are affected by what the church and its theologians say. Most importantly, the church and its theologians have an ongoing responsibility to preach, teach, practice, and fight for the equality and inclusivity of all people, in the name of the gospel of Jesus that forms the core mission for both.

Of all the issues under debate today, if there is one painfully unresolved one that requires careful, critical, and compassionate attention on the one hand, and bold action on the other, the topic of human sexuality and the right to marry is it. This is a high-priority reformation concern today. Lutherans can hardly shy away from it or wish for it to go away. The necessity of becoming involved in this discussion that affects human lives on so many levels comes with the turf of being first of all Christian—Christians care—and second by being Lutheran—Lutherans protest and reform after Luther's own model of personal involvement in action and fiery preaching on the issues that matter.

---

4. The reflections here are my own, designed as an introduction to the main part of the presentation, our conversation with Luther. A substantial amount of outstanding literature is available on the matters of human sexuality, as well as Reformation history and theology, but due to space limitations and in order to preserve the focus, these references are omitted.

5. Soon after his installation Pope Franciscus made a comment about sexuality matters dominating public conversation while more important issues were being ignored, namely solidarity with the poor and the alleviation of human suffering caused by poverty and related tragedies. While the Pope's point is well taken, until there is equality for people in their sexual orientations as men and women, in their most fundamental way of being, the urgency to address sexuality matters continues, and one could actually hope for an amplification of the discussion until the desired results are achieved.

Reformation in Luther's model is more about the well-being of the people in their daily God-given lives, and realization of the liberating power of the gospel in every person's life, rather than protecting the church's traditional view points and hermeneutics. Luther models a way to re-read the Scriptures in a daring manner in new situations and in light of new information, and thus reshape the tradition and hermeneutics where changes are called for.

In the sixteenth-century Reformations the primary concern that set the wheels in motion was the spiritual well-being of people. The "right to marry" was on top of the list of "must issues" to tackle—right there with necessary reforms in education, welfare, and worship, small but crucial steps taken towards democracy and equality in many ways, we could say. As the Reformers saw it, the well-being of human beings was at stake with the mutilation of the gospel message, and their theological reforms prefaced and enforced societal changes in this regard. The right to marry and have children was considered an urgent gospel issue, a theologically pertinent matter to resolve. The reforms in these areas central to daily life reflected significant changes in theological foundation and scriptural hermeneutics. The same is true today: what we think and say about marriage reflect our fundamental theological outlooks on life and reveal how we read our Bibles.

Speaking from a Lutheran perspective and in light of the original motivations for the sixteenth-century Reformations, the bottom line is: if the theology we preach and teach ceases to promote the freedom and the integrity of every person's life and no longer supports people's lives in their varied Christian vocations, then it is time for serious institutional self-reflection and thesis nailing. We live in that kind of a moment.

While our views and policies regarding marriage could and should reflect a radically emancipatory "Lutheran liberation theology," the opposite is often true. Listening to the arguments made back and forth about marriage, about pre- or post-marital sex, about sexual education in public schools, or about the marriage of gay and lesbian persons, it seems that Lutherans are at times in danger of slipping into a kind of medieval Catholic mindset, honoring celibacy over sexual happiness, confusing a human contract and a love affair between two individuals with the sacraments of the Catholic church, imposing the church's authority in marriage matters in areas that belong to the jurisdiction of the state, and in general, expressing confused and ambivalent views of sexuality as inherently bad and sinful (especially so when outside marriage or heterosexual relations). In many ways and in many corners of the Lutheran world, attitudes—and education—about sexuality are plagued with taboos of all sorts.

At the same time we as a society are vulgarizing sexuality in many ways, making sexuality a vanity issue or a "common thing" stripped of privacy and sacredness. Our ambivalence toward sexuality manifests itself especially in how we teach—or fail to teach—our children, in schools and the church. It also shows in what we require from our rostered leaders: abstinence or marriage. The ELCA's "Vision and Expectations" document in this regard has the flavor of a medieval Catholic document, and it unfortunately can be used in ways that violate our sense of integrity and rights as human beings, and lead to lies when people are unable to meet the written or unwritten "higher" expectations. For the sake of comparison, the written and unwritten norms around the sexuality of unmarried rostered leaders in the USA—or in North American culture more generally—are not necessarily shared with other Lutheran constituencies and global communities, particularly in northern Europe and Scandinavia.

If the church continues to place an unreasonable burden on people and causes distress in their consciences by forcing people to live with lies, we will have something like a *deja vu* of the problems our Reformers addressed already centuries ago. They explicitly rejected the celibacy requirement, preached positively on sexuality and the gift of marriage, and condemned the church's hurtful teachings that led people to live with shame in the dimension of life that was meant to be holy, enriching, and blessed by God.

Luther on Marriage as an External, Worldly Matter[6]

What can Luther teach us today? He wrote in 1530 in his *On Marriage Matters*:

> No one can deny that marriage is an external, worldly matter, like clothing and food, house and property, subject to temporal authority, as the many imperial laws enacted on the subject prove. Neither do I find any example in the New Testament where Christ or the apostles concerned themselves with such matters, except where they touched upon consciences, as did St. Paul in I Corinthians 7 [:1–24], and especially where unbelievers or non-Christians are concerned, for it is easy to deal with these and all matters among Christians or believers. But with non-Christians, with which the world is filled, you cannot move forward or backward without the sharp edge of the temporal sword. And what use would it be if we Christians set up a lot of laws and decisions, as long as the world is not subject to us and we have no authority over it? Therefore I simply do not wish to become involved in such matters at all and beg everyone not to bother me with them…. But since you persist so strongly in asking instruction of me, not only for yourselves and your office, but also for your rulers who desire advice from you in these matters, and ask me what I for my part would do if I were asked for advice—especially since your rulers complain that it is burdensome to their consciences to render decisions according to the spiritual or papal laws, which in such cases are unreliable and often run counter to all propriety, reason, and justice, and since the imperial laws too are ineffective in these matters—I will not withhold my

6. This article focuses solely on Luther's works, apart from explicit conversation with secondary sources on the topic, the rationale being to build an argument with Luther's own words concerning the specific questions at stake. The primary sources are: *Ein Sermon von dem ehelichen Stand // Sermon on the Estate of Marriage* [1519] (LW 44:7–14; WA 2:166–171); *Vom Ehelichen Leben // The Estate of Marriage* [1522] (LW 45:[13] 17–49; WA 10/2:275–304); *De captivitate babylonica ecclesiae // On the Babylonian Captivity of the Church* [1520] (LW 36:92–106 [= pp. on marriage]; WA 6:550,21–553,21); *Ein Traubüchlein für die einfältigen Pfarrherr // A Marriage Booklet for Simple Pastors* [1529], with Small Catechism, in *The Book of Concord*, ed. Robert Kolb and Timothy Wengert (Minneapolis, Mn: Fortress Press, 2000), 367–371; (LW 53:110–115; WA 30/3:74–80); *Von den Ehesachen // On Marriage Matters* [1530] (LW 46:265–320; WA 30/3:205–248); *De votis monasticis Martini Lutheri iudicium // Judgment on Monastic Vows* [1521] (LW 44:251–400; WA 8:573–669). For treatments on the topic in English, from different angles, see: Christopher Boyd Brown, "The Reformation of Marriage in Lutheran Wedding-Preaching," *SRR* 15/2 (2013): 1–25; Scott Hendrix, "Luther on Marriage," in *Harvesting Martin Luther's Reflections on Theology, Ethics, and the Church*, ed. Timothy Wengert, LQB (Grand Rapids, Mi: Eerdmans, 2003), 169–189; John Witte Jr., "The Mother of All Earthly Laws: The Lutheran Reformation of Marriage," *SRR* 15/2 (2013): 26–43 [and this volume pp. 111–125]; John Witte Jr., *From Sacrament to Contract: Marriage, Religion, and Law in the Western Tradition* (Louisville, Ky: WJK, 1997).

opinion from you. Yet I give it with this condition. . . . That I want to do this not as a judge, official, or regent, but by way of advice, such as I would in good conscience give as a special service to my good friends. So, if anyone wishes to follow this advice of mine, let him [her] do so on his [her] own responsibility; if he [she] does not know how to carry it out, let him [her] not seek shelter or refuge with me, or complain to me about it. . . . Let whoever is supposed to rule or wants to rule be the ruler; I want to instruct and console consciences, and advise them as much as I can.[7]

In sum, Luther addressed marriage as a "temporal realm" issue. He himself offered his advice specifically as a theologian and a pastor and a friend, with the concerns of conscience in mind. He considered this distinction important—only in this role would he get involved in discourse on an issue that belonged under the jurisdiction of the secular authority and law. He was also careful to make this point: he was offering his words on the matter because people had "dragged" him into the debates (and uttered opinions as if from his mouth and pen, which really infuriated Luther, every time it happened). For those who solicited his advice, they could have it here. For those who would ignore his first-hand arguments, they better not involve his name at all then.

It is curious that Luther wrote about marriage with significant force already before he was married himself (e.g., he preached on marriage in 1519). He was unusually knowledgeable for a bachelor, and he boldly thought outside the box. This was mostly due to his observations in his pastoral role and in friendships, and his first-hand reading of the human stories in the Bible. He actually became the leading voice for Protestant theology on marriage, as well as a kind of "Dear Abby" or "Dr. Phil" in marriage matters in his little town of Wittenberg.[8] He did it boldly, but with a healthy dose of holy terror as well.

"How I dread preaching on the estate of marriage!" wrote Luther in his 1522 treatise, *The Estate of Marriage*. "I am reluctant to do it because I am afraid if I once get really involved in the subject it will make a lot of work for me and for others." We know what he means! "But timidity is of no help in an emergency, I must proceed. I must try to instruct poor bewildered consciences, and take up the matter boldly."[9]

What was Martin Luther's significant offering in the matter, then? In a nutshell, he proposed that marriage is a human contract and a matter of the state, and as such it serves the well-being of the polis/human community. Luther did not wish to abolish the tradition of marriage but rather to uphold it as an essentially "good thing" that should be used, taught, and practiced with Christian integrity. He wished to purge the institution of marriage from false, onerous teachings that cast marriage and those who marry in an unwarranted negative light, and that prevented people from marrying regardless of their quite normal (i.e., created) human desires.

---

7. *LW* 46:265–267; WA 30/3:205,12–32 (printed in Wittenberg in 1530, then again in 1541, and twice more). Luther then concludes his introduction: "Well then, let us in God's name get down to the business at hand and summarize these opinions and this advice of mine in several articles and points, so that they may be understood and retained that much the better." (*LW* 46:267; WA 30/3:206,35–37).

8. See *LW* 46:265–320; WA 30/3:205–248.

9. *LW* 45:17; WA 10/2:275,2–4,8–9.

Most significantly, Luther argued (1) that the marriage contract and its recognition was an issue of the state, and (2) that it was a matter between two persons and—preferably—their families. Luther made it clear that the laws of the
land are to be followed and that the church has no business in confusing things.

In his *Marriage Booklet for Simple Pastors*, Luther writes: "For this reason,
because weddings and the marriage are worldly affairs, it behooves those of
us who are 'spirituals' or ministers of the church in no way to order or direct
anything regarding marriage, but instead to allow every city and land to continue their own customs that are now in use. . . . All these and similar things
I leave to the prince and town council to create and arrange as they want. It
is no concern of mine."[10] This is an example of how the two kingdoms doctrine plays out: the legitimacy of marriage and rules circumscribing it, the
conditions for its validity, and rules about eligibility for it are affairs that the
government decides (be it prince, duchess, city council, or president.) This is
so because marriage is a human contract, a *coram hominibus* issue, and not a
sacrament. If it was a sacrament, the church would decide. If marriage was
a sacrament, Luther would not leave it up to the state or the ruler to decide
about these matters.[11]

Luther on Marriage as a Voluntary Union

In addition to declaring marriage as a contractual worldly issue, the other
important point Luther made (in continuity with the Catholic church's teaching) was to underscore the validity of marriage as a union between two people
who join together with a promise to one another. That is where the marital
bond is formed, between two persons willing to love and care for each other.
This meant that Luther, reluctantly, accepted secret marriages and betrothals.
Promises are to be honored! Ordinarily though, it is to everyone's benefit that
such promises are made in broad daylight and in the knowledge and with the
approval of families, and with no force, of course.[12] This consideration was to
the particular benefit of women who often lacked choices in the making of marriage contracts.

As we well know, as much as marriage is a matter between two individuals committing to one another, it is also a matter between families as well as
a public contract. Luther wrote that "marriage is a covenant of fidelity" and
"the estate of marriage consists essentially in consent having been freely and
previously given to another."[13] For the protection of the private intimate union,
and for the sake of accountability, Luther considered it crucial that marriage

---

10. *Marriage Booklet for Simple Pastors*, in Kolb and Wengert, *The Book of Concord*, 367–368.
11. Luther explains that the Catholic view of marriage as a sacrament derives from confusion in
understanding the word *mysterion* in the New Testament epistles (e.g., Eph 5:31–32; 1 Cor 4:1) as
always meaning *sacramentum*. See his arguments in *De captivitate babylonica ecclesiae // On the Babylonian Captivity of the Church* [1520] (LW 36:92–106, esp 92–96; WA 6:550,21–553,21). The definition of
sacraments and their proper use being one of the main reforms Luther preached, the re-definition of
marriage was among the priority issues.
12. LW 44:7–14; WA 2:166–171. Luther offers that parents should make it explicit to their children that
they do wish to advise their offspring, and also, "My advice is that parents persuade their children not
to be ashamed to ask their parents to find a marriage partner for them." (LW 44:11; WA 2:169,20–24).
13. LW 44:10–11; WA 2:168,38; 169,11–13.

promises be given in public and with the approval of families or guardians. The validity of the marriage rests on the laws, which are public, and by marrying in public, the couple enters the protective orbit of the common law. The marriage, being at its heart a covenant between two willing hearts, serves both the individuals and the society, in accordance with the laws set for the protection of everyone concerned.

Luther gave specific advice on the matter (based on his theology and in light of the laws of the land):

1. There should be no secret engagements; they lead to no good![14]
2. If one does become engaged secretly, while being engaged to another in public, as a rule "public engagements take precedence over secret engagements."[15]
3. If one has twice made a promise to marry, then of the two public engagements, the first one is valid, and a punishment should be imposed on account of the second.[16]
4. Once engaged, "Intercourse with another man or woman after engagement is adultery" and punishable. Thus monogamy begins from the promise to spend life together.[17]
5. Forced engagements are not valid; parents should be reasonable here with their children.[18]

What should the church's role in these matters be? The church's role is to pray, bless, and support people in this holy estate. It is the church's role to teach and model to young people about marriage. The church's role is also to offer a ritual of celebration to mark the union and to explicitly support people in their new life in this particular Christian estate. As it is today, so also in Luther's time people wanted church ceremonies and found it meaningful to celebrate the beginning of the couple's life together in the church and with its public blessing.

Luther wrote in the *Marriage Booklet for Simple Pastors*, "However, when people request of us to bless them in front of the church or in the church, to pray over them, or even to marry them, we are obligated to do this."[19] We are obligated to do this, Luther said. That is an interesting statement—obligated why? Because that is what the church does; it walks with people. By its participation and with its rituals, the church both teaches and enforces the experience of the holy in marriage in particular, and also promises to support the couple's holy living in their marriage.[20]

---

14. LW 46:267, 268–280; WA 30/3:207,1–2 (30/3:207,15–217,32).
15. LW 46:267, 281–289; WA 30/3:207,3–4 (30/3:217,33–224,6).
16. LW 46:267, 289–297; WA 30/3:207,5–7 (30/3:224,7–230,15).
17. LW 46:267, 297–304; WA 30/3:207,8–10 (30/3:230,16–236.6).
18. LW 46:268, 303–310; WA 30/3:207:12–13 (30/3:236:7–240,9).
19. *Marriage Booklet*, in Kolb and Wengert, *The Book of Concord*, 368, 2–4.
20. Considering Lutheran marriage traditions today: The church's role has little if anything to do with the validity of the marital union in the eyes of the law, unless an arrangement is in place with the state that gives that authority to the clergy/church on behalf of the state. In some contexts the clergy serves as the official whose "officiating" and signature actually does make the marriage legal; but the church functions in that capacity only as far as the state authorizes it. This has been the case, e.g., in

Luther on the Holiness of Marriage and Sexuality

Marriage as a Christian estate according to Luther is serious business, and people need the church's help and guidelines for living in that vocation honorably. Holier than the vocation of the monastics and ascetics, marriage is important not only for the society's well-being; it entails God's holy intent on a larger scale. Marriage provides a structured platform for holy living, and in marital love one can experience and express sacredness in a unique way. Christians are to excel and model for others this holy vocation. The starting point for this is the public mutual agreement between two persons, bound in accordance with the laws of the state.[21]

Using the Bible as his primary sourcebook, Luther taught that the marital holy union and the honorable estate is created and instituted for the benefit of both men and women. Reading the book of Genesis (particularly chapters 1–2), Luther argued that God deemed it not good for the human being to be alone, thus God created partners, made of the same flesh and bone.[22] Men and women, created of the same flesh, by the same God, are commanded to love one another with the passion with which Christ loves the church, and to love their partner as they love their own bodies. Luther appreciated love, including physical love, as an essential force in human relations; he saw an explicit divine intent for human beings to love each other physically.[23]

It is important to notice that Luther's thinking about marriage does not start with sin. Marriage does not exist originally because of sin. Marriage continues regardless of sin. Post-fall, however, marriage involves sin just as is the case with other dimensions of life; the desire that was to unite lovers blissfully in paradise has now the potential to get out of whack and drag one with wrong impulses and in the wrong directions. Nevertheless, marriage is in God's orbit.[24] Luther wrote, "Intercourse is not without sin; but God excuses it by his [God's] grace because the estate of marriage is his [God's] work, and he [God] preserves in and through the sin all that good which he [God] has implanted and blessed in marriage."[25] Sexuality and marriage, thus, should not be considered in any way more tainted than other dimensions in life.

More problematic is the temptation of human beings to make ill-advised decisions with their desire(s), and this makes them vulnerable. In addition, most devastating is the satanic awareness that comes to cloud human beings' sense of who they are, in themselves and in relation to others. What sin brought

---

Finland. In some other contexts, e.g., in Germany, couples visit the town hall or an equivalent for the binding of the union first, followed by a church ceremony.

21. Luther considers marriage as fundamentally God's doing, something God instituted, since God "brought husband and wife together, and ordained that they should beget children and care for them." For this reason, it is notable, Luther interprets from Gen 1:28 that "The estate of marriage and everything that goes with it in the way of conduct, works, and suffering is pleasing to God." (*LW* 45:38; WA 10/2:294,27–30).

22. *LW* 44:7–8; WA 2:166,15–26; *LW* 45:17–19; WA 10/2:275,11–277,10.

23. See Luther's reflection on different forms of love: false love (that seeks for money and possession), natural love (parental), and married love (bride's love): "She says, 'It is you I want, not what is yours: I want neither your silver nor your gold; I want neither. I want only you. I want you in your entirety, or not at all.'" (*LW* 44:9; WA 2:166,29–30; cf WA 2:177,22–168,9).

24. E.g., *LW* 44:7–8; WA 2:166,15–168,12.

25. *LW* 45:49; WA 10/2:304,9–12.

to human life, including intimate relations and sexual expression, was not primarily a disorderly "lust" (although that is part of the post-fall human experience as well) but the diabolically distorted awareness and sense of ugliness of what originally was created good, a diabolical false awareness that filled human beings with an ungodly shame about who they are as God's images.[26]

The good news in the midst of the devastating alterations in post-fall human experience is this word about marriage: "this is your comfort, that you know and believe how your estate is pleasing and blessed in God's eyes."[27] Also good news is this: that the fall and the sin that entered human life did not change God's original intent that people unite, love one another, and procreate. The fall did not change what was the beauty of the created design for the images of God as men and as women, as sexual beings: "And God saw all that God had made, and look, it was all very good."[28]

This is an important point to keep in mind: in creation, everything was very good. When talking about human beings, regardless of age, sex, orientation, etc., we are talking about God's images whom God considered as Good. What would be the alternative? Surely there are not misfits or accidents in God's kingdom?

With his biblically based theological arguments, Luther continued to remind his listeners of the godly design of human beings, created in two sexes, and commanded to unite, in flesh. Luther concluded that God had seen a formal union between people as a good thing, an estate and an arrangement that God from the beginning of time desired for human beings' own good and protection. God had chosen such a union as a channel for an intimate blessing. The intimacy in such a union not only resembled divine love for human but also allowed for God to channel grace through the most intimate of human relations—the sexual relationship.[29]

---

26. Luther explains this, e.g., when interpreting Genesis 3 and Adam and Eve's reactions post-fall: Adam and Eve became ashamed of their nudity—their created beautiful state—and their most glorious organs, and made girdles for themselves. They wished to hide from God and their mutual relationship became tainted with shame, and an ongoing struggle for power ensued. Luther greaves over this calamity when interpreting Gen 3:7:
Therefore this is an excellent description of the corruption which has taken the place of original righteousness and glory. It was glory for man not to realize that he was naked. Moreover, what can be a greater depravity than that the nakedness which formerly was a glory is now turned into the greatest disgrace? No one blushes because of healthy and sound eyes. Distorted or weak eyes are regarded as less becoming and bring on shame. So in the state of innocence it was most honorable to go about naked. Now, after sin, when Adam and Eve see that they are naked, they are made ashamed, and they look for girdles with which to cover their disgrace. (*LW* 1:165–166; WA 42:124).
Out of this corruption which followed because of sin there followed another evil. Adam and Eve not only were ashamed because of their nakedness, which previously was most honorable and the unique adornment of man, but they also made girdles for themselves for the purpose of covering, as though it were something most shameful, that part of the body which by its nature was most honorable and noble. What in all nature is nobler than the work of procreation? This work was assigned by God neither to the eyes nor to the mouth, which we regard as the more honorable parts of the body, but to that part which sin has taught us to call the pudendum and to cover, lest it be seen. (*LW* 1:167–168; WA 42:126).
27. *Marriage Booklet*, in Kolb and Wengert, *The Book of Concord*, 371,15–16.
28. Ibid. Also, with Gen 1:27 Luther writes: "So God created man ... male and female ... divided mankind into two classes, namely, male and female, or a he and a she. This was so pleasing to him [God] that he himself [God] called it a good creation [Gen 1:31]." (*LW* 45:17; WA 10/2:275,18).
29. *LW* 44:7–8; WA 2:166,15–168,12. Also, *LW* 45:17–18; WA 10/2:275,11–276,31. The other area where people come as close to the experience of divine love is childbirth and parenthood, per Luther's observation.

Marriage is about a particular reality and expression and experience of holiness in life, while it is not sacramental holiness or a blessing in the way baptism and the Lord's Supper convey grace. Marriage, to Luther, is in a different category as a unique channel for God's grace to support people and society *coram hominibus*. As said before, it is not the church's means of grace—only two rituals rise to that level with Luther, baptism and the supper—but God's grace can be understood to be channeled to people's lives through the holy intimacy of two people, "outside" the church and its means of grace.

Luther on Necessities with Our Bodies

In marriage, even after sin, Luther saw a godly, blessed way to live out human relations, and thus sexuality. In defense of God's good creation plan and the gospel that was to liberate people to live fully in that plan again post-fall, Luther attacked the many rulings of the church and impediments that unnecessarily prevented people from marrying and thus hindered people from experiencing the God-created possibilities for men and women. When Luther talked about the right and need to marry, he made a point about all of this being in the same category with the necessity of bowel movements and eating and drinking.[30]

Luther wrote,

> It is more than a command, namely, a divine ordinance [*werck*] which it is not our prerogative to hinder or ignore. Rather it is just as necessary as the fact that I am a man, and more necessary than sleeping and waking, eating and drinking, and emptying the bowels and bladder. It is a nature and disposition just as innate as the organs involved in it. Therefore, just as God does not command anyone to be a man or a woman but creates them the way they have to be, so he [God] does not command them to multiply but creates them so that they have to multiply. And whenever men [people] try to resists this, it remains irresistible nonetheless and goes its way through fornication, adultery, and secret sins, for this is a matter of nature and not of choice.[31]

Luther talked about men and women and their natural desire to be with another human being in a physical way. He spoke of heterosexual unions. With our modern understanding of human nature and sexuality, we do not need to be hetero-normative; we can expand Luther's arguments to appreciate the nature of maleness and femaleness and sexuality more broadly, more inclusively based on the realities we know. We can apply Luther's arguments on (1) the natural desire in all human beings, and (2) his respect of the goodness of God's creation in every image of God, male or female, gay or straight, and (3) we can develop these arguments towards a contemporary Lutheran position that honors the natural desires and needs of gay and lesbian persons just as well as heterosexual persons, and protects their rights for love, for marriage, and for parenthood (when so desired).

---

30. *LW* 45:17; WA 10/2:275,11–276,31.
31. *LW* 45:18; WA 10/2:276,21–31.

Drawing from Gen 1:27, Luther reminded his listeners that God created humanity in two classes, men and women. God saw God's creation as pleasing and called the creation good. *"Therefore, each one of us must have the kind of body God has created for us. I cannot make myself a woman nor can you make yourself a man; we do not have that power. But we are exactly as he [God] created us: I am a man and you a woman."* Luther continued,

> Moreover, he [God] wills to have his [God's] excellent handiwork honored as his [God's] divine creation, and not be despised. The man is not to despise or scoff at the woman or her body, nor the woman the man. But *each should honor the other's image and body as a divine and good creation that is well-pleasing to God* himself [Godself]. . . . Again, as it is not in your power not to be woman, so it is not your prerogative to be without a man. *For it is not a matter of free choice or decision but a natural and necessary thing.* Whatever is a man must have a woman and whatever is a woman must have a man.[32]

What if we were to read these words without assuming that women always love men and vice versa, or that we are all always comfortable in our bodies and sex and gender notions, or that the only reason for our sex and sexuality is to generate babies? The words from Genesis and Luther's interpretation of them have been used to argue that only men and women can and should marry, and that they should do so mostly for the purpose of procreation. These words have been used to argue that there are clearly only men with men's bodies and women with women's bodies and that the two opposites—always, and only— are attracted to one another.

We know better than Luther in this regard. It is not so simple to define who is a woman and who is a man and what is meant by these concepts. Today we know that the physical features we are born with are really only one dimension of what constitutes our gender and sexuality. We know that we have ways to "adjust" our bodily existence to better match our identity. We know we cannot change natural forces of love and attraction. What comes to us naturally, comes to us naturally and inevitably, in terms of whom we love and how we experience ourselves as men and as women. We "know" certain things naturally, we feel on the basis of who we are. We can be attracted to the opposite sex, or we can be attracted to the same sex, and this is how it is from birth, in a most natural way.

Today we know too much to just keep holding on to the old assumptions of what Christian theology says about human sexuality and marriage. We can be Luthers in our day and dare to reinterpret our central concepts and experiences, such as maleness and femaleness, sexuality and sexual/gendered realities. Luther advanced his times' conceptions of these things; in his footsteps, so can we.

Once we acknowledge Luther's good efforts, and as long as we understand the words "man" and "woman," "maleness" and "femaleness" with fluidity and breathing room, we can in many ways appreciate the essentials of Luther's teaching on the beauty of gendered human experience and of the godliness and goodness of marriage, an institution resting on God's good intent, for the

---

32. *LW* 45:17–18 [emphasis added]; WA 10/2:276,1–5; also WA 10/2:275,18–276,8.

benefit of God's images, male and female, in heterosexual or homosexual relations—for those willing and suitable for the estate.

Luther's views are helpful already in terms of how to approach the topic, as well as what gravity to give to it in our most precious task: the education of children. Luther was very clear on this. Because of the holiness aspect of marriage, on the one hand, and because it is an honorable estate with legal binding, on the other, people need to approach it with proper respect, earnestness, and right intent. For these same reasons, young people need to be educated on the meaning and proper respect of marriage. Luther wrote,

> We honor this godly estate of marriage and bless it, pray for it, and adorn it in an even more glorious manner. For, although it is a worldly estate, nevertheless it has God's Word on its side and is not a human invention or institution, like the estate of monks and nuns. Therefore it should easily be reckoned a hundred times more spiritual than the monastic estate…. We must also do this in order that the young people may learn to take this estate seriously, to hold it in high esteem as a divine work and command.[33]

We can appreciate with Luther what an important task we have in educating our children on these matters and in instilling in them faith in the tradition. For example, in his *Estate of Marriage* (1522), Luther gave advice on how to encourage young people to overlook the many mundane rational reasons to wait for marriage, and just go for it, trusting in God who provides.[34]

Luther on the Right to Marry and Natural Necessities That Please God

In the *Estate of Marriage* (1522), Luther addressed the question that is very much on the table today: who has the right to marry, "which persons may enter into marriage with one another"? A second, related point that Luther addressed is the biblically founded incentive to "Be fruitful and multiply." The question for us is, what do we mean by "being fruitful and multiplying," does it refer to biological parenthood only, and does that define marriage?

We look at Luther's words (quoted above) again, and intentionally without the preconception that they refer only to heterosexual persons and relations:

> It is more than a command, namely, a divine ordinance [*werck*] which it is not our prerogative to hinder or ignore. Rather it is just as necessary as the fact that I am a man, and more necessary than sleeping and waking, eating and drinking, and emptying the bowels and bladder. It is a nature and disposition just as innate as the organs involved in it. Therefore, just as God does not command anyone to a man or a woman but creates them the way they have to be, so he [God] does not command them to multiply but creates them so that they have to multiply. And whenever men [people] try to resists this, it

---

33. *Marriage Booklet*, in Kolb and Wengert, *The Book of Concord*, 368,3–4.
34. See *LW* 45:17–49; WA 10/2:275–304. Luther advised boys to marry at 20, girls at 15–18, and not worry if they had enough funds to have children. "Let God worry about how they and their children are to be fed. God makes children; he [God] will surely also feed them." (*LW* 45:48; WA 10/2:304,2–5).

remains irresistible nonetheless and goes its way through fornication, adultery, and secret sins, for this is a matter of nature and not of choice.[35]

Natural disposition, innate, as created by God—these are powerful, important words to consider. If we take these words to heart, and consider them applying to persons who are gays and lesbians just as well as to heterosexual persons, we can make progress in preparing a way for all persons who so wish to enjoy the blessings of marriage and parenthood.

The concepts of nature and the natural are complicated and come with baggage. The confusion about these terms shows in debates on whether gay and lesbian persons should have the right to marry and be parents, since they cannot procreate the 'old fashioned' and 'natural' ways. One could read Luther's words to suggest that God created men and women only and exclusively for the purpose of multiplying, that therein lies the worth and purpose in this life as men and women; that marriage is only for men and women; or that only marriages that produce children are valid and blessed; or that sexuality is to be geared only for the purpose of producing children (meaning, no sex for fun, even in marriage); or that women's worth is only in becoming mothers, biologically speaking, and within marriage, etc.

Where to start to say, "No, that's not it"? Take the idea of procreation as being definitive for marriage. If we want to go that route, we should also take to heart Luther's idea that in Paradise women gave birth to a litter at once—and repeatedly! That was his sixteenth-century male perspective of an ideal situation—hardly appealing to any woman in any era. In addition, as we know for a fact, many marriages are enjoyed without children, and persons can live perfectly happy lives "single." And if we continue down this same road, no self-respecting woman would consider her primary purpose for existence to be in the role of "lust control" for men, even though Luther "sorrowed" for women for having to deal with this disorderly lust and the failed attempts to control it.[36]

We do not need to like some of these statements from Luther, while we can appreciate his effort and interest. Here are some ideas on how we can make sense of things with Luther, and with the Genesis texts. (1) We understand marriage as a bond between two persons, out of which children may or may not result, and as an estate well suited for men and women to have off-spring if they so wish and are able—whether from conception or in parenthood through adoption, surrogacy, or foster parenting. Luther—a biological and a foster father himself—had no idea how many options we would have with parenting and procreation, no idea at all. In addition, with Luther and especially the Reformation mothers, we can think of parenthood beyond biology by reckoning with "family" as a much larger category. For example, Katharina Schütz Zell talked about the office of a "church mother," a calling for those caring for the commonwealth and for their neighbors. As a Christian estate, parenting is a broad category and involves all citizens.

(2) We can understand Luther's powerful words about the necessity of marital copulation and baby-making as his way of addressing the innate sexual

---

35. *LW* 45:18; WA 10/2:276,21–31.
36. For Luther's discussion on the effects of the fall on sex, gender, and gender relations, see his interpretation of Genesis 3, e.g., *LW* 1:163–169; WA 42:122–127.

drive and nesting instincts he observed in human beings; already before his own marriage he was looking for constructive ways to handle it. He talked about this yearning and necessity as something that God made and that we cannot undo even if we tried. He actually worried that there is physical harm as a result of the sex-drive not being fulfilled. He had the opinion of his time's physicians to attest to this: use it or get foul![37] We can attest that while not all of us have a burning desire and necessity to have children, we all know what sexual desire is about and appreciate Luther's concern. We can swear by Luther's main insights that we are born with our sexuality and sexual desires and need to love and be loved (such was his main argument against the medieval church's celibacy rules). Unlike Luther, however, we can imagine the application of sexuality outside the marriage contract. Unlike Luther, we can imagine marriage and sexual intimacy between both heterosexual and homosexual persons; and not just imagine, we celebrate that reality.

(3) We take Luther's words on "men" and "women" with some grains of salt, when reading his interpretation of Genesis and words about marriage and gender. He considered human beings to have two sets of gender-specific gear that divides people in different "classes," as he says, but we know that sexual and gendered experiences are much more complex than the "two or three classes" Luther imagines.

Related to these kinds of questions, in his *Estate of Marriage* Luther made a point about eunuchs, with an attempt to imagine a "third category" for human beings. He recognized three kinds of eunuchs: those who have been so from birth, those made so by others, and those who have made themselves so. Luther excused only these people from the expectation to multiply. "Apart from these groups, let no man presume to be without a spouse."[38] He suggested that only eunuchs, castrated persons, can honestly live without sex. For the rest of the folks, sexless life is not an option, and even dreaming of such life is fooling oneself and leading into trouble and sins. These sins involve the church, in Luther's wise opinion, as the culprit of setting impossible standards with which people are prone to fail.

We cannot underscore enough what a huge discovery sexuality was for Luther, the one-time monk, and then a father of six and a happy spouse of Katharina. Once tasting the apple, he did not see it reasonable at all to expect sexless life from people—other than eunuchs and those with a special gift from God for God's purposes. Luther considered as a special group those people who "are equipped for marriage by nature and physical capacity and nevertheless

37. "It is certainly a fact that he who refuses to marry must fall into immorality." (*LW* 45:45; WA 10/2:300,23–24). This is so in light of what and why God created, Luther argues, referring to the physicians' observations:
> If this natural function is forcibly restrained it necessarily strikes into the flesh and blood and becomes a poison, whence the body becomes unhealthy, enervated, sweaty and foul-smelling. That which should have issued in fruitfulness and propagation has to be absorbed within the body itself. Unless there is terrific hunger or immense labor or the supreme grace, the body cannot take it; it necessarily become unhealthy and sickly. Hence, we see how weak and sickly barren women are (*LW* 45:46–47; WA 10/2:301,5–12).

38. *LW* 45:18; WA 10/2:277,5. In the same context Luther talks about men who seek women's company "and are quite effeminate." (WA 10/2:279,10). He wrongly assumes that these men surround themselves with women because of their desire for them. Regarding eunuchs, see *LW* 45:19–22; WA 10/2:277,1–278,9; 279,7–14.

voluntarily remain celibate." "Such persons are rare, not one in a thousand for they are a special miracle of God. No one should venture on such a life unless he [she] be especially called by God" (Jer 16:2).[39]

From the beginning with his initial dismissal of celibacy, Luther's advice on sexual matters was radical and fresh in many ways: for one, as he recognized the needs for sexual intimacy, he made an explicit point of recognizing women's needs and rights in this area. He was crystal-clear about the spouses' mutual responsibility to meet the sexual needs of one another, and he showed incredible flexibility in imagining alternate scenarios when people struggled. Quite radically, for example, Luther could advise the husband to come to reasonable arrangements to make sure this aspect of marriage was fulfilled for his wife, with him or with someone else; the same was true for both spouses.[40] While he was considering only heterosexual relations, we can expand his reasoning to include gay and lesbian and transgendered persons in our creative solutions.

The bottom line we gather with Luther is that people are created out of love and for love and with the capacity to love, and that physical love is a crucially important dimension of an individual's life. To try to hinder, ignore, or suppress that created desire—without a special gift from God—would be devilish. It is the devil, Luther claimed, who creates spider webs out of human commands and vows that confuse people and make them try to abstain and live unmarried, when it is against their nature and God's desire for their happiness. Not to consider marriage as God-ordained and pleasing to God is to fall into the devil's lies and into various sins.[41]

Who, then, gets to marry? Here is an area where we can really learn from Luther's progressive vision and his way of adjusting hermeneutics in a new situation. On the basis of his Reformation insights and Reformation theology, Luther severely criticized the Catholic church and its regulations in these matters, considering marriage to be the right of everyone. One by one, he demolished the so-called impediments, showing their "silliness."

The impediments for marriage that Luther criticized were many: Reasons of consanguinity or affinity through marriage, legal kinship, or spiritual

---

39. *LW* 45:45; *WA* 10/2:279,19–21.

40. Luther advised husbands unable to fulfill their conjugal duties towards their wives to let them have another arrangement to take care of this issue. He wrote, "If a woman who is fit for marriage has a husband who is not, and she is unable openly to take unto herself another ... she should say to her husband, 'Look, my dear husband, you are unable to fulfill your conjugal duty toward me, you have cheated me out of my maidenhood and even imperiled my honor and my soul's salvation; in the sight of God there is no real marriage between us.... Grant me the privilege of contracting a secret marriage with your brother or closest relative, and you retain the title of husband so that your property will not fall to strangers. Consent to being betrayed voluntarily by me, as you have betrayed me without my consent" (*LW* 45:20; *WA* 10/2:278,19–28). Luther went as far as to declare that if the husband refuses this arrangement and that way fails to honor his conjugal duty, the wife should flee to another country and marry again. This advice Luther had given already when still timid; now he was standing on firmer ground and wished to offer "sounder advise in the matter, and take a firmer grip on a man who thus makes a fool of his wife" (*LW* 45:20–21; *WA* 10/2:278,29–31; cf *WA* 10/2:278,32–279,2).

41. "This is why the devil has contrived to have so much shouted and written in the world against the institution of marriage, to frighten men away from this godly life and entangle them in a web of fornication and secret sins" (*LW* 45:37; *WA* 10/2:294,8–11). The devils' lies about marriage are in striking contrast to God's word about marriage: God says that God is pleased with marriage, and God does not lie. (*LW* 45:38, 42; *WA* 10/2:294,29–30; 298,9–18). "And whenever men try to resist this, it remains irresistible nonetheless and goes its way through fornication, adultery, and secret sins, for this is a matter of nature and not of choice." (*LW* 45:18; *WA* 10/2:276,29–31).

relationship—all these reasons Luther deemed foolishness. The same with other kind of impediments, such as unbelief, crime, episcopal prohibition, defective eyesight and hearing, limited mental capacities, etc. Luther's basic over-arching point was that it is important to marry, God wants us marry, thus the church should not stand in your way, so go ahead and take as your spouse whomever you wish, even a Turk, or a Jew, or a heretic (these are major compromises from Luther who condemned both the Jews and the Turks for ungodliness and thus damned).[42]

Most intriguingly, Luther demolished all kinds of impediments, even unbelief. His radical answer to a question that still has legs in our days, "May I marry a Turk?," was a firm "Yes!" He explained an important point: "Know therefore that marriage is an outward, bodily thing like any other worldly undertaking. Just as I may eat, drink, sleep, walk, ride with, buy from, speak to, and deal with a heathen, Jew, Turk, or heretic, so I may also marry and continue in wedlock with him. Pay no attention to the precepts of those fools who forbid it."[43]

While emphasizing the freedom to marry, Luther underscored that nobody should be coerced into marriage—neither by parents nor by the government. "That is to be sure no marriage in the sight of God."[44] Marriage is a union that must be voluntary. Without the will and "I do," there is no marriage. This is one of Luther's most basic arguments, as well as the central part of the wedding ritual he outlined in his *Marriage Booklet*. A choice and freedom are essential in establishing a marital union. This is one of the few areas in life where Luther underscored the factor of choice. It is also noteworthy that the choice would not work that well the other way around. Luther cherished the freedom to marry and to choose whom to marry, while he denied human beings' "own" freedom to stay celibate, that is, to abstain from sexual relations. With this conviction Luther ridiculed the futile vows of celibacy: "If you would like to take a wise vow, then vow not to bite off your own nose; you can keep that vow."[45]

The one impediment for marriage Luther considered with extra care had to do with sexuality. If people are unfit for marital relations, they should not marry. Luther says explicitly that if a wife or a husband is unfit for marriage—meaning sex—they could divorce, or not get married in the first place. The inability to fulfill the natural sexual needs of one's spouse would be grounds for a divorce. Here again we have proof of how important Luther deemed sexual life and happiness.[46]

Sins and crimes, on the other hand, should not be an impediment as sins and crimes do not change the person's natural being in this regard. Marriage should not be regarded as something only perfect, that is, non-sinning, persons would

---

42. *LW* 45:25; *WA* 10/2:283,1–7. On the various impediments dictated by the medieval Catholic church, see *LW* 45:22–30; *WA* 10/2280,16–287,11. Impediments he attacked are: blood relationship, affinity through marriage, spiritual relationship, legal kinship, unbelief, crime, public decorum/respectability, solemn vows/monastic, error, servitude, holy orders, coercion, betrothal, episcopal prohibition, restricted times, defective eyesight or hearing, and spouse unfit for marriage and for conjugal duties—the last one constituting grounds for divorce. (*LW* 36:96–103; *WA* 6:553,22–558,7).

43. *LW* 45:25; *WA* 10/2:283,8–12.

44. *LW* 45:28; *WA* 10/2:285,19.

45. *LW* 45:27; *WA* 10/2:284,22–23.

46. *LW* 45:33–35; *WA* 10/2:290,5–292,5; on grounds for divorce, *LW* 45:30–35; *WA* 10/2:287,13–292,6. Also, *De captivitate babylonica ecclesiae // On the Babylonian Captivity of the Church* [1520] (*LW* 36:103–106; *WA* 6:558,8–560,18).

quality for. Nor should church regulations put obstacles in people's way in this regard.[47] For example, regulations regarding times and episcopal prohibitions were, in Luther's opinion, plain rotten business: "It is a dirty rotten business that a bishop should forbid me a wife or specify the times when I marry, or that a blind and dumb person should not be allowed to enter into wedlock."[48] Marriage belongs to all, and the church should teach it and support those who marry, with full gusto, with gospel ammunition, and with common sense. This was Luther's solemn argument.

Concluding Thoughts

We see what Luther did with the impediments invented by the church. We see how he broke traditions, with a new reading of his Scripture, enlightened by his time's understanding of human life, and by his own experiences and observations of life.[49] His passion to preach the gospel of liberation and his trust in God's tangible grace in human life guided his re-visioning of the "holy while worldly" institution of marriage and human sexuality, with the best of intents.

We end with Luther's precious words on children. As a father himself, and even before, he saw children as a gift from God, "an eternal treasure" from God. He could not imagine the world without children who were the embodiment of God's grace. Similarly, he understood the well-being of the world to depend on the care of the children and their souls.[50] Any attempts to erect obstacles for parenthood, this most important responsibility and a gift with a theological bearing, was against Luther's gut-knowledge and biblical knowledge. It would be diabolical to prevent people from entering the calling of parenthood he deemed as most holy and most difficult and a central piece in God's design for human life on this earth.

Luther had an uncanny appreciation of the fundamental experiences parenthood brings about, and he was revolutionary in how he both saw a theological meaning in parental experiences and drew important theological insights from the parental realities for his imagination of God and God's love, sin and grace, and salvation. With Luther, we can argue, and forcefully so,

---

47. According to Luther, sex is good for any day for any condition. If one tries to regulate sexual activity with inane rules that lead to abstinence, which is impossible without God's special help anyway, such foolishness can lead to fornication and other transgressions as people look for ways to release their sexual energy; abstinence can also make one sick. (*LW* 45:45–46; WA 10/2:301,5–15).

48. *LW* 45:30; WA 10/2:287,3–11.

49. "I base my remarks on Scripture, which to me is surer than all experience and cannot lie to me. He who finds still other good things in marriage profits all the more, and should give thanks to God. Whatever God calls good must of necessity always be good, unless men do not recognize it or perversely misuse it" (*LW* 45:43; WA 10/2:299,10).

50. "God makes children." "Got macht kinder." (*LW* 45:48; WA 10/2:304,2). Quoting St. Cyprian, Luther wrote, "One should kiss the newborn infant, even before it is baptized, in honor of the hands of God here engaged in a brand new deed." (*LW* 45:41; WA 10/2:297,5–7). In his criticism of monastic vows and in illustrating holiness in marriage and parenthood, Luther made a radical argument that tells of his respect for parenthood and also of the godliness of children: "Therefore, I say that all nuns and monks who lack faith, and who trust in their own chastity and in their order, are not worthy of rocking a baptized child or preparing its pap, even if it were the child of a harlot. This is because their order and manner of life has no word of God as its warrant. They cannot boast that what they do is pleasing in God's sight, as can the woman in childbirth, even if her child is born out of wedlock" (*LW* 45:41; WA 10/2:297,10–15).

that excluding people from this gift and responsibility and foundational life-experience because of their sexual orientation is not theologically warranted. Regardless of how we consider the ultimate reason for marriage, or whether we personally want or can have children, we get Luther's point: we cannot afford nor do we have the rights to exclude any people so willing from this holy calling and responsibility. Rather we do well to support one another in that holy task, in our personal lives, in our societal ways, and in the church.[51]

Luther gives us much food for thought and building blocks for arguments to not only support but promote the right to marry and the right for parenthood for all people who so desire. Luther gives us many fruitful arguments to continue to consider marriage as a gift, as a choice, and as an institution worth having faith in. Remembering Luther and the sixteenth-century Reformations stirs us to think again about our church's role in marriage matters in the first place, and secondly, about the ways the church can support every person who wishes to enter that estate, which is noble, serious, and pleasing to God—Luther's words—while extremely complex.

51. E.g., Luther wrote, "A wife too should regard her duties in the same light, as she suckles the child, rocks and bathes it, and cares for it in other ways; and as she busies herself with other duties and renders help and obedience to her husband. These are truly golden and noble works" (*LW* 45:40; WA 10/2:296,12–15). Likewise, when a father washes diapers, he may be ridiculed by some as an effeminate fool, but God, with all his angels and creatures, is smiling—not because that father is washing diapers, but because he is doing so in Christian faith." (*LW* 45:40; WA 10/2:296,30–297,1; see also *LW* 44:12–14; WA 2:169,38–170,7 on the theological and spiritual importance of good parenting: for the eternal benefit of the parents themselves, for the good of society, and as a divine service for the child as a gift from God.)

Sharing the Sacraments

11. Luther and the Reformed Eucharist
What Luther Said, or Might Have Said, about Calvin

B. A. Gerrish

Ask a well-informed Presbyterian, What *is* this "Reformed church" to which you say you belong? and the answer will almost certainly be: It is the church that traces its pedigree back to John Calvin and the Reformation in Switzerland. Ask further, What about Ulrich Zwingli? and the puzzled response will be, Ulrich *who*? From denominational publications to the handouts in membership classes, Presbyterians agree—or assume—that Calvin is their theologian, and few of them know much, if anything, about Zwingli. It is curious, then, that the Lutheran-Presbyterian conversations of the 1960s were made public in a volume titled *Marburg Revisited*. (Perhaps it wasn't one of the Presbyterians who proposed the title!) Before I am done, I shall have to confess that the demons of Marburg have not been laid to rest: they continue to haunt the Presbyterians. But no Calvinists were present at the Marburg Colloquy of 1529. It was the culmination of a bitter controversy between Luther and Zwingli and their respective followers. Calvin himself had not yet joined the Evangelical cause, but (in his own choice language) was still "obstinately devoted to the superstitions of popery."

So I want to begin by revisiting not Marburg but *Strasbourg*, where from 1538 to 1541 Calvin served as pastor to the French refugees, worked closely with the Strasbourg reformer Martin Bucer, and attracted the attention of Martin Luther. From this beginning, we can look at the later relationship between Luther and Calvin and attempt a rough sketch of the dividing lines between Wittenberg, Zurich, and Geneva. Finally, we will consider Calvin's belief that he understood the essential point of harmony between Luther and himself on the Lord's Supper, so that he knew what Luther, if he were alive in 1554, would say about the quarrel between the Lutherans and the Reformed.

Strasbourg Revisited

Dismissed from Geneva in 1538, Calvin moved to Strasbourg. By then, relationships among the Evangelicals had changed. Zwingli was no longer in the picture: he had fallen on the field of Cappel in 1531. In 1536 the Wittenberg Concord had reconciled the Wittenbergers with Bucer and the south Germans. At first, Calvin had been suspicious of the Concord, which he thought left the door open to what he took to be Luther's crass language about the Eucharist. In the first edition of the *Institutes*, which appeared the same year as the Concord, he had taken his definition of a sacrament from Luther's *Babylonian Captivity* (1520): a sacrament is a sign that confirms the divine promise. And yet in his account of the Lord's Supper he had seemed to be critical of Luther, though not by name. Now in Strasbourg, three years later, young Calvin—he was not yet thirty years old—was surprised and delighted at the news that Luther held him in high esteem.

In a letter to Guillaume Farel, dated 20 November 1539, Calvin reports that Luther has asked Bucer to greet his young French associate for him: "Will you pay my respects (*salutabis reverenter*) to John Sturm and John Calvin. I have read their little books with singular enjoyment."[1] We can forget about John Sturm for the moment. Calvin exclaims with evident delight: "Just think what I say there about the Eucharist! Consider Luther's generosity (*ingenuitatem*)! It will be easy to decide what reason they have who so obstinately disagree with him." Calvin goes on to say that Philipp Melanchthon has confirmed the good news of Luther's high regard for him, and has instructed the letter-carrier to deliver an oral message, which Calvin reports in these words:

> Certain persons, to irritate Martin, pointed out to him the aversion with which he and his followers were alluded to by me. So he examined the passage in question and felt that he was there, beyond doubt, under attack. After a while, he said: "I certainly hope that he will one day think better of us. Still, it is right for us to be a little tolerant toward such a gifted man." We are surely made of stone [Calvin comments] if we are not overcome by such moderation! I, certainly, am overcome, and I have written an apology (*satisfactionem*) for insertion into my preface to the Epistle to the Romans.

Melanchthon persuaded Calvin (I'm not sure why) not to include the promised "apology" in the preface to his *Commentary on Romans*, but we know its content from the copy Calvin sent to Farel for his approval.

The intriguing question is, of course: *What* book of Calvin's had Luther read "with singular enjoyment"? There are two possibilities: either the new, 1539 edition of the *Institutes*, or Calvin's *Reply to Sadoleto*, published the same year. When Calvin was dismissed from Geneva, Cardinal Sadoleto urged the Genevans to return to the Roman church, where their prospect of salvation was better. Incredibly, the dismayed Swiss asked Calvin, who had been shown out of town in disgrace, to answer on their behalf; and this he did in an eloquent defense of the Evangelical cause. It is easy to suppose that Luther could have read it with approval. But scholarly opinion is divided on the choice between the *Reply* and the *Institutes*.

In his "apology" Calvin denies that he intended to attack the Germans in his *Institutes*, and some have held this to be persuasive evidence that it was Calvin's *Institutes* that Luther must have read "with singular enjoyment." It would certainly be an ecumenical boon if we could say that Luther approved of Calvin's *Institutes*. But the second edition was no longer a *libellus*, a "little book." And the case for the other alternative, the *Reply to Sadoleto*, it seems to me, is clinched by the fact that Luther's request to Bucer—"pay my respects

---

1. Translations throughout are those of the author.

to John Sturm and John Calvin," etc.—is followed immediately by the caustic remark, "As for Sadoleto, I wish he would believe that God is the creator of men even outside of Italy." It is possible that to spoil Luther's pleasure in reading the *Reply to Sadoleto*, trouble-makers showed him critical statements in the new edition of the *Institutes* that Luther took to be directed against him; but he refused to let that negate his high regard for the young French scholar. Calvin was wholly captivated by Luther's magnanimous response, and he insisted that he had never intended to attack the Lutherans.[2] Indeed, the remarkable thing is that Calvin now came to be seen as one of them—a Lutheran.

On his arrival in Strasbourg in early September 1538, Calvin must have been expected to assent to the Wittenberg Concord, and this would have entailed agreement with the Augsburg Confession (along with the *Apology* and the Tetrapolitan Confession of Strasbourg). It is no surprise, then, that when the emperor summoned ecumenical conferences between Roman Catholics and Lutherans at Hagenau, Worms, and Regensburg (1540–41), Calvin served on the Lutheran side with the representatives from Strasbourg. At Worms he was officially transferred from the Strasbourg delegation to the delegation of the Lutheran Duke of Lüneburg.

There is disagreement among scholars about how *formal* Calvin's assent to the Augsburg Confession may have been: Did he ever actually *sign*, and if he did was it the *versio variata* he signed, prepared with an eye to the imperial conferences by Melanchthon? In my opinion, Calvin must at least have indicated agreement with the *invariata*, with or without his autograph, because that is the only version there was in 1538. Subsequently, he may have given his formal assent—with pen and paper—to the *versio variata*.[3] In any case, the point is that during his Strasbourg period the Frenchman Calvin was accepted by the Lutherans as one of their own—all the more remarkable because he made no secret about the points at which he thought Luther's eucharistic language could be improved. In the new round of controversies that began in the 1550s, Calvin repeatedly recalled happier days, when he had Luther's approval and signed the Augsburg Confession. But, as it turned out, the promise of Strasbourg went unfulfilled.

2. A criticism is not necessarily an attack. But what *was* Calvin's supposed criticism? If we identify it with his insistence in both the *Reply* and the *Institutes* that Christ's body, if it is really a body, cannot be locally present everywhere, Luther could hardly have taken it as a personal attack—unless to reject it as mistaken—since he never intended a local, circumscribed presence of the body in the Eucharist. Moreover, Calvin's rejection of a local presence—again, in both the *Reply* and the 1539 *Institutes*—was explicitly aimed at Rome. In his later *Short Treatise on the Lord's Supper* (see below), the "criticism" is a wish: Luther should have cautioned that he did not mean the sort of local presence the papists dream of.

3. Following Calvin's example, some of the earliest collections of Reformed creeds included the Augsburg Confession. By then, understandably, preference went to the *versio variata*. Uncertainties remain about Calvin's attitude to the two versions. No doubt, he welcomed the language of *exhibere* in art. 10 of the altered version (*cum pane et vino … exhibeantur*). But he need not have objected, as is often assumed, to the statement in art. 10 of the *invariata* that the body and blood of Christ "are present … and distributed."

Hope Deferred

Calvin was back in Geneva by September 1541, and the city scribe who recorded his arrival wrote that (this time!) he offered himself to be forever the servant of Geneva. Obviously, we know more about Calvin's opinion of Luther in the following years than about Luther's opinion of Calvin. Luther had but five years left. They were years overshadowed, among other things, by an increasingly virulent renewal of controversy between Wittenberg and Zurich. In 1543 Luther announced that he intended to pray and teach against the Swiss till the end of his days (Luther to Christoph Froschauer, 31 August 1543). The next year, in his *Short Confession on the Holy Sacrament*, he described his adversaries as possessing an *eingeteuffelt, durch teuffelt, uberteuffelt, lesterlich hertz und Luegenmaul*. (That loses something in translation. We will leave it in German.) And in the year of his death Luther piously adapted the first Psalm: "Blessed is the one who walks not in the counsel of the sacramentarians, nor stands in the way of Zwinglians, nor sits in the seat of the Zurichers" (Luther to Jacob Probst, 17 January 1546). These, alas, were not good times for testing what had begun in the Strasbourg years as mutual respect between Luther and young Calvin.

For his part, Calvin feared that the "savage invective" of Luther's *Short Confession* was directed "against us all." He could only ask Heinrich Bullinger, on whom Zwingli's mantle had fallen, not to forget all they owed to Luther's greatness, and he added the much-quoted testimony: "I often say that even if he should call me a devil, I would still pay him the honor of acknowledging him as an illustrious servant of God.... It is our task so to reprehend whatever is bad in him that we make some allowance for those splendid gifts" (Calvin to Bullinger, 25 November 1544). "Those splendid gifts"! An interesting echo of Luther's first opinion of Calvin: "It is right for us to be a little tolerant toward such a gifted man." In actual fact, however, it is by no means certain that Luther's invective was meant for *all* the Swiss Evangelicals, Calvin included. And although Calvin stood alongside Bullinger in the storm of anger and invective that blew from Wittenberg (and, to be sure, blew back again), he could not quite believe he had fallen out of Luther's favor. He decided to write him a letter. The two never met, and this is the only letter addressed by one of the two Reformers to the other. It is dated 25 January 1545.

The occasion for writing was the news from France that some of Calvin's persecuted countrymen, fearing for their lives, were conforming outwardly to Roman Catholicism. They were called "Nicodemites" because, like Nicodemus, they came secretly to Jesus. Calvin admonished them that they must confess their faith openly and take the consequences. But they protested that Calvin's judgment was unreasonable (it came from his safe haven in Geneva), and they asked him to consult with the Wittenberg reformers—in person or by messenger—expecting a milder judgment from the Germans. It was a good topic on which to consult Luther and test the bond between him and Calvin, since it avoided the passion of the eucharistic controversy. Calvin wrote his letter and with it sent copies of his two tracts on the Nicodemite problem (1543, 1544). He addressed Luther as "most respected father" and showed himself willing to bow to Luther's authority if he would pronounce a verdict on the issue. He wrote: "How I wish I could fly to you there, so that I might enjoy your company for but a few hours! For I should prefer, and it would be much better, to discuss with you in person not this question only, but others too. But since it is not granted us here on earth, it will shortly be ours, as I hope, in the kingdom of God." That, I think we may say, is not the letter of someone who has given up hope of preserving a good relationship.

What, then, you may ask, did Luther make of Calvin's deferential letter? The answer is that he never received it, and probably never knew it had been written. Calvin had sent it, with another letter, to Melanchthon, who decided not to pass it on. By now, poor Melanchthon was terrified of Luther, and he would not risk throwing fuel on the fire. An interesting opportunity went by. But do we have evidence, anyway, of how Luther's attitude to Calvin may have fared in acrimonious times? An entry in the *Table Talk* asserts that "Calvin conceals his opinion on the question of the sacraments" (no. 5303); another that, "although a learned man, he is strongly suspect on the error of the sacramentarians" (no. 6050).[4] But there is also evidence of his unmixed praise for two of Calvin's writings. The first was Calvin's *Humble Exhortation to the Invincible Emperor, Charles V* (1544), popularly known as his treatise *On the Necessity for Reforming the Church.* There Calvin extols Luther as the man God raised up, along with others, to hold a torch over the path to salvation and purge the church of irreligious opinions about the merit of works. Small wonder that Luther repaid the compliment and gave the treatise his glowing praise!

The other writing of Calvin's that earned Luther's commendation is more important for our topic because it is directly pertinent to the eucharistic debate. In 1545 the Wittenberg bookseller Moritz Goltsch brought back from the Frankfurt Fair the Latin translation of Calvin's *Short Treatise on the Lord's Supper,* first written in French while Calvin was in Strasbourg and published in 1541 after his return to Geneva. Goltsch presented a copy to Luther, who, we are told, read with particular care the concluding section on the history of the eucharistic debate. Calvin, at his diplomatic best, says that Zwingli and Oecolampadius were so committed to the necessary task of rooting out the medieval belief in a carnal presence of Christ in the Lord's Supper that they neglected (Calvin says "they forgot"!) to show the true nature of the communion of Christ's body and blood in the sacrament. Luther thought they meant to leave nothing in the sacrament but bare signs without their substance. But Luther should have made it clearer, for his part, that he did not mean a local presence such as the papists dream of, and he could have been more cautious in his use of language that was a bit harsh and crude—although, Calvin admits, it is difficult to explain so high a matter without *some* impropriety. Once these mild reservations, addressed evenhandedly to each side, are duly noted, Calvin concludes that the controversy is over: "We all confess, with one mouth, that in receiving the sacrament in faith, according to the Lord's ordinance, we are truly made partakers of the proper substance of the body

---

4. The first entry indicates that Lutheran suspicion of Calvin's honesty goes back to Luther himself. The second, more ambivalent entry may mean that Calvin is suspected of misrepresenting, rather than sharing, the error of the sacramentarians: "Caluinus est vir doctus, sed valde suspectus de errore sacramentariorum."

and blood of Jesus Christ. How that happens, some can deduce better and explain more clearly than others." Luther is reported to have announced, as he read this gentle account of the controversy, that had Zwingli and Oecolampadius spoken like Calvin, there would have been no need for a long dispute.[5]

But, of course, that is not the way it worked out. In Switzerland, after Luther's death, Calvin turned his tireless ecumenical energies to resolving the differences between Geneva and Zurich. The Zurich Consensus, concluded in 1549 (published in 1551), brought harmony between the German- and the French-speaking Protestants in Switzerland. But success turned quickly to failure: the achievement of harmony in Switzerland cost Calvin some of his credit in Wittenberg. A number of Luther's theological heirs—by no means all of them—turned their heavy guns from Zurich to Geneva. The Zurich Consensus convinced them that Calvin had all along been a closet Zwinglian. Their opinion was to be immortalized in the Formula of Concord (1577) with its description of Calvinists, or Crypto-Calvinists, as "subtle sacramentarians," all the more dangerous for being subtle. Hope for a wider consensus between the Lutherans and the Reformed had to be deferred to the twentieth century. But that is another story. We must consider next where the stumbling blocks lay that hindered concord in Luther's and Calvin's time.

Carlstadt's Poison

As the sixteenth- and seventeenth-century eucharistic controversies progressed, they drew in a formidable number of issues and questions. It gets incredibly complicated, and there is always the temptation to salute the acumen and erudition of our forebears, but ourselves to make do with a few party slogans. However, my limited intention here is not to cover the field, only to trace the path leading to Calvin's persuasion that one thing would have been enough to win Luther's blessing. And I think it helps to go back to the time when the conflict was just beginning. In a letter to Nicholas von Amsdorf (2 December 1524), Luther growled: "Carlstadt's poison crawls far. Zwingli in Zurich ... and many others have accepted his opinion, continually asserting that the bread in the sacrament is no different from the bread sold in the market."[6]

Luther settled accounts with his colleague Andreas Bodenstein von Carlstadt in one of his greatest works, *Against the Heavenly Prophets* (1525). Carlstadt believed that medieval sacramentalism smothered the inwardness of true piety. He scorned dependence on the outward elements of water, bread, and wine and strove to get directly to the Spirit. The Lord's Supper, for him, was an act of remembrance, an occasion to fix one's thoughts on Calvary, not

---

5. Luther's reported verdicts on these two treatises of Calvin's may sound a little like Calvinist fiction, but they are well attested. For the sources, see my *The Old Protestantism and the New: Essays on the Reformation Heritage* (1982; reprint, London: T&T Clark International, 2004), 286 n.53, 287 n.66.

6. Documentation for what follows in this section (and some needed refinements!) will be found in my essay "Discerning the Body: Sign and Reality in Luther's Controversy with the Swiss" (1988), reprinted in B.A. Gerrish, *Continuing the Reformation: Essays on Modern Religious Thought* (Chicago, Il: University of Chicago Press, 1993), chap. 3.

a physical channel of divine grace. Luther retorts that while Carlstadt has swallowed the Holy Ghost feathers and all, he is so eager to get to the Spirit that he tears down the bridge by which the Spirit gets to us. Of course God deals with us inwardly through the Holy Spirit; God does it, however, by means of the external Word and sacraments, through which the blessings won by Christ on the cross are distributed. And remembering is not private meditation but public proclamation. Carlstadt's *memorialism* turns the sacrament into a devotional exercise and so has made the gift of God what it was for the papists: a human work. We have a new brood of monks and hypocrites, who trust in their own devotion.

What Zwingli added to Carlstadt's memorialist view of the Lord's Supper he borrowed from the Dutch theologian Cornelisz Hoen (Honius), whose controversial letter on the Eucharist Zwingli published at Zurich in 1525. Carlstadt had explained that when Jesus proffered the bread at the Last Supper and said, "Take, eat," he must have paused, pointed to himself, and said, "*This* is my body." Zwingli found Hoen's *symbolism* more persuasive: the bread *signifies* the body of Christ. And what, according to Zwingli, do signs do when they signify? Two things: First, by picturing them they call to mind things lying in the past. A sacrament is *factae gratiae signum*, a sign of grace "done." Thus, the symbolist view of the words of institution supports memorialism and faithfully observes Jesus' explicit, repeated injunction, "Do this in remembrance of me" (1 Cor 11:24–25). The sacrament reminds us that God's favor was procured for us by the death of Christ.

The second use of signs, according to Zwingli, is to declare our commitment—in the Lord's Supper our commitment to the Christ who died for us. Zwingli supported the second use of the term from the meaning of *sacramentum* in classical Latin, where it was used for a soldier's oath of allegiance. Signs, in short, are retrospective and declarative, not instrumental. In the Eucharist they point back to a *past* event and pledge our loyalty for the *future*: they are not means by which grace is given in the *present*—here and now, in the administration of the sacrament. Zwingli's fundamental principle is that the Spirit needs no channel or vehicle; and that, in Luther's eyes, was Carlstadt's poison. The bread of the Eucharist is just bread, no different from what you can buy at the baker's.

Now Luther himself had used the language of "sign" in, for example, the *Babylonian Captivity*. But there he used it in a somewhat peculiar way. He actually identified the sign with the presence of Christ's body and blood *under* the elements, not with the elements of bread and wine themselves. Since the presence of the body and blood is not visible, the entire Augustinian notion of a sacrament as a visible sign of an invisible grace is given up: the symbolic relationship of *signum* and *res*, sign and thing signified, is scrambled. Of course, Luther understood perfectly well what Augustine meant by a sign, and he utterly rejected Zwingli's appeal to him, because for the great church father a sign was not a sign of something absent—back there—but of something invisibly present *here*. Out of a sign, Luther scoffs, the fanatics make a mere badge or token of identification (Zwingli's second use): in appealing to Augustine they are only giving us something else to clout them on the head with, as though we did not have enough weapons already. But—and this is the intriguing thing—Luther is not interested in defending the real presence with a more authentically Augustinian view of signs: his single-minded purpose is to exclude sign talk from the interpretation of the words of institution and to stake everything on the sheer power of the words of institution themselves.[7] Calvin, by contrast, in this as in most things, was Augustine's disciple.

Remembrance of Things Present

Calvin's opinion of Zwingli and his sacramental theology was hardly less contemptuous than Luther's; only, he was not so public about it (mostly, you have to ferret it out from his correspondence). In the Strasbourg years, he pronounced Zwingli's explanation of the use of the sacraments "false and pernicious" (Calvin to Andrew Zebedee, 19 May 1539), and he confided to Farel his estimate of the relative worth of Zwingli and Luther as theologians: "You yourself know, if the two be compared, by what a distance Luther excels" (Calvin to Farel, 26 February 1540). Looking back in 1556, he tells his Lutheran adversary Joachim Westphal that when he learned from Luther that Oecolampadius and Zwingli left nothing in the sacraments but bare, empty figures, he could not even bring himself to read their writings. His opinion of their successors was no better: to Melanchthon he wrote that he found Bullinger's Zurich Confession,[8] written in reply to Luther's *Short Confession*, feeble and childish, distinguished more by stubbornness than learning (Calvin to Melanchthon, 28 June 1545). Harsh words!

The truth is that Calvin nursed a deep antipathy to Zwingli's confident explanations of what happens, and what doesn't happen, in the Eucharist. The reason has as much to do with Calvin's piety as with his theology (though he might not approve of the distinction). It is best conveyed, I think, in a letter to Pierre Viret (11 September 1542). Calvin admits that he hasn't read *all* Zwingli's writings (he couldn't, since he knew no German), and he grants Viret the possibility that Zwingli's sacramental teaching may have improved toward the end of his life. "But in his previous writings I remember how *profane* his teaching on the sacraments was."[9] How *profane*! That's a judgment in different words, but similar in substance to Luther's opinion of Carlstadt's teaching, which saw in the bread of the Eucharist nothing different from the bread you could buy at the baker's. It calls to mind John Williamson Nevin's remark that in the Puritan understanding of the Lord's Supper there is as little *mystery* as in a common Fourth of July celebration.[10]

---

7. The claim that Luther held a literal interpretation of the words "This is my body" is not strictly true. In actual fact, only Carlstadt did. For Luther the pertinent figure of speech was "synecdoche," naming the part for the whole, since the Word makes the bread one substance with the body of Christ (*Fleischbrot*). It should also be noted that although he saw no symbol in the words of institution, Luther did make use of the symbolism in Paul's metaphor of the one bread (1 Cor 10:17).

8. Commonly referred to as the Zurich Confession, its German title is *Warhaffte Bekanntnuß der dieneren der kilchen zu Zürych.*

9. Emphasis added.

10. John W. Nevin, *The Mystical Presence and Other Writings on the Eucharist*, ed. Bard Thompson and George H. Bricker, Lancaster Series on the Mercersburg Theology, vol. 4 (Philadelphia, Pa; Boston, Ma: United Church Press, 1966), 107. Nevin's *The Mystical Presence: A Vindication of the Reformed or*

For Calvin the Eucharist was a sacred mystery—to be adored, not explained. He was entirely at home in the strange Johannine language about eating the life-giving flesh of the Son of Man (John 6:53–58), and he was appalled that Zwingli could read no more in it than the necessity to believe that Christ died for our sins. According to Calvin, eating is not believing, but the effect of believing. "When he pronounced himself to be the bread of life, the Lord did not mean to teach only that our salvation rests on belief in his death and resurrection, but also that by a true communion with him his life passes into us and is made ours, just as bread, when taken for nourishment, dispenses vigor to the body."[11] The gift of the gospel is nothing less than "true communion" with the body and blood of Christ: the Lord's Supper is a means by which this communion is pictured and nurtured. In Calvin's eyes, Zwingli was mistaken about both the *reference* and the *function* of the signs of bread and wine in the Eucharist: for they point not only to the past deed of Christ, but much more to the mystery of our present *communion* with his body and blood; and they are not mere reminders that he died for our sins, but *instruments* by which the Holy Spirit nurtures our participation in Christ.[12]

It is astonishing that Calvin and Bullinger ever managed to agree about the Lord's Supper. In the years and months leading up to the Zurich Consensus, the two engaged in an exchange of candid criticisms, which might easily have been broken off in anger at any time. But they seem to have mastered the art of not letting theological disagreement become too personal. Bullinger started out as a loyal disciple of Zwingli: he rejected the notion that sacraments are vehicles of grace and took his stand on a strictly memorialist interpretation of the Eucharist. He wrote defiantly in his Zurich Confession that remembrance is the "real main part and purpose" of the sacrament, and he developed his views more fully in a treatise *On the Sacraments* that he sent to Calvin in 1546. Although he thought the Zurich Confession feeble, childish, and stubborn, Calvin was more tactful when he wrote to Bullinger himself (25 February 1547), but he was still surprisingly blunt. He ended his letter by remarking that, as a friend, he had not praised Bullinger where he was right but simply offered criticisms where he needed correction—a less colorful approach than Luther employed against Carlstadt's poison, but perhaps as effective (depending on what you want to accomplish).

To Bullinger's chief point—that the Lord's Supper is about remembering—Calvin replies disarmingly, "I say that in the Lord's Supper there is a remembrance of something present (*rei praesentis memoriam*)." That is good Augustinianism and obviously entails a correction of the Zwinglian understanding of signs. Bullinger argued that it is a mistake to ascribe to signs what belongs to God alone. Calvin replies that because God alone gives wisdom, does it follow that God's law does nothing? Do we transfer God's glory to created things when we say that God uses means to distribute his grace? "You exclude signs because it is by faith that we come to partake of the heavenly gifts. I say

---

Calvinistic Doctrine of the Holy Eucharist first appeared in 1846; it remains one of the best expositions of Calvin's understanding of the Lord's Supper.

11. *Inst.* 1559, 4.17.5.

12. It is interesting that the Augsburg Confession uses the expression *tamquam per instrumenta* not for the means by which the Spirit acts, but for the means by which the Spirit is given (art. 5).

the exact opposite: if it is by faith, then it is also through the sacraments. For faith comes from the Word and the sacraments." Calvin not only reaffirms his view that the sacraments are *instruments* through which God distributes grace; he also seeks to retrieve the scholastic teaching that the sacraments *contain* and *confer* grace by giving it an Evangelical interpretation: the sacraments contain grace as the gospel contains Christ, and they confer grace by exercising faith.

Such language could hardly commend itself to a disciple of Zwingli, and when Calvin sent him a set of twenty-four propositions on the sacraments, Bullinger bluntly replied (November 1548): "I do not see how your doctrine differs from the doctrine of the papists." He accused Calvin of binding grace to the elements. This, of course, was a misunderstanding: the point of Calvin's fondness for the term *instrumentum* was, in part, to make clear that it is *not* the signs as such that confer grace (*ex opere operato*), but the Spirit, who freely uses them. However, Calvin was willing to settle for the formula that *while* a sacrament is administered outwardly, the Spirit, in a parallel activity, is working within, and that is the position toward which Bullinger eventually moved.[13] But to use the terms I proposed in a paper written a long time ago (1966),[14] the Zurich Consensus goes beyond Zwingli's "symbolic memorialism" without making a clear choice between Calvin's "symbolic instrumentalism" and Bullinger's "symbolic parallelism." Article 9 of the Zurich Consensus states the formula Calvin and Bullinger were able to agree on: "Though we distinguish, as is proper, between the signs and the things signified, yet we do not separate the reality from the signs but confess that all who embrace by faith the promises there offered receive Christ spiritually with his spiritual gifts; further that those, too, who had long been made partakers of Christ continue and renew that communion."[15]

With this formula, the Reformed Eucharist officially left Zwinglian memorialism behind—but without wholeheartedly endorsing Calvin's persuasion that the Holy Spirit works *through* the symbolic acts as instruments and not merely at the same time (*simul*).[16] All three views are "symbolic" in the sense that they all take the notion of a sign or symbol as key to understanding a sacrament, but they differ in the way each relates the sign to the thing signified: whether the sign calls to mind a reality lying in the past (memorialism), or is the means by

13. Bullinger writes in his comments on Calvin's propositions: "There are two actions in the sacraments: the one external, the other internal." In his final statement, the *Fidei expositio* (1531), Zwingli himself had already developed his thoughts on the Eucharist in the direction of a kind of "parallelism," which enabled him to see the outward actions of the sacrament as picturing a *present* inward activity without connecting them as cause and effect. Of both the outer and the inward occurrences the subject is the communicant, not the Lord: "You do inwardly what you enact outwardly."

14. Reprinted in Gerrish, *The Old Protestantism and the New*, chap. 7. I suggested that Calvin's instrumentalism has an affinity with Thomist sacramental doctrine, Bullinger's parallelism with Franciscan occasionalism.

15. *Spiritualiter* here means "by the working of the Holy Spirit." See art. 8, which comes close to Bullinger's acceptance of parallelistic language. But see also art. 20, where a strict *simul* is denied since the grace of God, though assured, may bear fruit after the administration of the sacrament. In view of the distinction between *signum* and *res*, Calvin held that "This is my body" is an instance not of synecdoche but of "metonymy," by which one substitutes for a word ("bread") the name of the thing it suggests or points to ("body"). Cf. Consensus, art. 22. Note also that although communion with Christ is said to be drawing life from his flesh (art. 23), the location of Christ *sub pane* or *cum pane* is rejected as absurd (art. 24).

16. The Consensus avoids the word *instrumentum*, which Bullinger disliked, but still speaks of God's using the sacraments as *organa*, or working by the *ministerium* of the sacraments (arts. 12–13).

which the Holy Spirit brings the reality (instrumentalism), or simply indicates a reality that is going on at the same time (parallelism). The choice between the last two is nicely indicated by Nevin, who plainly preferred Calvin: "[T]he sacramental mystery as a whole … consists of two parts, the one outward and visible, the other inward and invisible. These, however, are not simply joined together in time, as the sound of a bell, or the show of a light, may give warning of something with which it stands in no further connection. They are connected by a true inward bond, so as to be different constituents only of one and the same reality."[17] But the Zurich Consensus did not choose between the two alternatives, and both can be found in other Reformed confessions.

The One Thing Needful

Like all compromise documents, the Consensus invited almost as many questions as it answered. It did not say all that Calvin himself liked to say, as is plain from his subsequent exposition and defense of it (1555). But article nine did state what to Calvin was the cardinal point: that sacramental signs cannot be divided from the reality they signify, so that when the sign is given the reality is given also. He liked to make the point by applying to sign and reality in the Eucharist the Chalcedonian formula concerning the two natures of Christ: there is "distinction without separation." Though he never claimed full agreement with Luther, Calvin believed that in the sacramental union of sign and thing signified he had found the hinge on which, for Luther as for himself, everything turned. It was the one thing needful for harmony among the Evangelicals, even if unresolved differences remained. Without it, the active agent in the sacrament, as Luther saw in his attack on Carlstadt, would be the devout worshiper trying to focus on Calvary, not the living Lord who offers his body as the sustenance of our souls. In a letter to the Lutheran John Marbach (24 August 1554), Calvin wrote:

> If Luther, that distinguished servant of God and faithful doctor of the church, were alive today, he would not be so harsh and unyielding as not willingly to allow this confession: that what the sacraments depict is truly offered to us (*vere praestari*), and that therefore in the sacred Supper we become partakers of the body and blood of Christ. For how often did he declare that he was contending for no other cause than to establish that the Lord does not mock us with empty signs but accomplishes inwardly what he sets before our eyes, and that the effect is therefore joined with the signs?

Here, of course, we have moved on from what Luther *said* about Calvin and his sacramental theology to what he *might* have said, if he were still living in 1554—or, in Calvin's optimistic judgment, what Luther assuredly *would* have said. His confidence was not mere wishful thinking: it rested on the experience of the Strasbourg years and on Luther's praise for the *Short Treatise on the Lord's Supper,* in which Calvin had already fastened on "naked signs (*les signes nudz*)" as the thought that provoked Luther to passionate rejection of the Zwinglian

17. Nevin, *Mystical Presence and Other Writings,* 182.

"heretics" (as he called them). Calvin left no ambiguity about his own conviction that sign and reality cannot be separated, that the union of sign and thing signified was the one thing needful for concord on the sacraments, and that, misunderstandings aside, unanimity on the subject had already been attained. The sequel proved that reconciliation was to be more difficult than he imagined, but he never changed his mind about the cardinal point. So far from being naked signs, sacramental signs are inseparable from what it is that they portray.

Not everyone was persuaded by Calvin's optimism, and there have been plenty of doubters ever since. They come from both sides of the confessional divide. In a deliciously patronizing letter (24 October 1554), the Zurich ministers blamed Calvin's optimism on his ignorance of German; otherwise, he would have known how crassly and barbarously Luther thought and wrote on the Lord's Supper. They cited a few helpful examples and gave the page numbers so that Calvin, as they said, could get someone skilled in German to translate for him word by word. "And if you do not possess the books, we have them and will be happy to lend them to you." For the men of Zurich, the chasm that separated them from Wittenberg could not be so easily crossed as their "dear brother" Calvin imagined.

From the other side came attacks on Calvin and the Zurich Consensus from the Lutheran polemicists Joachim Westphal and Tileman Heshusius. We cannot run through all the issues, arguments, and counter-arguments here.[18] I think the heart of Westphal's case was that because Calvin seemed reluctant to speak of eating the *substance* of Christ's body in the Eucharist, he really did, in fact, have nothing but empty signs left. Calvin heard this as a vain belief in the *local* presence of the actual physical mass of Christ's body in or under the bread. Sometimes (though not always) he preferred to say that, by the secret action of the Holy Spirit, life is infused into us *from* the substance of Christ's flesh.

An interesting addition to the controversy came from Heshusius, who launched his attack on Calvin in German. A third party thoughtfully sent Calvin some extracts translated into Latin, with the remark: "You, most learned Calvin, who are a Frenchman by race and do not understand German, no more understand the insults he spews out against you than I would if insulted in Arabic" (John Wolph to Calvin, 1 May 1560). But when Heshusius wrote that by the communication of properties (the *communicatio idiomatum*) ubiquity is ascribed *in concreto* to the whole person of Christ, the answer may have surprised him: Calvin replied that this was his own doctrine exactly. But for Calvin this meant that the presence of the God-Man did not require the physical mass of his body to be in or under the eucharistic bread. It remained in heaven, where (according to the Creed) it had ascended. This, to be sure, was not a scientific or cosmological assertion, but was intended simply to indicate distance (cf. Zurich Consensus, art. 25): until he comes again, the Lord is no longer present in the way he was present during his earthly ministry.

---

18. The main issues, apart from the understanding of signs and the interpretation of "This is my body" (see n. 15 above), concerned Lutheran teaching on the ubiquity of Christ's body and the eating of the body by the ungodly (the *manducatio impiorum*). See B.A. Gerrish, *Grace and Gratitude: The Eucharistic Theology of John Calvin* (1993; reprint, Eugene, OR: Wipf & Stock, 2002), esp. 134–45, 173–83.

Nearer to our own time, the formidable Lutheran theologian Hermann Sasse thought "it was a tragic error for Calvin to believe that he had found the solution" to the eucharistic impasse.[19] It is time, however, to make the confession I pledged to make as I began these reflections on Luther and the Reformed Eucharist: that the Reformed or Presbyterian churches have not exorcized the demons of Marburg. To put it bluntly: Just how Calvinist is the Reformed understanding of the Eucharist today? Just how Calvinist has it ever been? If I say that Presbyterians who are untroubled by theology tend to be Zwinglian by default, one could say as much of the adherents of most other Protestant churches. The simplicity and sweet reasonableness of a memorialist account of the sacrament lends it an immediate plausibility: talk of eating the life-giving flesh of Christ puzzles, or repels, or is translated into a harmless metaphor for believing in Christ.

Indeed, I must admit that the problem for the Calvinist goes deeper: Zwingli not only reigns by default in the pews but also has a firm hold on Presbyterian pulpits and academic lecterns. There have been eminent Reformed theologians who have expressly rejected Calvin's talk of the "life-giving flesh" of Christ. Charles Hodge, the supposed dean of American Calvinists in the nineteenth century, may speak for them all. When his former pupil Nevin undertook to expound and defend the Calvinist doctrine of the Eucharist, Hodge dismissed it as a private opinion of Calvin's, which soon died out: an uncongenial foreign element in Reformed theology, derived in part (note this!) from Lutheran influence. Up to a point Hodge was right. It is noteworthy that the *Book of Confessions* of the Presbyterian Church (U.S.A.), to which I belong, does not contain a single confession from Calvin's hand, or directly influenced by him, though there are ten to choose from in the *Opera omnia* besides Calvin's Geneva Catechism. Of the confessions included, only the Scots Confession of 1560 is vigorously and unambiguously Calvinist in its teaching on the Eucharist. It is there to reassure me that it is *possible* to be both a Presbyterian and a Calvinist, but hardly recommended.

It seems, then, that the supreme irony of my story is this: While many Lutherans mistrusted Calvin because he made peace with Zwingli's successors, there have been, and still are, Reformed theologians who renounce him because he was too much under the influence of the Lutherans. Of course, Calvin could still have been right about what *Luther* might have said of him and his eucharistic theology in 1554. Both of them were contending not only for a correct doctrine of the Lord's Supper, but for a conception of Christianity that does not equate Christian faith with right *beliefs* about Christ but sees the heart of Christian faith in what Calvin called *mystical union* with Christ. In reply to a query on the subject from Peter Martyr Vermigli, Calvin wrote (Calvin to Peter Martyr Vermigli, 8 August 1555):

What I say is that the moment we receive Christ by faith as he offers himself in the gospel, we become truly members of his body (*eius membra*), and life

---

19. Hermann Sasse, *This Is My Body: Luther's Contention for the Real Presence in the Sacrament of the Altar* (Minneapolis, Mn: Augsburg, 1959), 326.

flows into us from him as from the head…. Thus we draw life from his flesh
and blood, so that they are not undeservedly called our "food." How it happens, I confess, is far above the measure of my intelligence. Hence I revere
this mystery rather than labor to comprehend it—except that I recognize that
the life is transferred from the heavens to earth by the divine power (*virtute*)
of the Spirit.

Calvin goes on to speak of a "second communication," which is the fruit and
effect of the communication he has been describing.

Believers come into this communion on the very first day of their calling. But
in that Christ's life grows in them, he offers himself every day to be enjoyed
by them. This is the communication that they receive in the Holy Supper.

We might say, then, that Calvin taught a "real presence" of Christ even before
reception of the sacrament, and this may remind us that Luther, too, could say
that Christ is present in faith itself.

If Luther, "that distinguished servant of God and faithful doctor of the
church," consented to Calvin's confession on the sacraments, would it not be
because he recognized the understanding of Christian faith that lay behind it?

12. *Finitum est capax infiniti*
Luther's Radical Incarnational Perspective

Kurt K. Hendel

The Word and the sacraments were crucial aspects of Martin Luther's biblically-normed and experientially-informed theology. The Reformer viewed these means of grace as the unique gifts of God to the church through which the Holy Spirit creates and nurtures faith. They are, therefore, the constituent elements of the church's life and mission. The eucharist, in particular, captured Luther's attention because it was one of the great causes of dissension between the evangelical movement and the Church of Rome, as well as among the varied expressions of the Reformation. It was particularly in his conflict with fellow reformers, those to whom he referred in a derogatory manner as the sacramentarians, that Luther became an ardent defender of the physical presence of Christ in the sacrament. The notion of *finitum est capax infiniti* (the finite is capable of the infinite) or *finitum capax infiniti* was a central aspect of that defense and manifests the Reformer's radical incarnational perspective. The purpose of this essay is to explore Luther's literary debate with the Swiss reformers, especially Huldreich Zwingli and Johannes Oecolampadius. That debate marks the high point of Luther's theological defense of the real presence and in it the emphasis on *finitum capax infiniti* becomes readily apparent. In addition to highlighting the theological significance of this notion, I will also suggest some practical implications of this sacramental emphasis for the Lutheran movement's attitude toward and participation in contemporary society.

As I have already noted, Luther's eucharistic thought was developed in an intensely polemical context. In the early 1520's the Reformer addressed the medieval church's sacramental theology and practices. In the course of his conflicts with the Church of Rome he rejected five sacraments and affirmed only baptism and the eucharist. He militated against the notion of *ex opere operato* and stressed that faith is necessary for the efficacious reception of the sacraments. He dismissed the doctrine of transubstantiation as a philosophical explanation of a divine mystery and a misunderstanding of Aristotelian philosophy. He also advocated the distribution of both kinds in the eucharistic celebration and bitterly criticized the church's insistence that the sacrament is a sacrifice and a meritorious work.[1] By the middle 1520s, however, his major sacramental opponents were no longer the Roman theologians but the Swiss Reformer Huldreich

---

1. See *Babylonian Captivity of the Church*, 1520, in Jaroslav Pelikan and Helmut T. Lehmann, eds., *Luther's Works*, American ed., 55 vols. (Philadelphia, Pa: Fortress Press; Saint Louis, Mo: Concordia Publishing House, 1955–86), 36:3–126 (hereafter, *LW*).

Zwingli and his supporters, especially Johannes Oecolampadius.[2] The focus of the debate among the Reformers was the doctrine of the real presence. On the basis of his biblical interpretation, his humanist and rationalist tendencies and his own creative theological impulses, Zwingli proposed and defended a symbolic interpretation of Christ's eucharistic presence. While Oecolampadius, Andreas von Karlstadt, Martin Bucer and others formulated their own particular formulae in conceptualizing the eucharistic mystery, they all stood at Zwingli's side in his conflict with Luther. The latter emerged as an ardent and inflexible defender of a materialistic understanding of Christ's presence in his debates with the Swiss, even though he continued to reject the doctrine of transubstantiation. He, therefore, found himself much closer to the Roman side with regard to Christ's eucharistic presence than he did to his fellow reformers.

Luther and his opponents addressed a variety of issues in their sacramental writings, including the proper understanding of the words of institution, the meaning of the biblical concept of the right hand of God, the notion of ubiquity and the relationship of the two natures of Christ. I will focus particularly on their debate regarding the meaning of Christ's words in John 6:63. It is in his interpretation of this passage, which was central to the Swiss argument, and in his response to the Swiss position, as he understood it, that Luther formulated a highly positive understanding of the spiritual significance of created matter.

Prior to exploring the meaning of John 6:63 Luther made an important point regarding physical matter while addressing the Zwinglian interpretation of the right hand of God[3] and defending the scholastic notion of ubiquity. The Reformer noted that the biblical phrase "the right hand of God" does not denote a specific location or place but, rather, God's power. It is by means of this mighty power that God "creates, effects, and preserves all things."[4] Because it is God's work, all of creation is good and, therefore, neither condemned nor rejected by God.[5] As creator and preserver, God is also immanently present in all things. Luther is quite insistent: "Therefore, indeed, he himself must be present in every single creature in its innermost and outermost being, on all sides, through and through, below and above, before and behind, so that nothing can be more truly present and within all creatures than God himself with his power."[6]

2. The most important scholarly discussions of Luther's conflicts with the Swiss theologians are Walther Köhler, *Zwingli und Luther: Ihr Streit über das Abendmahl*, 2 vols., QFRG 6–7 (Leipzig: M. Heinsius Nachfolger, 1924; Gütersloh: C. Bertelsmann, 1953); Hermann Sasse, *This Is My Body: Luther's Contention for the Real Presence* (Minneapolis, Mn: Augsburg, 1959).
3. Note, for example, Oecolampadius' assertion: "The nature of a body is to be in one place. That body which can be in many places at the same time will not be considered to be a true body. A body has one location, unless it can be taught otherwise from Scripture." (*Reasonable Answer to Dr. Martin Luther's Instruction concerning the Sacrament*, in *Dr. Martin Luthers Sämtliche Schriften*, ed. Johann Georg Walch, 2nd ed., 23 vols. [Saint Louis, Mo: Concordia Publishing House, 1880–1910], 20:603); [hereafter, Walch]. Zwingli noted, "this word [until] binds him to the right hand of God until the predetermined day, so that we may easily understand that he will never be anywhere else than at the right hand of God until the judgment is completed." (*Reply to the Letters of Theobald Billican and Urban Rhegius*, in *Huldreich Zwinglis Sämtliche Schriften*, ed. Emil Egli et al. vol. 4 [Zurich: Theologischer Verlag Zurich, 1982], 907; [reprint of *Corpus Reformatorum*, vol. 4]). Hereafter referred to as *Zwingli's Sämtliche Schriften*. Unless otherwise indicated, all German and Latin translations are those of the author.
4. *LW* 37:57.
5. *LW* 37:237.
6. *LW* 37:58.

While God is present everywhere and in everything, it is also crucial to recognize that God is not circumscribed by any part of or even by the whole creation. After all, the divine "Majesty is so great that neither this world nor even a thousand worlds could embrace it and say, 'See, there it is!'"[7] Although he is careful to avoid the charge of pantheism, Luther insists that all material things are God's good creation in which God is intimately present. There is a creative and salvific relationship between the infinite and the finite. Obviously, this assertion was crucial for Luther's defense of the real presence. It also serves as one of the theological explanations for his positive view of matter.

Both Zwingli and Oecolampadius, who were Luther's chief sacramental antagonists, agreed with him that Scripture must be the ultimate source and norm of the church's teachings. Indeed, they attacked Luther by citing scriptural texts and drawing particular sacramental implications from them. Thus, Luther and the Swiss theologians agreed on what the norm of their theological positions should be. However, significant differences and disagreements emerged in their interpretations of that scriptural norm. In addition to the eucharistic passages and Eph 1:20[8], John 6:63 was a pivotal text in the sacramental debates between the Lutherans and the Swiss.

The sixth chapter of John, especially verse 63, was of particular significance as the Swiss theologians addressed the question of Christ's presence in the sacrament and the manner and significance of the believers' sacramental eating. The passage reads. "It is the spirit that gives life, the flesh is of no avail; the words that I have spoken to you are spirit and life" (John 6:63 RSV). Jesus' discourse in John 6 regarding the bread of life, his comments about eating his flesh and drinking his blood, the spirit/flesh dialectic which he develops and especially the phrase "the flesh is of no avail" in verse 63, raised important questions for the Swiss theologians and significantly shaped their understanding of the Lord's Supper, especially Christ's presence in that Supper. They argued that since the flesh is of no avail, the bodily, physical presence of Christ in the sacrament is neither necessary nor beneficial. Secondly, they stressed the flesh/spirit dichotomy and lauded the latter while denigrating the former. Thirdly, they maintained that spirit and flesh are such radically different entities that they cannot be united. Finally, they focused on spiritual and physical eating and noted that the former was much more crucial than the latter. Luther devoted a substantial portion of his two major eucharistic treatises, *That These Words of Christ, "This Is My Body," etc., Still Stand Firm against the Fanatics* of 1527 and his *Confession concerning Christ's Supper* of 1528,[9] to his own interpretation of John 6. In doing so, he examined and rejected the sacramental implications drawn by

---

7. *LW* 37:59. See also *LW* 37:228:

He is a supernatural, inscrutable being who exists at the same time in every little seed, whole and entire, and yet also in all and above all and outside all created things. There is no need to enclose him here, as this spirit dreams, for a body is much, much too wide for the Godhead; it could contain many thousand Godheads. On the other hand, it is also far, far too narrow to contain one Godhead. Nothing is so small but God is still smaller, nothing so large but God is still larger, nothing is so short but God is still shorter, nothing so long but God is still longer, nothing is so broad but God is still broader, nothing so narrow but God is still narrower, and so on. He is an inexpressible being, above and beyond all that can be described and imagined.

8. The passage speaks about Christ sitting at the right hand of God.

9. These two writings are the content of *LW* 37.

the Swiss theologians on the basis of these passages. What follows highlights crucial aspects of Luther's argument.

Since Jesus said that the flesh is of no avail, Zwingli and Oecolampadius concluded that Christ's flesh would not be sacramentally efficacious and is not present in the sacrament.[10] Luther responds that this passage is not applicable to Christ's flesh and, therefore, has no implications for the sacrament. He points out, first of all, that Christ says that "flesh is of no avail," not "my flesh is of no avail."[11] Thus, if the Swiss want to apply the passage to Christ's flesh, they must offer scriptural warrant for doing so. Of course, he implies that they are unable to provide such scriptural support. Secondly, Luther argues that Christ's flesh is not "fleshly" but spiritual. He notes that Christ was conceived by the power of the Holy Spirit. Therefore, the second part of John 3:6, "That which is born of the Spirit is spirit," applies to Jesus' flesh, not John 6:63.[12] Luther also recalls the promise of the angel to Mary that her child "will be called holy, the Son of God" (Luke 1:35 RSV). Thirdly, he warns that denigrating Christ's flesh will lead to dualism and docetism, as has happened in the past.[13] Finally, Luther points out the devastating implications of the Swiss assertion for the incarnation and for soteriology. He asks:

> If the flesh of Christ is not spirit, and therefore is of no avail since only the Spirit is profitable, how can it be profitable when it was given for us? How can it be useful if it is in heaven and we believe in it? If the reasoning is correct and adequate, that because Christ's flesh is not spirit it must be of no avail, then it can be of no avail on the cross or in heaven either! For it is quite as far from being spirit on the cross and in heaven as in the Supper. But since no spirit was crucified for us, therefore Christ's flesh was crucified for us to no avail. And since no spirit, but Christ's flesh ascended into heaven, we believe in an un-profitable flesh in heaven. For wherever Christ's flesh may be, it is no spirit. If it is no spirit, it is of no avail and does not give life, as Zwingli here concludes.[14]

The point is clear. If Christ's flesh is not beneficial in the sacrament, it is also not beneficial on the cross or even in heaven. Then the gifts of forgiveness, life and salvation have neither been won for us by Christ nor are they dispensed in the eucharistic celebration. Luther hoped that his readers would follow his logic, recognize both the error and danger of the Swiss position, reject the biblical interpretation proposed by his opponents and conclude with him that Christ clearly did not refer to his own flesh when he proclaimed that the flesh is of no avail. In light of his incarnational and soteriological perspective, Luther

---

10. Zwingli insisted: "The flesh of Christ profiteth very greatly, aye, immeasurably, in every way but ... by being slain, not eaten. Slain it has saved us from slaughter, but devoured it profiteth absolutely nothing." (*Commentary on True and False Religion*, in *The Latin Works of Huldreich Zwingli*, ed. Clarence Nevin Heller, vol. 3 [Philadelphia, Pa: Heidelberg Press, 1929], 209). Hereafter referred to as *Commentary*, LWZ 3. He articulates the same argument in his *Reply to the Letters of Theobald Billican and Urban Rhegius*: "The flesh of Christ is of no avail if it is eaten. Therefore those words of Christ, 'This is my body,' cannot be understood as if through them the flesh of Christ is eaten." (*LW* 37:130, n. 225; *Zwinglis Sämtliche Schriften*, 4:898).

11. *LW* 37:79.

12. *LW* 37:98–99; 236–237.

13. *LW* 37:99.

14. *LW* 37:246–247. See also *LW* 37:85.

argues that the flesh is, in fact, essential since it is in the flesh and by means of flesh that Christ has accomplished God's redemptive work. Hence the passage from John cannot be used to justify a rejection of the real presence, according to Luther. It also does not warrant a negative understanding of flesh or of created matter in general.

The Reformer clarifies his thinking further as he examines the spirit/flesh dialectic in greater depth. He notes that when flesh and spirit are placed in opposition in Scripture, flesh always refers to our sinful nature which is born of the flesh (John 3:6).[15] On the other hand, all that comes from the Spirit or is used by the Spirit for spiritual purposes, including flesh and other material things, is spiritual.[16] Luther summarizes his argument in the following passages:

> [We] do not call "flesh" that which can be seen by the eye or touched by the fingers, as the fanatics do when they call Christ's body useless flesh; but...all is spirit, spiritual, and an object of the Spirit, in reality and in name, which comes from the Holy Spirit, be it as physical or material, outward or visible as it may; on the other hand, all is flesh and fleshly which comes from the natural power of the flesh, without spirit, be it as inward and invisible as it may....[17] Because the Holy Spirit works in and through the Word of God and faith, everything that is connected with them is spiritual as well, no matter how physical or material it may be. Thus, all that our body does outwardly and physically, if God's Word is added to it and it is done through faith, is in reality and in name done spiritually. Nothing can be so material, fleshly, or outward, but it becomes spiritual when it is done in the Word and in faith. "Spiritual" is nothing else than what is done in us and by us through the Spirit and faith, whether the object with which we are dealing is physical or spiritual. Thus, "Spirit consists in the use, not in the object," be it seeing, hearing, speaking, touching, begetting, bearing, eating, drinking, or anything else. For if a person serves his neighbor and does it physically, it is of no avail to him, for the flesh is of no avail. But if he does it spiritually, i.e., if his heart does it out of faith in God's Word, it is life and salvation.[18]

The Holy Spirit, the Word and faith thus determine whether an object or a deed are spiritual or not, not the object or deed itself.

It is important to note that a basic perceptual and theological difference between Luther and the Swiss reformers is emerging here, namely, how they respond to the critical question of whether the finite is or is not a vehicle of the divine (*finitum est capax infiniti* or *finitum non est capax infiniti*). The fact that the two sides gave different answers to this central question largely explains their different sacramental theologies, especially with regard to Christ's presence in the eucharist. Their answers also had crucial implications for their attitude toward and perception of the material.

It is with these definitions of flesh and spirit, or of the fleshly and spiritual, in mind that Luther also addresses the Swiss claim that it is not fitting that

---

15. *LW* 37:95.
16. *LW* 37:94–95.
17. *LW* 37:99.
18. *LW* 37:92.

Christ's body and blood are present in bread and wine.[19] Here the issue of the finite holding the infinite comes to the forefront. Karlstadt had apparently set the stage for this debate in the following statement attributed to him by Luther. "My friend, you will not persuade me that God is in the bread and wine."[20] Oecolampadius also raised this central issue when he rejected the notion that Christ "is enclosed in the loaves and falling crumbs on many altars."[21] The Basel Reformer challenged Luther particularly by referring to the God of the Lutherans as a baked God, a bread-God, a meat-God and other similar terms.[22] From the Swiss perspective it was not consistent with Christ's divine glory to be physically present in the sacrament. Hence, they argued that it is neither fitting nor necessary that Christ's physical body and blood be in the bread and wine.[23] Luther retorted that if this is true then the incarnation and Christ's other saving acts are also not fitting or reasonable. And so he writes:

> To this first point I might say equally well that it is not reasonable that God should descend from heaven and enter into the womb; that he who nourishes, sustains, and encompasses all the world should allow himself to be nourished and encompassed by the Virgin. Likewise, that Christ, a king of glory [Ps. 24:10], at whose feet all angels must fall and before whom all creatures must tremble, should thus humble himself below all men and allow himself to be suspended upon the cross as a most notorious evil-doer and that by the most wicked and desperate of men. And I might conclude from this that God did not become man, or that the crucified Christ is not God.[24]

Questioning the reality of God's presence in and use of the material thus has dire consequences for the very heart of the Christian message and puts the salvation of humanity into doubt. The Swiss did not intend or envision such consequences, but Luther insists that these are precisely the implications of their eucharistic theology.

With regard to the Swiss contention that it is not necessary that Christ's body and blood are physically present in the sacrament, Luther cautions that they should let God decide what is necessary and what is not. If we start questioning

---

19. Zwingli claimed: "She [the church] will not even brook the question whether the body of Christ is in the Sacrament of the Eucharist in actual, physical, or essential form." (*Commentary*, LWZ 3:212).

20. LW 37:52. Luther asserts that Karlstadt said these words to an unidentified person, presumably someone who affirmed the doctrine of the real presence.

21. Quoted in LW 37:65, n. 108.

22. LW 37:52–53. See also LW 36:336; LW 38:29, 293, 295, 305. Oecolampadius argued that his description of his opponents as *gotsfleischesser* and *gotsblutsauffer* and of their God as *brötenen* and *gebachnen* was defensible. See his *Reasonable Answer to Dr. Martin Luther's Instruction concerning the Sacrament*, Walch, 20:582ff. Zwingli, too, argued that Lutheran sacramental theology suggested that God should be described in terms such as "edible," "impanated," "baked," "roasted" and "ground-up": "Si autem esculents deus, impanatus, coctus, frixus, aut pistus nusquam est." (*Reply to Letters of Theobald Billican and Urban Rhegius*, 1526 [*Zwinglis Sämtliche Schriften*, 4:934]).

23. LW 36:338. Oecolampadius asked. "What need have we of his body to be in that bread? I do not see what benefit accrues to us from this." (*Reply to Willibald Prickheimer on the Subject of the Eucharist* [LW 37:127, n. 216]; *D. Martin Luthers Werke: Kritische Gesamtausgabe*, 69 vols. [Weimar: Hermann Böhlaus Nachfolger, 1883–, 23:315] [hereafter, WA]. He notes further: "Moreover, the bodily presence of Christ is not necessary. As our adversaries themselves admit, the soul receives this [strengthening of faith] as often as the Word is preached in the gospel and received with faith." (*Reasonable Answer to Dr. Martin Luther's Instruction concerning the Sacrament* [LW 37:138 n. 236; Walch, 20:633]). Oecolampadius notes further: "Moreover, we do not at all need the bodily presence of the Lord in order to receive the spiritual gifts." (Walch, 20:603).

24. LW 36:338.

God regarding Christ's sacramental presence, we might well question why Christ was necessary at all since God could easily have overcome the power of sin by simply speaking a word. We could also assert that it was not necessary for Christ to be born of a virgin or that he be God since God could have enabled a human being to save us. This is what happens when people do not trust and believe God's clear word and draw conclusions about God's will and activity on the basis of their own reason. "Therefore," Luther insists, "one must close mouth, eyes and all the senses and say: 'Lord, you know better than I.'"[25]

The Swiss asserted that Christ's bodily presence in the sacrament was neither fitting nor necessary because they considered it to contradict Christ's glory.[26] Informed by his theology of the cross, Luther instructed his opponents what Christ's glory truly is. Christ's glory does not consist of sitting at the right hand of God "on a velvet cushion,"[27] insists Luther. Rather, his glory is manifest precisely when his body and blood are present in the Supper, when he permits the learned to become offended and hardened by his foolish words and works, when he makes the wise fools so that they are blinded precisely where they desire to be most wise. It is also Christ's glory to be so concerned about poor sinners and to show them such love that he is not only present among them but gives them his own body so that their bodies might have eternal life. Thus, the glory of God "is precisely that for our sakes he comes down to the very depths, into human flesh, into the bread, into our mouth, our heart, our bosom; moreover, for our sakes he allows himself to be treated ingloriously both on the cross and on the altar, as St. Paul says in I Corinthians 11[:27], that some eat the bread in an unworthy manner."[28] It is once again crucial to note Luther's incarnational perspective and his emphasis on the material as a means of God's immanence and of God's saving activity.

While Christ's eucharistic presence contradicts his glory according to the Swiss, Luther believes that his surprising, foolish, offensive divine glory is manifest particularly as he takes on flesh, suffers for us, is present in the sacrament and nourishes us with his own flesh and blood. The Reformer was so adamant and certain about this not only because of his theology of the cross but also because he was convinced that the physical and the spiritual, the material and the divine, are not irreconcilable opposites but are intimately yoked in God's saving and life-giving work. While the Swiss had difficulty imagining and, therefore, believing that the body could be in the bread, Luther insisted that God has specifically chosen to be present in and to work through the material. Hence, the Reformer can make the radical assertion that the Holy Spirit cannot be present with believers "except in material and physical things such

---

25. *LW* 36:345.

26. Oecolampadius cautioned: "If Christ is in the bread, then wherever the bread is placed or carried, it will be necessary for the body also to be carried to the same place, for it is bread; and one will be at liberty to play with it, so that it will be borne up and down, forward and backward in the bread, according to the whim of the administrant." (*Reply to Willibald Pirckheimer* [*LW* 37:65, n. 108]). Oecolampadius rejected the notion that Christ is "enclosed in the loaves and fallen crumbs on many altars" or that bread is a "wrapping" for Christ. See his *Genuine Exposition of the Words of the Lord, "This Is My Body," according to the Most Ancient Authors* (*LW* 37:65, n. 108). Oecolampadius also stated the position of the Swiss concisely in his *Apologetics*: "I know today a more glorious Christ than one who permits himself to be touched or carnally eaten." (*LW* 37:71, n. 118; *WA* 23:303).

27. *LW* 37:70.

28. *LW* 37:72.

as the Word, water, and Christ's body and in his saints on earth."[29] He also points out that God's word, which makes objects and works spiritual, is always accompanied by the physical or the material. Luther gives the examples of Abraham to whom God gave Isaac together with the word, of Noah to whom God made a promise and sent the rainbow and of the Supper where the word is accompanied by Christ's crucified body. And so he concludes. "You find no word of God in the entire Scriptures in which something material and outward is not contained and presented."[30] Luther presses his point even further and asserts that, as is the case with the Holy Spirit and the Word, faith, too, is always connected to a physical object.[31]

The philosophical law of identical predication, which stated that two differing substances cannot be united, had long challenged sacramental theologians as they sought to reconcile the presence of bread and wine as well as of body and blood in the eucharist. The medieval scholastics resolved the problem posed by identical predication through the doctrine of transubstantiation, which asserted that the substance of bread and wine is replaced by body and blood. Hence, only body and blood are present in the sacrament. During the fourteenth century, John Wyclif rejected transubstantiation, spoke of the elements as signs, suggested that Christ's body and blood are present "sacramentally," not physically, and argued that the sacramental elements remain bread and wine.[32] Not surprisingly, Zwingli, who also agreed with the law of identical predication,[33] cited Wyclif in support of his rejection of the real presence.[34] Luther not only disagreed with the scholastics as well as with Wyclif and Zwingli, but he also argued that the law of identical predication is irrelevant to the sacramental discussion. While reason and philosophical principles suggest that two diverse substances cannot become one, Luther argued that this is clearly a possibility, indeed, a reality, in divine matters. He points particularly to the incarnation in support of his position that bread and body and wine and blood, which are obviously distinct and different substances, can be united in the sacrament. While the physical elements are relationally changed by the sacramental union, they are not transubstantiated or destroyed. Body and blood as well as bread and wine are, therefore, present in the eucharist and together they are a new sacramental substance.

> For even though body and bread are two distinct substances, each one existing by itself, and though neither is mistaken for the other where they are separated from each other, nevertheless where they are united and become a new, entire substance, they lose their difference so far as this new, unique substance is concerned. As they become one, they are called and designated one object. It is not necessary, meanwhile, that one of the two disappear or be annihilated, but both the bread and the body remain, and by virtue of the

---

29. *LW* 37:95.
30. *LW* 37:135–136.
31. *LW* 37:292.
32. *LW* 37:294ff.
33. "The saying, 'this is bread and is, additionally, my body,' has no safeguard at all, either in God's word or in philosophy, for two substances cannot be one thing." (*Friendly Reminder* [Walch, 20:1111]).
34. "I hear (to mention this first) that Wycliffe earlier held and the Waldensians today hold this view, that 'is' was put here for 'signifies,' but I have not seen their Scripture basis for it." (*Commentary*, LWZ 3, 224).

sacramental unity it is correct to say, "This is my body," designating the bread with the word "this." For now it is no longer ordinary bread in the oven, but a "flesh-bread" or "body-bread," i.e., a bread which has become one sacramental substance, one with the body of Christ. Likewise with the wine in the cup, "This is my blood," designating the wine with the word "this." For it is no longer ordinary wine in the cellar but "blood-wine," i.e., a wine which has been united with the blood of Christ in one sacramental substance.[35]

According to Luther, then, the law of identical predication simply constitutes another fallacious argument in support of a denial of Christ's bodily presence in the sacrament. Divine truth obviously transcends philosophical principles. Hence, identical predication is irrelevant in divine matters and does not necessitate either a scholastic position, which rejects the presence of bread and wine, or a Zwinglian position, which denies the presence of body and blood. It also cannot be cited as justification for arguing that the divine and the material cannot be united.

While the Swiss continued to celebrate the eucharist and expected the people to participate in that celebration and partake of the sacrament, their sacramental theology caused them to emphasize spiritual, rather than physical, eating as the essential sacramental action of the believer.[36] Such spiritual eating, or faith, does not necessitate Christ's bodily presence in the sacrament. They also feared that the Lutheran stress on the real presence and on the physical eating and drinking of Christ's physical body and blood would lead to what was termed "Capernaitic eating." Indeed, they accused Luther and his followers of this error.[37]

In response to these assertions and concerns of his opponents, Luther defended the value of physical eating. Such eating, when done in faith, is, in fact, spiritual. Because Christ's body is eaten, the promise of forgiveness is also fulfilled through such spiritual physical eating.[38] Furthermore, as it partakes of the everlasting food which is the body and blood of Christ, the human body is also assured that it will live forever.[39] For Luther, then, the eucharist is not only spiritual food for the soul but also bodily nourishment which literally assures eternal life to the body. Physical eating is, therefore, essential and beneficial, but it is not sufficient. Those who partake must also eat spiritually. As they eat the bread and drink the wine physically, they must also believe that they are eating the body and drinking the blood of Christ.[40] Both physical eating and spiritual

35. *LW* 37:303.

36. Martin Bucer speaks in Christ's stead as he interprets John 6:63: "If faith and hence my spirit are lacking, you will not receive life, and the eating of my flesh will be of no avail. I have been speaking of that spiritual and life-giving eating of myself." (*Apology*, 18; *LW* 37:84, n. 144). Oecolampadius stressed: "We exhort to faith ... rather than to the eating of bread." (*Reply to Willibald Pirckheimer* [*LW* 37:86, n. 146]).

37. Oecolampadius asserts: "They are Capernaites, who promise themselves a fleshly table, as if the flesh of Christ were contained in the bread." (*Genuine Exposition* [*LW* 37:93, n. 153; *WA* 23:308]). Zwingli rejects any notion of physical eating. "That the symbolic bread is the flesh of Christ is so abhorrent to the mind of all believers that no one of us has ever truly believed it.... This idea of mangling the flesh the mind so rejects that one would not dare to chew but would spit it out of one's mouth." (*Zwinglis Sämtliche Schriften*, 4:493).

38. *LW* 38:46–47.

39. *LW* 37:71, 87, 93–94.

40. *LW* 37:85.

eating, or believing, are necessary if the sacrament is to be beneficial to both body and soul. Luther explains his position concretely:

> The mouth eats the body of Christ physically, for it cannot grasp or eat the words, nor does it know what it is eating. As far as taste is concerned the mouth surely seems to be eating something other than Christ's body. But the heart grasps the words in faith and eats spiritually precisely the same body as the mouth eats physically, for the heart sees very well what the uncomprehending mouth eats physically. But how does it see this? Not by looking at the bread or at the mouth's eating, but at the word which is there, "Eat, this is my body." Yet there is only one body of Christ, which both mouth and heart eat, each in its own mode and manner. The heart cannot eat it physically nor can the mouth eat it spiritually. So God arranges that the mouth eats physically for the heart and the heart eats spiritually for the mouth, and thus both are satisfied and saved by the same food.[41]

Luther clearly rejects the Swiss accusation that the Lutherans stress physical eating and neglect spiritual eating, and he also ardently denies the charge of Capernaitic eating. Although the Lutherans insist that the body and blood of Christ are physically present in the sacrament, they do not teach or envision a materialistic devouring of Christ's flesh in the eucharistic partaking, nor does their theology imply or lead to such a false understanding of the sacramental action. Luther explains, therefore, that when Christ's physical body is eaten physically in the Supper it is not torn into pieces, divided, corrupted, destroyed, chewed or digested. Christ's body is blessed, divine and incorruptible flesh which is unlike any other food. It is not consumed by the one who eats it, but it transforms that person into what it is, namely, something "spiritual, alive and eternal."[42] The charge that the Lutherans are Capernaites or that their eucharistic theology implies Capernaitic eating is both false and unfair, protests Luther.

In responding to the Swiss assertion that the flesh is of no avail and that it would be inconsistent with Christ's glory to be present in bread and wine, Luther formulated a theology of creation and incarnation which affirms matter as God's good creation, which emphasizes God's immanent presence in all created things and which maintains that God accomplishes God's saving work precisely through material means. The Reformer thus clearly differentiated himself from his sacramental opponents by insisting that the finite is capable of holding the infinite, *finitum est capax infiniti*.

As has become apparent, this crucial affirmation is informed by and confirms central themes in Luther's theology. The confession that God is the creator and preserver of all that is; the crucial importance of Christ's incarnation for God's self-revelation and God's saving acts; a conscious affirmation of Chalcedonian Christology, with a particular emphasis on the unity of the two natures; a focus on the means of grace and a physical, material understanding of Christ's eucharistic presence all reflect and necessitate his positive view of created matter and his insistence that the divine and the material are intimately and necessarily related. Luther was, therefore, an ardent proponent of the sacred, spiritual

41. *LW* 37:93.
42. *LW* 37:100.

nature of the material, not only as God's good creation but also as the unique means of God's intimate presence in the world and as the instrument of God's redemptive and justifying activity. The Reformer's soteriological perspective obviously necessitates an intimate relationship between God who is Creator and Redeemer and the creation. While he strives diligently to avoid pantheism and panentheism, he also rejects all dualistic and iconoclastic tendencies which have, too often, manifested themselves within the Christian tradition. The Reformer's stance has crucial implications for God's nature and work. Luther's God is a relational, immanent God, and this God works through means, the material means of God's creation. The notion that the finite is a vehicle of the divine also necessitates a particular attitude toward and relationship with the material and has very practical implications for the life and ministry of people of faith. For illustrative purposes I will note two such implications, one from the Lutheran historical heritage and one which suggests that the church should assume a leadership role in addressing one of the great challenges faced by our world today.

Luther's notion that the finite is a vehicle of the divine clearly shaped the Lutheran community's attitude toward and use of the arts. From its very beginning, the evangelical movement did not promote or tolerate iconoclasm.[43] Although the side altars, used primarily for the celebration of votive masses, were often removed, the churches which became Lutheran houses of worship were not stripped of their art work. Even when new evangelical churches were built, they did not differ significantly from already extant structures except that the pulpit was often located in the midst of the congregation. Quite obviously, this architectural feature reflected Luther's theological emphasis on the centrality and efficacy of the living Word and, hence, of proclamation in Christian worship. In light of the doctrine of the priesthood of all believers and his insistence that the sacrament was Christ's gift to the whole community, not a possession of the clergy, Luther also advocated that the altar should be moved away from the wall and that the priest should face the people during the sacramental liturgy.[44] In spite of its theological warrant, this innovation was generally not implemented among Lutherans until more modern times. With these minimal changes, Lutheran church buildings looked very much like those of the Roman church and retained the traditional artistic expressions, although these were informed by evangelical theology. Any fear of idolatry was transcended by the conviction that the material could be used to express a spiritual message and to celebrate God's saving acts.

The visual arts, especially woodcuts, were promoted by the Lutheran reformers, although primarily for didactic rather than aesthetic purposes.[45] The

---

43. See the eight sermons Luther preached when returning to Wittenberg from the Wartburg (*LW* 51:70–100). See also Carlos M.N. Eire, *War against the Idols: The Reformation and Worship from Erasmus to Calvin* (Cambridge, UK: Cambridge University Press, 1989). This is a fascinating study which compares the responses of the various Reformation movements to images. The author explores the different attitudes of the Lutheran and Reformed traditions and suggests that those differences are explained by their disagreement over the question of whether the finite holds the infinite.

44. *LW* 53:69.

45. The best and most thorough discussion in English of the German Reformation's use of and impact on artistic expression is Carl C. Christiansen, *Art and the Reformation in Germany*, Studies in the Reformation 2 (Columbus, Oh: The Ohio State University Press, 1981).

Bible, which was translated into German by Luther and his colleagues and was first published in 1534,[46] was not only an important theological, devotional and literary accomplishment. It also had artistic merit with its illuminated initials and 124 color woodcuts.[47] The Scriptures themselves, which were to have a central place in the church's life, thus became a means of affirming and promoting artistic endeavors, especially the visual arts. Luther's German Bible concretely demonstrated the Reformer's contention that the word pictures in Scripture are quite naturally formed into mental pictures by the believer and, in turn, foster the artistic depiction of biblical themes and scenes.[48] Woodcuts were also prevalent in the pamphlet literature of the time. This literary genre became a popular means of communicating Lutheran theological insights to the general public. The woodcuts portrayed the central message of the pamphlet in pictorial form. Thus, both the learned and those who could not read were taught the essentials of the faith. Albrecht Dürer and his school were particularly adept at this specific artistic medium. Unfortunately, the polemical and scatological use of pamphlets and of woodcuts also became quite popular during the Reformation period. It must be noted, however, that pamphlets, with their woodcuts, were often effective didactic and communication tools, even when they were employed in negative ways, and that they had an important impact on the culture and society of the time.

Artists, particularly Lucas Cranach the Elder and Lucas Cranach the Younger, not only provided posterity with portraits of the reformers and of contemporary ecclesiastical and political personalities, but they also produced religious art.[49] The altarpieces in St. Mary's Church, the city church of Wittenberg, and in St. Peter and St. Paul Church in Weimar are prime examples of evangelical sacred art. Important theological themes, such as the priesthood of all believers and the centrality of Word and sacraments, were presented in pictorial form by these artists. For example, in one of the panels of the altarpiece at St. Mary's Church, Philip Melanchthon, who was a layperson, is depicted baptizing one of his children. While the scene has no historical basis, it was a striking and effective visual depiction of Luther's doctrine of the universal priesthood which asserted that all the baptized have sacramental authority.[50] Artistic endeavors and visual images were affirmed by the evangelicals on the basis of Luther's theology, and they became integral parts of the worship spaces and worship experiences of God's people. The finite was clearly viewed and used as a vehicle of the divine.

The celebration and implementation of this theological principle was perhaps most readily apparent within Lutheran circles in the composition and use of sacred music as an essential part of worship, as an effective means of

---

46. The New Testament was translated by Luther in eleven weeks during his stay at the Wartburg. The first edition was published in September, 1522, and is generally known as the "September Testament." However, the whole Bible was not published until 1534 when it also appeared in a Low German version. For insights into Luther's work as a translator of Scripture, see Heinz Bluhm, *Martin Luther: Creative Translator* (Saint Louis, Mo: Concordia Publishing House, 1965).

47. Harold J. Grimm, *The Reformation Era 1500–1650*, 2nd ed. (New York, Ny: Macmillan Publishing Company, 1973), 186.

48. *LW* 40:99–100.

49. A fine collection of Cranach art is exhibited in the castle museum in Weimar, Germany.

50. *LW* 44:127–130; *LW* 36:112–113, 116; *LW* 40:18–35.

spiritual expression and as an important catechetical resource.[51] The long and illustrious tradition of Lutheran church music ranges from the popular hymns of Luther during the sixteenth century to the Christo-centric and spiritually moving hymnody of Paul Gerhardt in the seventeenth century to the majestic compositions of Johann Sebastian Bach in the eighteenth century, particularly his cantatas, organ preludes, passions, short masses and Mass in B Minor. These compositions proclaim the central themes of Luther's biblical message and reflect his theological and spiritual conviction that the material can be used for spiritual purposes.

The church no longer dominates society and culture as it did in medieval Europe or in the time of the Reformation. Theology no longer defines the contemporary world view nor does it play a major role in inspiring and shaping artistic expressions. Yet, the church continues to be a community which is called to be of service to the world. Christians continue to confess their faith and express that faith in worship, theological documents and practical witness. The church's theology thus continues to be a resource to the Christian community as it seeks to be the body of Christ in any particular time, place or culture. The confession that God is Creator, that God has taken on human flesh, that the creation is the dwelling place of the Holy Spirit and that God remains immanently present and active through such material means as water and bread and wine continues to enliven people and bring them hope. Therefore, these crucial theological affirmations which are so intimately related to the notion of *finitum capax infiniti* can still inspire the church to be an agent of cultural critique, transformation and expression. It will be precisely that when it again becomes a catalyst for artistic endeavors, whether sacred or secular, and when it opposes all forms of dualism which denigrate the material and justify its neglect and abuse. This last point brings me to the second implication which I want to highlight.

In addition to fostering artistic expression, and even more importantly, the church catholic and surely the Lutheran community should provide leadership in contemporary efforts to address the greatest and most fundamental challenge facing our world today, namely, the ecological crisis. There can be very little doubt that two centuries of industrial and economic activity has affected the earth in profoundly negative ways. God's wondrous gift of creation which has sustained life in its diverse complexity for so long has been compromised so radically that its very existence and, hence, the existence of life as we know it are endangered. Of course, Luther did not envision the contemporary ecological crisis nor does he address specific aspects of that crisis. However, because of his theology of creation, incarnation, redemption and the means of grace, the Reformer was profoundly respectful of all material things, and his love for the beauties of nature is readily apparent in his writings. The heritage which he articulated in such creative and passionate ways gives Lutherans a sound theological basis and serves as obvious inspiration for ecological consciousness and commitment. We are called to care for God's creation, not only for our sake and for the sake of future generations but also for God's sake. After

---

51. For Luther's and Lutheranism's contributions to sacred music, see Paul Nettl, *Luther and Music* (Philadelphia, Pa: Muhlenberg Publishing House, 1948) and Patrice Veit, *Das Kirchenlied in der Reformation Martin Luthers: Eine Thematische und Semantische Untersuchung* (Wiesbaden: F. Steiner Verlag, 1986).

all, the material continues to be a vehicle of the divine, and God continues to take simple water, connects it to God's Word and transforms it into life-giving water. Christ continues to add his promises to bread and wine and offers us his body and blood to nurture the gift of life within us. The Holy Spirit continues to be present in the means of grace and uses them to create and strengthen faith. When we respect and preserve the material world around us, we are stewards of the material vehicles of the divine. From a Christian perspective, the ecological movement is ultimately not a matter of political correctness, of practical necessity or of an altruistic sense of morality. It is a spiritual matter, a matter of faith, a divine matter, and we are reminded of this every time we come to the table, take the bread and wine and are assured that we receive Christ himself. *Finitum capax infiniti.*

Spiritual Care

13. Praying amid Life's Perils

How Luther Used Biblical Examples to Teach Prayer

Mary Jane Haemig

Luther's reformation of prayer has been relatively neglected in the study of the Reformation. Such neglect is odd, given the importance Luther assigned to prayer.[1] You are all (I assume) familiar with Luther's catechisms. What he terms the "three chief parts,"—what a Christian absolutely must know—come first. First in the *Small Catechism* comes God's law, as expressed in the Ten Commandments. The law tells us what God wants life on this earth to look like. Second comes "the faith," as expressed in the Apostles' Creed. Here Luther explains what God has done for us in creation, redemption and sanctification. Third comes our response to these—prayer, as exemplified in the Lord's Prayer. For what do we pray? For "faith and the fulfillment of the Ten Commandments."[2] Prayer is not an optional aspect of Christianity rather it is at the very center of how Luther understands the Christian faith.[3]

Much attention has been devoted to the Lord's Prayer in Luther's *Small* and *Large* Catechisms.[4] Scholars have also shown interest in his *Personal Prayer Book* (Betbuechlein) of 1522, seen as a predecessor to the catechisms.[5] Luther's letter to his barber (1535) on how to pray has also attracted attention.[6] But other places and occasions on which Luther taught prayer have received less notice.

1. Oswald Bayer has noted the significance of prayer for Luther's theology. Oswald Bayer, *Martin Luther's Theology: A Contemporary Interpretation*, trans. Thomas H. Trapp (Grand Rapids, Mi: Eerdmans, 2008), 346. The final chapter, "Promise and Prayer," studies Luther's understanding of prayer.

2. *The Large Catechism* in *The Book of Concord: The Confessions of the Evangelical Lutheran Church*, ed. Robert Kolb and Timothy J. Wengert (Minneapolis, Mn: Fortress Press, 2000), 440–441.

3. For further literature see, e.g., Martin Lehmann, *Luther and Prayer* (Milwaukee, Wi: Northwestern, 1985); Frieder Schulz, *Die Gebete Luthers: Edition, Bibliographie und Wirkungsgeschichte* (Gütersloh: Gütersloher Verlagshaus Mohn, 1976); Vilmos Vajta, "Luther als Beter," in *Leben und Werk Martin Luthers von 1526 bis 1546, Festgabe zu seinem 500. Geburtstag*, ed. Helmar Junghans, 2 vols. (Berlin: Evangelische Verlagsanstalt, 1983), 1:279–295; Rudolf Damerau, *Luthers Gebetslehre*, 2 vols. (Marburg: Im Selbstverlag, 1975–77); William R. Russell, *Praying for Reform: Luther, Prayer, and the Christian Life* (Minneapolis, Mn: Augsburg Fortress, 2005).

4. An entire volume of Albrecht Peters' five-volume commentary on the catechisms is devoted to the Lord's Prayer. Albrecht Peters, *Commentary on Luther's Catechisms*, vol. 3: *Lord's Prayer*, trans. Daniel Thies (Saint Louis, Mo: Concordia Publishing House, 2009–2012). Among American sources, see, e.g., Timothy Wengert, "Luther on Prayer in the Large Catechism," in *The Pastoral Luther: Essays on Martin Luther's Practical Theology*, ed. Timothy J. Wengert (Grand Rapids, Mi: Eerdmans, 2009), 171–197.

5. Jaroslav Pelikan and Helmut T. Lehmann, eds., *Luther's Works*, American ed., 55 vols. (Philadelphia, Pa: Fortress Press; Saint Louis, Mo: Concordia Publishing House, 1955–86), 43:3–45 (hereafter, LW). *Betbüchlein*, 1522, in *D. Martin Luthers Werke: Kritische Gesamtausgabe*, 69 vols. (Weimar: Hermann Böhlaus Nachfolger, 1883–), 10/2:375–406 (hereafter, WA).

6. *A Simple Way to Pray*, LW 43:187–211. *Eine einfältige Weise zu beten für einen guten Freund* (WA 38:358–375). William R. Russell, "Luther, Prayer, and the Reformation," *WW* 22/1 (2002): 49–54, focuses on the *Personal Prayer Book* and on *A Simple Way to Pray*. Russell's book, *Praying for Reform*, includes texts of the *Personal Prayer Book*, the *Booklet for Laity and Children* (1525), and *A Simple Way to Pray*.

Talking about prayer and teaching prayer is a consistent theme in Luther's work. Virtually everywhere one looks—in sermons, letters, biblical commentaries, etc.—one encounters Luther's instructions on why and how to pray.[7]

Luther realized the need to teach people how to pray very early in his career as a reformer. In Lent 1517 (before the 95 Theses!), Luther preached a series of sermons on the Lord's Prayer.[8] These became very popular, appearing at least 23 times between 1518 and 1525 in places as diverse as Basel, Leipzig, Wittenberg, Augsburg, and Hamburg.[9] Indeed, multiple editions of Luther's works on prayer show that they achieved public resonance. His 1519 sermon *On Rogationtide Prayer and Procession* was reprinted 13 times between 1519 and 1523 in Augsburg, Leipzig, Nuremberg, Wittenberg, Strasbourg, and Zurich.[10] Luther's *Betbuechlein* (Personal Prayer Book) was printed 17 times between 1522 and 1525 (in Augsburg, Erfurt, Wittenberg, Jena, and Strasbourg) and at least 44 times total by the end of the century.[11] Luther's writing on prayer extended to the end of his career. His *Appeal for Prayer against the Turks* dates from 1541, just five years before his death.[12] It was reprinted 10 times in 1541–42.[13] For the sake of contrast consider some printing statistics for some other pieces by Luther. His famous treatise on the *Babylonian Captivity of the Church* from 1520 was published 14 times in the sixteenth century.[14] The infamous *On the Jews and Their Lies* (1543) was only printed four times in that century.[15] Clearly, Luther's works on prayer were popular and widespread during his time.

Why did Luther need to devote such extensive effort to teaching prayer? One indication comes from the preface to his *Small Catechism* (1529). There he complained that during his visitations in rural Saxony he had learned:

> The ordinary person, especially in the villages, knows absolutely nothing about the Christian faith, and unfortunately many pastors are completely unskilled and incompetent teachers. Yet supposedly they all bear the name Christian, are baptized, and receive the holy sacrament, even though they do not know the Lord's Prayer, the Creed, or the Ten Commandments.[16]

Obviously Luther was distressed! And it was not just that people did not know how to pray. Previous efforts at teaching prayer had given them wrong ideas. In his 1522 *Personal Prayer Book* Luther attacked personal prayer books

7. See, e.g., Luther's suggestion of Solomon's prayer (1 Kings 3) to Prince John Frederick in his letter postscript to his commentary on the Magnificat (WA 7:603,17–604.9; *LW* 21:358). Christoph Burger, "Luthers Gebetsvorschlag für Herzog Johann Friedrich von Sachsen: Zur Bedeutung des Gebets in christlicher Theologie und zu Luthers Wertschätzung des Gebets," in *Oratio: Das Gebet in patristischer und reformatorischer Sicht*, ed. Emidio Campi et al. (Göttingen: Vandenhoeck & Ruprecht, 1999), 185–196.

8. *An Exposition of the Lord's Prayer for Simple Laymen* (*LW* 42:15–81). *Auslegung deutsch des Vaterunsers* (WA 2:80–130).

9. *Verzeichnis der im deutschen Sprachbereich erschienenen Drucke des XVI. Jahrhunderts* (hereafter VD) (Munich: Bayerische Staatsbibliothek; Wolfenbüttel: Herzog August Bibliothek; Stuttgart: Hiersemann, 1983–), 12:L4046–4068.

10. *LW* 42:83–93. *Ein Sermon von dem Gebet und Prozession in der* Kreuzwoche (WA 2:175–179). VD 16:L6325–L6339.

11. VD 16:L4081–L4124.

12. *LW* 43:213–241. *Vermahnung zum Gebet wider den Türken* (WA 51:585–625).

13. VD 16:L1934–1943.

14. VD 16:L4185–4198.

15. VD 16:L7153–7156.

16. Preface to the *Small Catechism* in Kolb and Wengert, *The Book of Concord*, 347.

as among "the many harmful books and doctrines which are misleading and deceiving Christians" and giving rise to "false beliefs." "They drub into the minds of simple people such a wretched counting up of sins and going to confession, such un-Christian tomfoolery about prayers to God and his saints![17]

At least five aspects of medieval prayer practice needed to be reformed: First, Luther emphasized that we pray to God rather than to the Virgin Mary and to the saints. Second Luther emphasized that God hears our prayers because God has commanded us to pray and promised to hear us, rather than because we are worthy to be heard. We are definitely not worthy, but since prayer does not depend on personal worthiness, we can pray. Third, Luther attacked the view that prayer was a good work, and, related to that, he, fourth, complained about the mindless repetition and babbling that he felt characterized prayer in his day. (If prayer was considered a good work, the number of times it was done became important). Luther commented in 1527: "In the past it has happened to us that we did not know how to pray but knew only how to chatter and to read prayers. God pays no attention to this."[18] Fifth, Luther rejected the idea that prayer should be left to monks and clerics. Repeatedly one sees Luther rejecting these harmful prayer practices and advocating for an evangelical prayer practice.

My focus in this paper is on Luther's use of biblical examples to teach prayer. Luther taught prayer using biblical examples in many kinds of writings. He focused both on the prayers used and on the people praying. Repeatedly he used biblical examples to portray prayer as frank and honest conversation with God. He saw calling upon God as an intimate and necessary part of the human relationship with God. By using biblical stories, Luther put some real human flesh on his instructions on praying. I have previously examined how Luther used the prayers in Genesis 15–19.[19] The prayers of Abram, questioning whether God would fulfill God's promise of an heir, showed a questioning human and a God faithful to his promise. The prayer of Abraham, pleading with God not to destroy Sodom for the sake of 50 or 40 or 30, etc. righteous men, and the prayer of Lot asking to be sent to a town rather than sent up into the hills, illustrated humans daring to argue with God—and a God who was willing to bend to their requests. In these examples, Luther stressed that humans should boldly and forthrightly approach God, posing blunt questions and arguing for a different result than the one presented to them.

In considering now how Luther used biblical examples to teach prayer, I want particularly to look at prayer in difficult and frustrating, even hopeless situations. What did Luther teach about prayer in the midst of perils, both bodily and spiritual?

Luther was well aware that such use of biblical figures might be frustrating to his audience. Were these examples too high and distant for the ordinary listener/reader in sixteenth century Germany? In his *Appeal for Prayer against the Turks* (1541) Luther reminded his readers that, though they may not be

17. *LW* 43:11. WA 10/2:375,5–8.
18. *LW* 30:324. WA 20:793,35–36.
19. Mary Jane Haemig, "Prayer as Talking Back to God in Luther's Genesis Lectures," *LQ* 23 (2009): 270–295.

the patriarchs of the Old Testament, nevertheless they can pray just as those figures did.

> True enough, we are not a Joshua, who through prayer could command the sun to stand still [Josh 10:12–13]. Nor are we a Moses, who through his fervent plea separated the waters of the Red Sea [Exod 14: 15–22]. Neither are we an Elijah, who by his prayer called down fire from heaven [2 Kings 1:9–12]. But we are at least the equal of those to whom God gave his word and whom the Holy Spirit has inspired to preach. Yes, we are no different from Moses, Joshua, and Elijah, and all the other saints because we have the same word and Spirit of God that they had. As preachers, ministers, and officials we serve the same God they served, even though they served him more gloriously than we. But they had no greater God than we have and were made of no better flesh and blood than we. They were human just as we are and were created by the same God.[20]

So the efficacy of prayer is not dependent on the one praying but rather on the Word and Spirit of God. Luther moved immediately to assure his listeners:

> And God must answer our prayer (if I may be so bold to put it that way) just as much as theirs, for we are members of his church, which is the bride of his beloved Son. He cannot ignore the church when it earnestly beseeches him. For that reason it is not impossible for God to accomplish deeds as great or greater through us.[21]

Look at the way Luther lined up examples in order to reach his conclusion. Joshua—Moses—Elijah—and you his church—these are the people whose fervent pleas God answers. We can be assured that God will hear us just as he heard Joshua, Moses, and Elijah. God might even accomplish greater deeds through us than he did through them!

Luther used biblical examples to teach prayer not only in treatises specifically on prayer but also in biblical commentaries and sermons. For example, in his lectures on 1 John from 1527,[22] Luther piled up a number of biblical examples when he commented on 1 John 5:14–15. Those verses read: "And this is the boldness we have in him, that if we ask anything according to his will, he hears us. And if we know that he hears us in whatever we ask, we know that we have obtained the requests made of him."

Luther used these verses to encourage his listeners toward confidence in the God who hears prayer. He quoted from the Gospel of John, James' epistle, Paul in Phil 4:6, and even Augustine to arouse such confidence that we will be heard. Then he used a string of biblical examples to teach the form and content of prayer and remind his listeners that God does indeed answer. First, he cited David and Jeremiah, saying that "he who desires to pray properly should not pray the canonical hours but should say brief prayers, as David and Jeremiah did, yet in such a way that he is persuaded that he will be heard."[23] Notice how the confidence that God hears us affects even the length of prayer!

---

20. *LW* 43:226–227. WA 51:598,16–599,9.
21. *LW* 43:227. WA 51:599,11–16.
22. *LW* 30:221–327. WA 20:599–801.
23. *LW* 30:322. WA 20:791,29–31.

Next, Luther used a biblical example of proper content for prayer. Solomon (1 Kgs 3:5–11) asked for an understanding heart. Luther noted: "This prayer pleased God." Because Solomon had prayed according to the will of God, God gave him what he had asked. But Luther hastened to tell his listeners: "it is not seemly to fix the manner and the time." Luther then used Abraham as an example of waiting patiently for the fulfillment of the promise. "We should only wait patiently and diligently. And this suffices for a Christian, because a Christian is content to know that he pleases God. And he is persuaded that his prayer is heard, that it is not neglected, but that it is accepted." Luther admitted that it is not always apparent that we have, as John says, "obtained the requests we have made of him.... Indeed, sometimes the opposite seems to be true."[24] God, when he was about to deliver the children of Israel from Egypt, first led them into difficulties. Luther drew the lesson: "Thus we, too, must say: 'Lord, Thou wilt give the where and the when, and in a better way than I shall understand.' The ways of deliverance are not known to us, yet meanwhile we should be sure that we shall be heard, yes, that we have been heard."[25]

These themes—that we should pray with confidence that we are heard, that we should pray according to the will of God, that we should not prescribe to God the time and manner of answering our prayers and that, indeed, we may perceive that God is doing the opposite of what we need—re-occur in Luther. In his *Appeal for Prayer against the Turks* (1541) Luther admonished his readers not to "tempt God, that is, we should not determine the when and where and why, or the ways and means and manner in which God should answer our prayer. Rather, we must in all humility bring our petition before him who will certainly do the right thing in accordance with his unsearchable and divine wisdom."[26] Luther assured his readers that "God hears our prayer, even if it may appear that he does not do so."[27] To support this, he drew on the example of Daniel. "The angel Gabriel says in Daniel 8[:23], 'At the beginning of your supplication, the command went forth,' etc. And Daniel's prayer was answered in much greater measure than he had dared to ask.... This is the way each one of us ought to pray in this present Turkish crisis."[28]

While Daniel's prayer was answered "in much greater measure" than he had dared to ask, Luther also knew that not all prayers were answered in this way. And sometimes the seemingly unresponsive God was in fact angry with the one praying. In his *Lectures on Deuteronomy*, first published in 1525, Luther used the story of Moses to teach about prayer that is, seemingly, "not heard" or "not answered."[29] In Deut 3:24–25 we hear Moses' request to the Lord when his people were at the brink of entering the promised land: "O Lord God, you have only begun to show your servant your greatness and your might; what god in heaven or on earth can perform deeds and mighty acts like yours? Let me cross over to see the good land beyond the Jordan". In Deut 3:26–28 Moses reports that "the Lord was angry with me ... and would not heed me" and that the

---

24. *LW* 30:323. WA 30:792,23–35.
25. *LW* 30:323. WA 20:793,27–30.
26. *LW* 43:230–231. WA 51:606,4–9.
27. *LW* 43:231. WA 51:606,9.
28. *LW* 43:241. WA 51:606,9–14.
29. *LW* 9. WA 14:497–744.

Lord said to him, "Enough from you! Never speak to me of this matter again!" God then tells him to go to the top of Pisgah and look over the Jordan but also tells him "you shall not cross over this Jordan." Finally, God tells him to encourage and strengthen Joshua.

Luther asked, "But why is the prayer of Moses not heard, since it is likely that he prayed in the Spirit?"[30] Answer:

> This is written for our example and consolation. For even though the Lord does not hear him and this causes Moses to realize that He is angry with him, as he says here, nevertheless He does not desert him; He commands him to climb the mountain and view the land, and to give orders to Joshua. So, since we do not know in what manner we should pray [Rom 8:26], let us not be surprised if we are not heard. At the same time, however, let us in no wise doubt that we are favored by, and dear to God; and let us grasp at the favor beneath the wrath, lest we lose heart.[31]

Notice that, according to Luther, God is angry with Moses and yet does not desert him. God still has things for Moses to do—climb the mountain, view the land, and give orders to Joshua. The message is paradoxical. Moses is not heard, that is, his request is not granted. Yet Luther acknowledged implicitly that Moses is heard and that beneath God's wrath toward Moses lies favor. In the midst of God's rejection of our requests, we are to have confidence that we are favored by God and dear to God. Grasping at the favor beneath the wrath will cause us not to lose heart.

I now want to examine in depth two longer considerations of prayer in the midst of life-threatening perils. One stems from the Old Testament and is found in Luther's lectures on Jonah. The other comes from the New Testament and is found in a sermon of Luther's on Matthew 26 concerning Christ in the Garden of Gethsemane.

In his *Lectures on Jonah* (1525) Luther reflected on this whole matter of experiencing God's wrath while at the same time grasping at the favor beneath the wrath.[32] Some of Luther's most powerful language on prayer comes in connection with the Jonah story. Luther lectured on Jonah in February 1525 and a German version of these lectures was published in 1526.[33] Jonah in the belly of the fish, crying out to God, offered Luther ample opportunity to reflect on the occasions and efficacy of prayer, the personal situation of the one praying, and the nature of the God who hears prayer.

Many of Luther's comments come in his discussion of Jonah 2:2 where Jonah states, "I called to the Lord out of my distress, and he answered me; out of the belly of Sheol I cried, and you heard my voice". Luther says that the first verse of Jonah's prayer teaches "important and necessary lessons."[34] The first lesson is that "we must above all else pray and cry to God in time of adversity and place our wants before Him."[35] Second "we must feel that our crying to God is

---

30. *LW* 9:42. WA 14:579,26.
31. *LW* 9:42. WA 14:579,27–32.
32. *LW* 19:3–104. WA 13:241–258. WA 19:185–251.
33. VD 16, vol. 2, B3891–3893, B3895 are Latin editions; B3903–3915 are German editions.
34. *LW* 19:71. WA 19:222,8–9.
35. *LW* 19:71. WA 19:222,9–10.

of a nature that God will answer, that we may glory with Jonah in the knowledge that God answers us when we cry to Him in our necessity."[36]

Jonah is an example of one praying in the midst of great need despite his unworthiness or lack of merit. Luther described Jonah's situation in these words:

> For there was nothing else to do in such need of both body and soul but cry out. Our desires, our powers are nothing, just as Jonah here called out in pressing need. No merit was present, for he had sinned very seriously against the Lord. And so the only thing to do was to cry out, to cry out "to the Lord." For the Lord is the only one to whom we must flee as to a sacred anchor and the only safety on those occasions when we think that we are done for.[37]

Jonah's situation was dire, and he was totally at fault for it. No merit was present. Precisely in this situation the only thing to do was to cry out to God.

Luther's first point was not simply about Jonah's (and our) dire situation. It was also about the nature of God. Luther noted, "For God cannot resist helping him who cries to Him and implores Him. His divine goodness cannot hold aloof; it must help and lend an ear."[38] Because God stands ready to help Luther can say:

> All depends on our calling and crying to Him. We dare not keep silent. Turn your gaze upward, raise your folded hands aloft, and pray forthwith: "come to my aid, God my Lord! Etc., "and you will immediately find relief. If you can cry and supplicate, then there is no longer any reason for worry to abide. Even hell would not be hell or would not remain hell if its occupants could cry and pray to God.[39]

Luther, as an experienced pastor, knew that the human tendency was not to pray to God but rather to remain sunk in despair and to seek another helper. "It is vain to lament and to bemoan your condition and to fret and to worry about your sad estate and to cast about for a helper. That will not extricate you from your woes; it will only drag you in deeper. Listen and hear what Jonah does."[40] At this point Luther moved to consider Jonah as a negative example—as someone who delayed seeking help from God. Luther commented:

> He, too, consumed himself a long time with his distress before he resorted to prayer. . . . If he had not delayed, he would presumably have been delivered sooner. He also bids and teaches you not to emulate his example in this respect but he immediately states that he prayed and thus was granted deliverance.[41]

Luther knew well that it is "hard and difficult" to pray as Jonah did. "To howl and to lament, to tremble and to doubt, and to cringe and to cower are easy for us; prayers, however, will not pass over our lips."[42] Our bad conscience

---

36. *LW* 19:73. WA 19:224,8–10.
37. *LW* 19:16–17. WA 13:249,20–26.
38. *LW* 19:71. WA 19:222,11–12.
39. *LW* 19:71. WA 19:222,12–17.
40. *LW* 19:71. WA 19:222,17–20.
41. *LW* 19:71. WA 19:222,20–24.
42. *LW* 19:71. WA 19:222,26–28.

and our sins weigh heavily on us. But these are not the only things that prevent us from praying. Luther knew that our perception of God also prevents us from praying. We feel that God is angry. Together these burdens "outweigh the entire world." Luther continued:

> In short, it is impossible for nature alone or for an ungodly person to throw off such impediments and at once to supplicate that same God who is angry and who punishes and to refrain from running to someone else. Thus Isaiah declares [Isa 9:13]: "The people did not turn to Him who smote them." Nature is far more adept at fleeing from God when He is angry and when He punishes. . . . It always seeks help from other sources; it will have nothing of this God and cannot abide Him. Therefore human nature forever flees, and yet it does not escape but must thus remain condemned in wrath, sin, death, and hell. Here you can glimpse a goodly portion of hell; you see how sinners fare after this life, namely, they flee from God's anger but never elude it, and yet they do not cry to God and implore Him.[43]

Luther made clear that praying does not come naturally to humans. Calling on God is impossible for us. We would rather flee God's anger—but Luther said we should act contrary to nature and flee *to* God—that is, we should call upon God. But by nature we cannot do it, we cannot conduct ourselves contrary to the way we feel. So when we feel God's anger and punishment, we view God as an angry tyrant: "Nature cannot surmount the obstacle posed by this wrath, it cannot subdue this feeling and make its way to God against God and pray to Him, while regarding Him its enemy. Therefore when Jonah had advanced to the point of entreating God, he had gained the victory."[44]

Did you hear that? Jonah's victory did not come when he was finally spit up from the belly of the fish, rather it came when he prayed. Luther immediately applied the lesson of Jonah to his listeners:

> And thus you, too, must be minded; thus you, too must act. Do not cast your eyes down or take to your heels, but stand still, rise above this, and you will discover the truth of the verse [Ps 118:5]: "Out of my distress I called on the Lord; the Lord answered me." Take recourse to the Lord, yes, to the Lord, and to no other. Turn to the very One who is angry and punishes, and resort to no other. The Lord's answer consists in this, that you will soon find your situation improved; you will soon perceive the wrath abating and the punishment lightened. God does not let you go unanswered so long as you can call upon Him, even if you can do no more than that. He does not ask about your merits. He is well aware that you are a sinner deserving of His anger.[45]

Luther saw a connection between our natural inability to pray and our natural longing to contribute something to our salvation. Just as we think we must do something to justify ourselves before God so also we think that we must do something (or be worthy in some way) before God will hear us. "Nature does

---

43. *LW* 19:72. WA 19:222,30–223,7.
44. *LW* 19:72. WA 19:223,14–17.
45. *LW* 19:72. WA 19:223,17–25.

not know and does not believe that it suffices to call upon God to appease His wrath, as Jonah teaches us here."[46]

Luther is already into the second lesson that Jonah's prayer teaches us, the lesson of what faithful prayer is. He contrasted this "natural" response (believing that we somehow have to be worthy to pray) to the other response—that which cries to God in faith. How can we, as Luther says, "glory with Jonah in the knowledge that God answers us when we cry to Him in our necessity"?[47] That happens when we "cry to God with the heart's true voice of faith; for the head cannot be comforted, nor can we raise our hands in prayer, until the heart is consoled."[48] The heart, said Luther, "finds solace when it hastens to the angry God with the aid of the Holy Spirit and seeks mercy amid the wrath, lets God punish and at the same time dares to find comfort in His goodness."[49] Luther emphasized repeatedly that it is difficult for us to see God's kindness and grace when we experience his anger and punishment. He uses imaginative and striking language:

> Take note what sharp eyes the heart must have, for it is surrounded by nothing but tokens of God's anger and punishment and yet beholds and feels no punishment and anger but only kindness and grace; that is, the heart must be so disposed that it does not want to see and feel punishment and anger, though in reality it does see and feel them, and it must be determined to see and feel grace and goodness, even though these are completely hidden from view. Oh, what a difficult task it is to come to God. Penetrating to Him through His wrath, His punishment, and His displeasure is like making your way through a wall of thorns, yes, through nothing but spears and swords. The crying of faith must feel in its heart that it is making contact with God.... One perceives that the spirit's words and works hit their mark and do not miss.[50]

Consider again how Luther used the story of Jonah to upset the "natural" ideas about prayer in his day. Jonah is dealing with an angry God—and God has good reason to be angry with Jonah. Instead of trying to placate this God with good works and/or proper meritorious existence, humans can simply call on this God. Instead of fleeing from the angry God Luther advocated fleeing to this God and thereby discovering God's help. Humans—like Jonah—do not have to be worthy to call on this God. Rather we have confidence that when we call upon God we will find an attentive God who hears and answers prayer mercifully.

Luther deals with the theme of praying to God when we are in great need and it seems God is angry with us in a sermon on Jesus in the Garden of Gethsemane in his House Postil, first published in 1544.[51] (This house postil became very popular in sixteenth century Germany.)[52] Luther discussed prayer

---

46. *LW* 19:73. WA 19:223,26–29.
47. *LW* 19:73. WA 19:224,9–10.
48. *LW* 19:73. WA 19:224,10–13.
49. *LW* 19:73. WA 19:224,13–16.
50. *LW* 19:73–74. WA 19:224,16–26.
51. WA 52:734–742.
52. VD 16:L4831–L4902. Most of these are editions in German, Latin, and Low German. Dutch, Polish, and Slovenian editions also appeared.

extensively under his third point, summarized as "we should pray in all temptation." Jesus is an example in several respects—Jesus prays in this situation of need, even though God seems angry with him. Jesus called to God as his father and trusts that the father is kindly inclined to him and will not let him suffer need. Further, Jesus, though he asked the father to take this cup from him, also added these words: Not my but thy will be done.

Luther declared that this story is very useful because it teaches us how to conduct ourselves in terror, temptation, and misery (*Angst, Anfechtung, und Not*). Luther described the situation Jesus faced: it is now the time that Judas will betray him, the Jews capture him, and the Gentiles nail him on a cross. What did Jesus do? Luther answered, "He is downcast and fearful, but he does not leave it at that, he goes ... and prays."[53] Luther admonished his hearers to learn this too, not to let the misery so deeply touch their hearts that they forget to pray. It pleases God, when we are in terror and misery that we do not despair but open our hearts to him and seek help from him. Luther cited Ps 91:15, "When he calls to me, I will answer him; I will be with him in trouble, I will rescue him and honor him."

Luther was realistic—he knew that when we face such situations we are disgusted (*sauer*). We object that God has led us into this situation of terror and misery, is angry with us and will therefore ignore our prayers. Using the example of Jesus, Luther firmly rejected that claim. "And here again you can console yourself ... for if God meant to be angry with us when he let us experience terror and misery, so it would have to follow that he was also angry with his dear son."[54] Instead, the opposite is true—as Solomon said, a father disciplines his son out of love. So, Luther counseled, don't let yourself be misled by thoughts that see God as an enemy because he lets you suffer. Rather see here that he lets his only begotten son suffer, feel the pangs of death, and tremble. Remember that you also are God's son and he is your father, even if he lets you suffer. Luther even hinted that we should feel privileged in suffering, asking rhetorically why God would want to deny you what he does not deny his own son. Luther drew the conclusion that we should follow Christ in praying. Just as you suffer terror and misery with him, so learn also to pray with him and do not doubt that God will graciously hear such a prayer.

How does Christ pray? Luther used Christ's prayer in the garden to offer a lesson on the form and content of prayer. Christ prays, "My father, if it is possible, so take this cup from me, but not my will, rather your will be done." This, declared Luther, is the proper form of prayer that we also should use in temptation and misery. We address God as father. Despite the fact that we see only God's anger and death, we still see him as our father who loves us and protects us. For that reason we hope to be delivered from this situation—if possible, take this cup from me, or help me to get out of this suffering! Just as Christ cries to his father, so also should we. We are, through faith in Christ, also God's

---

53. "Er ist betru(e)bt und engstig, Aber bey dem lest ers nit bleyben, Er gehet hyn, felt auff sein angesicht und bettet." (WA 52:739).

54. "Aber hie wider kanstu dich mit dem Olberg wider tro(e)sten und solches gedanckens dich erweren, Denn so es Got allweg mit uns bo(e)sz meinete, wenn er uns in angst und not lest kommen, so mu(e)ste folgen, er hette es mit seinem lieben Sun auch bo(e)sz gemeinet." (WA 52:739).

children and heirs. "For that reason we should not only use these words in our prayer but also trust with our hearts that he, as a father, is kindly inclined to us and will not let us, his children, suffer want."[55] To doubt this, to carry the thought in our hearts that God is not our father and does not care for us, is to dishonor God and to take his proper name—father—from him.

So, Luther advocated, cry to the Father as Christ cries to the Father. Do it in total confidence that God wants to help his children. But just as Christ asks the Father to take this cup from him, just as Christ expects good things from his Father and yet adds "not my will, rather your will be done," so also we should humble ourselves and not insist on our will. We should rather leave it to God whether he wants us to remain in misery longer and bear it patiently just as Christ did.

Here Luther made a key distinction between bodily matters and other matters. In matters that are not bodily matters—that God keep us in his word, save us, forgive us our sins, and give us the Holy Spirit and eternal life—in these matters God's will is already known and certain. God wants all humans to be saved, he wants all humans to recognize their sin and believe in forgiveness through Christ. So it is not necessary, when praying for these things, that one leave them to God's will whether he does them or not. We know and believe that he wants to do these. But we cannot have the same certainty as to what God's will is in bodily matters. We do not know whether God wants us to experience sickness, poverty, and other trials and whether those serve God's honor and our salvation. For that reason, ask for God's help but leave it to God's will, whether he wants to help immediately. Prayer in this situation is not in vain for if God does not help immediately he will strengthen the heart and give grace and patience so that one may endure it and finally overcome it—as the example of Christ teaches. God did not take this cup away from Christ but sent him an angel to strengthen him. Luther assured his listeners: "So it will also happen with you, even if God would delay or deny his help."[56]

Luther concluded this segment on prayer by commenting on the example of the disciples. They show that we learn these lessons slowly. They still had their temptations ahead of them and for that reason Christ admonished his disciples to "watch and pray that you may not enter into temptation." Prayer is the only and the best means to avoid this. But the flesh is lazy and when the need is greatest and praying is most necessary, we slumber and sleep—in other words fear overcomes us so that we think that prayer would be in vain. When this happens, we will deny the Lord, just as the disciples did. Luther, fortunately, did not leave his listeners/readers there but ended his discussion of prayer with the comment that the gracious and merciful God who promised us help and mercy through his son Christ Jesus wants to help us out of temptation.

55. "Derhalt sollen wir nit allein dise wort in unserm gebet fueren, sonder auch das hertz und das vertrawen haben, Er, als ein Vater, meine es gut mit uns und werde uns, als seinen kindern, keinen mangel lassen." (WA 52:740).

56. "Also soll es mit dir auch gehen, ob gleych Got mit der hilff verziehen oder auszbleyben wu(e)rde." (WA 52:742).

Conclusion

Luther used biblical examples to put human flesh on his teaching on prayer. Biblical figures prayed in situations of desperate need and hopeless outlook. They offered useful guidance on the why and how of prayer. What Luther teaches through these examples stands in sharp contrast to medieval prayer practice. Luther emphasized that we should not hesitate to pray to God (rather than the saints or the Virgin Mary). This God is a loving father, not an immoveable being, who hears and answers our prayer. We should pray in all situations of need and temptation and should not be discouraged by our unworthiness. We should even pray when we know that God is angry with us. God will hear our prayer despite our unworthiness and even despite God's own anger at us. Prayer is not a good work but rather honest communication with God, forthrightly declaring need and asking for help. Such prayer could be short and to the point! Finally, any Christian—not just the clerical experts—can and should pray in these ways.

In these biblical examples of pray-ers and prayers, we also hear the central themes of Luther's theology. God is a merciful God, justifying sinners while they are yet sinners, not waiting for them to achieve righteousness. For Luther this also means that the merciful God hears the prayers of sinners without regard to their worthiness. We also encounter in these discussions Luther's dialectic between the hidden and the revealed God. God can be angry, God's face and actions hidden. In this situation Luther advocates that we flee to (not from) God in prayer. In prayer we will find the loving Father who responds kindly to our requests, always caring for us, even when he denies our specific request and shows another way.

Luther's reformation of prayer has much to say about his Reformation generally. Luther rediscovered who God is and how God relates to humans. Luther used biblical examples to show us a God who is moved by prayer, who interacts with those praying and responds to their requests. The human relationship to God in prayer is one of confidence, boldness, honesty, intimacy, creativity, and trust. The biblical examples show humans praying—both those who run away from God's will (Jonah) and those ready to let God's will be done (Jesus). The wonder is that God hears and answers the prayer not only of his worthy and beloved son Jesus but also the prayers of people like Jonah, people like you and me.

14. Luther's In-Depth Theology and Theological Therapy

Using Self Psychology and a Little Jung

Peter D. S. Krey

Introduction

In this lecture I will present Luther's theology and show how it turns out to be all about the care of souls, how it encourages us to care about the mentally distressed, how like Luther himself in his *Anfechtungen*, his episodes of spiritual conflict, delves into the depths, just like his theology delves into the depths, and thus his theology "lies at the heart of the care of souls, because the care of souls is at the heart of his theology," as Gerhard Ebeling puts it in a nutshell.[1] Howard J. Clinebell Jr. writes, but without mentioning Luther, "The essential change force in any effective counseling relationship is the unearned freely given acceptance, which mediates divine grace."[2] Thus, in Lutheran language, it is justification by grace for Christ's sake through faith (*Augsburg Confession*, art. 4) that Clinebell is placing at the heart of all counseling itself.

I will also show how Luther's theology enters the midst of life, his *coram-relationships*, the existential rapture that I find in *Freedom of a Christian*, and finally, a Jungian analysis of what took place in Luther's *Anfechtung* of 1527—to preview the content, not the purpose of this lecture. My purpose is to move us away from being pastoral counselors that use a secular kind of psychology toward adopting a theologically informed counseling or therapy. To an extent secular healing may work for the body, but how can the inmost heart not have to be involved with Christ? I use the terms "theological counseling or therapy" to widen its scope beyond the ministry of the pastors, because we believe in the "priesthood of all believers." To be courageous, I can imagine a school or institute practicing and teaching a theological therapy derived from Luther. I am arguing that he provides Christianity with an in-depth theology that not only strengthens our counseling but brings spiritual growth for pastors and members of our congregations, for all our relationships.

I will present some of the basic features of Self Psychology in this paper as well, because a comparative analysis of Self Psychology with Luther's theology will show his theology to be in-depth. I also chose Self Psychology, as developed by Heinz Kohut and Ernest S. Wolf (among others), because it is

---

1. Gerhard Ebeling, *Luthers Seelsorge: an seinen Briefen Dargestellt* (Tübingen: J.C.B. Mohr [Paul Siebeck], 1997). In German: der theologische Grundzug der Seelsorge bei Luther (449) und der seelsorgerliche Grundzug von Luthers Theologie (472).

2. Howard J. Clinebell Jr., *Basic Types of Pastoral Counseling* (Nashville, Tn: Abingdon Press, 1966), 48.

more relational than what they call the "classical Freudian drive-and-defense psychology,"[3] and therefore it is more helpful for our theological purposes.

Self Psychology stresses empathy, defining it as vicarious introspection, where the understanding by the therapist is explained to the counselee, and then interpreted in accordance with a theory. This psychoanalytic approach developed directly from issues encountered in therapy,[4] much like Luther, whose theology developed out of the most difficult issues experienced and faced in life. By means of a comparative analysis of Self Psychology and Luther's theology, I believe Luther's in-depth dimension will stand out in bold relief.

Robert Goeser, my late mentor, used to say that Luther's theology was concrete,[5] occasional,[6] performative,[7] and relational.[8] I hope to convince you that it is also therapeutic.

Compassionate Empathy

Many a "letter of spiritual counsel," to use the title of Theodore Tappert's fine volume,[9] can be read as a case study, where Luther exhibits a phenomenal capacity for empathy (*Einfühlungsvermögen*) for the depressed, the suicidal, and the dying. He even empathizes with women grieving and hurting over miscarriages. Luther had suggested that Bugenhagen include such a consolation in one of his writings, but he could not handle the topic, so Luther wrote a consolation himself, which Bugenhagen attached to his writing.[10]

Luther's compassionate empathy and ours in our counseling, is received by grace, and is like that stressed in Self Psychology. Such empathy includes understanding and explanation,[11] and would use interpretation from Luther's theology in terms of incremental experiences of justification by grace on a person's way to a gracious birth of his or her New Being, the renewed self in Christ.

3. Heinz Kohut and Ernest S. Wolf, "Disorders of the Self and Their Treatment: An Outline," *International Journal of Psycho-Analysis* 59 (1978): 414.

4. Ibid., 413.

5. *Concrete* can be understood in all the nuances, instances, properties together, none of which are abstracted away. Thus Luther does not speak of the Spirit abstractly, but as the concrete Spirit, the Word, enfleshed, embodied.

6. *Occasional*: Luther always writes addressing a specific crisis, issue, or situation at hand. A letter can be a good example of occasional writing.

7. *Performative*: The Word in powerful speech-act promises and commands, makes reality reflect what it says, brings into existence what it proclaims. Think of Luther's language of address!

8. *Relational*: Persons do not have their being in themselves but receive it from the outside and the also have their being for others, in the coram-relations.

9. Theodore G. Tappert, *Luther: Letters of Spiritual Counsel*, LCC 18 (Philadelphia: The Westminister Press, 1955).

10. Jaroslav Pelikan and Helmut T. Lehmann, eds., *Luther's Works*, American ed., 55 vols. (Philadelphia, Pa: Fortress Press; Saint Louis, Mo: Concordia Publishing House, 1955–86), 43:245 (hereafter, *LW*). For Luther's *Comfort for Women Who Have Had a Miscarriage*, see LW 43:247–250; *D. Martin Luthers Werke: Kritische Gesamtausgabe*, 69 vols. (Weimar: Hermann Böhlaus Nachfolger, 1883–), 53:205–208 (hereafter, WA). Even today women find that there is no language to talk about miscarriages. See "A Secret Planet of Pain, Where No Words Are Quite Right," The Science Times Section in the New York Times (10/21/2008), D-5.

11. Ernest S. Wolf, *Treating the Self: Elements of a Clinical Self Psychology* (New York, Ny: The Guilford Press, 1988), 99–100.

The Internal Dimension

I am convinced that Luther has an in-depth theology. While writing my dissertation, *Sword of the Spirit, Sword of Iron*, I very much confirmed my thesis that Luther carved out an internal realm of freedom. He speaks of an inward living faith, an internal church, a spiritual, internal Christianity; an internal mass, where Christ is worshiped in spirit and truth; internal communion, the internal word, the internal teacher, the internal person.[12] For example, immersed in the inner life, Luther allots almost all of the first 19 sections (3–19) of his popular version of the *Freedom of the Christian* (found in our book, pages 69–90) exploring the internal dynamics of the inner person, the next six for the outward person or the body; and the last four, for their outward economic relations.[13] I believe it is possible to situate what the sociologist, Robert Bellah, called the deep self and the social, extensive self,[14] into this internal realm charted by Luther. An in-depth theology, therefore is more comprehensive, holistic, and relational, than the narrow intra-psychic scope of an in-depth psychology, but also, includes it.

A Theological Concept of the Unconscious

I believe that Luther had a theological concept of the unconscious. Luther's *Fourteen Consolations for Those Who Labor and Are Heavy Laden* (1519) is astonishingly perceptive. He wrote it for the Elector Frederick the Wise, after the Elector had returned very sick from the Imperial Diet in Spain, where Charles V had been elected the emperor.[15] Tell me if you do not think that Luther was aware of the unconscious, a theological unconscious, if you will! He argues that God shelters us from knowing and feeling all the evils that are inside us, even our innermost evils. One symptom of evil is nothing in comparison to a thousand evils hidden from us by God. "Although these evils are deeply hidden, they bear fruit that is clearly seen."[16] On the blessing side of the consolations, Luther says: "To have faith is to have the Word and truth of God's self, the Maker of all. If all these blessings in their fullness were revealed to the soul, it would in a moment break free of the body, because of its exceeding abundance of sweet pleasure,"[17] and "[s]ince this life of ours cannot bear to have [the fullness of

---

12. Peter Krey, *The Sword of the Spirit, the Sword of Iron: Word of God, Scripture, Gospel, and Law in Luther's Most Often Published Pamphlets [1520–1525]*, (PhD. Dissertation, Graduate Theological Union, Berkeley, CA, 2001), 320–322.

13. Philip D.W. Krey and Peter D.S. Krey, trans. and eds., *Luther's Spirituality* (New York, Ny: Paulist Press, 2007), 267, n. 9, (hereafter, *LS*). (This is "our book," often referred to in this paper.)

14. The concepts of the deep and extensive selves come from a course by Prof. Robert N. Bellah in the Sociology of Religion at the University of California at Berkeley, Spring Semester, 1996.

15. *LW* 42:119.

16. *LW* 42:127. See also *LW* 42:133 where Luther writes,

Until now we have seen in all the evils we endure only the divine goodness which is so great and so near to us that all of the countless evils which surround and tightly imprison us in this life, only a few—and even these not all the time—are permitted to assail us. . . . Is it not a miracle to be struck only now and then by one of the countless blows aimed at us? It is indeed a blessing not to be struck by all. It is a miracle to be struck by but a few."

I believe that these kinds of statements point to Luther's version of the unconscious.

17. *LW* 42:147. For the Latin text of the *Fourteen Consolations*, see WA 6:104–134.

these blessings] revealed, God mercifully keeps them hidden from us."[18] (Even the soul, "the king's daughter," as Luther describes the soul, "all glorious within; her clothing of wrought gold,"[19] is sheltered from our sight.) Yet, you see how only a few evils and blessings that our conscious mind can sustain are available to us, and to plummet into the abyss on the left or receive rapture on high, on the right, would possibly explain an early sixteenth-century manic-depressive experience. Thus according to Luther, God mercifully shelters us so that we stay in our right minds. (In a Jungian sense of the unconscious, ever more of it would have to become conscious, in order to grow and mature. Here Luther is referring to onslaughts of the unconscious that the psyche has not been able to integrate.)

Self Psychology in a Nutshell

Self Psychology was worked out by the psychoanalyst, Heinz Kohut (1971), whose "unique achievement [it is]," writes Ernest S. Wolf, "to have developed the 'subjective' point of view into a comprehensive psychology."[20] Kohut argued that Freudian psycho-analysis was not reaching a number of persons suffering from self-disturbances and even causing misdiagnoses and therapeutic failures. The self and selfobjects, or selfobject experiences, are the dynamic center of his Self Psychology. Roughly, selfobject experiences[21] are intra-psychic and strengthen the core of the personality, i.e., the self.[22] According to Kohut, the self had a bi-polar structure, "one pole for mirroring (for ambition and acceptance), the other for merger and idealizing (for values and ideals). A tension arc stretches between these poles, because the poles (the one of acceptance and affirmation for mirroring and the second for merger with a perfect ideal for idealizing) push and pull the self in different directions.... Along the tension arc are arrayed the inborn talents and acquired skills." The action agenda issues out of the tension arc between these poles in the self. That is metaphorically speaking, according to Ernest Wolf in *Treating the Self*.[23] What Kohut and Wolf call the nuclear self, Luther calls the inmost heart. For Luther, the heart is the center of the responsible self, according Prof. Robert Goeser.

Perhaps you already sense how merger with a perfect ideal in idealizing and acceptance and affirmation in mirroring and the tension arc of the action agenda makes Lutheran ears tingle. Idealizing brings to mind Christ's marriage with the soul in *Freedom of a Christian* and Augustine's dictum, "Our hearts are restless until they rest in Thee." Mirroring brings to mind experiences of grace,

18. Ibid. I substituted "God's self" for "God himself."
19. Ibid.
20. Ernest Wolf, *Treating the Self: Elements of a Clinical Self Psychology*, 24, n. 3.
21. "Precisely defined, a selfobject is neither a self nor an object, but the subjective aspect of a self-sustaining function performed by a relationship of self to objects who by their presence or activity evoke and maintain the self and the experience of selfhood. As such, the selfobject relationship refers to an intrapsychic experience and does not describe an interpersonal relationship between the self and other objects." (Wolf, *Treating the Self*, 184).
22. Other definitions include "an independent center of initiative and recipient of impressions," (ibid., 182) and "the center of an individual's psychological universe," but essentially unknowable. Heinz Kohut, *The Restoration of the Self* (Madison, Ct: International Universities Press, 1977), 310–311.
23. Wolf, *Treating the Self*, 50.

accepting being accepted. Self Psychology argues that the self is at issue rather than its action: its cohesion, vigor, and harmony as opposed to its fragmentation, enfeeblement, and disorganization. Has anybody counted how many times Luther stresses the gracious change of the person via faith over works in the *Freedom of a Christian*? Note that Self Psychology deals with the weakness or strength of selves over what they do, their action agenda. In Luther's language, they separate the person from works. Selfobject experiences strengthen the weak self and internalize and repair a person's self-structure. The unconscious structure of the self, which I believe is a narrative structure, needs to become conscious to the self, according to Kohut.[24]

Christ's Mandate to Care for the Suffering

Why should the priesthood of all believers, the church itself care about people suffering with weak and enfeebled selves or with damaged self structures? Why should we care about people who are psychotic, bi-polar, or those who have personality and behavioral disorders? Healing such suffering people— who certainly also make us suffer, was part of what Jesus did in one encounter after another in the New Testament.

Thus Luther writes, "Our Lord Jesus has left us a commandment, which applies equally to all Christians, namely, . . . that we are to render works of mercy [Luke 6:36] to those that are afflicted and in a state of calamity, and that we are to visit the sick, try to free the captive, and do similar things for our neighbors so that the evils of the present may be somewhat lessened."[25]

You hear an echo of Jesus' inaugural there (Luke 4:18–19). Then Luther writes to Frederick the Wise: "Your Lordship has been stricken by a grave illness [and] Christ is also sick in you. I cannot pretend that I do not hear the voice of Christ calling to me out of your body and flesh, 'Look, I am sick.' Such evils as sickness and the like are borne not by us Christians, but by Christ himself, our Lord and Savior, in whom we live and who plainly testifies in the Gospel, 'What you have done for the least of these, you have done for me' [Matt 25:40]."[26] Thus those who suffer mental distress, who have lost their minds and have sustained injuries to their souls, have the voice of Christ crying out to us in the same way.

An Autobiographical Note

In my ministry in St. Paul's Evangelical Lutheran Church in Coney Island, mentally challenged people filled my Bible study, and I had to take one person after another to the Coney Island Hospital, because they were decompensating and experiencing another episode of their mental disturbance. We also

---

24. Kohut, *The Restoration of the Self*, 210–211: "when thinking only in terms of knowledge—then the unconscious becomes conscious—does not fill in the structure of the self and restore it." The point is "to make conscious the unconscious structure—[underlying] the conscious self experience."
    25. *LW* 42:122–123.
    26. *LW* 42:122.

rented our facilities to the South Beach Psychiatric Clinic from Staten Island, and I believe our church could have been called St. Paul's Psychiatric Lutheran Church in those days. In our inner-city conference held in Manhattan on June 24–26, 1985,[27] I invited the pastors to deal with some of our mentally challenged church members. It was an excruciating experience for me as I sat between them and they exhibited the sickness of their minds. But they pleaded with the pastors there not to give the last word over them to the psychiatric community.

I studied the way Jesus healed the demon-possessed in the Gospels and found it rewarding. A fine article by Paul W. Hollenbach[28] shows how these mental disturbances could have been oblique political protests, e.g., to the possession of Judea and Galilee by Roman legions. Hence the demoniac called himself "Legion" and Jesus sends the 2,000-strong legion of evil spirits in him into the pigs and gives them leave to jump off a cliff and into the drink (Mark 5:1–20).

We also need to understand that the word "house" in the New Testament is used to designate the soul as well as a dominion. Ched Meyers interprets Mark's Gospel from the vantage point of binding the strongman so Jesus can plunder his "house."[29] In our concern for the care of souls, we need to widen our scope from psychology to theology for the hope of healing persons such as the fellow who called himself Legion.

Self Psychology distinguishes between secondary and primary disturbances of the self, the ones that can be healed and the others that cannot.[30] That healing is impossible for those persons with primary disturbances is hard to accept. But even Luther says (and I paraphrase), some injuries to the soul are like scratches easily healed, others like a broken bone that will take some time; while others are like a broken back, from which one cannot recover.[31]

Luther encourages us to care about those who suffer in this way. In mental disturbances we have, in the words of Luther, "the misfortunes that assail . . . even our very mind, which after all is the main target of all evils and the one trysting place of sorrow and every evil."[32]

Luther's *Anfechtung*: An Episode of Spiritual Conflict

Luther himself plummeted into the depths when he felt crushed in his spiritual conflict (*Anfechtung*) between Satan and Christ. Gerhard Ebeling spends 82 pages analyzing this *Anfechtung* from many different angles.[33] Here is a very

---

27. There my mentor, Pastor Leslie C. Schulz, D.D., of Cincinnati, was the keynote speaker. See peterkrey.wordpress.com for my introduction of him.

28. Paul W. Hollenbach, "Jesus, Demoniacs, and Public Authorities," *JAAR* 49/4 (1981): 567–588.

29. Ched Meyers, *Binding the Strongman: A Political Reading of Mark's Story of Jesus* (Maryknoll, Ny: Orbis Books, 1988).

30. Kohut and Wolf, "Disorders of the Self and their Treatment: an Outline," 416.

31. I have not been able to relocate this source in Luther. Perhaps it was in the *Table Talks*. This is one example, however, of many for what Alexander S. Jensen calls "Luther's intuitive use of psychological concepts." See his article: "Martin Luther's 'Sin Boldly' Revisited: A Fresh Look at a Controversial Concept in the Light of Modern Pastoral Psychology" (undated but after 1996) on p. 1 of his sample article in the online journal, *Contact: Practical Theology and Pastoral Care*, www.contactpracticaltheology.org/sample_index.html.

32. *LW* 42:128.

33. Ebeling, *Luthers Seelsorge*, 364–446. The following page numbers in this section refer to this book.

brief account: this spiritual conflict lasted from the middle of 1527 until deep into 1528,[34] by far the worst of his life (365 and 409). The plague was rampaging in Wittenberg (starting late in July and climaxing early in November), but Luther refused to leave the souls who were sick and dying, who depended on his care, even when the Elector commanded him to flee to Jena with the rest of the faculty. Luther felt left alone because all the students fled as well, except that Bugenhagen and his family moved in with them (378). Imagine an empty Wittenberg University, like a ghastly gospel! Luther needed the company and support of his friends and students. His and Katie's home, the Black Cloister, where he gave all his table talks, became a hospital filled with the dying. The wife of the mayor, Tilo Dene, died almost in his arms.[35] George Rörer's wife, Hanna, had a miscarriage and died soon afterwards (378). The sack of Rome took place May 6, but Luther writes about it on July 13. Then on August 16, 1527, Luther received the news that Leonhard Kaiser, a promising graduate freshly promulgated from Wittenberg was burned at the stake in Passau for his evangelical faith (390). "Why was he, Luther, himself not worthy of martyrdom?" was Luther's excruciating question to God. The letter is in Latin, but significantly, he writes this question in German (393). "Why was I not worthy to shed my blood" was also the first thing he said after awakening from unconsciousness (393). When Agricola sent his disturbed wife, Else, to join the Luthers for a change of atmosphere, Luther wrote that her sickness was more spiritual than physical (374). Else and Katie, too, argued that the Word of God did not concern them directly, but really the men who protected them (402). In a half joking tone, Luther said that they should know that precisely they also were addressed, when the gospel was preached (402).

On July 6, 1527, the *Anfechtung* started by his life-strength draining out of him and his going unconscious (366, 372–373). Being held in the arms of Katie and his friends, he thought he would die. It seemed like Luther slipped down into the unsheltered abyss, where for weeks he felt like a ping-pong ball bouncing between death and hell. His limbs and his whole body shook and he felt as if the whole Christ was gone[36] (368 and 373). He felt like a rudderless ship tossed about in the floods and waves of a storm of despair and blasphemy (368 and 407–408). He said that Satan assaulted his person because he had not been able to prevent the gospel truth from being proclaimed (404), so Satan clobbered him with his fists.[37]

Even when the plague was being overcome, late in 1527 and students were returning, Luther felt hell within. Outside the world was again healthy, inside are the devil and all his angels, (he wrote). Outside the enemies plague us and inside (as weak and few as we are) the devil is among the children of light (403).

---

34. Ibid., 426.

35. *LW* 43:115.

36. I associate his allusion to the "whole Christ" with his passive righteousness in the experience of justification and to having Christ, in the sense of being in the power of Christ. Cf. Tillich: "The power which makes acceptance possible is the resource of all pastoral care. It must be effective in him who helps and it must become effective in him who is helped. . . . This means that both the pastor and the counselee . . . are under the power of something that transcends both of them. One can call this power the new creature or the New Being. The pastoral counselor can be of help only if he is grasped by this power." (quoted in Clinebell, *Basic Types of Pastoral Counseling*, 306–307).

37. One could say that Luther experienced a demonic spiritual *ad hominum*. The *ad hominum* fallacy in thought attacks the person when the argument cannot be refuted.

Luther asked everyone in his letters to pray for him. Not that the *Anfechtung* would cease, but that Christ would not leave him. But his connection to Christ was by a gossamer thread and the devil had a chain and an anchor on his leg dragging him into the abyss (371 and 408).

Luther finally recovered again late the next year, having once again received a gracious God and having had a first hand experience of the in-depth dimension, the in-depth theology, that from experience counted on the grace of Christ, whose strength was manifest in Luther's weakness that made the devil's victory a defeat. I will return to Luther's *Anfechtung* at the end and try to explain it with Carl Gustav Jung's psychological approach using the theory of opposites.

A Theology Facing the Issues of Life

Because theologians are tempted to ignore Luther's conviction that theology concerns these issues faced in the midst of life for the sake of life, he says, "Speculative theology belongs to the devil in hell."[38] And we also know his famous words about how one becomes a theologian, "Not grasping [material], reading, and speculation, but living, nay, dying and being damned, make a theologian."[39] How do you deal with being declared an outlaw of the empire and being excommunicated from the Holy Catholic Church? These kinds of experiences make his diabolical dialectic understandable in his commentary on Psalm 117: "The word shines in a dark place, indeed, a very dark place. . . . Ultimately, God cannot be God unless he becomes the devil beforehand; and we cannot come into heaven unless we've first gone to hell.[40] . . . and the devil is not and does not become the devil without first being God."[41] And then, of course, what a vision! "God has built a great new heaven over those of us who believe, and it is called the heaven of grace!"[42] Luther's in-depth theology issues not only into life, but directly into therapy.

Luther's Theology as *Seelsorge* (Care of Souls)

There is a sense in which the gospel can be understood comprehensively from this care-of-the-soul perspective.[43] Gerhard Ebeling argues that the care of souls or *Seelsorge* is at the heart and moves Luther's theology, and basically, his

---

38. *LW* 42:x. See also Luther's *Table Talks*, *LW* 54:22, #153 and WA TR 1:72, #153.
39. WA 5:163,28f. (1519).
40. I used to say, "The only trouble with heaven is that you have to go through hell to get there!" And then I would add that that is something Luther would say. Then I translated his Psalm 117 and found that he really said it!
41. *LS*, 142.
42. Ibid., 138.
43. For the "soul," we could substitute the Greek word, *psychē*, inner person, or self. If we assert that there is more to the gospel than helping injured souls and people suffering from mental disturbances, then that's because we no longer see an earthly state as an individual soul writ large, the way antiquity did. We now understand that very different principles are involved in psychology as opposed to political science. For us the "house" as dominion and the "house" as the self seem completely separate.

theology lies at the heart and moves us to the care of souls,[44] because (1) his theology empowers it, (2) it connects us with Christ, (3) it makes us be at home in the Word of God, and (4) it gives us exercise in the care of souls, by (a) informing our consciences,[45] (b) having us take life seriously, and (c) giving us an existence in prayer.

(1) Even Luther's theology of the cross is concerned about the care of souls: "The cross is the word of comfort and the most certain sign by which to recognize that comfort."[46] Luther is thinking in terms of opposites. Resistance confirms that the gospel is afoot! Ebeling writes, "The care of souls is not a practical application of the theology of the cross, but the sole reason for its development."[47] Thus, rejoice, if you now completely despair of your own abilities. You are ready for the grace of God (*Heidelberg Disputation* article 18).[48] You are now ready to live out of God's strength, rather than your own effort (Luther's explanation of article III of the Creed).

(2) Luther notes that Christ's life is bound up with our lives.[49] We are possessed and enlivened not by legions of evil spirits (Mark 5:1–20), but by the Holy Spirit. Luther writes: "Thus we should take comfort, those of us who believe in him, that we know we are not our own selves, but belong to him who died for us [Rom 14:7]." So that if we are sick we are not sick ourselves, and if we are healthy we are not healthy ourselves. Like a little sick unconscious child in crisis matters more to its parents, [Luther explains] our sickness touches the One to whom we belong much more than us.[50] So tightly are we bound up with Christ that we exclaim, "The One in us is greater than the one in the world" (1 John 4:4) and "Christ dwells only in sinners!"[51] That is vintage Luther.

(3) "To live out of the Word of God," says Ebeling, in fact, is possible only to those rooted and at home in it."[52] "They will not get into the rut of talking to themselves and certainly won't become speechless."[53] "Scripture gives us the impulse to speak with fellow human beings and with God."[54]

(4a) Luther made rescuing terrified consciences a driving force in the Reformation.[55] They are free and are to be informed by the gospel, not to be coerced and violated.

---

44. Ebeling, *Luthers Seelsorge*, 449. I had a great deal of difficulty translating "der theologische Grundzug der Seelsorge bei Luther and der seelsorgerliche Grundzug von Luthers Theologie."
45. Ibid., 463. According to Ebeling, Luther uses the word "conscience" to show where and how a person is addressed by the gospel, and what kind of response is asked. "This aim certainly also applies to his words 'soul' or 'heart,' which do not refer to parts of the human being, but in a strict sense to the person him or herself. Luther uses both of these expressions ['soul' and 'heart'] interchangeably with 'conscience,' and all three terms are derived from biblical usage, and converge related in intention" (463). Luther's care of souls is oriented to responsibility for the world and making the heart the center of the responsible self. (All translations of Ebeling are mine.)
46. Ibid., 457.
47. Ibid., 456. Also, "[The cross], [o]nce honored as a relic, was now both the content of life and a life following the gospel."
48. *LW* 31:40 and 51. Also in Timothy Lull, *Martin Luther's Basic Theological Writings* (Minneapolis, Mn: Fortress Press, 1989), 31, 42–43. WA 1:361,22–24.
49. The way Jacob was with Benjamin in Gen 44:30.
50. Ebeling, *Luthers Seelsorge*, 457.
51. Ibid., 458.
52. Ibid., 460.
53. Ibid., 426.
54. Ibid.
55. I thank the Graduate Theological Union doctoral candidate, Pastor Dan Smith, for making me mindful of this point.

To touch only one more point, (4b), ours is a prayer existence in a covenant of prayer, a *Gebetsverbund*, to use Ebeling's word in German, and he continues, "Luther's theology is a prayer theology."[56] The care of souls drives us into an existence of prayer and requires prayer to carry out.[57]

What is Luther's experience of justification by grace through faith, Ebeling asks, if not his concern for a gracious God for himself and all believers, One who did not look down from the sky at them (like a monster) in the guise of a wrathful judge to terrify them? What was Luther's campaign against indulgences, if not the concern for the souls of those being misled and deceived?[58] Why did Luther burn the canon law along with the Summa Angelica (1486), the compendium for the care of souls for the outgoing fifteenth century,[59] if not because of their harrowing affect on the care of souls? "They murdered souls rather than saving them!," Luther exclaimed.[60] As Jane Strohl writes in the introduction to our book, "One could describe Luther's career as the mounting of a life-long pastoral malpractice suit against the church's authority at every level of the hierarchy.[61]

A Theology inside of Life

Gerhard Ebeling states that "[a]ccording to Luther, theology has its place essentially in the midst of life,"[62] which it illuminates completely for the sake of the "art of arts," which entails one sorrow after another, one anger after another,"[63] and that art is: the care of souls. This heavy burden, however, is given us by Christ, the shepherd and bishop of our souls (1 Peter 2:25).[64] Luther says that we find it to be the Christophorus burden on our shoulders, having a secret blessing.[65] You cannot see reality through glory and success, but what God is doing is revealed to you through the cross and suffering.[66]

This internal dimension is carved out by Christ's making present the presence of God, while God is the One who makes present the presence of Christ,[67]

---

56. Ebeling, *Luthers Seelsorge*, 441. "Three dimensions should here be noticed: the God-relatedness [of prayer], one's own heart being moved, and the involvement and participation of all believers [in one's prayer]."

57. For his book, *Luthers Seelsorge*, Ebeling made a magisterial study of Luther's ca. 3,000 letters!

58. Ibid., 475.

59. Ibid.

60. Ibid.

61. *LS*, xxiii.

62. Ebeling, *Luthers Seelsorge*, 3–4.

63. Ibid., 46.

64. Ibid., 45.

65. Ibid., 46. St. Christopher's story can be found in our book in the "Sermon at Coburg on Cross and Suffering," *LS*, 155–157.)

66. See the *Heidelberg Theses*, art. 20 and 21.

67. Ebeling speaks about a "presence that makes one present" in *Luther: Einführung in sein Denken* (Tübingen: Mohr, 1964), 227. In the English version: "the presence which makes its object present. And the presence which makes its object present is God alone." (Gerhard Ebeling, *Luther: An Introduction to His Thought*, trans. R.A. Wilson [Philadelphia, Pa: Fortress Press, 1970], 199). I believe that Wilson's translation is inadequate, unless "object" is understood psychologically. Ebeling writes, "Coram thinking [relates] not only in fellowship, as little as the face to face encounter cannot be excluded, but it is the present making of presence, i.e., God, upon which this thinking is directed." (Ebeling, *Luther: Einführung*, 227). This line of thought also came to me from John Ellis Large, *The Church and Healing* (Cincinnati, Oh: Forward Movement Miniature Book, 1959), 62, where he writes about "the divine infusion of the Presence."

as we also become Christs, really present to each other. Christ is within his Kingdom the internal teacher and healer in our hearts.[68] What is the word of God? It is when Christ is preached in accordance with the gospel, so that you hear your God speaking to you![69] Luther would surely agree, if we extrapolated further saying, "Christ is the internal therapist in our hearts." (The internal Counselor: that would be the Holy Spirit!) Thus, Luther says to Matthias Weller, "May [God] say all these things in your heart, which I hereby, speak in your ear."[70] This power of God makes it possible for us to be present as selves before God, before ourselves, before others, and before the world (*coram deo, coram meipso, coram hominibus, et coram mundo*). Because "[t]rue theology is practical and its foundation is Christ. . . ."[71] Luther's theology is not theoretical needing application. It revolves concretely in the immediate concerns of life. The more difficult our life becomes, the more effective Luther's theology is. (I learned that from Timothy Lull.) Luther's theology charts its course through the heart of life in its internal and external dimensions by means of his *coram*-relations. Here I am following Ebeling, who writes powerfully on this subject.[72]

The *Coram*-Relations

In the *coram*-relations, "[t]he truth of our very being experiences the event, the encounter of our becoming known [by God, by ourselves, by others, and by the world]."[73] The four *coram*-relations, before God, before oneself, before others, and one's image in the world, transcend and have a wider scope than ego-states like the superego, the ego, and the id, which are only intra-psychic. The *coram*-relations would be analogous to them, however, for Luther's in-depth theology. Each *coram*-relation places the person in a forum of existence and evaluation, the *fora*, the plural of "*forum*," ranging from the internal over into the external dimension. For example, becoming a Christ is in part III of a *Freedom of a Christian*, where Luther describes outward relations with others!

The Latin preposition "*coram*" means "before," but in Luther it is most often used in the Hebrew sense of "being before the face of," "existing in the eyes of," "in the sight of," either God, oneself, others, or the world.

Ebeling explains these *coram*-relations as the heart of how Luther's theology opens directly into life-experience.[74] *Coram deo* is one's existence in the eyes of God. How one is seen by God, how one lives before the face of God. Ebeling has a whole rhapsody of insights about what goes on in the face. If God's eyes go down, we know God disapproves of us and that constitutes our conscience.

---

68. [Christ] "teaches us inwardly in our hearts." From *Freedom of a Christian*, in *LS*, 77.
69. I paraphrased this citation. See *LS*, 72.
70. *LS*, 12.
71. *LW* 42:x. See also Luther's *Table Talks*, *LW* 54:22, no. 153.
72. Ebeling, *Luther: An Introduction to His Thought*, 192–209.
73. This is my translation. German: "In der coram-Relation ist es begründet, dass das Sein als Erkanntwerden das geschehen seiner Wahrheit ist." (Ebeling, *Luther: Einführung*, 225). R.A. Wilson's translation misses the event and the encounter involved in the truth of our existence: "It is because man exists in this coram-relationship that man only truly exists by being recognized." (Ebeling, *Luther: An Introduction to His Thought*, 197).
74. Ebeling, *Luther: An Introduction to His Thought*, 192–209.

Is our conscience defined only by how others look at us? We can save face, lose face, fall on our face; someone can even turn his or her back on us. These four *coram*-relations take place in *fora*, (again plural of *"forum"*). They are not mutually exclusive relations, because the person is in all of them at one and the same time, *simul*, i.e., simultaneously. Sometimes one has to turn one's back on others, *coram hominibus*, to set one's face toward God, *coram-deo*. But to live *coram deo* is to respond to the needs of others, *coram hominibus*. For some people the *coram-hominibus* is determinative because of peer pressure, keeping up with the Jones's. We can let others define our existence. In this respect, those living in the eyes of God have an advantage. Importantly we also exist in our own eyes, *coram meipso*. For some of us this *forum* is very weak and our self-definition derives almost completely from our living in the eyes of others. Bismarck is said to have had a strong *coram-meipso*-self. Perhaps, when he introduced universal health coverage back in the 1800s and unemployment insurance or perhaps other legislation, the parliament would go off into a tirade of noisy protest. He would take out the newspaper and read it until the raucous was over and then continue with his speech. *Coram meipso* can be absorbed into *coram deo* as *coram hominibus* can be, in *coram mundo*.

Interestingly enough, we do not see and know ourselves the way God does. We are naked in the eyes of God, because God sees the heart. Self-knowledge follows after God's knowledge of us, takes time, and is difficult to attain. Hence, we learn to know ourselves fully, even as [by God] we have [already] been fully known (1 Cor 13:12). In-depth therapy would therefore require a theological self-analysis and strict supervision to start. (That would require a real challenge for pastors. Now we mostly make referrals.) But these are the *coram*-relations, to which Ebeling relegates most of a rewarding chapter.[75] I submit that these *coram*-relationships, these *fora*, because of their spiritual and relational character, hold real promise for Luther's in-depth theology and therapy.

In other words, the *coram*-relations are more comprehensive, holistic, spiritual, and relational than just intra-psychic ego states, like the superego, ego, or the ego-ideal that do not even work out the structure of the self. Even the intra-psychic exploration of the self of self psychology does not integrate the deep self, the extensive, social self,[76] nor the kingdom within, where we live out our world self and our Christ self. Traversing the depth of the internal into the external, the *coram*-relationships feature whole persons in relation to their evaluative *fora*, where the gracious experience of justification does away with the self damage of judgment and condemnation and issues into recovery and wholeness, and that from one qualitatively higher level of existence to another. This internal dynamic described by Luther in the *Freedom of a Christian* entails strengthening of the self, indeed, the whole person.[77] These could be called Christobject experiences, because Christ is completely ours (*pro nobis*), always for us, and we are completely *extra nobis*, ecstatic in God, beside ourselves,

---

75. Ibid.

76. "As such, the self object relationship refers to an *intrapsychic* experience and does not describe the interpersonal relationship between the self and other objects." (Wolf, *Treating the Self*, 53).

77. Luther tells Justus Jonas, who just lost his son, that he "should take care to notice, that he will be strengthened in Christ." (Ebeling, *Luthers Seelsorge*, 359).

outside ourselves, but always in God and God's love.[78] Our translation of *The Freedom of a Christian*, i.e., the popular version of this pamphlet, makes the ascent and descent, higher integrations of our being, stand out in bold relief.[79]

Existential Rapture and Descent

In my analysis of the *Freedom of the Christian*, I argue that there is an existential rapture in receiving the nobility of spirit. It proceeds from receiving the first-born-status in Christ,[80] to becoming royalty, then receiving priesthood, to being a Christ for others and finally entering into God through faith. The descent through the same levels of existence takes place via love, faith providing the strength for love, as faith becomes active in love. Like ascending through the magnitudes of stars from the sixth to the first, for example, this existential "promotion" correlates with the ascent and descent of the angels, which I will mention next.[81] Understanding the ascent through faith and the descent through love gives a whole new meaning to: "Lift up your hearts!," and Christ lifts us up as whole persons, "like the poor are lifted up from the dust heap to sit with princes" (Ps 113:7–8), Christ lifts us up as whole persons, from the center of our responsible selves, as we are "changed from glory into glory, lost in wonder praise and love."[82]

When you read about "Jacob's Ladder" at the end of the "New Spirituality" section of our book, you will discover that Luther really introduces you to a new dimension of spirituality.[83] The ascent and descent of the angels into the God in heaven coming down to the God on earth in Christ, takes place in the internal space that is beyond that space circumscribed by the deep self and the extensive, social, relational self. It deepens into the kingdom of heaven within you, out of which we express our selves in the world self and our Christ self, postulated by Luther.[84]

Therapy and Active Listening

Now, counseling and therapy, theological or otherwise, is not a matter of giving advice. Skilled and disciplined, active listening is required.[85] I also believe

---

78. See the last paragraph of the *Freedom of a Christian*, LS, 90.

79. See *LS* sections 7–19 and 27.

80. *LS*, 77.

81. Peter Krey, *Sword of the Spirit, Sword of Iron*, 372–374. See also the third diagram under the subcategory "Ethics" in Peter Krey, "'Groundwork for a Metaphysic of Morals' and 'Freedom of a Christian': Kant and Luther" (May 13, 2002), https://peterkrey.wordpress.com.

82. From the hymn, "Love Divine All Loves Excelling." Our hymnals: *Lutheran Book of Worship*, #315, *Evangelical Lutheran Worship*, #631, last verse. Designated here is not only a spiritual high. Luther says, although these are spiritual possessions, "temporal goods are not thereby excluded." (*LS*, 77). Thus you could be more helpful and crucial for people than the governor of your state and yet be outside that office. It is paradoxical, however: the higher your level, the deeper your service.

83. See *LS*, 172–181.

84. To explain: the tension between the world self and Christ self, coming about because of the two kingdom theory, can never exclude love of neighbor, or allow for an autonomous law, excluding our life in God's sight. But some of our decisions and actions have to take place for the sake of our neighbors as world persons, while we cannot take them for our own self-interest as a Christ person.

85. See "Positive 'I' Messages and Active Listening" and Les Schulz Keynote speaker of the 1985 Inner-City conference in Manhattan, N.Y., www.peterkrey.wordpress.com.

that hearing the gospel is possible as well as preaching it.[86] In our listening with empathy, Christ the internal Word and therapist, can speak to the counselee's heart and enter it even while the theological therapist is listening.

Very roughly, when in a listening session we speak of transference feelings, those of the counselee for the therapist; and counter transference feelings, those of the therapist for the counselee, in the deepening relationship, a recapitulation of harmful experiences of the counselee can be worked through in incremental experiences of grace. These are usually painful, but a great deal of training is required for bringing up only what the counselee can handle in the strength of the acceptance and self knowledge of the therapist.

Recognizing and Providing Experiences of Grace

Because Luther's justification by grace for Christ's sake through faith is not only a doctrine for Luther but also an experience, he has many ways to express it, and it became the lightening flash, which spread a heaven of grace over an unreformed Christianity. "Those who hear the Word, become like the word, pure, good, and just."[87] That happens by grace. Using other language, God throws a marriage celebration between Christ and our soul, in which his holy and divine attributes are marvelously and graciously exchanged for our human, sinful, and corrupt ones. So forgiveness includes transformation. The New Testament is not only the book, but Christ's last will and testament, making us inherit his heavenly possessions.[88] Thus, the whole gospel is in the word "testament."

What Kohut called mirroring and idealizing self-object experiences, similarly resemble gracious experiences of acceptance. Because of Luther's experience of condemnation and justification he immersed himself into the inner life and with his capacity for empathy gained further access to it. Thus his language of address, derived from the Scriptures, spoke directly into people's hearts and moved them. By mirroring self object experiences they received sweet-hearts, their hearts became sweet, for their gracious God. Luther also offered believers "the opportunity for merger with an idealized, omnipotent, self object,"[89] to use the language of Self Psychology for the marriage of Christ with the believer's soul in the *Freedom of a Christian*.

What Kohut calls the nuclear self, Luther calls the inmost heart of the inner person. Self Psychology explains that someone's nuclear self can be completely helpless and vulnerable while the inner self can be fierce and raging with many a narcissistic injury. In therapy the empathy of the therapist can lead that self to having empathy for his or her inmost self, nuclear self, i.e., *coram meipso*, bringing about recovery.

---

86. Perhaps via the internal word, listening to the gospel becomes possible. "You may ask, 'Which is the word that gives such abundant grace and how shall I use it?' The answer: it is nothing but the preaching of Christ in accordance with the gospel, spoken in such a way that you hear your God speaking to you." (*Freedom of a Christian, LS*, 72).

87. Ibid., 75, 268 n. 18.

88. Krey, *The Sword of the Spirit, the Sword of Iron*, 395–399.

89. Kohut, *The Restoration of the Self*, 265.

I believe there could be gracious Christ-selfobject experiences of accepting being accepted for mirror-hungry persons, and gracious experiences of merging with Christ in the marvelous exchange, for those whose idealizing pole of the self is weak, to use the model of Self Psychology. Because Luther gives the soul a word-faith structure[90] the internal Christ could pronounce a self structure back into existence or into its first existence, if it were diffuse, fragmented, dysfunctional, or disorganized. That is a spiritual frontier to be explored.

The Coincidence of Opposites

Let me end with Luther's delight in placing opposites together.[91] The tension arc is so very interesting for Luther's theology, because for him it does not only issue into the action agenda, but he places tension right into the self, the God-encountered-event-of-the-self in the union of opposites, human and divine, sovereign but slave, raptured but groaning in the spirit. We know the sinner and saint opposition best, in the formula *simul iustus et peccator*. Luther continually places opposites together in the *Freedom of a Christian*, and he insists that they are in us at one and the same time! Did you notice his putting together "confident despair" in George Spenlein's letter in our book?[92]

This tension, which Luther brings directly into the self, is key to the dynamic growth of a person's maturity in Christ, from human to divine. Luther enfolds believers inside his Christology. "For the Word of God comes, whenever it comes to change and renew the world,"[93] but also "the Word of God comes, whenever it comes, to change and renew the person."

To consider Luther's *Anfechtung* once more, now the opposing powers of Christ and the devil fight inside him. Carl Gustav Jung has a theory about the union of opposites required for differentiation and integration of the psyche.[94] (Note that when needed, Kohut sees no problem in complementing Self Psychology with the classical psychoanalytic approach,[95] when the [Freudian] guilty self needs to be treated along with [Self Psychology's] tragic self.)[96] Jung's opposites, which are relevant here, are the conscious and unconscious. The directedness of the conscious mind always has an opposite countering it in the unconscious.[97] "When the tension increases as a result of too great [a] one-sidedness, the counter tendency breaks through into consciousness, just at the

---

90. I believe that in Ebeling's *Luthers Seelsorge*, I read his saying that for Luther the soul was "Wort-förmig." But, "Those who hear the word become like the word," as just quoted from the *Freedom of a Christian*, in which Luther also writes: "as the word is so shall the soul be because of it." (*LS*, 75).

91. From a static kind of logic, these opposites are viewed as crass contradictions. Luther states, "What is our teaching to unbelievers than a pack of contradictions?" (Ebeling, *Luthers Seelsorge*, 460).

92. *LS*, 4.

93. From Luther's *Bondage of the Will*, LW 33:52; WA 18:626,25–27, 31–32. What follows about the person I have extrapolated from this Luther citation.

94. Joseph Campbell, ed., *The Portable Jung*, trans. R.F.C. Hull (New York, Ny: Penguin Books, 1971), 273–300. I thank Pastor Rod Seeger of Mill Valley, CA, for making me aware of the usefulness of the integration of opposites, *simul iustus et peccator*, in therapy.

95. Kohut, *The Restoration of the Self*, 279.

96. Ibid., 206.

97. Ibid., 276.

moment when it is most important to maintain the conscious direction."[98] Jung is speaking of an unconscious balance where opposition in the unconscious accompanies the direction taken in the conscious.

Thus using this theory of opposites, I believe Luther went too far into the direction of his Christ and the gospel in many ways without the support of his close companions, and then the devil broke through from his unconscious. When Luther found a more refined integration of justification by faith, as the one who proclaimed the pure gospel precisely because he was a most wretched sinner, the integration of these opposites brought back a gracious God.

Jung says that the tendencies of the conscious and unconscious are the two factors that make up the transcendent function[99] and it manifests as a quality of conjoined opposites.[100] The shuttling to and fro of arguments and affects (Luther felt like a ping pong ball, his whole self bouncing back and forth) represents the transcendent function of opposites. The confrontation of the two opposites, Jung continues, generates a tension charged with energy and creates a living third thing—not a logical stillbirth, but a movement out of the tension between opposites, a living birth that leads to a new level of being. So long as (the opposites) are kept apart, naturally for the sake of avoiding conflict, they do not function and remain inert.[101]

The opposing powers, Christ and the devil, fought over Luther, until he received a new integration in a higher level of being in faith for a deeper level of service in love.

Jung seems to explain the engine of our growing and maturing into the stature of Christ. Gracious, while painful, Christ self experiences written about and lived by Luther, bring hope, I believe, alongside secular treatment, for those who also have primary disturbances of the self.

I know how far short I fell of developing a Lutheran therapy along the lines of Luther's in-depth theology. But really it needs to be worked out in the actual experience of doing theological therapy. Meanwhile practice such empathy in your Christian conversation with each other, that you rescue me from Luther's condemnation of my speculation.

---

98. Ibid.
99. Ibid., 279.
100. Ibid., 298.
101. Ibid.

The Word Transforming
the World

15. "Christ Has Nothing to Do with Politics"
Martin Luther and the Societal Order

Hans J. Hillerbrand

"Christ has nothing to do with politics." Martin Luther said it, perhaps as was his wont at times all too casually, at the dinner table, and one of the student boarders in the Luther household took down the sentence, all too eagerly, as if he were taking down lecture notes in one of Professor Luther's courses. "Christ has nothing to do with politics."[1] Really? Jesus has nothing to do with how we as Christians relate our faith to our daily lives, to our vocations, our professions? What principles should inform the body politic? Surely, Luther did not mean that!

Once again the devil is in the details—all depends on how Luther's comment is interpreted. If it means that the gospel, the good news, is about justification of the sinner by faith, the sentence will stand, for this good news will stand, uninfluenced by whatever may be going on in society. If, on the other hand, the sentence means that the good news of Jesus has no bearing on the body politic, the sentence is precarious; there will be disagreement, especially from Catholics and Calvinists, and comfort only from the Anabaptists. And that, of course, is precisely how the sentence has been interpreted. No wonder, then, that Luther's understanding has been controversial almost from the day he first formulated it. In Germany, the topic triggered extensive scholarly attention especially since the end of the Nazi regime, which put what was understood as Luther's notion to a severe test. Nothing less than the silence of the German Lutheran churches in the face of Nazi totalitarianism and the Holocaust was blamed on Luther's teaching. In this country, deeply influenced as it has been by Calvinist/Reformed notions, it has been seen as an aberration.

The issue has had a rather specific point of departure: Martin Luther and the German peasants' uprising of 1524/25. Scholars have discussed the reformer's views with particular reference to his writings about secular government and against the peasants. Indeed, his relationship to the insurgent peasants in

---

1. This is a free translation of "Christus kümmert sich nicht um die Politie," as quoted in Walther Köhler, *Dogmengeschichte als Geschichte des Christlichen Selbstbewusstseins: Das Zeitalter der Reformation* (Zurich: M. Niehan, 1951), 64. This essay confines itself deliberately to the (limited) time of 1518–1525; the broadening of the chronological perspective beyond 1525 would have yielded interesting shifts as well as re-affirmations in Luther's thinking, e.g., as related to his exposition of the Sermon on the Mount (Jaroslav Pelikan and Helmut T. Lehmann, eds., *Luther's Works*, American ed., 55 vols. [Philadelphia, Pa: Fortress Press; Saint Louis, Mo: Concordia Publishing House, 1955–86], 21:3–294 [hereafter, *LW*]; *D. Martin Luthers Werke: Kritische Gesamtausgabe*, 69 vols. [Weimar: Hermann Böhlaus Nachfolger, 1883–], 32:299–544 [hereafter, WA]). There is, of course, no doubt but that the topic deserves amplification to encompass all of Luther's writings. However, the period here under consideration surely offers the most incisive segment of Luther's ideas.

1524/25 is tangled up in one of the orthodoxies of Reformation scholarship.[2] It has argued that the peasants (and the "common man" in the towns) were fatally mistaken when they took Luther's reform ideas as justification for their attempt to redress, on the basis of the Bible, longstanding economic and social grievances. They failed to understand the religious nature of Luther's reform impulses and wrongly took him to be their ally. Despite the extensive use of biblical references in the *Twelve Articles*, the agenda of the insurgency, and its declaration that the demands should be judged by the Word of God, the peasants misunderstood the connection between Scripture and the world of fishing rights, land use, death taxes. The most recent German biographer of the Wittenberg reformer sees it simply as the peasants' failure to understand Luther's fundamental dictum that the "world cannot be governed with the gospel."[3] This judgment is in keeping with the scholarly consensus that suggested that Luther's views were a consistent unfolding of his understanding of the "two kingdoms," the notion in other words that God relates to creation in two ways, through "orders" inherent in creation, such as family and government, and through revelation.[4]

Luther's literary involvement proved to be a heavy burden (if not a catastrophic turn) for the Reformation movement, for it was in the wake of the failed uprising that an ominous connection between reform and the disruption of law and order was made. Catholic rulers, both secular and ecclesiastical, harped on this connection and insisted that the suppression of the Lutheran heresy and of a future insurgency was one and the same task. Luther's role in the conflagration came in for fierce criticism. Catholic polemicists were satisfied that he had been the cause of it all.[5]

Luther's Catholic nemesis Cochlaeus noted that "many peasants had been slain in the uprising . . . who perhaps would still all live as good Christians had Luther not written."[6] Disappointment also prevailed in the reform camp about Luther's aggressive disengagement from those who meant to follow his lead in the matter of reform. Luther's strident language in the tract *Against the Robbing and Murdering Hordes of Peasants* came in for criticism, and his stance led to the

---

2. The classic statement is by Paul Althaus, *Luthers Haltung im Bauernkrieg*, 3rd ed. (Darmstadt: Wissenschaftliche Buchgesellschaft, 1969; [1942]). For an extensive evaluation of the scholarly sentiment, now somewhat outdated, see Kyle C. Sessions, "The War over Luther and the Peasants: Old Campaigns and New Strategies," *SCJ* 3 (1972): 25–44. See also Heiko A. Oberman, "Gospel of Social Unrest: 450 Years after the So-called German Peasants' War of 1525," *HTR* 69 (1976): 103–129.

3. Volker Leppin, *Martin Luther* (Darmstadt: Wissenschaftliche Buchgesellschaft, 2006), 221. (Unless otherwise noted, all translations are those of the author).

4. See Franz Lau, "The Lutheran Doctrine of the Two Kingdoms," *Lutheran World* 12/4 (1965): 355–372; Per Frostin, *Luther's Two Kingdoms Doctrine: A Critical Study*, STL 48 (Lund: Almquist and Wiksell, 1994); and the study by William J. Wright, *Martin Luther's Understanding of God's Two Kingdoms: A Response to the Challenge of Skepticism* (Grand Rapids, Mi: Baker Academic, 2010). Luther himself appeared to be altogether impatient with those who found this teaching puzzling: in his *Sendbrief* he seemed exasperated about having to propound his understanding of the two kingdoms once more. (WA 18:389; LW 46:70).

5. See Johannes Cochlaeus, *Antwort auf Luthers Schrift "Wider die räuberischen und mörderischen Rotten der Bauern"; Ein kurzer Begriff vom Aufruhr der Bauern* (Cologne, 1525); Hieronymus Emser, *Wie Luther in seinen Büchern zum Aufruhr getrieben* (Dresden, 1525); Johannes Fundling, *Anzeigung zweier falschen Zungen Luthers* (Landshut, 1526). Support came to Luther from Johannes Poliander, *Ein Urteil über das harte Büchlein Martin Luthers* (Nürnberg, 1525).

6. Johannes Cochlaeus, *Sieben köpffe Martin Luthers, von sieben sachen des Christlichen glaubens* (Dresden: W. Stöckel, 1529), bij (v) as quoted in Mark U. Edwards Jr, *Printing, Propaganda, and Martin Luther* (Berkeley, Ca: University of California Press, 1994), 149.

end of the Reformation as a popular movement.[7] It may well be, as has been argued, that the distraught surviving peasants succumbed to the appeal of the incipient Anabaptist conventicles and their insistence on the separation of the true Christians from the world.[8] Certainly, the number of pamphlets, the lifeline of the reform movement, dwindled to a trickle after 1525.[9] As one observer wrote, "Dr. Martin has fallen into great disfavor with the common people, also with both learned and unlearned; his writing is regarded to have been too fickle."[10] Later, Luther, his head bloody but unbowed, insisted that it was the peasants' fault that pope and papacy had not been completely destroyed, adding that he still shuddered at what would have happened had the peasants succeeded in their uprising.[11] It surely was not Luther's finest hour.

This paper focuses on Luther's pronouncements on social and political issues between 1519 and 1525.[12] It will be (the reader should be forewarned) a bit revisionist. Two preliminary observations must set the stage in order to establish the context of Luther's thought. One is the reminder that, at the time, Luther's 95 Theses were by no means the only expression of reform concerns. Reform, in church and society, was the concern of some, which led partisans of the Reformation ever since to the dictum that everybody in the early sixteenth century was crying out for reform, so that there would have been a Reformation if Martin Luther had died in the cradle. (Those are my own words when I was a young scholar).[13] It is a distorted understanding of the Reformation, no matter how ubiquitously perpetrated in confirmation classes and Sunday School. To be sure, voices pled for reform, but a crucial ingredient was missing: there was no pervasive sense of a crisis in church and society, and it was not until Luther came along that such a pervading sense of crisis surfaced. And in a stunningly short time, there was not merely a trickle but a flood of voices calling for all manner of reform.

Secondly, Luther's own literary activities must be placed into the context of this reform literature, especially that appearing after 1518. Luther got caught up in the maelstrom of what he himself had triggered, namely his conviction

---

7. *LW* 46:49–55; *WA* 18:357–361.

8. Franz Lau, "Der Bauernkrieg und das angebliche Ende der lutherischen Reformation als spontaner Volksbewegung," *LuJ* 26 (1959): 109–134, vigorously argued the continuing impact and success of the Reformation movement as evidenced by the towns and territories that turned Protestant in the 1530s. The problem with this view is that it equates the formal introduction of the Reformation in a number of places in the 1530's with an expression of popular sentiment. That, I would argue, is not the way the course of events must be seen. The evidence of widespread disappointment with Luther in 1525 seems overwhelming, focusing on the blatant reality that his third pronouncement, the *Sendbrief von dem harten Büchlein wider die Bauern* (Wittenberg, 1525) revealed a Luther stubbornly reiterating the harshness of his treatise on the murderous and plundering hordes of the peasants.

9. See the telling statistics in Edwards, *Printing, Propaganda, and Martin Luther*, esp. chap 7.

10. Tom Scott and R. W. Scribner, eds., *The German Peasants War: A History in Documents* (Atlantic Highlands, Nj: Humanities Press, 1990), 322.

11. This, of course, is the sentiment of Luther's final pronouncement, the *Open Letter on the Harsh Book against the Peasants* (*LW* 46:63–85; *WA* 18:384–401).

12. Both the chronological and thematic delimitation of this essay is important, even though a chronological expansion of our theme would have yielded important further perspectives. A broad introduction to Luther's advice to rulers (with ample bibliographical references) is found in Eric W. Gritsch, "The Use and Abuse of Luther's Political Advice," *LuJ* 57 (1990): 207–219.

13. The sentence occurs in my first foray into the world of the Reformation, Hans Hillerbrand, *The Reformation: A Narrative History* (New York, Ny: Harper and Row, 1964), 16.

that reform had to be put on the front burner. His was a two-pronged concern: he called for a revitalized Christian faith, yet at the same time for reform also in society. Luther's early "religious" or "devotional" pamphlets—which catapulted him to prominence—were devoted to reform concerns, so that each title could have the word "proper" inserted: how one should "properly" confess? How one should "properly" understand the Lord's Prayer? How one should properly prepare for dying? What is a "proper" Christian marriage?[14]

At the same time, Luther also addressed topics of societal reform, for the crisis of which he convinced his contemporaries was not confined to matters of faith. In 1519 he published a *Sermon vom Wucher* (Sermon on Usury) in which he discussed the most pressing economic-religious issue of the time: the legitimacy of taking interest. Luther's point was simple. Fiscal and business matters were not autonomous forces; their principles had to be related to the gospel. The Golden Rule must dominate the Christians' economic pursuits, and therefore no interest can be charged for the use of borrowed money. Luther's notions were drawn from the world of medieval reflection; he showed little empathy for the new world of economics that increasingly characterized the early sixteenth century.[15] Luther castigated those who charged "seven, eight, nine, ten percent."[16]

The details of Luther's pronouncements are less important than the fact of his engagement in a controversial economic issue. The very fact that he denounced the taking of interest indicates that "the holy gospel of Christ" and "the natural law" offered the grounds on which to make economic judgments; Luther's pamphlet signaled that socio-economic issues were part and parcel of needed reform.

Hardly a year later, Luther published his *To the Christian Nobility of the German Nation concerning the Reform of the Christian Estate*, one of the famous "Reformation treatises" of 1520.[17] It was his most popular publication, judging from the two dozen reprints in a strikingly short time. Truly, a best-seller. A masterpiece of rhetoric and polemic, its intention was to solicit support among the "Christian nobility" for the cause of reform. Luther dedicated the treatise to none other than the new German emperor, Charles V, as the foremost representative of the "Christian nobility," who might side with those committed to reform. Luther was aware that the church's deliberations about him were about to be concluded. In this setting, his treatise meant to convince his readers that the church had assumed too much power in society and much was awry, politically, economically, socially, in the body politic, an argument on which Luther could be sure to receive support.

---

14. I note at random: *Kurze Unterweisung, wie man beichten soll* (WA 2:59–65); *An Exposition of the Lord's Prayer for Simple Laymen* (LW 42:19–81; WA 2:80–130); *A Meditation on Christ's Passion* (LW 42:3–14; WA 2:136–142); *A Sermon on the Estate of Marriage* (LW 44:7–14; WA 2:165–171); *On Rogationtide Prayer and Procession* (LW 42:87–93; WA 2:175–179); *A Sermon on Preparing to Die* (LW 42:99–115; WA 2:685–697). Luther's stereotypical use of the word "sermon" in his titles must have created anticipation on part of literate readers for additional publications.

15. "Ist eyn unchristenlich furnehmen wider das heylig evangelium Christi, ja widder das naturlich gesetz." (WA 6:5,7–8).

16. "Hie wirt das arm gemeyn volck heymlich auss gesogen und schwerlich unter drugckt." (WA 6:7,1–2).

17. *LW* 44:123–217; WA 6:404–469.

The title of the treatise bore out Luther's strategic objective; it was addressed to the Christian nobility who were to become engaged in the "improvement," "reform," of the "Christian estate," the "Christian people." The title, in other words, expressed that the treatise was about the need for a comprehensive reform in society, including the role of clergy and laity in church affairs. And since the Roman church had failed to provide leadership, the secular authorities had to step in. Luther's appeal for support was not to the "people" but to the "nobility," the ruling elites. Shrewdly, Luther reminded the "Christian nobility" of the restlessness of the common people, because reform in church and society was not forthcoming.

The twofold structure of the treatise unfolded Luther's strategy and program. The first section "tore" down the three "paper" walls of the "Romanists," in effect rejecting the notion of the superiority of the "ecclesiastical" or "spiritual" estate over the laity, perhaps Luther's most revolutionary attack on the Roman church.[18] Historically, the theological insights of this first section have tended to overshadow the far lengthier second section, where Luther laid out the reforms necessary in society.[19] In other words, Luther addressed the ramification of the first part—the Christian ruling class was to undertake reform in society. The specifics ranged widely. Point 9 declared that "the Pope has no power over the Emperor" while point 10 demanded "that the kissing of the Pope's feet should also no longer take place." Some of Luther's notions were hardly calculated to receive rousing popular support; point 18, for example, proposed that "one should do away with all festivals and retain Sunday alone" and "that all begging should be done away with throughout Christendom."

Toward the end of the treatise the focus of the argument shifted. Luther listed a number of topics in need of reform that had nothing to do with either church or religion. For example, point 25 noted that "the universities are also in need of a good, strong reformation," perhaps a timeless pronouncement, but here a thinly veiled attack on the centrality of Aristotle and canon law in the university curriculum. Luther bewailed the heavy cost of the import of spices from abroad and painted a gloomy picture of adverse economic consequences. It was as if Luther sought to evoke the "good old days" when he wrote that

18. Luther writes: "[A]ll Christians are truly of the spiritual estate, and there is no difference among them except that of office. Paul says in I Corinthians 12[:12–13] that we are all one body, yet every member has its own work by which it serves the others. This is because we all have one baptism, one gospel, one faith, and are all Christians alike; for baptism, gospel, and faith alone make us spiritual and a Christian people. The pope or bishop anoints, shaves heads, ordains, consecrates, and prescribes garb different from that of the laity, but he can never make a man into a Christian or into a spiritual man by so doing. He might well make a man into a hypocrite or a humbug and blockhead, but never a Christian or a spiritual man. As far as that goes, we are all consecrated priests through baptism, as St. Peter says in I Peter 2[:9], 'You are a royal priesthood and a priestly realm'" (*LW* 44:127; WA 6:407).
    Timothy Wengert's little book *Priesthood, Pastors, Bishops: Public Ministry for the Reformation and Today* (Minneapolis, Mn: Fortress Press, 2008) reads the sources somewhat idiosyncratically, leading to the conclusion that Luther did not advocate the universal priesthood of all believers.
19. It is telling that an online study guide to Luther's tract focuses exclusively on the first part of the treatise with questions such as
1. Warum und mit welcher Intention wendet sich Luther an den Adel? Was ist sein Anlass? . . . 3. Von welchen drei Mauern spricht Luther? Was prangert er an? 4. Welche Auffassung hat Luther vom Priestertum? Wer ist Priester und wie wird man seiner Meinung nach Priester? 5. Welche Aufgaben und Rechte hat die weltliche Gewalt? 6. Wie äußert sich Luther zum Papsttum? (www.br-online.de/wissen-bildung/collegeradio/medien/geschichte/*luther*/arbeitsblaetter).

there also was no reason why enormous amounts of money were expended on silk, velvet, golden ornamentations from abroad, merely to sew ever fancier clothes.[20] Soberly, he opined that no action was necessary since before too long these extravagant imports will impoverish the nobility and the rich, and the issue will be moot.

In short, the treatise does not allow us to speak of an "apolitical" Luther, therefore, or of a Luther carefully bracketing his opinions on social issues. His concern for societal reform is altogether evident. He understood "reform" broadly so as to include not only matters of theology and ecclesiastical practice but also of society. Luther, the theologian and professor, did not hesitate to offer comments on, and even solutions for, societal issues.

The flood of pamphlets that swept across the German countryside at the time calling for reform differentiated little between reform needed in society and in the church.[21] The slogan of "reform" meant comprehensive reform.[22] Luther shared this presumption, both with his own pamphlets and (just as important) with his failure to oppose those who advocated broad societal reform on the basis of the Bible. Contemporaries, whether nobility or common folk, had to arrive at no other conclusion than that he sided with those who demanded comprehensive societal reform.

Nothing illustrates Luther's stance better than that he returned twice to the topic, which he had written about in 1519, of usury, making it the number one topic of his publications prior to 1525. Within weeks of the "brief" *Sermon on Usury* of 1519, Luther turned to the topic again and enlarged the treatise, then recycled it four years later by making it part of a new treatise, the tract on *Kaufshandlung und Wucher* (Trade and Usury).[23] Once again Luther pontificated at length about usury, undoubtedly also with his arch nemesis John Eck in mind; Eck after all defended taking interest.[24] The two writings were part of Luther's propaganda strategy to persuade his contemporaries that the state of affairs in society called for reform.[25] Luther, in other words,

---

20. *LW* 44:212ff.; *WA* 6:462ff.

21. Importantly, Bernd Moeller, "Was wurde in der Frühzeit der Reformation in den deutschen Städten gepredigt, *ARG* 75 (1984): 176–193; also idem, *Städtische Predigt in der Frühzeit der Reformation: eine Untersuchung deutscher Flugschriften der Jahre 1522 bis 1529* (Göttingen: Vandenhoeck & Ruprecht, 1996).

22. So, e.g., in the *Gesprächsbüchlein*, "Wohlauf, ihr frommen Teutschen nun, Viel Harnisch hab'n wir, und viel Pferd, Viel Helebarden und auch Schwerd, Und so hilft freundlich Warnung nit," in *Ulrich von Hutten, Auserlesene Werke* (Leipzig: Georg Reimer, 1822), 351. Ulrich von Hutten plainly challenged the common people to take an active role in bringing about change and reform. Unfortunately, there is no recent biography of Hutten, perhaps the result of a bifurcation of scholarship—literary scholars, historians, and theologians having focused on particular aspects of his life and thought. Most useful is Eckhard Bernstein, ed., *Ulrich von Hutten: Mit Selbstzeugnissen und Bilddokumenten* (Reinbek bei Hamburg: Rowohlt, 1988). A selection of carefully edited pamphlets is found in Adolf Laube et al., eds., *Flugschriften der frühen Reformationsbewegung [1518–1524]* (Berlin: Akademie-Verlag, 1983).

23. In 1540 Luther turned to the topic of usury again in his tract *Trade and Usury* (*LW* 45:245–295; *WA* 15:293–313; 321–322), an indication of the continuing relevance of the topic for him. We should note that Luther, of course, was not the only theologian who took up the topic of usury, which may well be considered to have been the foremost social issue in the early sixteenth century. An important contributor to the discussion was Jakob Strauss, whose *Haubtstuck vnnd Artickel Christlicher leer wider den vnchristlichen Wucher, darumb etlich pfaffen zu Eysnach so gar vnrüwig vnd bemüet seind*, marked by the convergence of "Christlicher leer" and a social issue, appeared in Augsburg in 1523.

24. See here Eric Kerridge, *Usury, Interest, and the Reformation* (Burlington, Vt: Ashgate, 2002). This monograph includes helpful selections from the writings of the major reformers.

25. They are found in *WA* 6:36–60 and 15:293–313; 321–322 respectively (*LW* 45:245–295; 295–310).

called attention to the crises and to the source of their solution, namely the Word of God.[26]

Alongside his comments on usury, Luther reflected on economic life in general. What he had to say about *Kaufshandel* (commerce, trade) expressed deep concerns about developments in society. Echoing notions already expressed in his appeal to the Christian nobility, Luther distinguished between proper and improper commerce and trade. Proper commerce dealt with items "which cannot be done without and serve a Christian purpose", such as trade in cattle, butter, milk, wool.[27] Luther rejected trade in luxury items.[28] He castigated those who traded with such places as "Calcutta and India" and imported goods "that only serve for show and serve no purpose."[29] Luther demanded that the governmental authorities should intervene and end the costly imports of useless foreign goods. He was gloomy, however, about the likelihood of governmental intervention and action. He plaintively observed that the problem will take care of itself when we run out of money—when, in other words, European wealth had moved overseas.[30]

The picture then, is of a Martin Luther deeply involved in advocacy of societal reform. It is not, however, the Luther we know. What happened?

The answer takes us to Luther's clandestine visit to Wittenberg from his hiding place on the Wartburg in December 1521.[31] At that time, a new theme surfaced which was, in the end, to dominate his views. At issue was not a theological insight, but the awareness that at some places the agitation for reform, even religious reform, was accompanied by disruption of law and order, as for example in Zwickau in May 1521.[32] The ugly word *Aufruhr* (uproar, rioting) made its appearance and increasingly took center stage. It had hovered over the deliberations at Worms and in fact had given Luther breathing room. Back in Wittenberg, he wrote Georg Spalatin, the elector's secretary, that he was pleased by what he had seen there. But that was not the whole story. He had also heard rumors, however, about a growing restlessness among peasants and townspeople. *Aufruhr* seemed to be around the corner. In January he received word about happenings in Wittenberg that subsequently entered history books as the "Wittenberg Disturbances," riots and agitation, which so

---

26. In my judgment the case cannot be made strongly enough that Luther's role was not that he put into words what everyone thought at the time, but rather that Luther succeeded in making his contemporaries aware of something that they had not been deeply aware—that church and society were in crisis.

27. One may surmise that the reference to the "old law," subsequently so prominent in the *Twelve Articles* of the peasants, may well have been derived from the point Luther is making in the usury treatise, that is that in earlier days the workings of society were more just.

28. LW 45:245–246; WA 15:293–294.

29. "...wares like costly silks, articles of gold, and spices—which minister only to ostentation but serve no useful purpose..." (*LW* 45:246; WA 15:294,1–2).

30. LW 45:246–247; WA 15:294. See here also the remark of Bonifazius Amerbach, the Basel humanist and jurist: "Faxit deus, ut tumultus sedari possit; quod nisi fiat, periimus omnes," in *Die Amerbachkorrespondenz*, vol. 3: *Die Briefe aus den Jahren 1525–1530*, ed. Alfred Hartmann (Basel: Verlag der Universitätsbibliothek, 1947), 19, 63.

31. An interesting contemporary source, probably published in January 1522, was entitled *Zeitung aus Wittenberg*, but it says nothing about public disturbances. Its focus is on the appearance of the so-called Zwickau "prophets." See Nikolaus Müller, *Die Wittenberger Bewegung 1521 und 1522* (Leipzig: M. Heinsius, 1911), 151ff.

32. The surmise is that the Zwickau events had been influenced by Thomas Müntzer. See Paul Wappler, *Thomas Müntzer in Zwickau und die "Zwickauer Propheten"* (Gütersloh: Mohn, 1966 [1908]), 43.

the story goes were taking the town to the brink of lawlessness and chaos.[33] The actual reality was quite different. What happened will be familiar to anyone who has been on a college campus after a successful athletic event: students acting disorderly, roaming town in search of action, in the process pushing a priest from the altar as he was celebrating Mass.[34] Luther trembled and got hot under the collar.

Luther clearly became concerned about the connection of reform and the disruption of law and order. *Aufruhr* seemed to be making the rounds, endangering the gospel. Societal reform could not put religious reform at risk. It is telling that immediately upon learning of public disturbances, Luther informed Spalatin of his intention to write a treatise about *Aufruhr*. He engaged in politicking here, for Spalatin, to whom Luther wrote more letters than to anyone else between 1520 and 1522, would obviously inform Elector Frederick of Luther's disapproval of rioting in support of the gospel.

Luther's treatise appeared in early 1522 and was entitled *A Sincere Admonition by Martin Luther to All Christians to Guard against Insurrection and Rebellion*.[35] It is not too much to say that the treatise reoriented the movement of reform. In the opening pages Luther observed that numerous misdeeds and tyrannies of the church—of "priest, monk, bishop"—had been brought to the light of day. Anger had found expression in riots and demonstrations which, however, were not directed against secular authorities but against the tyranny of the Roman church. Luther acknowledged that at some places public agitation had accompanied the demand for "evangelical preaching." He went out of his way to explain. It was understandable, he wrote, that some of those who wanted to be faithful to the Word might be tempted to demonstrate publicly in the streets to end the tyranny of the pope and demand reform.

To do so, however, was no longer necessary nor was it prudent. Now that the "pure gospel" had been rediscovered, the tyranny of the Roman pope had also come to an end. It was up to the secular authorities to accept their responsibility and do away with all papal perversion of the gospel. Luther declared himself in sympathy with those who had taken public action, but such was no longer necessary or appropriate. Luther found harsh words for those who failed to understand that things had changed, prompting his colleague Andreas

---

33. For divergent perspectives on what happened, see James S. Preus, *Carlstadt's Ordinances and Luther's Liberty: A Study of the Wittenberg Movement 1521–22* (Cambridge, Ma: Harvard University Press, 1974); Ulrich Bubenheimer, "Luthers Stellung zum Aufruhr in Wittenberg 1520–22 und die frühreformatorischen Wurzeln des landesherrlichen Kirchenregiments," *ZSGRG* 102 (1985): 148–214.

34. While still in Wittenberg (Dec. 5, 1521) Luther wrote Spalatin:
    Everything else that I hear and see pleases me very much. May the Lord strengthen the spirit of those who want to do right! Nevertheless I was disturbed on the way by various rumors concerning the improper conduct of some of our people, and [therefore] I have decided to issue a public exhortation on that subject as soon as I have returned to my wilderness. (*LW* 48:351; *D. Martin Luthers Werke: Kritische Gesamtausgabe, Briefwechsel*, 18 vols. [Weimar: Hermann Böhlaus Nachfolger, 1930–1985], 2:410,18–22 [hereafter, WA Br]).
    Luther mentioned his intention to write against any disruption of law and order in conjunction with the implementation of religious reform.

35. *LW* 45:57–74; WA 8:676–687. Interestingly, Luther refers in the introductory paragraphs to both readers and "listeners" of his tract, an indirect reference to the means by which reform notions were propagated.

Bodenstein von Carlstadt to publish a tract in defense of his role in introducing reform in Wittenberg.[36]

As Luther saw it, reform could only succeed in harmony with the political authorities. Perhaps he saw a parallel between his situation (his own fate hinged on the support of the Saxon elector) and the larger cause of reform (which was impossible without governmental support). To make matters crystal clear, Luther took to the pen again in 1523. His treatise *Concerning Temporal Authority, to What Extent It Should Be Obeyed* arguably offered the most rigid exegesis of Romans 13 in Christian history.[37] Notwithstanding his own grandiose declaration that no one had ever taught as clearly about governmental authority as he had, the treatise was pure St. Augustine. But the real significance of the treatise was found in something else.

At issue was not secular government as such. As the title makes clear, the focus was "in how far one owes it obedience," a pertinent issue since numerous governmental authorities were suppressing the preaching of the gospel. Luther's dedication of the treatise to Duke Johann of Saxony, brother (and co-ruler) of Elector Frederick, surely was to convey that the religious reform movement posed no threat to the political and social order. Johann, who would become the ruler of Ernestine Saxony two years later, was to be assured that Scripture commanded Christians to be obedient to governmental authority. Only when the gospel itself was at stake could Christians refuse obedience.

This, then, formed the background for Luther's 1525 involvement in the "revolution of the common man." He had affirmed religious and social reform, even when broadly defined, but had rejected any challenge of divinely ordained governmental authority. But that was, of course, precisely what the peasants and the "common man" in the towns were doing; they pursued reform by force. Then came the *Twelve Articles* which placed the peasants' social, economic, and political demands into the context of Luther's own record of advocating broad understanding of reform.[38] Behind the heavy dose of biblical citations in the *Twelve Articles* stood the notion expressed by Luther any number of times—that the Word alone must be the yardstick for all of life, both religious and social.

It is easy to see how the *Twelve Articles* posed a challenge for Luther's understanding of how reform could be achieved, and why he became so emotional. The document echoed the quest for the kind of societal reform that he himself had endorsed and seamlessly juxtaposed societal and religious concerns. At the same time, the Articles were not simply an intellectual statement, but a clarion call for support. Luther retreated from his own earlier definition of reform, declared the peasants' grievances to be a matter for legal experts, and

---

36. *Entschuldigung D. Andres Carlstats des falschen namens der auffrür, so jm ist mit vnrecht auffgelegt. Mit ainer vorred D. Mar. Luth* (Augsburg, 1525). Before long Carlstadt concluded, however, that reform was not introduced with appropriate speed—and penned another tract, whose title conveyed the timeless passion of all who find themselves impatient with the larger course of events: *Ob man gemach faren* (1524).

37. LW 45:81–129; WA 11:245–280.

38. Several years ago I ventured the observation that the overwhelming majority of the local peasant grievance documents recorded only economic and social demands: "The Reformation and the German Peasants' War," in *Social History of the Reformation*, ed. Lawrence P. Buck and Jonathan W. Zophy (Columbus, Oh: Ohio State University Press, 1972), 106–136. I still believe my notion to have been correct, except that I might have emphasized better that the peasants saw in Luther's theological argumentation the validation of their own economic and social concerns.

denounced the insurrection. When Duke Johann asked Luther if there was not anything positive to say about the *Twelve Articles* (which included not only the notion of the utter primacy of the Word but also the right of a congregation to elect its minister, both demands taken straight out of Luther's book), Luther disagreed. The disturbance of law and order had rendered everything moot. Theologically, Luther found that the peasants confused the two "kingdoms" or "realms" that he had delineated in his tract on secular government. In other words, Luther refuted his own treatises on usury and trade as well as his letter to the Christian nobility, while affirming his treatises on avoiding riots and obedience to secular government.

Luther's responded no less than three times to the challenge of the *Twelve Articles*. In principle, he could not find the peasant grievances and demands problematic. Accordingly, the *Admonition to Peace: A Reply to the Twelve Articles of the Peasants in Swabia* (1525) expressed sympathy for the plight of the peasants and took their side against their lords.[39] In the second treatise, however, his position shifted. The peasants had become—as the title of the treatise had it—a horde of disobedient murderers and insurrectionists. The notion of societal reform based on Scripture disappeared and was rejected. Luther now embraced the principle that had been discernible in his treatise on secular government: the world cannot be ruled by the gospel or, "Christ's gospel has nothing to do with politics." Luther's treatise was the last step in the evolution of his position, which became the hallmark of Lutheran social ethics. Society has its own laws; introducing the gospel as criterion for rule and law spells trouble. At the same time, Luther never surrendered the notion that the government must not only allow and support the proclamation of the gospel but must also rule according to "Christian" principles.

In so arguing the case, Luther failed to recall that half a decade earlier he had as a theologian, not as an expert in the law or economics, offered pronouncements and recommendations on societal issues.[40] In his letter to the Christian nobility no less than in his tracts on usury and trade, he had put forward stinging critiques of current socio-economic practices. He was not only concerned about spiritual corruption and theological aberration in the Roman church; he also wanted a new society since the present one had strayed from biblical principles. Accordingly, he had confronted established interests and, be they faculties at universities or merchants in South German towns, denounced them for their lack of adherence to biblical values. Luther surely would have embraced the peasants' reform proposals if the demands had remained intellectual pronouncements and had not impinged on the authorities who were making the Reformation possible.

It was the phenomenon of *Aufruhr* (rioting, civic disobedience) that caused the problem and put Luther on the way to negating his earlier concern for a more orderly and just society. He was led on that path by his conviction that

---

39. *LW* 46:17–43; *WA* 18:291–334.

40. Luther's Catholic protagonists promptly called attention to Luther's shift; for example, Johannes Findling, general commissioner of the infamous indulgence proclamation and sale, belabored the point in his *Anzaigung zwayer falschen zungen des Luthers, wie er mit der ainen die paurn verfueret, mit der andern sy verdammet hat* (Landshut, 1515). Findling repeated the sentiment with his *Assercionis Lvtheranae Confvtatio centum locorum, In quibus ipse Lutherus sibiipsi contradicit* (Augsburg, 1528).

any confrontation with the secular authorities would be seen as disruption of law and order that had to be squelched. Luther thus performed a precarious balancing act, extolling a biblical vision of a just society, while placing the realization of this vision solely in the hands of the properly established political authorities.

We misinterpret Luther if we see him as categorically abrogating normative biblical principles for society. His earlier writings indicated that he did not wish to withhold such principles from society nor fail to acknowledge that there were normative core values that ought to be operative in society. However, in the end Luther was furious with the peasants' acts of civil insurrection and was thereby driven to reject what he understood to be the underlying assumption of the insurgent peasants, namely that the Bible offered guidelines for economic and political issues. In so doing he offered a distorted reading of the *Twelve Articles*, for a close reading of that document reveals that most demands were not based on the Bible, the rich biblical citations on the margins of the document notwithstanding, but on the law (the "ancient law"). The one article that got knee-deep into theology dealt with the "desire to be free" since, so the commentary, Christ shed his blood and freed all humankind, a reading that Luther promptly labeled "carnal." Clearly, however, the biblical references in the *Twelve Articles* were not meant to define but to confirm the arguments based on traditional law.

What, then, are our conclusions? First and foremost, Luther's public pronouncements prior to the 1524 insurgency were in keeping with his own declaration that both church and society were in crisis and reform was sorely needed. That he so argued is not surprising. The Christian faith includes also the Christian life, and Luther never grew tired in insisting that the Christian profession has to be lived in the world. The monitor of values and the agent of change was not the individual Christian, however, but government. Luther initially ignored the question as to who was to be the agent of change, assuming it would all fall into place. He was concerned to trumpet to his contemporaries that everything needed renewal. It was precisely his broad call for renewal—in church as well as in society—which turned a narrow focus on the church practice of indulgences into a broad movement of reform.

But Luther's overriding focus came to be the maintenance of public law and order in the process of reform. Luther realized as early as January 1522 that reform—defined as the public establishment of new forms of worship together with the dis-establishment of Catholic institutions, such as monasteries—would not succeed against the will of the political authorities. Accordingly, he gave priority to a concept of reform which had reformers and government proceed hand in hand, a concept even more strikingly exemplified in Zwingli's Zurich or Calvin's Geneva. In Lutheran territories and towns the territorial rulers (or the city councils) became the de facto heads of the church in their jurisdiction, the summepiscopus, the *Notbischof*. It must remain an open question if Luther was driven by his intense reading of Romans 13 (during the Nazi period in Germany a key problem for some of the devout Lutheran Christians who participated in the anti-Nazi resistance) or by the conviction that riots, not to mention insurrection, would alienate those, who in the final analysis would make possible the implementation of reform. The significance of the peasant uprising in Luther's mind went far beyond the immediate issue of social and economic demands and grievances. The uprising turned him into a staunch believer in the government and the impossibility of mixing the Christian faith and the social order.

It remains a pity, I believe, that Luther's reflections about societal issues faded from the scene in the context of the peasants' uprising. Lutheran commentators ever since have concluded that the one unpardonable sin for Lutherans is to confuse the two "realms" or kingdoms," as was done by the insurgent peasants. "Christ," as we heard from Luther's lips, "has nothing to do with politics." No doubt, Lutheranism's withdrawal from the public square allowed Lutheran social ethics to bracket questions banal and tricky—is there a biblical warrant for the 70 mph speed limit on interstate highways or for determining the marginal tax rate on incomes over $78,500, or for stem cell research, or for legitimizing gay marriages? However, by withdrawing from the public square Lutheran theology tended to ignore the rich panoply of issues in the realm of social ethics, declaring that the Christian faith has no specific word to offer.

Of course, any pronouncement on a societal issue that requires technical expertise found eminently outside the church is bound to trigger controversy and disagreement. One need only consider the reception of the social statements of the ELCA or other Protestant denominations. They tend to leave some of the faithful bewildered, detached, even angry. And that not only because of disagreement with the conclusions of such statements, but also because the values of the men and women in the pews are frequently derived from Fox News, or MSNBC, or the *New York Times*, or the *Wall Street Journal*, Rush Limbaugh or Bill Clinton, and not from their pastors or their teaching theologians.

In the long haul, however, errors of judgment on certain specific societal issues may be less disastrous than silence. But when we reflect on the legacy of Lutheran silence, we do well to contrast it with a courageous reformer who was convinced that biblical principles could and must be brought to bear on the public square and who was willing to speak out in their support. One wonders, of course, what would have happened if Luther had been able to deal with the issue of *Aufruhr* separately from the question of whether the Christian faith has a word for the social and political realm. German history and the history of the church in it would have been different? Certainly Dietrich Bonhoeffer, writing in 1933 on the "Jewish Question," would have been pleased to have Luther help him to put a hand on the spoke in the wheel.[41]

Luther's repudiation of the peasants, properly seen, should not be taken as an abrogation of the relevance of the gospel in the public square, though that, of course, is the way Luther allowed himself to be understood. Rather, it was the repudiation of the peasants' ignoring of the plain text of Romans 13. Luther affirmed the relevance of the gospel for the social and political order, a relevance that might well mean the advocacy of change and reform. But Romans 13 constituted for him the limit of what was possible in the face even of injustice and tyranny, for government could not be opposed even if it was blatantly

---

41. It was not until the German invasion of Norway in 1940 that the Norwegian Lutheran bishop, Eivind Berggrav, delineated a new understanding of Romans 13 for the Lutheran tradition. His most important work in English was *Man and State*, trans. George Aus (Philadelphia, Pa: Muhlenberg Press, 1951).

unchristian. Only when government overstepped its legitimate boundaries or hindered the proclamation of the gospel could faithful Christians oppose it. Otherwise, they were bound to accept and even suffer. Luther's distrust of the high and mighty, *"die grossen Hansen,"* the bigshots, the elites, the Caesar Augustuses and Pontius Pilates, the popes and emperors of this world, comes through loud and clear.

This distrust was not incidental to his thought; it lay at the very heart of his understanding of the gospel. Luther never tired of reminding his fellow Christians of Jesus—who had suffered deep agony, had not called upon the legions of angels and archangels but had prayed that his Father's will be done. In the most moving of his writings, written in hours of loneliness on the Wartburg, he laid out with warmth, thoughtfulness, and sensitivity what Mary's Magnificat was all about. He praised Mary for her humility, her willingness to accept what God had chosen. In this respect, she was for Luther a role model for Christians in society—Christians who derive from Scripture the legitimation of a just society, boldly assert it, but who in the end must always take their seat with the lowly, the powerless, the humble. I think it a pity that Luther, his eyes blinded by the peasants' disruption of law and order, was unable to appropriate the powerful dynamic that is the gospel both in the individual believer and in the public square.

16. Luther on Government Responsibility for the Poor

Carter Lindberg

A Reformation woodcut portrays Luther as a "Wild Man" carrying a huge club. The "Wild Man" image is an icon of "the reversible world," the world turned upside-down.[1] When Luther overturned the late medieval world he included its values concerning money and poverty.

Luther was a "wild man" with respect to money, poverty, and social welfare because he attacked every expression of the counterfeit gospel that a person's worth depends upon his or her accomplishments. His "club" was the good news that human worth is independent of success whether it is measured in terms of renunciation or acquisition of the world. Luther therefore fought a two-sided battle against monastic asceticism on the one hand and early modern capitalism on the other hand. The first battle is well-known, but the second one has been obscured by the common association of the "Protestant ethic" with the "spirit of capitalism." But to Luther, both really belong to the same coin—salvation by works.

The claim for Luther's ethical significance in relation to economics, poverty, and social welfare runs counter to the received tradition epitomized by that dynamic duo of the history and theory of social ethics: Ernst Troeltsch and Reinhold Niebuhr. They claimed that Luther was a social conservative whose two kingdoms theology promoted subservience to divinely willed authorities and an ethical quietism.[2] Another prominent critic, Karl Barth, claimed that while Luther may have taken a radical stance toward usury this was only lip service because "in acts he stood on the side of the princes and other authorities; above all when the people tried to carry out his teachings."[3]

Luther a socio-economic conservative, even reactionary? How then do we account for Luther's constant criticism of early capitalism as a systemic injustice, his call for government regulation of business and banking, and his contribution to social welfare legislation? A list of some of his writings shows his engagement with the burning financial and welfare issues of his day. *The Blessed Sacrament of the Holy and True Body of Christ, and the Brotherhoods*, written in German "for the laity" related worship and welfare. Published in 1519 with a Latin

---

1. The wild man image is printed in Richard Cole, "Pamphlet Woodcuts in the Communication Process of Reformation Germany," in *Pietas et Societas: New Trends in Reformation Social History: Essays in Memory of Harold J. Grimm*, ed. Kyle Sessions and Phillip Bebb (Kirksville, Mo: Sixteenth Century Journal Publishers, 1985), 113.

2. See my response to their charges in *Beyond Charity: Reformation Initiatives for the Poor* (Minneapolis: Fortress Press, 1993).

3. Karl Barth, *Eine Schweizer Stimme [1938–45]* (Zollikon-Zürich: Evangelischer Verlag, 1948), 328. Cited by Günther Fabiunke, *Martin Luther als Nationalökonom* (Berlin: Akademie Verlag, 1963), 127.

translation in 1524, this tract went through 14 editions in German by 1525.[4] Luther attacked profiteering in the *Short Sermon on Usury*, also published in 1519, appearing in three editions, and the *Long Sermon on Usury*, 1520, both of which were incorporated into his major attack on monopolies and profiteering in his 1524 tract, *Trade and Usury*,[5] that appeared in seven editions. In 1523, in response to the request of the town council of Leisnig, Luther wrote the preface to the town's "Ordinance of a Common Chest" that provided legislation for social welfare.[6] Obviously by this time people looked to Luther for guidance for reform of economic and welfare issues. Thus, in 1525 the town council of Danzig requested his advice on profiteering and legitimate interest rates.[7] In the meantime, he wrote *To the Christian Nobility of the German Nation* (1520) in which he proclaimed that taking interest is the work of the devil and the greatest misfortune of the German nation.[8] He continued with the *Freedom of a Christian* (1520); *Temporal Authority: To What Extent It Should Be Obeyed* (1523); and *To the Councilmen of All Cities in Germany That They Establish and Maintain Christian Schools* (1524); not to mention his biblical and sermon commentaries, e.g., on Deut 15:4 that there should be no poor among you (1525), and his exposition of the seventh commandment in his *Treatise on Good Works* (1520) and *Large Catechism* (1529). Finally, there is the explosive tract at the end of his life that exhorts pastors to excommunicate usurers, *Exhortation to the Clergy to Preach against Usury* (*An die Pfarrherrn wider den Wucher zu predigen, Vermahnung*, 1540) that went through four editions plus a translation into Latin. His criticism of the tax policies of the German princes which demanded the same rate regardless of the economic vicissitudes of the time, and his promotion of fairer tax rates were deemed radical enough to be omitted from the Wittenberg edition of his writings, which bowdlerized several of his writings on political as well as doctrinal grounds.[9]

We might add that while Luther was quite happy to have Katy be the family's domestic "finance minister,"[10] he was not unacquainted with financial and management concerns. As prior and district vicar of the Augustinians, a position to which he was elected in 1515, he was responsible for some eleven cloisters in Thuringia and Meissen. Thus, in those years, alongside his ongoing work as a theology professor and preacher, his days were filled with practical and administrative activities. Luther's extensive economic and commercial correspondence in this regard required at least two constant secretaries.[11]

4. Jaroslav Pelikan and Helmut T. Lehmann, eds., *Luther's Works*, American ed., 55 vols. (Philadelphia, Pa: Fortress Press; Saint Louis, Mo: Concordia Publishing House, 1955–86), 35:47–73 (hereafter, *LW*); D. *Martin Luthers Werke: Kritische Gesamtausgabe*, 69 vols. (Weimar: Hermann Böhlaus Nachfolger, 1883–), 2:738–758 (hereafter, WA).

5. *LW* 45:233–310; WA 15:279–313; 321–322.

6. *LW* 45:159–94; WA 12:11–30.

7. D. *Martin Luthers Werke: Kritische Gesamtausgabe, Briefwechsel*, 18 vols. (Weimar: Hermann Böhlaus Nachfolger, 1930–1985), 3:483–486 (hereafter, WA Br). Luther's response was to emphasize equity and a limit of 5%.

8. *LW* 44:213; WA 6:466.

9. See *LW* 9:139, note 7.

10. Katherine's management of the Black Cloister—including the renting of rooms, handling of the large sums of money for the procurement of food and drink, et al.—as well as her buying and developing various properties is presented in Martin Treu, *Katharina von Bora* (Wittenberg: Drei Kastanien Verlag, 1995), 46–58.

11. Fabiunke, *Martin Luther als Nationalökonom*, 32.

Since Luther was clearly involved in the economic issues and concerns of his day, why is the negative stereotype of Luther as social ethicist so widespread? I suppose the reputation of his modern critics has some weight in this connection. As does the fact that Luther's writings on economics have until recently been largely neglected. And while his writings on this topic were obviously important to his contemporaries, they are not easily accessible today.[12] There are inexpensive editions of his 1520 tracts but not of *Trade and Usury*. And his last effort, exhorting excommunication of *laissez faire* capitalists, is largely unknown and available only in German, and then only in the Weimar, Erlangen, and Walch editions. This is not particularly surprising in a society that extols capitalism to the extent that CEOs receive hundreds of times the amount of income as their employees; where credit card companies made a 78 billion dollar profit in the last year; and where there is wholesale government deregulation promoted by the Reagan and Bush administrations.[13] There may be no interest in Luther's political-economic writings because they condemn the American way of life as conceived by those who attribute social problems to government regulations and programs, and who claim that the solution is free enterprise supplemented by charity.[14] The latter is what the present administration calls "faith-based charity."[15] Given the present American privatization of health care and the effort to privatize social security, the faith-based charities will have to cough up a lot more money!

Luther on economics is probably just too much of a "socialist" for us. Indeed, a century ago, Gustav Schmoller, one of the intellectual fathers of Prussian social legislation under Bismarck, remarked that Luther's keen perspective on economics and its ethical dimension is significant for the discussion of political

12. Leopold von Caprivi, "Mit scharfen ökonomischen Blick: Luthers Schrift vom Kaufhandlung und Wucher bleibt aktuell," *Lutherische Monatshefte* 21 (1982): 382–85. Hans-Jürgen Prien, however, notes that in 1947 the CDU republished *Von Kaufshandlung und Wucher* ("On Trade and Usury") in booklet form. Prien cites one of the editors of the reprint: "When Luther speaks of the necessity of a 'stringent, hard temporal government' of economics, when he expressly conferred on the state monopoly formation and finally when he recognized productivity as the criterion for the formation of a set price, he touched on the questions which are as burning in the contemporary discussion over socialism as in his own time." Prien goes on to caution about a fundamentalism that does not recognize historical contexts and the difference of 400 years. Hans-Jürgen Prien, "'Lieber mit Gott arm denn mit dem Teufel reich sein': Überlegungen zu einer Wirtschaftsethik Martin Luthers" in *"Wach auf, Wach auf, Du Deutsches Land!": Martin Luther, Angst und Zuversicht in der Zeitenwende*, ed. Peter Freybe (Wittenberg: Drei-Kastanien-Verlag, 2000), 86–108, here 86–87. On the other hand, Prien sees Luther's concern for the poor evident in the Latin American preferential option for the poor. There was also the recent exhibit in the Luther museum in Wittenberg, "Die Güter dieser Welt." See Martin Treu, ed., *Martin Luther und das Geld: Aus Luthers Schriften, Briefen und Tischreden* (Wittenberg: Drei Kastanien Verlag, 2000).

13. Thomas Oliphant provides a quick review of the "usury industry" and why MBNA and the mortgage companies have so far provided more than $25 million to the Bush campaign. Thomas Oliphant, "The Fleecing of Credit Card Users," *The Boston Sunday Globe* (August 29, 2004), D11.

14. See Norman Faramelli, "Neo-Conservatives in the Church," *The Ecumenist* 21/1 (November–December 1982), 1–5, 1.

15. If—a large "if" to those who rightly hold a hermeneutics of suspicion with regard to the present administration—the "faith based charity" program is not a cynical manipulation of popular piety in order to cut the domestic budget, this is a theology of glory. Religious faith in itself does not guarantee wisdom. One can be both faithful to one's religion and clueless regarding social issues and the causes of poverty, homelessness, and other social ills. There is also now a federal faith-based health plan according to Catholic tenets that will begin this November in Illinois. See Ellen Goodman, "Mixing Medicine and Faith," *Boston Globe* (September 30, 2004), A17. What is called for from Luther's perspective is the use of critical reason and the proper distinction of law and gospel.

economics, but that Luther's advocacy of government regulation evokes a sense of communistic tendencies.[16] Karl Marx's admiration of Luther as "the first German political economist" may also have been less than helpful.[17]

The following remarks are an effort to respond to these criticisms. We shall begin with Luther's critique of monastic asceticism, followed by his attack on capitalism, and conclude with his contribution to social welfare legislation.

Luther's Attack on Monastic Asceticism

Medieval monasticism narrowed the spiritual athleticism of the early church to renunciation of the world. Poverty was idealized into a kind of spiritual capital for poor and rich alike. The poor were on the preferred path to salvation, and the rich earned merit for salvation by almsgiving. The highest denomination of the medieval poverty movement was certainly Francis of Assisi whose rejection of money served to radicalize discipleship and to alleviate the anxiety of early capitalists by providing atonement for violating the canon law against usury through the outlet of philanthropy.

Luther's response to the mendicant movement in general and to Francis in particular was unequivocal. "Many people, of both low and high estate, yes, all the world were deceived by this pretense. They were taken in by it, thinking: 'Ah, this is something extraordinary! The dear fathers lead such an ascetic life; …' Indeed, if you want to dupe people, you must play the eccentric."[18] The deception Luther saw in the mendicant orders was exacerbated by the begging practices described in the 1510 *Liber Vagatorum* (Book of Vagabonds) to which Luther later wrote a preface.[19] This is the context for his admonition not to give to those "who already have or could have enough. For it is particularly in our time that there are beyond all measure many evil swindlers who present themselves as poor, needy, and beggarly, and thereby con the people."[20]

Luther thought that Francis was foolish in supposing money was evil in itself, and in displacing the free forgiveness of sin through Christ by a new law of renunciation. "If silver and gold are things evil in themselves, then those who keep away from them deserve to be praised. But if they are good creatures of God, which we can use both for the needs of our neighbor and for the glory of God, is not a person silly, yes, even unthankful to God, if he refrains from them as though they were evil? For they are not evil, even though they have

16. Caprivi, "Mit scharfen ökonomischen Blick," 383.

17. Marx's admiration was based not just on Luther's excoriation of early capitalism as a plunder system but also on Luther's sense that the "essence" of capitalism is to buy work and reproduce itself. See Hermann Lehmann, "Luthers Platz in der Geschichte der politischen Ökonomie," in *Martin Luther. Leben—Werk—Wirkung*, ed. Günter Vogler et al., 2nd ed. (Berlin: Akademie Verlag, 1986), 279–94; and Gisela Kahl, "Martin Luther, 'der älteste deutschen Nationalökonom'," *Wissenschaftliche Zeitschrift* 33/3 (1984): 315–26. For recent theological analyses of Luther's views on economics see Andreas Pawlas, *Die lutherische Berufs- und Wirtschaftsethik: Eine Einführung* (Neukirchen-Vluyn: Neukirchener Verlag, 2000); Hans-Jürgen Prien, *Luthers Wirtschaftsethik* (Göttingen: Vandenhoeck & Ruprecht, 1992), and idem, "'Lieber mit Gott arm denn mit dem Teufel reich sein' . . ."

18. *Sermons on the Gospel of St. John*, 1537 (LW 22:50).

19. See my *Beyond Charity*, 182–85, and Robert Jütte, *Abbild und soziale Wirklichkeit des Bettler- und Gaunertums zu Beginn des Neuzeit: sozial-, mentalitäts- und sprachgeschichtliche Studien zum Liber Vagatorum [1510]* (Cologne: Böhlau, 1988).

20. *An die Pfarrherrn* (WA 51:383,1–3).

been subjected to vanity and evil.... If God has given you wealth, give thanks to God, and see that you make right use of it."[21] The problem here is not money but its use. The greedy misuse the world by striving to acquire it, the monastics by struggling to renounce it.[22] The end result for both is personal insecurity because trust is placed in self-achievement rather than in God. Meanwhile the neighbor is neglected.

Luther's Attack on Early Capitalism

The medieval ideology of voluntary poverty as the path to salvation had been entrenched for centuries, but the idea that money can make money was relatively recent. The medieval church's condemnation of the profit economy, termed usury in theology and canon law, was reiterated as late as the Fifth Lateran Council in 1515. But by all accounts, by then the entrepreneur was well-established. Hence the popular saying, "einen Bürgen soll man würgen"— roughly translated: loan sharks should be strangled.[23]

Luther detested the calculating entrepreneur. He was convinced that the capitalist spirit divorced money from use for human needs and necessitated an economy of acquisition. From his *Brief Sermon on Usury* (1519) to his *Admonition to the Clergy to Preach against Usury* (1540), Luther consistently preached and wrote against the expanding money and credit economy as a great sin. "After the devil there is no greater human enemy on earth than a miser and usurer for he desires to be God over everyone. Turks, soldiers, and tyrants are also evil men, yet they must allow the people to live ... indeed, they must now and then be somewhat merciful. But a usurer and miser-belly desires that the entire world be ruined in order that there be hunger, thirst, misery, and need so that he can have everything and so that everyone must depend upon him and be his slave as if he were God."[24] "Daily the poor are defrauded. New burdens and high prices are imposed. Everyone misuses the market in his own willful conceited, arrogant way, as if it were his right and privilege to sell his goods as dearly as he pleases without a word of criticism."[25]

This "lust for profit," Luther observed, had many clever expressions: selling on time and credit, manipulating the market by withholding or dumping goods, developing cartels and monopolies, falsifying bankruptcies, trading in futures, and just plain misrepresenting goods.[26] Luther's shorthand for these practices was "usury," the common medieval term for lending at interest. However, the

---

21. *Lectures on Genesis*, 1537 (LW 2:327; 331).
22. *Lectures on I Timothy*, 1528 (LW 28:370–72); *Lectures on the First Epistle of St. John*, 1527 (LW 30:248).
23. Caprivi, "Mit scharfen ökonomischen Blick," 384.
24. *An die Pfarrherrn* (WA 51:396,12–397,3). Greed is the sin of idolatry and unbelief. See Ricardo Rieth, "Luther on Greed," in *Harvesting Martin Luther's Reflections on Theology, Ethics, and the Church*, ed. Timothy J. Wengert (Grand Rapids, Mi: Eerdmans, 2004), 152–68; and idem, *"Habsucht" bei Martin Luther: Ökonomisches und theologisches Denken, Tradition und soziale Wirklichkeit im Zeitalter der Reformation* (Weimar: Böhlau, 1996).
25. *The Large Catechism* in *The Book of Concord*, ed. Theodore Tappert (Philadelphia: Fortress Press, 1959), 397.
26. See *Trade and Usury*, 1524 (LW 45:231–310).

focus of Luther's attack was not medieval usury per se but the contemporary financial practices related to large scale national and international commerce.

Such usury, Luther argued, affects everyone. "The usury that occurs in Leipzig, Augsburg, Frankfurt, and other comparable cities is felt in our market and our kitchen. The usurers are eating our food and drinking our drink." Even worse, however, is that by manipulating prices, "usury lives off the bodies of the poor."[27] In his own inimitable style, Luther exploded, "The world is one big whorehouse, completely submerged in greed" where the "big thieves hang the little thieves."[28] Thus he exhorted pastors to condemn usury as stealing and murder, and to refuse absolution and the sacrament to usurers unless they repent.[29]

The context for Luther's call to excommunicate profiteers was the spring drought of 1539 that led to a steep rise in food prices and a famine in Wittenberg and surrounding areas.[30] Grain was being held off the market in order to gain higher prices.[31] Luther requested communal assistance from the city council and received the reply that it was not responsible. Luther then appealed to his prince, Johann Friedrich, pointing out that grain had been bought and then kept off the market "to the ruin of your electoral grace's land and people."[32] The extent of Luther's effort to change the situation may be seen in "the very sharp sermon" he preached the following Sunday against the avarice of the usurers. "They were all to be cursed and damned for they are the greatest enemies of the land" and "are strangling many people with shameful miserliness and usury." In order to spread his criticism as widely as possible, he wrote a pamphlet exhorting preachers to preach against the usurers.

Preachers are to preach against the "great sin and shame" of usury that is ruining and destroying Germany. They are to make it clear that those who take more than five percent profit in interest are idolatrous servants of mammon and shall not be blessed unless they repent. The prohibition of usury corresponds to Old Testament law, secular law, and the teaching of Christ in Luke 6:34–35 ("If you lend to those from whom you hope to receive, what credit is that to you? ...[L]end, expecting nothing in return."), a passage to which Luther continually returned. Preachers should stand firm against the rejoinder that if the taking of interest is condemned then "nearly the whole world would be damned." For the practice of the world contradicts the law and the word of God, and therefore one is not to preach according to the customs of the world but must express what the law demands and should be done.[33] The gospel explodes the categories of the world! In the case of famine the civil authority has to intervene, for the refusal to sell the grain is equivalent to stealing and robbing. What is done against God's word and the valid law is never a good deed, and the preachers

---

27. *An die Pfarrherrn* (WA 51:417,11–17).
28. *Commentary on the Sermon on the Mount*, 1532 (LW 21:180); *Lectures on Romans*, 1516 (LW 25:172).
29. *An die Pfarrherrn* (WA 51:367,10–368,16).
30. *An die Pfarrherrn* (WA 51:325). Much of the following discussion of this tract depends upon Gerhard Müller, "Biblische Theologie und Sozialethik," *Evangelische Theologie* 59/1 (1999): 25–31; and Eberhard Schendel, "Martin Luther und die Armen: Sein Beitrag zur sogenannten sozialen Frage," *Lutherischen Kirche in der Welt* 36 (1989): 112–124.
31. Cf. WA TR 4:329,22–332,9.
32. WA Br 8:403–405, especially 404,21–22.
33. WA 51:325, 332–336.

should clearly say so. Luther is not naively assuming that the CEOs of his day will change their ways. "We preachers can easily counsel but no one or few follow."[34] If it is said that the world cannot be without usury, this is true. But Christ says, woe to the person by whom offense comes (Matt 18:7), and Luther concludes, "There must be usury, but woe to the usurer!"[35]

Luther's concern was not merely about an individual's use of money, but about the structural social damage inherent in the idolatry of the "laws" of the market. Ideas of an "impersonal market" and "autonomous laws of economics" were abhorrent to Luther because he saw them as both idolatrous and socially destructive. He saw the entire community endangered by the financial power of a few great economic centers. That his perspective was not an isolated one is reflected in the saying of the day that "a bit should be placed in the mouth of the Fuggers,"[36] the central bank of the empire at that time. The rising world economy was already beginning to absorb urban and local economies, and to threaten an as yet unheard of opposition between rich and poor. He saw economic coercion—we call it globalization—as immune to normal jurisdiction and thus perceived early capitalism as a "weapon of mass destruction"[37] aimed at the common good, the ethos of community. That is why Luther considered early capitalism to constitute a *status confessionis* for the church, in spite of the fact that many of his contemporaries thought he was tilting at windmills.[38]

On the other hand, an analysis of a contemporary broadsheet by Jörg Breu, "A Question to a Minter," suggests that Luther's views were not so far afield. The print shows a minter striking money; to the right is a mounted indulgence seller displaying the papal bulls validating his wares; to the left is a merchant or banker taking money. The minter is asked why Germany complains of lack of money when he is continually minting it. The minter answers that if we weren't so blind we would see the enemies that drain money from the land: the pope, new customs, and foreign goods. The pope sells salvation; the merchant sells imported luxury goods and an abundance of new fashions. The minter

> provides a critique of early modern capitalism and its attendant consumer culture. Money is spent, but not on necessary, life-sustaining items; instead it is wasted on wares purchased for their power to signify status. Monetary excess is equated with moral excess. The minter describes the consequences of this consumer culture as particularly dire: Germans will be turned into fools, they will become arrogant, wars will break out, and God will turn against them.[39]

34. WA 51:353,29–31.
35. WA 51:354,28.
36. *To the Christian Nobility* (LW 44:213).
37. The Rev. Dr. James Forbes, Pastor of Riverside Church in New York City, in an interview with Bill Moyers on *Now* described poverty as "a weapon of mass destruction."
38. See *Beyond Charity*, 114, 191; Prien, "Lieber mit Gott," 94, 107 note 33; Hermann Barge, *Luther und der Frühkapitalismus* (Gütersloh: Bertelsmann, 1951), 51; Werner Elert, *Morphologie des Luthertums*, 2 vols. (Munich: C.H. Beck, 1958), 2:477–83; Theodor Strohm, "Luthers Wirtschafts- und Sozialethik," in *Leben und Werk Martin Luthers von 1526 bis 1546*, ed. Helmar Junghans (Berlin: Evangelische Verlagsanstalt, 1983), 205–23, 219; Ulrich Duchrow, *Global Economy: A Confessional Issue for the Churches?* (Geneva: WCC Publications, 1987).
39. Pia F. Cuneo, "Constructing the Boundaries of Community: Nationalism, Protestantism, and Economics in a Sixteenth-Century Broadsheet," in *Infinite Boundaries: Order, Disorder, and Reorder in Early Modern German Culture*, ed. Max Reinhart (Kirksville, Mo: Sixteenth Century Journal Publishers,

Here Reformation propaganda constructed Protestant identity and community along national, moral, social, and economic lines.

Although Luther did not directly connect indulgences, purgatory, and usury, the development of the doctrine of purgatory may have drastically reduced the inhibition of usury.[40] Before the doctrine of purgatory, the usurer could only go to hell, but now through the purifying punishments of purgatory he could pass the threshold to heaven. Even better, by the purchase of indulgences the stay in purgatory could be lightened or passed—the capitalist could have his cake and eat it too![41] Indeed, according to Jacques Le Goff's "provocative opinion," the doctrine of purgatory contributed to the birth of capitalism by allowing the salvation of the usurer.[42]

Luther believed that not only was the church called publicly and unequivocally to reject these economic developments, it was also called to develop a constructive social ethic in response to them. Luther's endeavor to do this began quite early, already in 1519, with his suggestions for developing a common chest for community welfare. He and his colleagues then developed social welfare policies and legislation that spread rapidly through the legislation of the Church Orders where the Reformation was enacted.[43] In this process, Luther overcame his bias against lawyers as they shouldered his cause and gave "institutional and legal form to the best theological teachings of the Reformation."[44]

At the same time, Luther and his colleagues promoted public accountability of large business through government regulation. Here Luther is not rejecting the profit economy out of hand, but rather promoting government control that would limit the interest rate to 5% in contrast to the 30–40% of the time.[45] Luther proposed a state-controlled economy in the form of price-freezes or price controls.[46] The biblical principle for Luther is love to the neighbor that in the realm of the law is governed by equity.[47]

1998), 171–85, 179. Luther voiced these concerns in many of his tracts. See, for example, *Treatise on Good Works* (LW 44:95–96).

40. In his ironically titled tract *Ein Widerruf vom Fegfeuer: Allen unseren Nachkommen*, 1530 ("A Cancellation of Purgatory: To All Our Descendents"), Luther links the development of purgatory to the drive for money. (WA 30/2:360–390).

41. Prien, "Lieber mit Gott arm," 91, with reference to Jacques Le Goff, *Your Money or Your Life: Economy and Religion in the Middle Ages* (New York: Zone Books, 1988).

42. Jacques Le Goff, *La naissance du Purgatoire* (Paris: Gallimard, 1981), 409.

43. See Stefan Oehmig, "Der Wittenberger Gemeine Kasten in den ersten zweieinhalb Jahrzehnten seines Bestehens [1522/23 bis 1547]," *Jahrbuch für Geschichte des Feudalismus* 12 (1988): 229–69; 13 (1989): 133–79; idem, "Die Wittenberger Bewegung 1521/22 und ihre Folgen im Lichte alter und neuer Fragestellungen," in *700 Jahre Wittenberg: Stadt, Universität, Reformation*, ed. Stefan Oehmig (Weimar: Böhlaus, 1995), 97–130. The concern for communal health is treated in Wolfgang Böhmer and Friedrich Kirsten, "Der gemeine Kasten und seine Bedeutung für das kommunale Gesundheitswesen Wittenbergs," *Wissenschaftliche Zeitschrift Universität Halle*, 34/2 (1985): 49–56; and Ole Peter Grell and Andrew Cunningham, eds., *Health Care and Poor Relief in Protestant Europe 1500–1700* (London: Routledge, 1997).

44. John Witte Jr., "An Evangelical Commonwealth: Johannes Eisermann on Law and the Common Good," in *Caritas et Reformatio: Essays on Church and Society in Honor of Carter Lindberg*, ed. David Whitford (Saint Louis, Mo: Concordia Publishing House, 2002), 73–87, here 74. See also idem, *Law and Protestantism: The Legal Teachings of the Lutheran Reformation* (Cambridge: Cambridge University Press, 2002).

45. Prien, "Lieber mit Gott arm," 92–95.

46. See Igor Kiss, "Luthers Bemühungen um eine sozial gerechtere Welt," *Zeichen der Zeit* (1985): 59–65; and Schendel, "Martin Luther und die Armen," 116.

47. See Matthieu Arnold, "La Notion d'*Epieikeia* chez Martin Luther," *Revue d'histoire et de philosophie religieuses* 79/2 (1999): 187–208; 79/3 (1999): 315–325.

Social Welfare Policies and Legislation

The widespread poverty, vagrancy, and underemployment of the late medieval period was legitimated by the church's ideology of poverty and exacerbated by the new economic developments. The medieval schema of salvation that presented poverty as the ideal of Christian life and anchored it in society through the promises of earthly and heavenly rewards due the almsgiver, inhibited recognition and alleviation of the social distress of poverty.

For example, one of the great French Dominican preachers of Luther's time, Guillaume Pepin (1465–1533), explained the inequalities of economic life in terms of the medieval ideology of almsgiving and salvation. "Why does God want some in this world to be rich and others poor? . . . I say that God has till now ordained that some are rich and others poor, so that each one has the material at hand to merit the kingdom of God. The rich by giving alms to the poor, the poor by patiently doing their work, and praying that the rich will sustain them."[48] The rich could buy salvation with charity.[49] Even Juan Luis Vives, the Spanish Catholic humanist known for among other things his effort to provide an impetus to civic welfare, repeated this mantra that there is a "heavenly reward . . . prepared as a recompense for almsgiving that proceeds from charity."[50]

Luther's doctrine of justification by grace alone apart from works cut the nerve of this medieval ideology of poverty. Salvation is received not achieved, and thus is the foundation for life rather than its goal. Since salvation is purely a gift of God, both poverty and almsgiving lose their soteriological significance. Furthermore, this also undercut the explanatory function of the medieval ideology of poverty that fatalistically presented poverty and riches as the divine plan. By de-spiritualizing poverty, the Reformers could recognize poverty in all its forms as a personal and social evil to be combated. Under the rubrics of justice and equity, Luther and his colleagues quickly moved in alliance with local governments to establish new social welfare policies.[51]

The first major effort in this direction was the Wittenberg Church Order of 1522 that established a "common chest" for welfare work. Initially funded by the expropriation of medieval ecclesiastical endowments and later supplemented by taxes, the Wittenberg Order prohibited begging; provided interest-free loans to artisans, who when established were to repay them if possible; provided for poor orphans, the children of poor people, and poor maidens who needed an appropriate dowry for marriage; provided refinancing of high-interest loans at 4% annual interest for burdened citizens; and supported the

48. Larissa Taylor, *Soldiers of Christ: Preaching in Late Medieval and Reformation France* (New York, Ny: Oxford University Press, 1992), 150.

49. Marco H.D. van Leeuwen, "Logic of Charity: Poor Relief in Preindustrial Europe," *Journal of Interdisciplinary History* 24/4 (1994): 589–613, here 598.

50. Juan Luis Vives, *De Subventione Pauperum sive De Humanis Necessitatibus*, Libri II, ed. C. Matheeusen and C. Fantazzi (Leiden: Brill, 2002), 143. The above examples are reflecting the long tradition stemming from the early church fathers that regarded almsgiving as a "donor-centered" "pious usury" that atoned for sin, enabled philanthropy, and transferred one's wealth to heaven. See Boniface Ramsey, O.P., "Almsgiving in the Latin Church: The Late Fourth and Early Fifth Centuries," *Theological Studies* 43 (1982): 226–59, reprint in Everett Ferguson, ed., *Acts of Piety in the Early Church*, vol. 17 (New York, Ny: Garland Publishing, 1993), 276–309.

51. See Lindberg, *Beyond Charity*.

education or vocational training of poor children.[52] To the objection that this was open to abuse, Luther replied: "He who has nothing to live on should be aided. If he deceives us, what then? He must be aided again."[53] Other communities quickly picked up these ideas. By 1523 there were common chest provisions for social welfare in the Church Orders of Leisnig, Augsburg, Nuremberg, Altenburg, Kitzingen, Strasbourg, Breslau, and Regensburg.

These ordinances for poor relief were efforts to implement Luther's conviction that social welfare policies designed to prevent as well as remedy poverty are a Christian social responsibility. Under the motto "there should be no beggars among Christians," the early Reformation movement set about implementing concern for personal dignity and public alleviation of suffering.[54] Luther and his colleagues[55] taught that the giving of alms was no longer bound up with appeasement for sin, redemption, nor expectation of divine reward, but rather that faith active in love is expressed in regulated, centralized communally administered social welfare.[56]

Civic Control of Capitalism

While Luther's efforts to develop welfare legislation were well-received in the cities and territories which accepted the Reformation, his efforts to encourage civic control of capitalism did not gain comparable support. Of course, it is hardly surprising that when interest rates could soar to 40%, bankers turned a deaf ear to his call for a 5% ceiling on interest. Also, Luther's criticism of capitalism included far more than exorbitant interest rates. He argued that social need always stood above personal gain. "[I]n a well-arranged commonwealth the debts of the poor who are in need ought to be cancelled, and they ought to be helped; hence the action of collecting has its place only against the lazy and the ne'er-do-well."[57] But the common good was being undermined by the activities of large businesses that could not be held accountable even by the emperor.

Luther experienced that it is easier to motivate assistance to individuals than it is to curb the economic practices that create their poverty. Poverty's squalor calls out for redress whereas the attractive trappings of business muffle criticism. Yet the effects of early capitalism could be felt. In Wittenberg between 1520 and 1538 prices doubled but wages remained the same. Luther called this

---

52. Hans Lietzmann, ed., *Die Wittenberger und Leisniger Kastenordnung* (Berlin: De Gruyter, 1935).

53. *Lectures on the First Epistle of St. John*, 1537 (LW 30:278).

54. See Karlstadt's tract by this title with my introduction and translation in Carter Lindberg, ed., *Piety, Politics, and Ethics: Reformation Studies in Honor of George Wolfgang Forell* (Kirksville, Mo: Sixteenth Century Journal Publishers, 1984), 157–66.

55. Johannes Bugenhagen was particularly important for the institutionalizing of these concerns. See Kurt Hendel, "Johannes Bugenhagen, Organizer of the Lutheran Reformation," *LQ* 18 (2004): 43–75.

56. Hans-Otto Schembs, ed., *Der Allgemeine Almosenkasten in Frankfurt am Main 1531–1981: 450 Jahre Geschichte und Wirken einer öffentlichen milden Stiftung* (Frankfurt am Main: Verlag Waldemar Kramer, 1981), 36. Schembs continues by stating that the Reformation establishment of the common chest in Frankfurt was the start of a new epoch, a turning point in the history of the city and a turning point in the development of social welfare.

57. *Lectures on Deuteronomy*, 1525 (LW 9:243).

disguised murder and robbery.[58] "[H]ow skillfully Sir Greed can dress up to look like a pious man if that seems to be what the occasion requires, while he is actually a double scoundrel and a liar."[59] "God opposes usury and greed yet no one realizes this because it is not simple murder and robbery. Rather usury is a more diverse, insatiable murder and robbery.... Thus everyone should see to his worldly and spiritual office as commanded to punish the wicked and protect the pious."[60] As a pastor and biblical scholar, Luther proceeded to incorporate this conviction in his explanation of the seventh commandment in his *Large Catechism*.

In his 1525 advice to the Town Council of Danzig, Luther stated that government regulation of interest should be according to the principle of equity. For example, a mortgage of 5% would be equitable, but it should be reduced if it does not yield this return. At the same time, one should consider persons. The well-to-do could be induced to waive a part of his interest, whereas an old person without means should retain it.[61]

But these views were of minimal influence. Legislation introduced in Dresden in 1529 prohibited 15–20% interest in favor of a 5% rate, and in turn influenced the reform of the Zwickau city laws in 1539. Yet it was also noted how often such legislation was violated.

That these examples may indicate more failure than success is confirmed by the 1564–1565 controversy in Rudolstadt. The Lutheran pastor there refused to commune two parishioners who lived by "usury." The theological faculties of Wittenberg, Leipzig, and Jena were requested to give their opinions. They concluded against the pastor, who then had to leave town; and they did not recognize Luther as an authority on this issue. After this there was never again a serious effort to acknowledge Luther's position on usury. Luther's followers first ignored and then forgot his position against early capitalism.[62] On the question of money, even Luther's followers thought he was too much of a "wild man."

Conclusion

Luther's efforts to turn the early capitalist world upside-down by insisting on government regulation of business was countered by the powerful of his day, the analogues to our financial, energy, and pharmaceutical industries. Luther was not utopian in these matters. Nevertheless, throughout his career Luther fought against what he saw as the two-sided coin of mammonism: ascetic flight from money and the acquisitive drive for it. His foundation for this battle was the good news that a person's worth is not determined by what he or she does or does not possess, but rather by God's promise in Christ.

58. Barge, *Luther und der Frühkapitalismus*, 35.
59. *Commentary on the Sermon on the Mount*, 1532 (LW 21:183). *Treatise on Good Works*, 1520 (LW 44:107): "[G]reed has a very pretty and attractive cover for its shame; it is called provision for the body and the needs of nature. Under this cover greed insatiably amasses unlimited wealth."
60. *An die Pfarrherrn* (WA 51:422,15–423,2).
61. WA Br 3:485–86.
62. Barge, *Luther und der Frühkapitalismus*, 40–44.

That is the gospel. But as you all know, Luther held gospel and law together in dialectical tension. The gospel is for "despairing consciences," and the law is for "hard and stubborn minds." God's law of equity and justice, written on the hearts of humankind, finds positive expression through the use of reason. As Luther emphasized, it is not necessary for social well being that the emperor be Christian but that he be able to reason. "Christians are not needed for secular authority. Thus it is not necessary for the emperor to be a saint. It is not necessary for him to be a Christian to rule. It is sufficient for the emperor to possess reason."[63] Thus, it stands to reason that an ounce of prevention is worth a pound of cure. Unfortunately, our present government is against prophylactic measures, whether they apply to economics or sex. We may simply illustrate this by the old maxim that it is better to teach a person to fish than to give her a fish; in contemporary terms this is the "leave no fisherperson behind" mantra. But what does such "compassionate conservatism" say about mercury levels in the fish we catch or the actions that put such poisons in the environment or the globalization of fishing that corners the fish market? To Luther these are spiritual questions to be addressed by the civil use of laws and regulations designed to restrain greed and promote the common good.

63. *Sermon on Matthew* 22, 1528 (WA 27:417–418).

17. Martin Luther's Concept of *Sola Scriptura* and Its Impact on the Masses

A Dalit Model for Praxis-Nexus[1]

Surekha Nelavala

As a religious movement the Reformation had an enormous impact on the masses. Its primary leader, Martin Luther, was a biblical scholar whose approach to the Bible and theology was embraced and accepted by the common people. But what was it about Luther's theology and biblical interpretation that caused it to resonate so well with common people? What did he actually address in his theology that enabled him to gain the trust and confidence of the masses? In his capacity as a scholar, how did Luther reach out to the people? How did his theology and biblical hermeneutics become praxis-nexus[2] in their character? How does Luther's approach compare to contemporary contextual and people-centered theologies and hermeneutics, such as the Dalit perspective, which are yet struggling in their praxis-nexus? How might Luther's approach during the Reformation apply to present day contextual and critical approaches, which attempt to reach out effectively to the masses? In this brief article, I aim to address the above questions as a Dalit feminist reader of the Bible, making particular use of Luther's concept of Scripture and its effectiveness within faith communities.

Martin Luther's Concept and Understanding of Scripture

Martin Luther's principle of *sola scriptura* is widely evoked even today by Christians who believe that the Bible is the word of God and that it serves as corrective and judge for Christian life. Luther was a biblical scholar who both affirmed Scripture and responded to it as a committed person of faith. His approach to Scripture was not a two-fold interpretive approach that created a binary opposition between scholarship and faith.

It is evident from his works that there was an indissoluble bond between Luther and the Scripture that he loved and studied so fiercely. He could often use "the word of God" as a synonym for Scripture, without making any major distinction between them. However, when keenly observed, he chose

---

1. [Editors' note: This article derives from the author's work on a project entitled, "The Future of Lutheran Theology and the Lutheran Communion in India," sponsored by the *Gurukul Journal of Theological Studies*. The objective of the project is to interpret/reinterpret some of the key theological insights of Luther in light of the diverse theological challenges in Indian churches in general and in Lutheran churches in particular.]

2. "Praxis-nexus" refers to the interconnection between theory and practice, when a theory is used as a successful strategy to bring about desired change.

to use Scripture and "the word of God" in particular contexts with a distinct purpose.[3] Luther's sense of the word of God includes both the oral and the written word that proclaims Christ. His theology is undoubtedly Christ-centered, and for him, therefore, Scripture's sole purpose is to proclaim Christ. Thus "*sola scriptura*—Scripture alone" is in fact his conviction and dedication to "Christ alone." For Luther, "Scripture alone" is based entirely upon the biblical proclamation of "Christ alone." Therefore, he grants the utmost authority to Scripture, because of its function.[4] Luther did not have any reservations about seeing Scripture as the word of God,[5] as opposed to a perspective that says that the Bible *contains* the word of God, a position of much contemporary critical hermeneutics. For him, however, Scripture is judged by its theological content, not by the canonization process or by tradition. Luther presents the relationship between Scripture and Christ in a peculiar way, that is, Scripture as "servant" and Christ as "King."[6] Thus for Luther, Scripture is not at the center of his Christian understanding but rather "Christ alone", and "Christ alone" is possible because of his belief in "Scripture alone." His usage of Scripture is absolutely christocentric, that is, Scripture exists with the sole purpose of proclaiming Christ.[7] Thus Luther's scholarship and his faith were integral to all of his proceedings as an ecclesiastical person. In presenting himself primarily as a member of a faith community, Luther followed a methodology of biblical interpretation whereby his intellectual analysis and his spiritual beliefs formed an indivisible part of his hermeneutics.

Luther's principle of *sola scriptura* had significant influence on his method of biblical interpretation, because he did not place tradition on par with Scripture but instead asserted that Scripture must be the sole authority and doctrinal guide for the church.[8] For Luther, sacred Scripture is not essentially a literary work or a historical document but rather a book of faith that is given in faith and must be received in faith. Therefore, Luther treats Scripture as part of his spirituality rather than merely as literature that is open to critical approach and interpretation. His affirmation of "*sola fide*—by faith alone" is inseparably related to his spirituality, which is also connected to the word of God/Scripture.[9] Thus Luther in his hermeneutical principle provides a scope for identifying a Canon within the Canon,[10] qualifying Scripture for its purpose of being a witness of and to Christ, which he claims is Scripture's primary function.

According to Luther, however, "gospel" is not restricted to Scripture but extends beyond it. Thus Luther grants authority to oral tradition as well as

3. David W. Lotz, "Sola Scriptura: Luther on Biblical Authority," *Interpretation* 35/3 (July 1981): 258–273.
4. Ibid.
5. See Jaroslav Pelikan and Helmut T. Lehmann, eds., *Luther's Works*, American ed., 55 vols. (Philadelphia, Pa: Fortress Press; Saint Louis, Mo: Concordia Publishing House, 1955–86), 34:112 (hereafter, *LW*): "The Scriptures must be understood in favor of Christ, not against him. For that reason they must either refer to him or must not be held to be true Scriptures." Note that Luther disqualifies as Scripture any text that is not self-revealingly christological.
6. Martin Luther, *Lectures on Galatians*, 1535 (*LW* 26:295).
7. Martin Luther, *A Brief Instruction on What to Look for and Expect in the Gospels*, 1521 (*LW* 35:123).
8. See *LW* 26:57, 66; *LW* 30:166.
9. Kenneth Hagen, *Luther's Approach to Scripture as Seen in His "Commentaries on Galatians: 1519–1538"* (Tübingen: Mohr, 1993), 69.
10. Gary M. Simpson, "'You Shall Bear Witness to Me': Thinking with Luther about Christ and Scripture," *WW* 29 (Fall 2009): 380–388.

to biblical interpretation while maintaining his christocentric hermeneutic. He gives equal importance to the spoken word of God and to written Scripture in terms of proclaiming Christ. He states:

> And the gospel should really not be something written, but a spoken word which brought forth the Scriptures, as Christ and the apostles have done. This is why Christ himself did not write anything but only spoke. He called his teaching not Scripture but gospel, meaning good news or a proclamation that is spread not by pen but by word of mouth.[11]

Luther is not bound or limited in his approach to Scripture, but rather he qualified Scripture through his Christian understanding and faith. Thus according to Luther Scripture exists for Christ, not the other way around, and similarly Christ exists for Christ's teachings that promote the values of equality, freedom, love, liberation, peace, and justice. Any text that speaks against these Christian values cannot be counted as Scripture, because Scripture cannot proclaim Christ on the one hand and injustice on the other. A text must be qualified in order to become Scripture, and thus Luther's hermeneutic of "Scripture alone" can also serve as the foundational and normative basis for all liberationist approaches that turn to Scripture for their proclamation.

At this intersection, as a liberationist, Dalit feminist reader, I see the points of convergence with Luther's principle of "Scripture alone," although his interpretations may differ in some ways from modern-day interpretations that use contextual, cultural, and ideological hermeneutical perspectives. As a liberationist reader, however, who comes from a Lutheran confessional background, I uphold Luther's concept of "Scripture alone" because Scripture proclaims Christ, and therefore Scripture perpetuates liberation and justice. As a Dalit feminist and liberationist scholar, I affirm that any text that proclaims Christ will by default advocate for liberation and justice. To compromise on the values and teachings of Christ is to compromise on Christ himself. Trusting that God's word advocates for freedom, liberation, and justice, but not for bondage or injustice, it is liberating for me to regard "Scripture alone" as the normative principle of Dalit feminist hermeneutics, as it seeks, through Scripture, for liberation and justice to prevail in society.

Dalit Theology towards Praxis-Nexus: An Analysis

Contextual theologies are particularly liberationist in their perspective, but they have not been assertive in their deliberations about the "Scripture alone" concept on the same level as Luther's affirmation. Contextual hermeneutics emphasizes the primacy of the reader and the reader's context in biblical interpretation,[12] while liberationist hermeneutics qualifies a text as Scripture only when it has the potential for gleaning a liberation motif from it. Thus each method projects

---

11. *A Brief Instruction* (LW 35:123).
12. See Fernando Segovia, "Cultural Studies and Contemporary Biblical Criticism: Ideological Criticism as Mode of Discourse," in *Reading from This Place: Social Location and Biblical Interpretation in Global Perspective*, ed. Fernando F. Segovia and Mary Ann Tolbert (Minneapolis, Mn: Fortress Press, 1995), 7.

a different explicit agenda in its methodology of the proclamation of Christ, although this is implicit in all readings of Scripture. Even though contextual perspectives and the liberationist readings of the Bible are people-centered, they have not come across effectively with the masses, particularly among the faith communities which, for the benefit of their spirituality, should be the primary audience and practitioners of people-centered hermeneutics. As a Christian, a member of a faith community from the Lutheran ecclesiastical tradition, and as a Dalit feminist reader of the Bible, I propose the need to follow Luther's model of uplifting Scripture, by saying that "Scripture alone" is the essential point of connection to the masses. This approach places the scholars together with the people to create a praxis theology that is meaningful to their lives and communities.

It comes as no surprise that the Bible is at the center for a practicing Christian. More Christians than we know begin and end their days by paying tribute to Scripture, by reading, reflecting, and meditating on the word that Scripture contains. However, the method that each one uses for this personal reflection or meditation differs, influenced by numerous factors that create a highly individualized Christian spiritual formation. Although many claim that their reading is literal, they tend to read the text through the lens that was given to them, a lens reiterated by preachers from their understanding of spirituality or bhakti practices of Christianity. Popular Christians on the one hand honor the Bible as their sacred Scriptures, a faith document, but on the other hand they also tend to believe that it is historically accurate and that everything that is written there is, in fact, historically factual. Any deviation from this scripture-centered point of view is deemed hurtful to their spirituality and, therefore, a popular Christian resists critical interpretations of the Scripture that do not confirm and affirm such scripture-centeredness. Thus in order to make contextual, feminist, and liberationist perspectives realistic and to create praxis-nexus hermeneutics and theology, it is mandatory to affirm the authority of Scripture as the norm and as central to biblical interpretation and theology.

This situation makes it even more pressing for trained biblical readers to approach the Bible in faith and respect and with a willingness to verbalize the same, while also approaching it critically and systematically so as to interpret Scripture in such a way that it can come alive for existing faith communities. Therefore, I deem it necessary to approach the Scriptures, first as a Christian in faith, then as a Lutheran by tradition, a biblical scholar by education, and a Dalit-feminist-liberationist reader. Generally, the tendency is to approach the text from only one identity while the other identities take a back seat, thus creating a bifurcated or even dualistic approach to the Bible rather than a holistic one. My aim is to address and discuss the needed interconnectedness of all these perspectives—namely, Christian, traditional (ecclesiastical), critical/scholarly, and ideological—such that together they are active in producing the outcomes of each biblical interpretation. I aim to do this by taking Luther's faith affirmation, "*sola scriptura*", as the foundation for Christian understanding of Scripture.

While Dalit theology itself has evolved in the last four decades,[13] it has always affirmed that Dalit theology is a people-centered theology directed

---

13. See A. P. Nirmal, ed., *A Reader in Dalit Theology* (Madras: Gurukul, 1992); G. Koonthanam, "Yahweh the Defender of the Dalits: A Reflection on Isaiah 3.12–15," *Jeevadhara* 128 (1992): 112–123;

towards justice and liberation. Similarly, Dalit theology has always been Bible-centered, seeking liberative motives to develop its theology while claiming the experiences and pathos of Dalits and marginalized people as the quintessential normative factor. K.P. Kuruvilla summarizes Dalit theology in a three-fold definition. He writes: "First of all, it is a theology about Dalits or theological reflection upon the Christian responsibility to the depressed classes. Secondly, it is theology for the depressed classes or the message addressed to the Dalits to which they seem to be responding. Thirdly, it is a theology from the depressed classes, that is, the theology they would like to expound."[14] Although various theologians use a different methodology to do Dalit theology and biblical interpretation, the above definition sums up the objective of the Dalit approach to theology and Scripture.

Since its emergence, a paradigm shift in theological studies in India has taken place under the influence of Dalit theology, but it has had negligible impact on ecclesiastical faith communities. Even though Dalit theology is, without question, a people-centered theological phenomenon, it has not reached out to the masses and thus has not yet proven to be effective in its praxis objective. It is a popular opinion that scholarly or intellectual theology fails to be effective in ecclesiastical communities of faith and can be used only in classroom settings. If this opinion is true regarding Dalit theology, which, as it makes particular use of the suffering of the people, is a people-centered theology, it is time to evaluate the objectives and methods of Dalit theology. If it cannot appeal to the masses, what then is its purpose? If its core objective is to do praxis-nexus, that is, to bring theology into practice, Dalit theology must use the tools that bring Scripture to life in the reality of suffering people. Dalit theology must claim Scripture as its basis and the ecclesiastical faith communities as its location for praxis-nexus.

G. Soares-Prabhu, "The Table Fellowship of Jesus: Its Significance for Dalit Christians in India Today," *Jeevadhara* 128 (1992): 140–159; M. Gnanavaram, "Dalit Theology and the Parable of the Good Samaritan," *JSNT* 50 (1993): 59–83; David M. Carr, "A Biblical Basis for Dalit Theology," in *Indigenous People: Dalits*, ed. James Massey (Delhi: ISPCK, 1994), 231–249; James Massey, *Towards a Dalit Hermeneutics: Re-reading the Text, the History and the Literature* (Delhi: ISPCK, 1994); M. Arul Rajah, "Towards a Dalit Reading of the Bible: Some Hermeneutical Reflection," *Jeevadhara* 151 (1996): 29–34; V. Devasahayam, ed., *Frontiers of Dalit Theology* (Chennai: Gurukul, 1997); Sathianathan Clarke, *Dalits and Christianity: Subaltern Religion and Liberation Theology in India* (Delhi: Oxford University Press, 1998); Monica J. Melanchthon, "The Indian Voice," in *Reading the Bible as Women: Perspectives from Africa, Asia, and Latin America*, Semeia 78 (Atlanta: SBL, 1997), 151–160; M. Arul Raja "Reading Bible from a Dalit Location: Some Points of Interpretation," *Voices From the Third World* 23/1 (2000): 71–91; George Oommen, "The Emerging Dalit Theology: A Historical Appraisal," *Indian Church History Review* 34/1 (2000): 19–37; J. Susaimanickam, "Dalit Hermeneutics: A Proposal for Reading the Bible," *Vaiharai* 5/3–4 (2000): 3–24; K. Jesurathnam, "Towards a Dalit Liberative Hermeneutic: Re-reading the Psalms of Lament," *Bangalore Theological Forum* 34/1 (2002): 1–34; Surekha Nelavala, *Liberation beyond Borders: Dalit Feminist Hermeneutics and Four Gospel Women* (Cologne, Germany: Lambert Academic Publishing, 2009); Peniel Rajkumar, *Dalit Theology and Dalit Liberation: Problems, Paradigms and Possibilities* (Farnham, England: Ashgate, 2010); Sathianathan Clarke, Deenabandhu Manchala and Philip Vinod Peacock, eds., *Dalit Theology in the Twenty-First Century: Discordant Voices, Discerning Pathways* (Delhi: Oxford University Press, 2010); Monica J. Melanchthon, "Dalits, Bible and Method," accessed online: http://www.sbl-site.org/Article.aspx?ArticleId=459; Evangeline Rajkumar, "Skin, Body, Blood: Explorations for Dalit Hermeneutics," accessed online: http://www.womenutc.com/evangeline_anderson_rajkumar_3.htm; Surekha Nelavala, "Jesus Asks the Samaritan Woman for a Drink: A Dalit Feminist Reading of John 4," *Lectio Difficilior* 1 (June 2007), accessed online: http://www.lectio.unibe.ch/07_1/surekha_nelavala_jesus_asks_the_samaritan_woman.htm. The list of works cited here is not exhaustive.

14. K.P. Kuruvilla, "Dalit Theology: An Indian Christian Attempt to Give Voice to the Voiceless," accessed online, http://www.csichurch.com/article/dalit.htm.

Dalit theology has a specific role to play that is different from Dalit social activism, as it approaches Scripture and has religious significance and spiritual importance. Therefore, it is critical to evaluate its significance for the Christian masses as we move forward with the commitment for seeking justice and liberation for Dalits through Scripture and theology. Therefore, first, I strongly affirm the need to emphasize the scriptural base for Dalit theology by saying "*sola scriptura*" as strongly as Martin Luther did. Second, it is mandatory that Dalit theology and Dalit hermeneutics be praxis-oriented. Third, it is not enough that Dalit experience is used as the normative factor for doing theology. Actually taking this theology to the masses for evaluation and practice ought to be equally normative, because doing that will make the Dalit perspective the praxis perspective also.

Tat-siong Benny Liew states: "Interpretation or reception of texts is not private and individual, but public and communal. Such public and communal reception also has a public effect or affect on communities."[15] Contextual readings carry both obligation and accountability to their communities. Therefore, contextual hermeneutics must be praxiological, as opposed to self-imposed, as a reader represents the people of a particular context. Similarly, each contextual reading has to be context specific, and therefore it is important to describe the particular context in which the hermeneutical process happens. If Dalit theology and Dalit feminist-hermeneutics aim to reach out to the people, and if Dalit theologians and biblical scholars have a role to play in faith communities, it is then important to take their context into consideration from all angles, including their faith tradition.

The effect that Luther had on the masses, the praxis-nexus that he was able to achieve, challenges my own hermeneutical principle as a contextual reader, particularly as a Dalit feminist scholar, and particularly as Dalit and feminist theologies and hermeneutics have not been able to make their way to the people. Thus I believe that in order to reach out to the critical masses of faith communities, it is important to recognize and establish the essential aspects of spirituality while continuing to be theologians and scholars, all the while following Luther's model of bringing his theology into practice.

---

15. Tat-siong Benny Liew, "More Than Personal Encounters: Identity, Community and Interpretation," *USQR* 56/1–2 (2002): 41–44.

Critical Issues to Embrace

18. Suffering and the Theology of the Cross from a Feminist Perspective

Anna Madsen

It is with great honor and great trepidation that I stand before you this afternoon. When Kirsi Stjerna spoke to me on the phone about coming to this grand event, and informed me that she would like me to speak about Luther, and sex, and violence, and feminism, and then listed all of the other crazy-illustrious names with which my name would mingle, I gulped, and said, "Um, Kirsi, I'm not like them. That's a whole different league. Might even be a whole different sport!" And then she said, "Anna, I've read your blog. I think you can do Luther, sex, violence, and feminism just fine." Hmm. I decided not to ask exactly what she meant by that.

Just two weekends ago, I presented at the South Central Wisconsin Synod's Bishop's Convocation. My friend who accompanied me asked if I ever get nervous when I present. I said, "Nah . . . unless I have to present at an academic forum. Then I do, but only during the question and answer period. But I have developed a strategy for such occasions. If someone asks a question that either makes no sense, or addresses an area about which I am not exactly clear, or when it is obvious that the question is really posed more to garner a platform for the questioner than it is about any possible answer I could provide, then I simply lean in, put my hand on my chin, and say, 'Well, that is really interesting.... Tell me more about what moved you to ask that.' Then either I get further clarity about the question, further time to get further clarity about what I could possibly say to the question, or further time for the questioner to offer the coveted clarification of his or her own agenda!"

Now, let me be clear. This prelude to my presentation is no stereotypical female fare, no expression of an embedded cultural habit of self-deprecation. This prelude is rather an expression of confidence about what I do, and about what I don't do; or, perhaps rather, what I don't do very often. In fact, it has been exactly seven years since I have had an offering at an academic feast-hall such as this, and, not coincidentally, I couldn't even make it. The day that little Else and I were to fly off to the San Diego American Academy of Religion Annual Meeting, where my co-authored paper was to be presented, she came down with a terrible strep throat, and my son had medical complications that simply needed a mama's presence. And so, a proxy had to be sent.

Thus rather than attempt to do what I have not done for years, and, frankly, no longer is my schtick anyway, I am going to do what I do do. I am going to tell a story that is mine, and yet that is not only mine.

My dissertation was completed in 2003. Prior to revving up, so to speak, my doctoral studies, I served in a tiny rural parish in South Dakota. It was tempting to spring right into Ph.D. work, but even in the waning days of seminary, I realized that any further academic work I would do had to be tethered to real life, to people's real experiences, real sufferings, real questions, real yearnings. My dissertation had to matter beyond my own thirst for intellectual inquiry. I had a personal hunch that if I really wanted to teach, pastoral experience would help me discern that, and shape it, and fasten it to something less ethereal than theory. And who knows? Maybe I really was called to be a parish pastor.

And so Badger, South Dakota, hosted my late husband and me for three years. There I began to know a bit more of life than I had in my previous twenty-seven years. Sudden deaths by cardiac arrest, diabetic shock, drunken snowmobile accidents killing fiancés and fathers-to-be; I learned that sometimes talking about the weather is not just small talk, but is life and death for farmers and ranchers; in a small town, change might sound good on paper, but then it turns out it is not just a question of Sunday morning service times, liturgical rituals, and hymns, but is about communal and familial allegiances, political persuasions, and generational loyalties. I learned that baptisms always make me cry: a baby bundled up in blankets and future and grace. And I discovered that I am not called to be a parish pastor.

Through a series of serendipitous connections and conversations and events, Bill, my late husband, and I ended up in Regensburg, Germany, where for four years I studied various and morphed forms of the theology of the cross. That was my settled topic, after I threw the net far and wide, asking mentors and colleagues and friends what they thought had not received enough theological wondering. Theologian Michael Root said to me, "Well, the term 'the theology of the cross' is used all the time, but there is no real clear sense of what it means. Maybe you should check that out." And so I did.

For four years I poked around at this "thin tradition," nodding to Douglas John Hall, this thin tradition that surfaces by name only fleetingly in the first few pages of Luther's career. I sought to find the Big Bang of his thought in the writings of Paul, and learned that Paul tends to employ references to the cross in a variety of ways, depending on the recipients and intents of his letter. That was both enlightening and confounding and premonitory. I looked at Luther, who, although he clearly bound the theology of the cross most intentionally to the forgiveness of sins, as well as to *Anfechtung*, summed up a somewhat broader vision for it in his explanation to the second article of the creed:

> I believe that Jesus Christ, true God, begotten of the Father in eternity, and also a true human being, born of the Virgin Mary, is my Lord. He has redeemed me, a lost and condemned human being. He has purchased and freed me from all sins, from death, and from the power of the devil, not with gold or silver but with his holy, precious blood and with his innocent suffering and death. He has done all this in order that I may belong to him, live under him in his kingdom, and serve him in eternal righteousness, innocence, and blessedness, just as he is risen from the dead and lives and rules eternally. This is most certainly true.[1]

---

1. Robert Kolb and Timothy J. Wengert, eds., *The Book of Concord: The Confessions of the Evangelical Lutheran Church* (Minneapolis, Mn: Fortress Press, 2000), 355.

I studied Von Loewenich, and Kitamori, and Moltmann, and learned that World War II changed everything in theology, that the theology of the cross has to speak to the oppressed as it does to the oppressors, and if you cannot say what you want to in Auschwitz with the ashes of Jews on your shoulders, then stop talking. I studied feminist theologians and liberation theologians, the likes of Elisabeth Moltmann-Wendel, and Dorothee Sölle, and Mary Grey, and Elizabeth Johnson, and Jon Sobrino, and Gustavo Gutiérrez, and North American theologians like Douglas John Hall, and I learned that the theology of the cross speaks to abuse and poverty and loneliness and depression and consumptive wants that transform, that mutate, into needs.

Almost to a theologian, the theology of the cross declared that there, precisely there—wherever the "there" was for that specific theologian—God was at work. I looked up at my husband and I said, one day, "It sounds really good, but if something were to happen to you and to the children, would it be enough?" And I presented my dissertation, and with a few tweaks here and there and here again, it was accepted, and I defended my understandings of process theology and Buddhism, and as the final culmination of my worthiness as a *systematische Theologin* from a German *Universität*, I proved that I could tap a keg.

We stayed on for one more year in order to help with my doctoral advisor's *Geburstagsfest* (birthday celebration), and while at a gathering with my then still breastfeeding eight-month-old daughter, Else, in Neuendettelsau in the waning days of that event, one month before we were to return to the States where I was to begin teaching at Augustana College in Sioux Falls, a car screamed into my husband and my about-to-turn-three son. Bill died, and Karlchen suffered a traumatic brain injury, from which he is still and will evermore be recovering. As will Else, and will I.

I discovered that sometimes, Easter—the core, frankly, of my theology—*isn't* enough. And alone, the cross tempts people to become like Boot Strap Bill Turner, the pirate who finally became part of the ship, settling into a moorless grief that promises no lighthouse, and only perpetual stormy seas. I discovered, as the trajectory of that accident's event continued to shoot through my family, my planned vocation as an academic, my personal tangle with grief and hopelessness and loneliness and emptiness, and, for the first time, a visceral understanding of apocalyptic, that my experience, my story, was not just mine. Suddenly, all suffering was one. The whole creation *was* crying out. It really was. I hadn't heard it before. How could I not have heard it before? And why isn't everyone hearing it with me now? And suddenly, the theology of the cross became real. It became tangibly, inescapably, incontrovertibly real.

Today, I stand before you as an academic, to be sure. I have the credentials. I know how to footnote. I know whom to quote. I know which theologians come out of which school and which theologians like which other theologians, and I know the litmus tests to determine the orthodoxy of any given school of thought or theological leaning. Und, ich kann sogar Deutsch sprechen, und Luther *auf Deutsch* lesen! And, let us not forget, I know how to tap a German Lutheran keg. But before the accident, I did not know the theology of the cross in any way except from the safety of a desk and behind a pulpit. Even while I had been in Badger, I had certainly been present in other people's Good

Fridays, but I always returned to my Easter life. Nothing bad had really happened to me, you see, short of the Minnesota Twins never picking it up after their World Series streaks. My Grandmother died at 92, but she had lived a life filled with akvavit and butter.

After June 19, 2004, however, that all changed. Suddenly, the theology of the cross was no theory. It was nothing to footnote, and God knew it was no footnote. It was, it is, daily life.

Still, confronted by Kirsi with this task of presenting about the theology of the cross from a feminist perspective, my first tendency, even after all of these years of not needing to live the life of academic pursuit, of having to "publish or perish" (a theme which itself could be addressed under the notion of the theology of the cross, by the way), of having to prove my theological worth by proving how many people I can reference, of living my topic day in and day out, what was my first tendency? Slog around dozens of books. And not just slog them around. But read them. And I tried to read them. Really, I did. I read a good bunch of them. Skimmed more of them. But while I tried to absorb them, highlight them, cull from them, I was preparing for a series of lectures with New Testament theologian, Ray Pickett, for a Bishop's Convocation in Wisconsin last weekend, my son's brain injury was causing him a spate of stomach uck, and my mother's pancreatic cancer was gaining in its fearfully strong cadence to hospice, just this past week, and death now, at any time.

Let me be clear: I am not complaining about the commitment to be here or the preparation it took to come. It is rather that the theology of the cross has become my daily existence, this trust that under the ick and ish and pain and grief and exhaustion of life, God must be there. In some ways, frankly, the theology of the cross seems to me to be more accurately named the theology of Holy Saturday. You see, the accident put everything into a new perspective. For example, Kirsi asked me a few weeks ago whether, given Mom's illness, I could still come. I told her that after the accident, every and any commitment for *anything* in the future seemed an audacious thing, so, yes, insofar as I could promise to come, I would!

And another example: Little boy Karl, who, like his sister is about as perfect as can be, can, on occasion, make me positively insane with frustration and irritation and downright anger. And when those rare moments happen, I look at him, and my little spirit's lips, all pursed, say within myself, "I am so glad that you are alive to piss me off!" Or another example: I understand that there are those who have these beautiful embroidered pictures in their kitchens, the ones that go something like, "I thank you, God, for all the dirty dishes in my sink and on my counter, for they signify that I have food to eat, and friends to eat it with," and so on and so forth. As for me? I have a framed German postcard that says, simply, in bold red letters, "Abwaschen sucks!"

But more to the point of this presentation's expected thrust: before the accident, I figured that the promise was enough. It would tide anyone over when death, in any of its forms, came around and paid a visit. The empty tomb was about hope and perseverance and faith. But after the accident, I learned that Easter can be an insult. "Why do you look for the living among the dead?" I had so often retold at bedsides, over tears at coffee tables, and in funeral sermons. "He is not here, but is risen!" Isn't that good news? Well …

Is it good news to put an arm—with full sincerity and presence—around a mother holding a starving child and tell her that it is truly a travesty that there is nothing to feed her son or daughter in the moment . . . but! . . . soon and very soon, Jesus will come again, and let me tell you about the feast then! Is it good news to say that God heals, and then say to those with no health insurance that on that day but not before, they will deserve it? Is it good news to promise that God forgives sins, and preach and teach that there is nothing we can do to save ourselves, but not screw up the courage to preach and teach that the converse then is also true: there is nothing that we can do to damn ourselves either? Is it good news to a wife and a mother who has lost a husband and a perfectly healthy son?

I learned, then, that sometimes promises are not enough, at least not in the moment of deep darkness, or in dark moments strung together that might last days, or months, or even years.

I have heard it said that if we just *believed*, though, just trusted in the news that Jesus is risen, then it would make all the difference in the world. That may well be a full crock when you are standing in the Ground Zero of shocking suffering.

Part of my motivation for beginning OMG[2] was determining that people are yearning for relevance. They are yearning for authenticity. They want good theology, they really do, theology that makes a difference, that has a power to help them discern how to parent, how to be in relationship with a partner, how to comfort, how to advocate. But they don't want platitudes, they don't want clichés, they don't want obscure theology that makes no intersection with real life, real suffering, real grief, real pain. Life cannot be lived without an acknowledgement of pain, nor can that pain be assuaged by theological maxims or promises of redemption that will *eventually* come to pass.

A year and a half or so after the accident, I was venting via email, and not just a bit, to a good friend and colleague down the hall about my sudden deeply tough situation, not least of all because of the logistics of being a single mother of a precocious then three-year-old and a special needs then five-year-old, also as a then tenure-track professor. I had recently moved to a new community, had no deep friendships, was suddenly a first-time home-buyer forced to undergo a remodel to make the house handicapped accessible and who was living therefore a nomadic life imposing on friend and foe alike for temporary housing for a period of seven weeks, and who was, in a few words, overwhelmed and exhausted in body, mind, and spirit, losing herself in the swirl of it all, with nary a moment even to sit and grieve. My friend had this to offer—with full sincerity and presence: "Just recall the scripture," wrote he, "'Be still, and know that I am God.'" Oh, was I pissed. I pursed my lips and briskly typed back (I'm sure he heard the email down the hall before he received it), "I will be still, IF *God* preps for classes, grades papers, creates books and journal articles in my name, writes bills, fills out forms, ensures that I find worthy care-givers, transfers Karl to his countless therapies, brings and picks up Else-girl to school, pushes a wheelchair and a grocery cart to get food for my family, plays with both, does the dishes, laundry, and pick-up, and brings the car in for an oil

---

2. OMG: Center for Theological Conversation. http://omgcenter.com/about/.

change, and as an indulgent bonus, finds me time to sit with a cup of coffee to breathe! THEN I'll be still!"

Tom Stoppard's play *Rosencrantz and Guildenstern Are Dead* helps explain why I was so bothered. It contains a marvelous passage, a heartbreaking passage, of actors who reconvene with Rosencrantz and Guildenstern at Elsinore after the two snuck away during their impromptu performance in the woods. The lead actor said to them:

> PLAYER: You don't understand the humiliation of it—to be tricked out of a single assumption, which makes our existence viable—that somebody is watching. . . . Don't you see?! We're actors—we're the opposite of people! . . . We pledged our identities, secure in the conventions of our trade, that someone would be watching. And then, gradually, no one was. We were caught, high and dry. No one came forward. No one shouted at us. The silence was unbreakable, it imposed itself upon us; it was obscene.[3]

The text has been used to get at the feelings of abandonment we would feel if we were to learn, or at the very least believe, that there is no God watching. It's a powerful tool in that way. But it can also be used to demonstrate, I think, how people feel if the church, the incarnate presence of God, looks away, doesn't notice the action in people's lives, the drama, cares more about footnotes than washing the feet.

It is well to remember that Jesus came to offer salvation, which in the Greek is *soteria*, which means health, healing, and wholeness. Note, by the way, that definition changes the meaning of the question: Are you saved? Instead of being a veiled inquiry about whether you think you are going to heaven or hell, the question really asks, "Are you well?" But we can't ask the question if we aren't watching people's plays—not watching in the sense of popping corn to tune into a voyeuristic Big Brother, but in the sense, rather, of being in relation to and with another.

You see, that Jesus came to offer *soteria*, health, healing, and wholeness, suggests that the opposite is often more true: disease, decay, brokenness, and death. I am convinced that Jesus is risen from the dead. And I am convinced that in that event, he announced that death no longer has the last word—all evidence to the contrary. We might live as if it does, death might like to present itself in the form of fear, threat, intimidation, and hopelessness and in so doing try to convince us that it does. But the Christian confession, our *gospel*, is that Jesus is risen. And the gospel has meaning *now*. It is *news*. There must be a reason to listen: whatever that reason is, it must by definition have relevance. And I am convinced that relevance has everything to do with relationship. It is not fundamentally about the self, but it is about the self and its relationship to others and to God. You cannot know what is relevant to someone if they are irrelevant to you.

Sometimes the church is called to point out the relevance—the on-the-ground-relevance—of one's theology where one might not ever have otherwise noticed it. That is, relevance has a prophetic element to it. The Word of God speaks to unique situations, calling awareness to matters that either were

---

3. See the text in full in Tom Stoppard, *Rosencrantz and Guildenstern Are Dead* (New York, Ny: Grove Press, 1967), 63–64.

unseen or intentionally ignored. An Old Testament professor of mine, Lynn Nakamura, pointed out that the only commandment that we have ever gotten right was, "Be fruitful and multiply." But we've done that. We've had great fun doing that. We've done that exceedingly well. And now the world is overcome by our fruit, and there are those who cannot, for any number of reasons, multiply. "Would," she asked, "God still speak the same word to us today?"

So, what does the cross mean to us today? What are its implications? Does it affect only the sinners or the ones sinned upon? Does it have anything to do with love? hope? reconciliation? justice? mercy? grief? vocation? avocation? pain? loss? parenting? loneliness? alienation? connection? emotions? addictions? doubt? brokenness? health? relationships? renewal? rebirth? joy? The flesh of life? Its essence?

If not, we have spiritualized the incarnate. I can't think of much more that could be relevant than God incarnate, and to help figure out what that means to the rest of us incarnate folks. If we don't, we have made the supremely relevant not only irrelevant, but we have lost an opportunity for relationship.

My hope for purveyors of theology in these days is that we discover that theology must be relevant and that relevance has everything to do with relationship to wherever there is death or the promise of it. It has to do with *soteria*. God's word relates to us. Could we in the church, including the theological world—even, perhaps, the academic world of grades and pre-tenure and promotions and institutional politics—create a culture of *relationship* where the gospel, that is, news that is terribly salvatory, terribly relational, which heals, serves, feeds, binds up, forgives, encourages, aids, and offers hope uniquely, concretely, and contextually, defines our *esse*? This is prolepsis-in-motion, this enacting out of the promise of the future, of bringing forth Easter into a presently persistent Holy Saturday, the union of Cross and Tomb.

Now. I understand that my topic is supposed to be about feminism and the theology of the cross. Thus far, perhaps, it has been so only obliquely. Let me make the connections more explicit. Feminist theology is born out of the experiences and perspectives of women. It has, thankfully, morphed from a movement of white women with privilege to a broader acknowledgment of and advocacy against oppression against all people, and against creation.

The objection to oppression is not only because it is wrong *an sich*, but also because feminism has emphasized and recognized the crucial and intrinsic nature of creature-to-creature/creation relationship. We are not in this alone. Even our actual dying is not ours to have in isolation, for our physical death causes emotional and spiritual deaths within the spirits of those who must learn to love us *in absentia*.

Some years back, I began to punch around at the idea of the intersection of theology and psychology and neurology, particularly by way of sin. I found a new voice in ethicist Seyla Benhabib. In her book, *Situating the Self: Gender, Community and Postmodernism in Contemporary Ethics*, she makes the obvious and yet oddly novel statement that "the moral self is not a moral geometrician but an embodied, finite, suffering and emotive being."[4] She continues:

---

4. Seyla Benhabib, *Situating the Self: Gender, Community and Postmodernism in Contemporary Ethics* (New York, Ny: Routledge, 1992), 50.

Current constructions of the "moral point of view" . . . exclude all familial and other personal relations of dependence from their purview. While to become an autonomous adult means asserting one's independence vis-à-vis these relations, the process of moral maturation need not be viewed along the fictive model of the nineteenth-century boy who leaves home to become "a self-made man" out "yonder" in the wide, wild world. Moral autonomy can also be understood as growth and change, sustained by a network of relationships.[5]

Benhabib goes on to formulate an ethical principle that is based on dialogue, fostering an appreciation of the context of moral decision-making, a complex method based on the supremely basic question of a parent to a child—"What if others threw sand in your face or pushed you into the pool, how would you feel then?"[6] This question is not necessarily accusatory, but curious. Simple inquiry moves the questioner into an empathic role, one who recognizes the nuances— the messiness—of life and that decisions are made neither in a moral nor a relational vacuum.[7]

In other words, vis-à-vis sin, it takes no imagination at all blithely to name something sinful. That is low-hanging fruit. It is far more complex and far more nuanced and far more potentially humbling, to ask, not accusingly, but openly, and curiously, "How did this happen?"

That is a relational question. It is a cross-question. "Father, forgive them, because they have no clue what they are doing." Any simpleton could name the crucifiers sinners. But the factors that got Jesus on the cross were multi-layered, multi-flavored, multi-colored. They had no clue. Or consider those who suffer oppression and injustice. If we as Christians are ambassadors of salvation, we realize that where there is death, we are called to steward life, recognizing even that that might mean altering our status quo manners of living. Or consider how "family values" in political parlance is clearly code for anything to do with sex: abortion, single mothers, anything-other-than-straight sexuality. Living in sin still means "shacking up!" As if we are not all living in sin.

Our synod is like any synod, legally and prudently obligated to send out a letter naming clergy who have been removed from the roster because of any inappropriate (even if consensual) sexual contact. We just had a round of two letters in the last two weeks. I understand the level of precaution necessary in the event that there is a pattern of boundary violations that harm vulnerable people. I cannot emphasize enough my awareness of this need to both free victims to come forward and support them once they do. These public letters are but one way to ensure that victims are protected and have institutional avenues for healing. Still, these letters do conjure up another response in me, causing me

---

5. Ibid., 51.
6. Ibid., 53. A critical facet of Benhabib's thesis is the moral framework of many women. She notes that women tend to think morally in terms of primary relationships by way of empathy; see idem, 149, and Carol Gilligan, "Moral Development in Late Adolescence and Late Adulthood: A Critique and Reconstruction of Kohlberg's Theory," *Human Development* 23 (1980): 77–104.
7. In this way, Carol Gilligan has been instrumental in reframing conversations of ethics. She states incisively: "Since everyone is vulnerable both to oppression and to abandonment, two moral visions— one of justice, and one of care—recur in human experience." (Carol Gilligan, "Moral Orientation and Moral Development," in *Woman and Moral Theory*, ed. E.F. Kittay and Diane T. Meyers [Totowa, Nj: Rowman and Littlefield, 1987], 20). Referenced in Benhabib, *Situating the Self*, 189.

to cock my head, wondering why, to be consistent, we do not also get a letter every time it becomes clear that rostered clergy are not tithing to the poor, or that they support politicians cutting food stamps from the tables of the poor, or that they fail to speak up forcefully for the hungry, thirsty, and naked—the very forms of service addressed in the one place in the Gospels where Christ sits on the heavenly throne (Matthew 25). Vulnerable, vulnerable victims exist also, you see, in the lack of advocacy and aid to the ones about whom Jesus called the least of these.

I am more concerned, that is, on ensuring that everyone has a home with a bed in it upon which they can sin (and here I speak only of consensual sex) than that someone is (consensually) sinning on a bed! And yet even the notion of sending out letters makes me curious about the effect. How is this process lending itself toward reconciliation rather than shame? What are the effects of such letters on those who are yet still hiding in sin (be they sexual, or abuse of substances, gambling addictions, etc.), and yet need confession, forgiveness, and hope for a new path?

Or consider the way that Valerie Saiving Goldstein, a female graduate student in theology in 1960 (!) reframed sin. She observed that "feminine sins" are born precisely out of the exhorted antidote, humility, to a sort of sin that is uniquely masculine in experience and expression. Humility, she said, is the very thing which women are culturally instructed to embody anyway, yet o.d.-ing on it serves up a lack of self-worth, and a tendency toward pettiness and manipulation, a very different understanding of the traditional definition of sin.[8]

Perhaps the way to define a feminist take on the theology of the cross is to speak of relation: its presence, its lack, its incarnational promise. After the accident, I planted a garden—my first adult garden!—in the backyard of the house that my late husband Bill and Karl picked out when they flew to Sioux Falls, leaving my daughter and me in Germany, so that all would be ready when we all arrived just four months later. Except only three of us arrived, and a very broken three of us. So there I sat in the dirt of my garden. I had bags of shit—literally and figuratively—all around me. I had seeds of all sorts of good things—literally and figuratively—all around me. And I had water. Water from my hose and from my eyes, dripping down into the dirt. And it dawned on me that rich, fine rich soil is nothing more than composted once-alive-but-now-dead things. And that out of this compost, this swirl of stink that with tending, and watering, and turning, becomes hummus, comes new life. A composted banana does not grow a banana. But it does grow something else. And that is a promise to which I hope you can all relate.

---

8. Valerie Saiving, "The Human Situation: A Feminine View," in *Womanspirit Rising: A Feminist Reader in Religion*, ed. Carol P. Christ and Judith Plaskow (San Francisco, Ca: Harper and Row, 1979), 25–42.

19. "Like a Sow Entering a Synagogue"

Brooks Schramm

Luther in the Discussion

In the field of critical biblical studies, there was a time when it was considered off limits to refer to pre-critical—pre-modern—biblical commentators in any kind of positive or constructive way.[1] The field regarded itself as having moved beyond all biblical interpretation that had come before it. And, in certain respects, that is in fact true. As critical biblical studies took root in the wake of the European Enlightenment, two major—yet basic—methodological questions dominated the field. First: *The Question of Composition*. How did the Bible come to be? How, and when, and by whom, were the biblical texts actually written? Second: *The Question of Historicity*. Did things really happen in the way they are described as happening in the Bible, miracles and all? With this second question in particular the Bible came to be studied with all of the tools of modern critical historiography. Leopold von Ranke famously described the task of critical historiography as ascertaining *"wie es eigentlich gewesen?"* ("how it actually happened").[2] The force of this new, nineteenth-century critical question can be felt when held up alongside the statement of the fifth-century BCE Greek historian, Hecataeus of Miletus, who stated: "Thus I write, as the truth seems to be to me..."[3] The distance between these two approaches to matters historical is wide indeed, and it corresponds to the distance between modernity and pre-modernity. Recognition of this distance is also what stands behind the refrain of one of my former teachers, Gösta Ahlström, who loved to remind his students in a strong Swedish accent: "[T]he modern idea of history did not exist in ancient times."[4] It is to this new nineteenth-century historical approach to the Bible that we owe what are still the foundations of critical biblical study even today: the Documentary Hypothesis in Old Testament studies, with all of its consequences, and the Synoptic Problem and the related quest of the historical Jesus in New Testament studies, with all of their consequences.

---

1. This article is dedicated to Eric H. Crump and Nelson T. Strobert: friends in need, friends in deed.
2. "Man hat der Historie das Amt, die Vergangenheit zu richten, die Mitwelt zum Nutzen zukünftiger Jahre zu belehren, beigemessen: so hoher Aemter unterwindet sich gegenwärtiger Versuch nicht: er will blos zeigen, wie es eigentlich gewesen." Leopold von Ranke, *Sämtliche Werke*, vol. 33/34 (Leipzig: Duncker and Humblot, 1885), 7.
3. Felix Jacoby, *Die Fragmente der griechischen Historiker*, vol. 1 (Leiden: Brill, 1957), 7. See the programmatic use of this quote in Gösta W. Ahlström, *Ancient Palestine: A Historical Introduction*, JSOTSup 146 (Sheffield, UK: Sheffield Academic Press, 2002), 1.
4. Ahlström, *Ancient Palestine*, 1.

When these new historical critics looked at their great predecessors, like Irenaeus, Origen, Gregory of Nyssa, Augustine, Bernard, Thomas, Nicholas of Lyra, Luther, and Calvin—as intellectually brilliant as they were—they found their work to be based on assumptions about the text and about historicity that could no longer be sustained, barring a *sacrificium intellectus*. As a result, these great pre-critical interpreters dropped out of the scholarly conversation in biblical studies, for all practical purposes. If they were referred to, they functioned primarily as foils. But biblical criticism, not being a static phenomenon, continued to grow and evolve. Once there was broad agreement on the possible ways in which biblical texts were produced, and once there was broad agreement on the distinction between mythology and history, critical study began to turn again to biblical texts in their final forms. Given what we know about the possible ways in which these texts came to be, what then can we say about these texts as texts? What kinds of questions does it make sense to ask of them? What kinds of meaning—what kinds of truth—can be derived from them? Scholars began to critique their own assumptions about the final forms of the biblical texts. Without denying that our texts have a long and complex pre-history, far from it, they began to ask questions like: Were the final redactors/editors of the texts really as mechanical and wooden as the early critics had always assumed? Are the Pentateuch and the Gospel of Mark, for example, really as un-readable in their final forms as the source critics had always assumed? Is it possible, rather, that we need to learn *how* to read them? This latter question, one could say, is the primary question that drove redaction criticism and its successors in the twentieth century.

In many ways this question was already anticipated early in the century by the German Jewish philosopher, Franz Rosenzweig, who argued that the traditional scholarly abbreviation "R" for *Redaktor* (or Editor) really should be understood to stand for "*Rabbenu*" (the Hebrew term meaning "our Teacher" or "our Rabbi").[5] This was an aesthetic judgment by Rosenzweig, and it signaled a crucial shift in the evaluation of the final form of the biblical texts. Once this shift in focus became possible, then it also became possible for critical scholarship to retrieve the great commentators from the past and allow them to help us learn *how* to read these texts anew. And, *mutatis mutandis*, help us they can. Why? Because they knew the biblical text so well, and they knew how to read very very closely. In addition, and not incidentally, they also believed in God.

In my own work on the Old Testament I find myself, a contemporary critical biblical scholar, in regular conversation with two different kinds of pre-critical commentators. The first are the eleventh-, twelfth-, and thirteenth-century medieval Jewish commentators (*Ha-Mefarshim*), that is, those whose interpretations are collected in standard Rabbinic Bibles and who function as the touchstone of Jewish biblical interpretation, and the second is Martin Luther. It is the latter about whom I will speak today.

So why Luther? An undervalued and sometimes even little-known aspect of Luther is the fact that the heart of his life's work was the Old Testament. Heinrich

---

5. See John Barton, *Reading the Old Testament: Method in Biblical Study*, rev. ed. (Louisville, Ky: WJK, 1996), 46–47. For a critique of Rosenzweig on this issue, see Gerhard von Rad, *Genesis: A Commentary*, rev. ed., trans. John H. Marks, OTL (Philadelphia, Pa: Westminster, 1973), 40–42.

Bornkamm has stated that if Luther were on a theological faculty today, he would be in the Old Testament department.[6] Heiko Oberman thought that Luther would be in Practical Theology, but Oberman is wrong.[7] Throughout Luther's professorial career, no matter what else was demanding his time and attention, he was constantly at work lecturing on, writing commentaries on, preaching on, and being meticulously involved in translating the books of the Old Testament. The God whom he worshiped, the God whom he feared in the marrow of his bones, and the God whom he zealously struggled to love with all of his heart, soul and mind, was no other than the God of Genesis, Exodus, the Psalms, and Isaiah. Martin Luther was as far from Marcion as it is possible to be.

Part of what makes Luther such a puzzle is that he was in many respects a liminal figure. Sometimes he sounds thoroughly medieval (e.g., he thought Copernicus should be executed as a heretic and witches should be burned), and sometimes he sounds virtually modern (e.g., it is better to have a wise pagan ruler than a stupid Christian ruler). There are even times when he can give a good post-modernist plenty to think about (e.g., when he speaks about the inextricable relationship between the existence *of* God and faith *in* God). Where the Bible is concerned, though, and chiefly the Old Testament, I find Luther to be endlessly fascinating. And one area of his thought here that most intrigues me is his relationship with the Jewish interpretive tradition. The sixteenth century was the age of the birth of *Christian Hebraism*, that intellectual movement within Christianity that sought—and eventually gained—expertise not only in biblical Hebrew but also in the Hebrew and Aramaic of classical rabbinic sources and in their systems of thought, as well as in the great medieval Jewish biblical commentators.[8] The sixteenth century was the first time in history that Jewish scholarly material relevant to the study of the Old Testament became widely available to Gentile Christian scholars. Luther's career spanned the beginnings of this movement, and he himself benefited from it and, to a limited extent, contributed to it. But when it came to matters of theology, Luther adopted a rigidly antagonistic stance toward Jewish interpretation. Luther clearly loved the Old Testament, and he was a vocal advocate for the study of the Hebrew language, but he detested Jewish theological readings *of* the Old Testament. This fascinates me, and I am trying to understand it better. Kirsi Stjerna and I have made some preliminary claims in this area, but considerable work remains to be done.[9] Needless to say, Luther's complex legacy regarding the Hebrew language and the Jewish interpretive tradition is still very much with us, albeit in subtle and often unconscious ways. The fact that

---

6. Heinrich Bornkamm, *Luther and the Old Testament*, ed. Victor I. Gruhn, trans. Eric W. and Ruth C. Gritsch (Mifflintown, Pa: Sigler Press, 1997), 7.

7. ☺.

8. See now especially Stephen G. Burnett, *Christian Hebraism in the Reformation Era (1500–1660): Authors, Books, and the Transmission of Jewish Learning* (Leiden; Boston: Brill, 2012); Bruce Gordon and Matthew McLean, eds., *Shaping the Bible in the Reformation: Books, Scholars, and Their Readers in the Sixteenth Century* (Leiden; Boston: Brill, 2012), [esp. Stephen G. Burnett, "The Strange Career of the Biblia Rabbinica among Christian Hebraists, 1517–1620," 63–84].

9. See Brooks Schramm and Kirsi I. Stjerna, eds., *Martin Luther, the Bible, and the Jewish People: A Reader* (Minneapolis, Mn: Fortress Press, 2012).

Hebrew has never been a required language throughout the 187-year history of Gettysburg Seminary is an aspect of this complex legacy.

Eyn unterrichtung, wie sich die Christen yn Mosen sollen schicken

My current research is part of the new *Annotated Luther* project from Fortress Press, six volumes of Luther's most essential writings, newly introduced, edited, annotated, and published by Reformation Day 2017. Kirsi Stjerna is one of the three general editors of the project, along with Tim Wengert and Hans Hillerbrand. The first writing of Luther's for which I am responsible is entitled *How Christians Should Regard Moses* ("Eyn unterrichtung, wie sich die Christen yn Mosen sollen schicken").[10] This document originated as a sermon preached by Luther in Wittenberg on August 27, 1525. In 1523–1524 Luther had preached all the way through Genesis. Immediately upon completing that series, he began with Exodus in the fall of 1524, and by late summer of 1525 he had reached Exodus 19, Israel's arrival at Mt. Sinai and the preparations for receiving the divine law. This sermon, *How Christians Should Regard Moses*, served as Luther's introduction to Exodus 19–20, and thus to the Ten Commandments themselves.[11] It is an essential text for many reasons, certainly not least because here Luther takes up the ancient and perennial Christian problem of which Old Testament laws are binding on Christians. If anyone thinks that this issue is passé, just have a look at what the ELCA has been arguing about for the better part of twenty-five years: *Mirabile dictu*, Lutherans in public debate quoting the purity laws of Leviticus as binding!

1525 was a tumultuous year for the forty-one-year-old Martin Luther. Some brief highlights. In January he finishes the major treatise, *Against the Heavenly Prophets in the Matter of Images and Sacraments*. In February he finishes his *Commentary on Deuteronomy*. In March the Peasants' War, which had been ebbing and flowing, finally explodes. In April he begins a series of treatises against the Peasants. On May 5, Frederick the Wise, his protector, dies. Shortly thereafter he writes the notorious treatise, *Against the Robbing and Murdering Mobs of Peasants*. On May 15 the peasants are crushed at the Battle of Frankenhausen, and on May 27 Thomas Müntzer is beheaded at Mühlhausen. Over the course of the long war, estimates are that something like 100,000 peasants have been killed. On June 13, less than a month after the war ended, Luther and Katharina von Bora are married. In July, he "kinda sorta" apologizes for the notorious treatise against the peasants. In the fall he writes the seminal treatise called *De servo arbitrio* (On the Bondage of the Will) against Erasmus. And throughout this entire time, he is preaching his way through Exodus at the town church, while

10. *D. Martin Luthers Werke: Kritische Gesamtausgabe*, 69 vols. (Weimar: Hermann Böhlaus Nachfolger, 1883–), 16:363–393 (hereafter, WA); Jaroslav Pelikan and Helmut T. Lehmann, eds., *Luther's Works*, American ed., 55 vols. (Philadelphia, Pa: Fortress Press; Saint Louis, Mo: Concordia Publishing House, 1955–86), 35:161–174 (hereafter, *LW*).

11. The sermon would take on something of a life of its own, as it was subsequently printed separately, and then later as a companion-piece to other of Luther's writings, especially his 1528 *Exposition of the 10 Commandments* (WA 16:363–393).

at the university he is lecturing through Hosea. This would make for quite the annual faculty report to the Dean.

In *How Christians Should Regard Moses*, Luther concisely formulates his essential principles for distinguishing antithetically between Law and Gospel, Moses and Christ, the worldly external kingdom and the spiritual internal kingdom, the Old Covenant and the New Covenant; in other words those fundamental principles that will drive his theology for the remainder of his career. And all of this is being worked out in the midst of major real-life events, with the Peasants' War being the most serious one.

The problem of biblical interpretation that Luther was facing in 1525 is as follows. Some Protestant preachers were beginning to quote Old Testament legal texts and claim that certain Old Testament laws were binding on Christians on the grounds that these laws were the word of God.[12] "Gott(i)s Wort, Gott(i)s Wort!," they said.[13] For example, in Exodus and Deuteronomy God through Moses commands the people to destroy its arch enemy, "Amalek". Some Protestant preachers, in the context of the Peasants' Revolt, argued that the lords and landowners of sixteenth-century Germany were the contemporary incarnation of Amalek. Therefore when we kill these lords and landowners, we are only obeying the word of God. This is of course a simplification of the position of his opponents, but Luther uses it and other real-life current examples to carve out essential principles on how Christians should relate to the Old Testament in general and to Mosaic law in particular. Luther's answer to the question—"Which Mosaic laws are binding on Christians?"—may surprise you: None of them! "Not one little dot in Moses pertains to us."[14] Here is Luther's categorical claim:

> The law of Moses does not bind pagans but only Jews[15].... Moses was an intermediary for the Jewish people alone. It was to them that he gave the law. Therefore one must shut the yaps of the mob-spirits who say, "Thus says Moses," etc. Here you simply reply: "Moses does not pertain to us." If I were to accept Moses in one commandment, I would have to accept the entire Moses.[16] Thus the consequence would be that if I accept Moses as master, then I must have myself circumcised, wash my clothes in the Jewish way, eat and drink and dress thus and so, and observe all that stuff. So, then, we will neither observe nor accept Moses. *Moses ist tod* ('Moses is dead'). His rule ended when Christ came. He is of no further use.[17]

The principle here enunciated by Luther is that Mosaic law was temporally constrained. It was never intended for the pagan world in the first place but for

---

12. Of particular relevance here is the polemic against Karlstadt in part one of *Against the Heavenly Prophets*.

13. *Against the Heavenly Prophets*, 1525 (WA 18:73,30; 88,20; *LW* 40:91, 105); *How Christians Should Regard Moses* (WA 16:388, 10; *LW* 35:171).

14. *LW* 35:166; "keyn puenctlin gehet uns an ym Mose." (WA 16:375,14).

15. In this, ironically, Luther is in complete agreement with the entirety of Jewish tradition.

16. Here Luther is drawing on Gal 5:3, where Paul states that the entire Torah is binding, and one cannot pick and choose. This is standard rabbinic teaching.

17. WA 16:371,13; 373,4–13 (italics added); see *LW* 35:164–165. [Translations from WA are those of the author. Quotes from *LW* have been slightly amended by the author].

the Jews alone,[18] and, in addition, once the Christ comes, Mosaic law terminates in its entirety.[19] Luther's pregnant phrase, "Moses is dead", means that Moses no longer has any claim, not even on the Jews.[20] But, though Moses is dead and not binding on us, we Christians who come from the pagan world are still free to learn from him.

> I dismiss the commandments given to the people of Israel. They neither constrain nor compel me. The laws are dead and gone, *except insofar as* I gladly and willingly accept something from Moses, as if I said, "This is how Moses ruled, and it seems fine to me, so I will follow him in this or that part."[21]

Thus, for Luther, Christians are in no sense bound by Mosaic law, any of it, but we are free to learn from it and to adopt and adapt it where appropriate; not by constraint but freely, willingly, and reasonably. Our contemporary religio-political public discourse could learn a great deal from Luther on this point.

This principle just discussed is part of a much larger one that Luther establishes: just because something is God's word does not make it God's word to me, that is, it does not make it applicable to me. How I wish I had known this when growing up in a sea of fundamentalists:

> One must deal and proceed cleanly with the Scriptures. From the beginning the word has come in various ways. One must not simply consider whether it is God's word, whether God has said it; rather much more [one must consider] *to whom* it has been spoken, whether it concerns you [or somebody else][22].... In the Scriptures the word is of two kinds: the first does not pertain or apply to me, the second kind does apply to me.[23]

As an example of this principle at work, Luther draws on the story of the binding of Isaac: "God commanded Abraham to strangle his son; but that does not make *me* Abraham such that I should strangle *my* son."[24] The claim that Luther is making is that no law is binding on us in a religious sense that is either temporally constrained, like the whole of the Mosaic legislation, or that was directed to a specific person or circumstance, like commands given to Abraham or to David or even to the lepers healed by Christ. Stated positively, the only commandments that are applicable to us in a religious sense are those that are universally applicable to all people, no more and no less.

What are these universally applicable laws, and where do we find them? This is precisely where things start to become interesting. Simply stated, the

---

18. It is in this context that Luther refers to Mosaic law as the *Sachsenspiegel* (the customary law) of the Jews.

19. Luther's interpretation of Rom 10:4.

20. For a similar expression, see the 1535 *Lectures on Galatians* (WA 40/2:18,13–14; LW 27:15) – "[W]e do not grant [Moses] any authority over our conscience. Let him remain where he lies dead and buried, and 'no one knows the place of his burial' (Deut 34:6)." Cf. *LW* 26:151. Luther states many times that post-biblical Jews are unable to keep Mosaic law, because there is no temple, and because Jews now live outside of the land of Israel.

21. WA 16:376,8–12 (italics added); see *LW* 35:166.

22. Reading with WA 24:12,17.

23. WA 16:384,19–385,9; 385,12–14 (italics added); see *LW* 35:170.

24. WA 16:384,11–12 (italics added); see *LW* 35:170.

universally applicable laws are the Ten Commandments themselves.[25] But, for Luther, the Ten Commandments are not applicable to us because they are in the Bible, or because Moses gave them, but rather because they represent what Luther calls Natural Law. These are the laws that are written by nature on the conscience of all human beings since the creation of the world.[26] Strictly speaking, therefore, the Ten Commandments are not "Mosaic" (or "Jewish"), it is just that Moses has written and arranged them in a particularly fine way.

> Why does one then keep and teach the Ten Commandments? Answer: Because the natural laws were never so finely and orderly written as by Moses. Therefore one rightly follows the example of Moses.[27]

Thus the Ten Commandments are binding on us, Gentile Christians, because they cohere with Natural Law, and Natural Law is what is binding on all human beings.[28]

But there is a twist. For Luther, even the Ten Commandments themselves contain material that is temporally constrained and thus no longer binding. This is material that Luther referred to as "zeitlicher Schmuck," normally rendered into English as "temporal adaptation," but better is "temporal adornment." Think back to Confirmation when you learned the Ten Commandments from Luther's Catechism. If you had an accurate Catechism that rendered the commandments precisely as Luther did, and if you then compared Luther's wording with the wording of the actual commandments in Exodus 20 and Deuteronomy 5, you would find that a substantial amount of material is missing in the former. Luther was not trying to save space, nor was he trying to make it easier to memorize the commandments. All of the material in Exodus 20 and Deuteronomy 5 that is missing in Luther's Catechism is that which he regarded as temporal adornment, that is, material that was relevant and binding on the Jews in the biblical period but which is no longer binding on or applicable to us.

Two brief examples. In the Bible, the fourth commandment reads: "Honor your father and your mother, that your days may be long in the land that the LORD your God is giving you." The land referred to here is, of course, the land of Canaan. That portion of the commandment is regarded as a temporal

---

25. On the distinctiveness of Luther's treatment of the Ten Commandments vis-à-vis the preceding church tradition, see Albrecht Peters, *Commentary on Luther's Catechisms: The Ten Commandments*, ed. Charles P Schaum, trans. Holger K. Sonntag (Saint Louis, Mo: Concordia, 2009), 55–87.

26. Luther here, as everywhere on this topic, sees himself as merely repeating what Paul writes in Rom 2:14–15. See also *Against the Sabbatarians*, 1538 (*LW* 47:89–90). To be sure, however, this natural law written on the heart/conscience is well-nigh illegible, due to the fall. This is why Luther regularly emphasized that the Gospel is required to clarify exactly what the Law is and demands.

27. *Against the Heavenly Prophets*, 1525 (WA 18:81,18–20; LW 40:98). See also *Against the Sabbatarians*, 1538 (WA 50:331,13–17; LW 47:90): "He is the common God of all the pagans, who gives the common Ten Commandments – which prior to this had been implanted at creation in the hearts of all – to this particular people orally as well. In his day Moses fitted them nicely into his laws in a more orderly and excellent manner than could have been done by anyone else." One of Israel's perquisites is that it and it alone has the Natural Law *in writing*.

28. Whereas Luther's claim that the Mosaic legislation as a whole is not binding on pagans was in agreement with standard rabbinic teaching, here his claim for the Ten Commandments places him at odds with the rabbis, for whom only the "Noahide Laws" were binding on non-Jews. The Noahide Laws would be a rough rabbinic equivalent of what Luther's "Natural Law" means. It is noteworthy that Luther regards the first three commandments, the most Israel-specific commandments of all, as written on the human conscience by nature.

adornment and is no longer applicable. Thus the commandment in Luther's Catechism reads only: "You are to honor your father and your mother."[29]

The third commandment is even more illustrative. In Exodus: "Remember the Sabbath day, by sanctifying it." In the Catechism: "You are to sanctify the day of celebration/holiday."[30] In Luther's translation of Exod 20:8 in his German Bible, he uses the word "Sabbattag", but in the Catechism he changes "Sabbattag" to "Feierta." Why? Because, as his explanation makes clear, the Sabbath itself was a temporal adornment given to the Jews alone; it has been abrogated and is no longer applicable. What remains of this commandment is merely the setting apart of a regular time to worship God and to learn God's word. Sunday is fine, because it is customary, but there is no necessity that Sunday be the day. The Sabbath itself, however, is gone. Thus when Luther speaks of *The Law* that is the counterpart and the antithesis to *The Gospel*, he means the Ten Commandments minus their temporal adornments. It is this that constitutes the universally applicable divine law, which in turn is identical to Natural Law.

". . . wie eine saw jnn die Jueden Schule"

We turn now finally to the heart of the matter, which is a particular aspect of Luther's treatment of the First Commandment, and more specifically the Prologue to the First Commandment. "I, YHWH, am your God, who brought you out of the land of Egypt, out of the house of slavery." The entirety of Jewish tradition and the entirety of critical biblical interpreters are in agreement that this Prologue is the "because" of a "because-therefore" statement: "*Because* I, YHWH, am your God, who brought you out of the land of Egypt, out of the house of slavery, *therefore* you shall have no other gods but me." YHWH's prevenient act of liberation constitutes the rationale for imposing on Israel its covenantal obligations: "*Because* I have done this for you, *therefore* you are obligated to do this for me."[31] This is the language of a vassal treaty, with YHWH in the role of suzerain and Israel in the role of vassal. Because of YHWH prior act of liberation, Israel now owes YHWH its exclusive fidelity.

How does Luther deal with the strict Israel-specific logic of this language? In exactly the same way as in the other commandments. "I am the LORD your God" and "You shall have no other gods but me" apply to us; "who brought you out of the land of Egypt, out of the house of slavery" is a temporal adornment that does not:

> We and all pagans are just as duty-bound as the Jews to keep the first commandment, so that we have no other gods than the only God. But we pagans have no use and can have no use for the phrase with which he *adorns* this

---

29. Elsewhere Luther is able to derive a general truth from the promise of the land of Canaan: "We also observe that countries and governments, yes, also families and estates, decline or survive so remarkably according to their obedience or disobedience; and it has never happened otherwise than that he fares badly and dies an evil death who dishonors father and mother." *Against the Sabbatarians*, 1538 (*LW* 47:95; WA 50:335,1–5).

30. "Du solt den feyertag heiligen." (WA 30/1:130,9).

31. This raises the difficult question of whether it was possible for Israel to reject God's "offer."

commandment and which applies only to the Jews, namely, "who brought you out of the land of Egypt, out of the house of slavery." For if I [a pagan] were to approach God and say, "O Lord God, who brought me out of Egypt, out of misery," etc., I would be just like a sow entering a synagogue, for God never performed such a work for me. God would [even] punish me as a liar; I would be making an imaginary god out of him. Yet I must recite and keep all the other words of the first commandment. I *may* also say, "You are my God, the God and also the Creator of us all, who, to be sure, led the children of Israel out of Egypt, but not me; however, you did lead me out of my Egypt and my misery." Thus the first commandment remains common to both Jews and Gentiles. It is especially *adorned and fitted* to the Jews with reference to the exodus from Egypt, just as everyone after their own exile can and should name and praise the common God as their own God and helper.[32]

Like a sow entering a synagogue. So much to say, and so little time. Let it suffice for now, on the positive side, to voice agreement with Luther's main claim here: We Gentile Christians are not Jews, nor should we try to be. Circumcision, the Sabbath, the Passover, the Exodus, taking the land of Canaan, the Temple, the laws of *kashrut*, the Exile and return, are Israel's stories and practices and they address us only by analogy, not directly.

On the negative side, Luther's insistence that the words "I am the LORD your God" represent the direct address of the God of the whole world to the conscience of all human beings brings with it some problematic consequences. When Luther writes that Moses is dead, what he really means by that is that *Judaism is dead.* Thus the peculiar and particular name of God used in the Prologue to the First Commandment morphs into generic terms available in any language: κύριος, dominus, Herr, lord, or simply God, and the particular "you"

---

32. *Against the Sabbatarians*, 1538 (WA 50:331,20–36; LW 47:90–91; italics added). This is a more extensive and colorful elaboration of the same point made in *How Christians Should Regard Moses*, 1526 (WA 373,14–374,8; LW 35:165):

> That Moses does not bind the pagans can be demonstrated from the text in the Second Book of Moses in the 20th chapter, where God himself speaks, 'I am the LORD your God, who brought you out of the land of Egypt, out of the house of bondage.' This text makes it clear that even the Ten Commandments do not pertain to us. For [God] never led us out of Egypt, but only the Jews. The mob-spirits want to saddle us with Moses and all the commandments. We will just skip that. We will regard Moses as a teacher, but we will not regard him as our lawgiver— unless he agrees with both the New Testament and the natural law.

In addition, see esp. the introduction to Luther's 1525 sermon on Exod 20:2 (WA 16:424,11–32):

> Wir wollen die Zehen gepot kurtz uberlauffen. Zum Ersten ist zu mercken, das uns Heyden und Christen die Zehen gepot nicht betreffen, sondern alleine die Jueden, Das bezeuget und zwinget der Text, so er spricht: Ich byn der HERR dein Gott, der dich aus Egypten lande aus dem diensthauss gefurt habe. Das ist ja war und klar genug, das wir Heyden durch Gott nicht auss Egypten gefurt sind, sondern allein das Juedisch volck Israel. Darumb deuttet Mose die zehen gepot allein auff das volck, welchs durch Gott auss Egypten ist gefurt. Das wir aber gleich auch den Gott, den die Jueden ehren, der sie auss Egypten gefurt hat, erkennen, anbeten und ehren, haben wir nicht durch Mosen oder aus dem geschriben gesetz, sondern auss andern schrifften und auss dem gesetz der natur. Das rede ich abermal daruemb, das ich den falschen geistern were, die uns Mosen auff den halss mit gewalt woellen legen, yhn zu halten mit allen seinen gepoten, das wollen wir aber lassen und yhn mit dem aller minsten titel nicht annehmen denn so ferne wo er mit dem natuerlichen gesetz uber einstymmet. Wir wollen yhn wol lesen wie einen andern lerer frey und ungezwungen, Aber fur unsern gesetzgeber wollen wir yhn nicht haben, den wir haben vorhyn yhm newen Testament gesetz genug, daruemb wollen wir yhn nicht haben ynn unserm gewissen, sondern das Christo alleine rein behalten. Also ist es ja klar, das die zehen gepot allein den Jueden geben sind und nicht uns, trotz allen Rottengeistern, das sie mit warheit anders sagen.

is swallowed up by the universal "you." Stated differently, the problem of the election of Israel is "solved" by viewing it as temporally constrained, and YHWH's love for fleshly Israel is itself regarded as "zeitlicher Schmuck", temporal adornment.[33] "YHWH the God of Israel" recedes and "the God of the whole world" comes to the forefront.[34] One can even say that for Luther the Jewishness of Jesus itself is, finally, regarded as temporal adornment. It should not be a surprise, therefore, that the aspect of rabbinic Judaism, post-biblical Judaism, that most disturbs Luther and against which he writes most vehemently is precisely that of the eternal election of Israel, which in biblical language refers to God's love for Israel. In the final analysis, Luther's theology has no room for the ongoing existence of Judaism in any theologically positive sense. That aspect of his thought, deep and wide though it is, cannot be our way.

Christian theology, if it is to be true to the Old Testament itself and to the First Commandment, cannot speak of "the God of the whole world" if it is not willing simultaneously to speak of the "God of Israel," and to do so in the present tense.[35] The Old Testament itself and the First Commandment hold these two aspects of God's identity inextricably together. Holding these aspects together simultaneously, and in the present tense, does not solve the problem of Jew and Gentile, synagogue and church, but it does place the theological discussion on different footing, and changes the rules of the game. It is to that discourse that I have dedicated my life and my work. And it was Luther, after all, who said: "In the future life all commandments will cease— except the first."[36]

33. For an excellent study of the tension between monotheism and the election of Israel, see Joel Kaminsky and Anne Stewart, "God of All the World: Universalism and Developing Monotheism in Isaiah 40–66," *HTR* 99/2 (2006): 139–163. See also R. Kendall Soulen, *The Divine Name(s) and the Holy Trinity* (Louisville, Ky: WJK, 2011).

34. On this, see Heinrich Bornkamm, "The Father of Jesus Christ as God of the Entire Scripture," in *Luther and the Old Testament*, 195–200.

35. On this issue, see esp. R. Kendall Soulen, "'They are Israelites': The Priority of the Present Tense in Jewish-Christian Relations," in *Between Gospel and Election: Explorations in the Interpretation of Romans 9–11*, ed. Florian Wilk and J. Ross Wagner, WUNT 257 (Tübingen: Mohr Siebeck, 2010), 497–504.

36. "In futura vita omnia praecepta cessabunt excepto primo." *D. Martin Luthers Werke: Kritische Gesamtausgabe, Tischreden*, 6 vols. (Weimar: Hermann Böhlaus Nachfolger, 1912–1921), 1:159,31–32, #369.

Index